ROYAL HISTORICAL SOCIETY

STUDIES IN HISTORY 67

TYRONE'S REBELLION

IN MEMORY OF MY GRANDFATHER
HUGH CLOSE

TYRONE'S REBELLION

THE OUTBREAK OF THE NINE YEARS WAR
IN TUDOR IRELAND

Hiram Morgan

THE ROYAL HISTORICAL SOCIETY
THE BOYDELL PRESS

First published 1993

A Royal Historical Society publication
Published by The Boydell Press
an imprint of Boydell & Brewer Ltd
PO Box 9 Woodbridge Suffolk IP12 3DF UK
and of Boydell & Brewer Inc.
PO Box 41026 Rochester NY 14604 USA

ISBN 0 86193 224 2

ISSN 0269-2244

British Library Cataloguing-in-Publication Data
Morgan, Hiram
Tyrone's Rebellion:Outbreak of the Nine Years War in
Tudor Ireland. – (Royal Historical Society Studies in History,
ISSN 0269-2244;No.67)
I. Title II. Series
941.505
ISBN 0-86193-224-2

Library of Congress Cataloging-in-Publication Data applied for

The paper used in this publication meets the minimum requirements
of American National Standard for Information Sciences –
Permanence of Paper for Printed Library Materials, ANSI Z39.48–1984

Printed in Great Britain by
St Edmundsbury Press Ltd, Bury St Edmunds, Suffolk

Contents

	Page
List of maps and genealogies	vii
Acknowledgements	viii
Note on conventions	ix
Abbreviations	x
Maps	xii

INTRODUCTION
| 1 Historiographical background | 3 |
| 2 Political background | 16 |

PART ONE: CROWN POLICY
| 3 The apotheosis of Perrot | 29 |
| 4 The nemesis of Fitzwilliam | 55 |

PART TWO: ULSTER OVERLORDS
| 5 The rise of Hugh O'Neill | 85 |
| 6 The realignment of Tirconnell | 113 |

PART THREE: STRUCTURAL CRISIS
7 Conspiracy and crisis in Ulster	139
8 The outbreak of war	167
9 The aborted peace	193

Conclusion	214
Appendix	223
Bibliography	226
Glossary	239
Index	243

The Society records its gratitude to the following whose generosity made possible the initiation of this series: The British Academy; The Pilgrim Trust; The Twenty-Seven Foundation; The United States Embassy's Bicentennial funds; The Wolfson Trust; several private donors.

Maps and Genealogies

		Page
1	North of Ireland: site references c. 1590	xii
2	North of Ireland: physical features and woodland c. 1590	xiii
3	North of Ireland: political c. 1590	ix
4	The O'Neills of Tyrone	86–87
5	The O'Donnells of Tirconnell	114–115

Acknowledgements

This attempt to explain the outbreak of the Nine Years War – the greatest conundrum in Irish historiography – would not have been possible without the assistance and indulgence of many individuals and institutions. First and foremost there is my wife, Dorothy Convery. She has shown infinite patience, borne financial hardships and done meticulous proof-reading. At school Tim McCall first excited my interest in Early Modern Ireland and at university Brendan Bradshaw was an omnicompetent supervisor of the original thesis. At the research stage, Bob Hunter gave me the benefit of his amazing knowledge of local history and Micheline Walsh pointed me to the relevant manuscript material in Spain. During the writing phase, Ciarán Brady, Nicholas Canny and Steven Ellis made valuable criticisms. Indeed, I must acknowledge my debt to Brady, whose work on the period immediately preceding this one has been an inspiration. I must also thank Colin Smith and Brian Scott for translating vital documents, Tony Sheehan for his computer wizardry, Jill Alexander for drawing the maps and Olivia Lammey for plotting the genealogical tricks. At Queen's University, Belfast I received help and encouragement from my colleagues, especially Pete Jupp and Art Hughes. I am also grateful to various librarians and archivists in Ireland, England and Spain. The doyens of the Royal Historical Society also deserve a mention, most notably Sir Geoffrey Elton, who has shown a continued interest in my work, and Christine Linehan, who has laboured hard to prepare this manuscript for publication. Financially, I am beholden to the British Academy, who granted me a post-doctoral fellowship in the second year of which this book was completed. Research trips to Spain and Portugal were paid for by the Cambridge Historical Society and by 'a small personal research grant' from the British Academy. On a broader plane, my generation is indebted to an educational system which has given equality of opportunity and freedom of choice.

Hiram Morgan
Belfast
1992

Note on Conventions

The following should be noted:

1. Spelling in quotations has been modernised.
2. Dates have been given in old style unless otherwise stated.
3. All currency denominations have been given in pounds sterling unless otherwise stated.

Abbreviations

AFM	*Ánnála rioghacta Eireann: annals of the kingdom of Ireland by the Four Masters from the earliest times to the year 1616*, ed. and trans. J. O'Donovan, 7 vols, Dublin 1856
AGS	Archivo General de Simancas
APC	*Acts of the Privy Council of England*, ed. J. R. Dasent, 32 vols, London 1890–1907
BLO	Bodleian Library, Oxford
BL	British Library
ULC	University Library, Cambridge
C, Carew	*Calendar of the Carew Manuscripts preserved in the archiepiscopal library at Lambeth, 1515–1624*, ed. J. S. Brewer and W. Bullen, 6 vols, London 1867–73
CPCRI	*Calendar of Patent and Close Rolls of chancery in Ireland*, ed. J. Morrin, 3 vols, Dublin 1861–3
CPRE	*Calendar of Patent Rolls, Elizabeth, 1558–80*, by various editors, 8 vols, London, 1939–86
CSP, Scot.	*Calendar of State Papers relating to Scotland and Mary, Queen of Scots, 1547– 1603*, by various editors, 13 vols, Edinburgh and Glasgow, 1898–1969
CSP, Sp.	*Calendar of State Papers, Spanish, Elizabeth*, ed. M. A. S. Hume, 4 vols, London 1892–9
CSPD	*Calendar of State Papers, Domestic*, ed. R. Lemon and M. A. E. Green, 12 vols, London 1856–72
CSPI	*Calendar of State Papers, Ireland*, ed. H. C. Hamilton, E. G. Atkinson and R. P. Mahaffy, 24 vols, London 1860–1912
DNB	*Dictionary of national biography*, ed. N. Stephens and S. Lee, 22 vols, London 1917
Fiants	Calendar of Fiants of the reigns of Henry VIII . . . Elizabeth in the appendices of 7th to 22nd *Reports of the deputy keeper of the public records in Ireland*, Dublin 1875–90
HMC	Historical Manuscripts Commission Reports
IHS	*Irish Historical Studies*
Lambeth	Lambeth Palace Library
LCS	*Leabhar Chlainne Suibhne*, ed. Paul Walsh, Dublin 1920
Life	Lughaidh Ó Cléirigh, *The life of Aodh Ruadh Ó Domhnaill*, ed. Paul Walsh, 2 pts, Dublin 1948–57
NLI	National Library of Ireland
NRO	Northamptonshire Record Office
PRIA	*Proceedings of the Royal Irish Academy*
PRO	Public Record Office, Chancery Lane, London

PRONI   Public Record Office of Northern Ireland
RIA   Royal Irish Academy
SP 63   Irish State Papers, Eliz. to Geo III
SP 65   Miscellaneous Irish papers

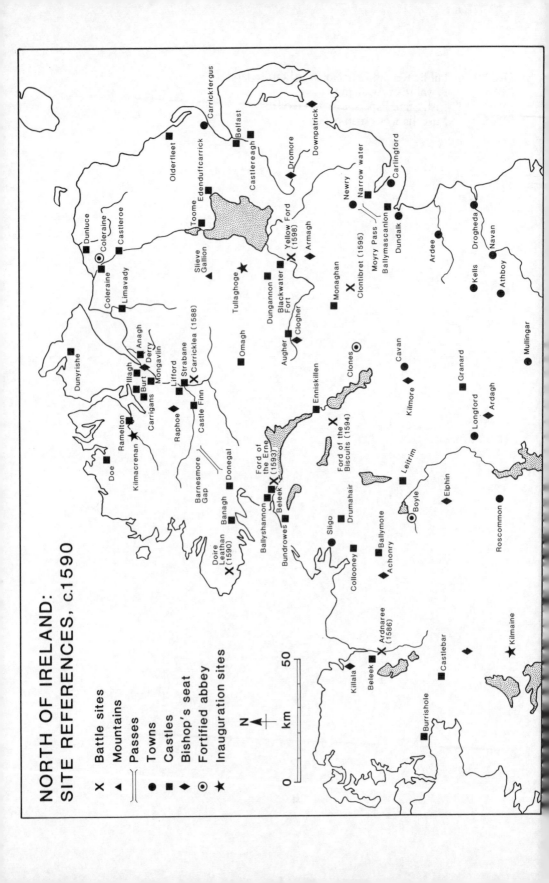

NORTH OF IRELAND:
SITE REFERENCES, c.1590

X   Battle sites

▲   Mountains

)(Passes

●   Towns

■   Castles

◆   Bishop's seat

◉   Fortified abbey

★   Inauguration sites

N

km

0   50

Carrickfergus
Belfast
Olderfleet
Edenduffcarrick
Castlereagh
Dromore
Downpatrick
Dunluce
Coleraine
Castleroe
Toome
Narrow water
Newry
Carlingford
Coleraine
Limavady
Yellow Ford (1598)
Armagh
Clontibret (1595)
Moyry Pass
Ballymascanlon
Dundalk
Ardee
Drogheda
Kells
Navan
Athboy
Slieve Gallion
Dunyrishe
Tullaghoge
Dungannon
Blackwater Fort
Monaghan
Anagh
Derry
Mongavlin
Omagh
Augher
Clogher
Illagh
Burt
Lifford
Strabane
Carricklea (1588)
Enniskillen
Clones
Cavan
Granard
Mullingar
Carrigans
Raphoe
Castle Finn
Ramelton
Kilmacrenan
Barnesmore Gap
Kilmore
Longford
Ardagh
Doe
Donegal
Banagh
Ford of the Erne (1593)
Ford of the Biscuits (1594)
Leitrim
Elphin
Boyle
Roscommon
Doire Leathan (1590)
Ballyshannon
Beleek
Bundrowes
Drumahair
Sligo
Collooney
Ballymote
Achonry
Ardnaree (1586)
Killala
Beleek
Castlebar
Kilmaine
Burrishole

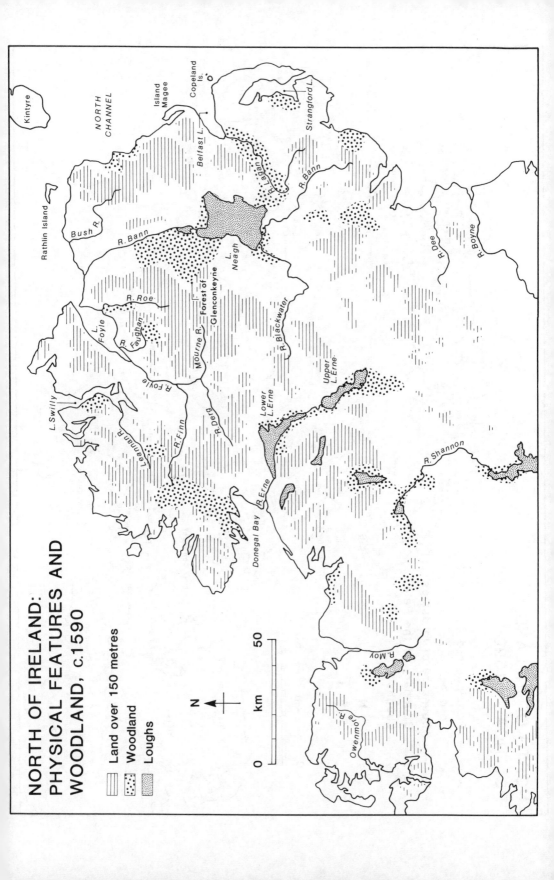

NORTH OF IRELAND: PHYSICAL FEATURES AND WOODLAND, c.1590

Land over 150 metres

Woodland

Loughs

km

0   50

N

North Channel

Kintyre

Rathlin Island

Bush R.

Island Magee

Copeland Is.

Belfast L.

Strangford L.

R. Lagan

R. Bann

R. Bann

R. Roe

R. Faughan

L. Foyle

L. Neagh

Mourne R.

Forest of Glenconkeyne

R. Blackwater

R. Dee

R. Boyne

Leannan R.

L. Swilly

R. Foyle

R. Finn

R. Derg

R. Erne

Lower L. Erne

Upper L. Erne

Donegal Bay

R. Shannon

Owenmore R.

R. Moy

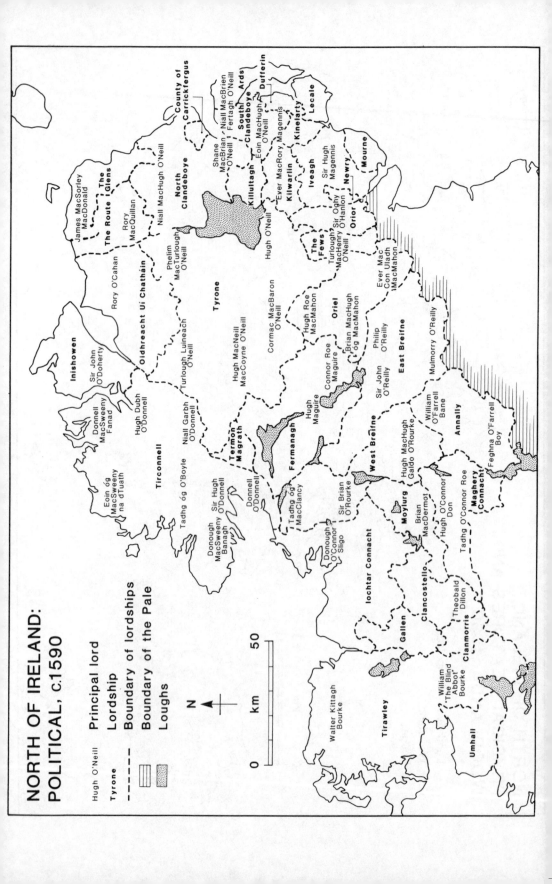

NORTH OF IRELAND: POLITICAL, c.1590

Hugh O'Neill — **Principal lord**

Tyrone — **Lordship**

– – – **Boundary of lordships**

░░░ **Boundary of the Pale**

▒▒▒ **Loughs**

N

km
0   50

James MacSorley MacDonald

Sir John O'Doherty

Inishowen

Donnell MacSweeny Fanad

Eoin óg MacSweeny na dTuath

Hugh Dubh O'Donnell

The Route

The Glens

Rory O'Cahan

Oidhreacht Uí Chatháin

Niall MacHugh O'Neill

Rory MacQuillan

North Clandeboye

Phelim MacTurlough O'Neill

Shane MacBrien O'Neill

Niall MacBrien Fertagh O'Neill

Eoin MacHugh O'Neill

South Clandeboye

Ards

Dufferin

Lecale

Ever MacRory Magennis

Kilwarlin

Kinelarty

Iveagh

Sir Hugh Magennis

County of Carrickfergus

Mourne

Newry

Killultagh

Hugh O'Neill

Turlough? MacHenry O'Neill

Sir Oghy O'Hanlon

The Fews

Orior

Tyrone

Turlough Luineach O'Neill

Hugh MacNeill MacCoyne O'Neill

Cormac MacBaron O'Neill

Hugh Roe MacMahon

Ever Mac Con Uladh MacMahon

Oriel

Brian MacHugh óg MacMahon

Niall Garbh O'Donnell

Termon Magrath

Tadhg óg O'Boyle

Donnell O'Donnell

Tirconnell

Donnell O'Donnell

Tadhg óg MacClancy

Fermanagh

Hugh Maguire

Connor Roe Maguire

Philip O'Reilly

Sir John O'Reilly

East Breifne

Mulmorry O'Reilly

William O'Farrell Bane

Annally

Feghna O'Farrell Boy

Donough MacSweeny Banagh

Donough O'Connor Sligo

Sir Brian O'Rourke

West Breifne

Hugh MacHugh Galdo O'Rourke

Moylurg

Brian MacDermot

Hugh O'Connor Don

Tadhg O'Connor Roe

Maghery Connacht

Iochtar Connacht

Clancostello

Gallen

Clanmorris

Theobald Dillon

William "The Blind Abbot" Bourke

Tirawley

Walter Kittagh Bourke

Umhall

INTRODUCTION

1

Historiographical Background

This study deals with relations between the English crown and the Gaelic lords of Ulster in the 1580s and their breakdown into a disastrous conflict in the 1590s. The crown spent £2,000,000 to gain final victory and thousands of lives were lost. The military struggle achieved what half a century of political reform had failed to do: the establishment of functional English sovereignty through-out Ireland. The outbreak of these hostilities has never been the subject of thorough investigation. Rather it has been treated as a component of general histories or as an episode in biographies. Since the conflict saw the completion of the English conquest of Ireland, it has naturally been the subject of dispute, not least over its causes and over the character of the main protagonist, Hugh O'Neill.

The contemporary historians were partisans.[1] William Camden, the official historian of Queen Elizabeth's reign, was patronised by Lord Burghley and had access to state papers.[2] He said that the rebellion was caused by the desire of the Gaelic lords to prevent the imposition of English law which would have prevented their tyrannical government over their own people. He cited the cases of MacMahon and O'Rourke as trigger factors. Camden dismissed com-plaints against the excesses of English officials and the cause of religion as mere cloaks to cover rebellious intentions. On the contrary, he claimed that Hugh O'Neill, the earl of Tyrone, had been conniving secretly with the Spanish since the time of the Armada.[3] He gave this description of O'Neill: 'He had a strong body, able to endure labour, watching and hunger: his industry was great, his soul large and fit for the weightiest businesses: much knowledge he had in military affairs, and a profound dissembling heart: insomuch as some did prognosticate of him, that he was born either to the very great good or the great hurt of Ireland.'[4] An itinerary, Fynes Moryson's travelogue of Europe written in 1617, contained a large section entitled 'The rebellion of Hugh earl of Tyrone and the appeasing thereof'. Moryson had come to Ireland in 1600 as private secretary to Mountjoy, the lord deputy who had suppressed the revolt. He followed Camden's account in describing O'Neill's personality. However he also had access to state papers and in examining the causes of the conflict gave far greater credence to the complaints of the Irish against English maladmin-

---

[1] An excellent guide to the historiography of this period is found in R. W. Dudley Edwards and Mary O'Dowd, *Sources for early modern Irish history, 1534–1641*, Cambridge 1985.
[2] John McGurk, 'William Camden: civil historian or Gloriana's propagandist?', *History Today*, xxxviii (1988), 47–53.
[3] William Camden, *History of the most renowned and victorious princess Elizabeth, late Queen of England*, London 1675, 447, 478–9.
[4] Ibid. 446.

istration, especially under Sir William Fitzwilliam. Of course all this served to put the government of his late master in the best possible light.[5] Another book written in praise of a former Lord Deputy was *The government of Ireland under Sir John Perrot* by the unidentified E. C. S. It used state papers to establish Perrot as an energetic reformer and implied that the Irish war was caused by his successors.[6] However, the most common source of information about Perrot was by way of his inclusion amongst the favourites of Queen Elizabeth in Sir Robert Naunton's memoirs of her reign, *Fragmenta regalia*.[7] Also widely circulated was Thomas Gainsford's short pot-boiler, *The history of the earle of Tyrone*. It was based mainly on Camden and came out in 1619.[8]

The losing side also had its proponents. Peter Lombard's *De regno Hiberniae, sanctorum insula, commentarius* cannot strictly be described as a history. Although it was published posthumously in 1632, it had been originally written as a propaganda tract in 1600 to win Papal support for the Irish cause. It began as a classical account describing Ireland's geographical position, the character of its inhabitants etc. It emphasised Ireland's contribution as the island of saints to the development of Western Christianity and how Pope Adrian had granted the island to the kings of England who had eventually ended up schismatics and heretics. Lombard attributed the current conflict to the escalation of English religious and political persecution in Ulster which had hitherto been isolated from it.[9] Remarkably, his assessment of O'Neill coincides with Camden's:

> If one looks to his education . . . it was of such kind that he is most thoroughly versed in the politics and affairs not only of Ireland but also of England, in all matters relating to peace and war. If one considers his age, it was ripe for command, for though he had just passed his fiftieth year, yet he was as fresh and active as if he had not as yet attained forty. If one observes his qualities of mind and body, he is brave, spirited, ready, temperate, wary, patient, prudent, generous, affable, and has his feelings under control that if it were necessary for the matter in hand to appear serious or joyful, pleased or angry, he can most readily and in the most natural manner exhibit these emotions. Indeed he quite captivates the feelings of men by the mobility of his looks and countenance, and wins the affection of his soldiers or strikes terror into them.[10]

In fact, stripped of its blatant religious propaganda, Lombard's account of the outbreak of the war is reasonably accurate. Vatican sources indicate that he had

---

5 Fynes Moryson, *An itinerary*, 3 pts, London 1617, II/i, 1–15.
6 E. C. S., *The government of Ireland under Sir John Perrot 1584–1588*, London 1626.
7 Sir Robert Naunton, *Fragmenta regalia or observations on the late Queen Elizabeth her times and her favourites*, 3rd edn, London 1653, in *English reprints*, ed. Edward Arber, London 1870, 41–4.
8 Thomas Gainsford, *The true, exemplary and remarkable history of the earle of Tyrone*, London 1619.
9 Peter Lombard, *De regno Hiberniae, sanctorum insula, commentarius*, ed. P. F. Moran, Dublin 1868.
10 M. J. Byrne (trans.), *The Irish war of defence 1598–1600: extracts from the 'De Hibernia Insula commentarius' of Peter Lombard, archbishop of Armagh*, Cork 1930, 27–9.

the use of information forwarded by O'Neill.[11] However, Philip O'Sullevan Beare writing in 1621 was far less accurate. His *Historiae catholicae Iberniae compendium* was structured in a similar way to Lombard's commentary. Its third tome related 'the Fifteen Years War' between Irish Catholic lords and the Protestant crown of England between 1588 and 1603 but contained far too many errors to be of much value in establishing what really happened.[12] In a resulting dispute about the early church, Archbishop Ussher referred to O'Sullevan Beare as 'a worthy author to ground a report of Antiquity upon; who in relating matters that fell out in his own time, discovereth himself to be as egregious a liar as any (I verily think) that this day breatheth in Christendom'.[13]

These contemporary or near-contemporary sources were the major influences over what was written until the middle of the nineteenth century. However, where historians had access to manuscripts or to new printed sources, their perspective was liable to change in spite of any contrary predilection. Sir James Ware in his *Annals* followed Camden and Moryson and contributed no new insights.[14] Richard Cox was a Protestant exile in England from the Jacobite ascendancy in Ireland when he wrote *Hibernia Anglicana* in 1689 to urge a reconquest. He had access to the papers of Sir George Carew, one of Queen Elizabeth's most outstanding servitors in the Irish wars. Cox's view of O'Neill as a duplicitous and ungrateful rebel was a standard one. More significantly, he adopted a positive view of Perrot's government and a negative one of Fitzwilliam's. He viewed Fitzwilliam as regarding government as a preferment not a service and pointed to allegations of bribery in the cases of O'Donnell's escape and MacMahon's hanging.[15] In the mid-eighteenth century Abbé James MacGeoghegan presented a Catholic alternative to Cox's history but no new insights into what he called the Fifteen Years War.[16] A recasting of the period was worked by the appearance of two new printed sources. In 1727 Richard Rawlinson published a life of Sir John Perrot which had survived in manuscript and had probably been written by the deputy's bastard son to vindicate him posthumously.[17] Equally significant was the long memorial by Captain Thomas Lee attacking Fitzwilliam's government of Ireland contained in John Lodge's *Desiderata curiosa Hibernica or a select collection of state papers* (Dublin 1772).[18] The new sources were utilised in Leland's history. Perrot was firm but fair, Fitzwilliam was corrupt and the execution of MacMahon emerged as the key

[11] J. Hagan, 'Some papers relating to the Nine Years War', *Archivium Hibernicum*, ii (1913), 290.
[12] Philip O'Sullevan Beare, *Historiae catholicae Iberniae compendium*, Lisbon 1621, ed. Matthew Kelly, Dublin 1850.
[13] James Ussher, *A discourse of the religion anciently professed by the Irish and British*, 4th edn, London 1687, 69.
[14] Sir James Ware, *The annals of Ireland*, Dublin 1705, 38–50.
[15] Richard Cox, *Hibernia Anglicana or the history of Ireland from the conquest thereof by the English to this present time*, London 1689, 370–400.
[16] James MacGeoghegan, *Histoire de l'Irlande, ancienne et moderne*, 3 vols, Paris 1758–1762, iii. 468–510.
[17] Richard Rawlinson (ed.), *The life, deedes and death of Sir John Perrot*, London 1727.
[18] Thomas Lee, 'A brief declaration of the government of Ireland . . . 1594', in *Desiderata curiosa Hibernica*, Dublin 1772, i. 87–150.

event in the outbreak of hostilities: 'the condemnation of this chieftain confirmed the Irish in their aversion to English polity, which they considered as a system of baleful tyranny and cruelty'.[19] Sylvester O'Hallaron in his famous critique *Ierne defended* attacked Leland as having 'furnished us with an account of the transactions of the English Pale' by ignoring the Gaelic sources for Irish history. This was unfair to Leland's book which was for its day an outstanding and unrivalled piece of synthesis.[20] Indeed his depiction of Fitzwilliam as a corrupt governor gave writers such as Curry and Taafe who favoured Catholic emancipation the opportunity to portray Hugh O'Neill not as an ungrateful rebel but as a loyalist forced into insurrection.[21]

It was not until the 1840s that O'Neill's life attracted individual attention. The poet-clergyman James Wills was paid £1,000 to write a national biographical history of Ireland following the successful completion of similar projects for England and Scotland. The resulting *Lives of illustrious and distinguished Irishmen* contained a thoughtful, unbiased biography of O'Neill.[22] Wills included a crucial misconception about O'Neill – that he had been brought up in England. This was a simple misreading of the sources which had already surfaced in the works of MacDermot (publ. 1823) and Taylor (publ. 1831).[23] The account presented the now standard view about the divergent governmental approaches of Perrot and Fitzwilliam, the latter having caused the conflict by his seizures of O'Gallagher and O'Doherty and especially by his execution of MacMahon. In the case of O'Neill himself, Wills reckoned his marriage to Mabel Bagenal as the more decisive event without explaining why. He portrayed the earl as practising acts of dissimulation against both English and Irish and thereby earning the mistrust of both. He regarded him as wavering at the onset of hostilities caught between 'the restless suspicions and despotic temper of Lord-deputies and the fierce remonstrances of his countrymen' but having eventually to make a choice because of the forceful conduct of Hugh Roe O'Donnell, the inspirational young leader of Tirconnell. Wills had reached this conclusion by obtaining his information about O'Donnell, who was the subject of another biography in the same volume, from the manuscript of Ó Cléirigh's life of the Tirconnellian lord in the library of the Royal Irish Academy. The influence of Wills's compendium of lives which was republished twice is difficult to assess. His fellow poet Tom Moore certainly used his biography of O'Neill when writing a history of Ireland, a companion to popular histories of England and

19 Thomas Leland, *A history of Ireland from the invasion of Henry II*, 3 vols, Dublin 1773, II/iv, chs iii, iv.
20 S. O'Hallaron, *An introduction to the study of the history and antiquities of Ireland*, 3 vols, Dublin 1810, i. 7, 552.
21 J. Curry, *An historical and critical review of the civil wars in Ireland from the reign of Queen Elizabeth to the settlement under King William*, London 1786, 15–27; Denis Taafe, *An impartial history of Ireland*, Dublin 1809–11, i. 466–526.
22 James Wills, *Lives of illustrious and distinguished Irishmen from the earliest times to the present period, arranged in chronological order and embodying a history of Ireland in the lives of Irishmen*, 6 vols, Dublin 1840–7, II/i. 94–155.
23 Martin MacDermot, *A new and impartial history of Ireland from the earliest accounts to the present time*, 4 vols, London 1823, iii. 75–6; W. C. Taylor, *History of the civil wars of Ireland*, 2 vols, Edinburgh 1831, i. 210.

Scotland by Mackintosh and Scott respectively. However Moore put a patriotic gloss on O'Neill as 'one who was destined, not only to rally round him the hearts of his fellow countrymen, but to show for once an instance of Irishmen conquering in their own cause'.[24] In 1846 O'Neill was also the subject of a biography by the Protestant nationalist politician, John Mitchel. He said that he was writing from the viewpoint of Irish clansmen rather than that of the Dublin government. The denigration of Fitzwilliam was now complete: 'All historians of both nations concur in representing him as one of the most flagitious, greedy, cruel and corrupt governors that an English monarch ever sent to Ireland.' Mitchel did not seek to castigate or explain away O'Neill's dissembling behaviour. Instead, he provided a nationalist interpretation of O'Neill 'striving to heal the feuds of rival chiefs and out of those discordant elements create and bind together an Irish nation'. In the same spirit of unity, Mitchel exploited Lee's memorial to downgrade O'Neill's Catholicism and to make him a politique in religion.[25] By contrast O'Neill's Catholicism was exaggerated in a French biography by Guénot in 1863 which presented a romanticised portrait of the earl as a patriotic, Counter-Reformation warrior.[26]

The emergence of modern history writing was facilitated by the institutional developments of the Victorian era. In 1838 the Public Record Office was established in London, to be followed thirty years later by a counterpart in Dublin and then after partition in the twentieth century by one in Belfast. These institutions gave scholars access to the records of government for the first time on a regular basis. Furthermore, the HMSO gave even greater prominence to the existence of such primary sources by embarking upon the publication of calendars. Of particular relevance here are The Calendar of State Papers, Ireland, (published 1860–1912), The Calendar of the Carew Manuscripts, (publ. 1867–73), and The Calendar of State Papers, Spanish, (publ. 1892–9). Yet these calendars had many deficiencies. The early calendars of the Irish state papers were mere summaries of documents, the later ones were erratic with some transcribed mysteriously into the third person. The calendars of the Carew manuscripts at Lambeth Palace were fuller but this document collection was itself only a personal selection copied in the early seventeenth century from the state papers. M. A. S. Hume made a calendar of state papers relating to England, Scotland and Ireland in the Spanish national archives at Simancas but failed to include all the relevant documents and those he did include were not always summarised precisely or even translated correctly. The Victorians also established the Historical Manuscripts Commission to publish source materials in private hands. The first and major achievement was the publication of the papers of William Cecil, Lord Burghley, and his son, Sir Robert, held at Hatfield House by their descendant, the Marquis of Salisbury (publ. 1883–1973). A successor

---

[24] Thomas Moore, The history of Ireland from the earliest kings of that realm down to its last chief, 4 vols, London 1835–46, iv. 99. I owe this reference to Murray Smith, a postgraduate student at University College, Dublin, who has begun research on the historiographical reputation of O'Neill in the nineteenth and twentieth centuries.

[25] John Mitchel, The life and times of Aodh O'Neill, prince of Ulster, Dublin 1846, preface, 77–101.

[26] C. Guénot, Le comte de Tyrone, Tours 1863.

native institution was the Irish Manuscripts Commission which after independence published materials from private and public archives, including *The chronicle of Ireland, 1584–1608*, (publ. 1933), *The compossicion booke of Conought*, (publ. 1936) and *The Walsingham letter-book*, (publ. 1959). Gaelic sources also became available in print and often in translation. The greatest triumph was the publication of the compilation of Irish histories dating from 1634 known as *The annals of Four Masters*. They appeared in 1848 edited and translated by the Celtic scholar, John O'Donovan. In 1871 William Hennessy translated a late sixteenth-century work, *The annals of Loch Cé*. In 1893 Denis Murphy brought out in English one of the sources used by the four masters, Lughaidh Ó Cléirigh's biography of O'Neill's ally Hugh Roe O'Donnell, which has since been superseded by Paul Walsh's edition of 1948. In addition to these major publications, many important documents have been published by learned societies in their journals over the last one hundred and fifty years.

The accessibility and increasing availability of source material represented in many respects a false dawn. The amount of material was too awesome for most historians to grapple with and therefore they either reworked established versions of the past or risked even greater distortions by using an exiguous part of the material. A learned, academic history was developed by a few individuals but it never wholly diverged from popular Irish history. In these circumstances there was considerable latitude for creative interpretations or even wholesale misconceptions. For instance, Martin Haverty's *History of Ireland* (publ. 1860), which trumpeted its use of primary sources, simply gave a Catholic slant to Mitchel's nationalist interpretation of O'Neill.[27] More seriously, the errors of fact and interpretation contained in Wills's biography were compounded rather than corrected. The belief that Hugh O'Neill was educated in England gained greater prominence with its inclusion in Thomas D'Arcy McGee's book *A popular history of Ireland* (publ. 1869) and in James Anthony Froude's polemic *The English in Ireland in the eighteenth century* (publ. 1872). As a result this misconception became an established truth to be repeated by the next generation of popular historians.[28] It was fossilised by inclusion in Robert Dunlop's account of O'Neill in *The dictionary of national biography* (publ. 1895).[29] The assumption that O'Neill was educated in England had of course profound implications. These were evident in McGee and Froude. For the nationalist McGee, the English-educated O'Neill became 'a patriot of Ulster rather than of Ireland' and an ambivalent figure trying 'to play the Celtic prince north of the Boyne, and the English earl at Dublin or London'.[30] The imperialist Froude had a different

---

[27] M. Haverty, *History of Ireland, ancient and modern, derived from our native annals, from the most recent researches of eminent Irish scholars and antiquaries, from the state papers and from all the resources of Irish history now available*, Dublin 1860, 452.

[28] For example: Justin MacCarthy, *An outline of Irish history*, London 1883, 42; William Francis Collier, *History of Ireland for schools*, London 1884, 172–3; Charles G. Walpole, *A short history of the kingdom of Ireland*, London 1885, 153; W. Stephenson Gregg, *Irish history for English readers*, London 1886, 44; Emily Lawless, *Ireland*, London 1888, 199; William O'Connor Morris, *Ireland, 1494–1868*, Cambridge 1898, 108–9.

[29] *DNB*, xlii. 188.

[30] Thomas D'Arcy McGee, *A popular history of Ireland from the earliest period to the emancipation of the Catholics*, 2 vols, Glasgow 1869, ii. 36.

view based on the same misconception. His diatribe against Ireland departed radically from the rigorous method of his *History of England from the fall of Wolsey to the defeat of the Spanish Armada* (12 vols, London 1856–70). He wrote:

> In Hugh O'Neill, earl of Tyrone, Elizabeth was now to find the most formidable Irish antagonist which either she or her predecessors had encountered. To her he was indebted for life, rank and fortune. He was son of the baron of Dungannon, whom Shane had murdered, and the grandson of the first earl, Con. Beyond doubt, he would have shared his father's fate, had he not been sent to England, and thus taken care of. He was brought up at the Court as a Protestant, in the midst of the most brilliant circle which any capital in Europe could show. No pains were spared to make him a fit instrument for the reclamation of his country and when of age, he received the patents of his grandfather's earldom and returned to Ireland. The wolf which is treated as a dog remains a wolf.[31]

In other words O'Neill remained an unreconstructed Irishman in spite of his education in England. And by implication his great success in arms was not the result of natural intelligence or organisational ability but only because of his education in England!

A more academic approach can be seen in Richey's *Lectures on the history of Ireland* (publ. 1870).[32] Alexander Richey, a professor of law at Trinity College, Dublin, was one of the first to make extensive use of the newly printed sources. For his ninth lecture on 'the war of Hugh O'Neill', he utilised the *Carew calendars* and *The annals of the Four Masters*. These sources were difficult to exploit. The state papers copied for Carew included many of the most important documents but they were a small part of the whole and so divorced from their context. *The annals of the Four Masters*, which purported to be a Gaelic history of Ireland, was in fact written from the standpoint of the O'Donnell family. Indeed the result was a mosaic of long citations supported by editorial glosses rather than a sustained analysis. Richey did use – somewhat uncritically – the complaints of the Irish lords contained in Carew to show the excesses of Fitzwilliam as the main cause of the war.[33] However, his interpretation of O'Neill was informed by a strange mixture of Victorian racial stereotyping and national pride. As a result of O'Neill's alleged sojourn at Court, 'he was, by education, habits and interest, English'. This meant 'he was essentially not a Celt; he possessed none of the enthusiasm or instability of his nation . . . he exhibited the very un-Irish quality of appreciating existing facts . . . Yet, after every allowance, he was undoubtedly the ablest man the Celtic race since the arrival of the English has produced'.[34]

In a different league from Richey's dabbling was Bagwell's three volume *Ireland under the Tudors* (publ. 1885–90).[35] It was more terrazzo than mosaic.

---

[31] J. A. Froude, *The English in Ireland in the eighteenth century*, 2 vols, London 1872–4, i. 58–60.
[32] Alexander G. Richey, *Lectures on the history of Ireland from A.D. 1534 to the date of the plantation of Ulster*, London 1870, 390–445.
[33] Ibid. 398–400.
[34] Ibid. 416–17.
[35] Richard Bagwell, *Ireland under the Tudors*, 3 vols, London 1885–90.

Although Bagwell disclaimed any political allegiance in his treatment of the subject, he was touched by the prevailing Social Darwinism as evidenced by his reference to 'the inevitable doom of the Celtic race'.[36] He used all the published source material and the archives where possible by using the calendars as a guide to produce the fullest possible history. Bagwell's work could be described as a 'Castle-centred' history of Ireland since it is derived largely from official papers. Even then it is less a sustained analysis of policy than a series of anecdotes. Bagwell had little to say about Hugh O'Neill's supposed education in England save that it took place 'at headquarters'.[37] As a cause of hostilities, he over-emphasised O'Neill's marriage to Mabel Bagenal whom he characterised as 'the Helen of the Elizabethan wars'.[38] He did hold that the treason charges against Perrot were trumped-up but on the other hand he tended to mitigate the charges of corruption against Fitzwilliam, especially in the case of MacMahon, stating that 'this old-world gossip wants confirmation'.[39] Possessed of a guide to the subsequent state papers, Bagwell might have come to a different conclusion because when he wrote the process of calendaring had only reached 1592. As a result he relied on the Carew calendars and so refused to accept the Irish allegations contained therein at face value. As such it is fair to say that the last eleven years of Bagwell's history is too reliant on annals and contemporary accounts even though he did have access to the papers of the marquis of Salisbury at Hatfield House.[40] In which case Bagwell's third volume should be supplemented by Lord Ernest Hamilton's *Elizabethan Ulster* (publ. 1919) which had the benefit of the requisite calendars. This was a good solid account but it should not be viewed in isolation from the extreme political bias of his sequel *The Irish rebellion of 1641* (publ. 1920).[41]

Reacting against this type of history writing was the great scholar, Standish O'Grady. His book *Red Hugh's captivity* (publ. 1889) is as important for its introductory critique as its contents.[42] He wanted to write popular history because what he called 'philosophical history' was killing genuine interest in the subject by its dull and tedious approach. He attacked Bagwell head-on: 'Has the reader ever rambled through *Ireland under the Tudors* on a holiday? Does he desire another pleasure trip of the sort?' And he took Froude down a peg or two by showing that a reference to Irish events in his *History of England* was completely wrong. He objected to uncritical reliance on official documentation: 'The state papers, so multifarious are they, and so representative of all sorts of minds, that from them quotations may be selected which will support any view which the historian may think true. I will prove from the same authorities that any conspicuous character of the age, Englishman or Irishman, was a scoundrel and also prove from the same authorities that he was a saint.' He insisted that Elizabethan Ireland contained plenty of tragedy and romance

---

36 Ibid. i. preface.
37 Ibid. ii. 40.
38 Ibid. iii. 223–5.
39 Ibid. iii. 196–7, 201–3, 227–32, 241.
40 Ibid. iii. preface.
41 Lord Ernest Hamilton, *Elizabethan Ulster*, London 1919; idem. *The Irish rebellion of 1641*, London 1920.
42 Standish O'Grady, *Red Hugh's captivity*, London 1889, 1–30.

and that he himself had sufficient grasp of the sources to write history that was more interesting even than fiction. His general view of the period would have been shared by many other Victorians:

> The Elizabethan conquest of Ireland was, in my opinion, as inevitable as salutary, and the terrors and horrors which accompanied it, to a considerable extent, a necessary condition of its achievement. These petty kings and princes had to be broken once and for all. In blood and flame and horror of great darkness it was fated that Ireland should pass from barbarism to civilisation, from the wild rule of the 'monocracies' to the reign of universal law.

However, he felt that the Gaelic lords involved had not been given sufficient attention and that the neglected figure of Hugh Roe O'Donnell was a suitable subject for his humanising and dramatising technique. As regards the Nine Years War, he believed that 'the grand driving force of the rebel movement was the fiery young chieftain'. Indeed it was in *Red Hugh's captivity* that O'Grady coined the term 'the Nine Years War' for the great struggle at the end of Elizabeth's reign. It is either because of the popularity of the book or because O'Grady used the term again in his introduction to *Pacata Hibernia*, a seventeenth-century account of the final suppression of the revolt, that it has stuck and become accepted as the preferred alternative to 'Tyrone's rebellion'.[43]

In the 1930s the troika of R. D. Edwards, T. W. Moody and D. B. Quinn having imbibed new knowledge as postgraduate students at the Institute of Historical Research in London set out to transform the writing of Irish history. So the story goes. With their inspiration, the Ulster Society for Irish Historical Studies and the Irish Historical Society were founded in Belfast and in Dublin respectively in 1936 'for the advancement of Irish historical learning on scientific principles'. Under the auspices of these societies, Edwards and Moody established and edited *Irish Historical Studies* to publish the results of original research because of 'the absence of any journal exclusively devoted to the scientific study of Irish history'.[44] The work of these men was significant but it is itself the subject of historical misconception in the hands of current devotees. The passport into the scientific study of history was the postgraduate dissertation. One such dissertation was J. K. Graham's 'An historical study of the career of Hugh O'Neill' which was awarded the degree of master of arts at Queen's University of Belfast in 1938. However this only made use of the printed sources.[45] His one resulting publication was a short piece on the birth-date of Hugh O'Neill in the 'historical revisions' section of the first *IHS*. This established the year of the earl's birth as c. 1550 rather than c. 1540 but failed to challenge his alleged education in England which Graham now assumed to have been between the ages of twelve and eighteen.[46] Worse was to come in the shape of Sean O'Faolain's ever popular biography, *The Great O'Neill* (publ.

---

[43] Thomas Stafford, *Pacata Hibernia*, London 1633, ed. Standish O'Grady, 2 vols, London 1896, i. pp. xxxii–xxxiii.

[44] Preface, *IHS*, i (1938–9), 1–3.

[45] J. K. Graham, 'An historical study of the career of Hugh O'Neill, 2nd earl of Tyrone, c. 1550–1616', unpubl. MA thesis, Queen's University, Belfast 1938.

[46] Idem. 'The birth-date of Hugh O'Neill, second earl of Tyrone, *IHS*, i (1938–9), 58–9.

1942). He attempted to write a popular account of O'Neill's life borrowing substantially from Graham's postgraduate work. However, O'Faolain had no historical training whatsoever; he was a novelist whose model was more that of Sir Walter Scott than Standish O'Grady. His book is full of wild inaccuracy, crass romanticisation and faulty revisionism. Unable to reject the received notion of O'Neill's education in England, he embroidered it with fanciful references to life at the Court and country-houses of Elizabethan England. In short, O'Faolain more than anyone else has been responsible for the image of Hugh O'Neill as an ambivalent individual caught helplessly between the inexorable advance of Renaissance civilisation and the obstinate resistance of a traditional society.[47] Yet it wasn't all bad. When reverence is paid today to the Holy Trinity of Edwards, Moody and Quinn, acknowledgment is scarcely afforded G. A. Hayes-McCoy, the father of Irish military history. His first book *Scots mercenary forces in Ireland, 1565-1603* (publ. 1937) showed how important the troops hired from the highlands and islands were in sixteenth-century Irish warfare.[48] In the writings that followed he made a major contribution to the understanding of the tactics and strategy of the Nine Years War.[49] Another military historian who made his mark was Cyril Falls. His book *Elizabeth's Irish wars* (publ. 1950) was based mainly on the calendars of state papers but he did make use of manuscripts in Spain.[50] The first substantial inroad into these Spanish archives was however made by John Silke. As well as his book on the climax of the war, *Kinsale* (publ. 1970), he wrote a significant article emphasising the role of Catholic bishops in its genesis.[51] Since the beginning of the 1970s a sustained revival of scholarly interest in Tudor Ireland has been underway. The result has been four significant studies. Nicholas Canny and Brendan Bradshaw have examined the ideology of Tudor rule and more recently, Steven Ellis and Ciarán Brady have looked at the development of policy through changes in the administrative process.[52] In this spate of research, the climacteric of the Tudor period – the Nine Years War – has been surprisingly neglected.

Writing in the last decade of the twentieth century, it is obvious that

47 Sean O'Faolain, *The Great O'Neill*, London 1942. O'Faolain's book has since given rise to 'Making History', a play by Brian Friel (first performed, 1988). O'Faolain provided the germ of the idea for the play in his preface: 'Indeed, in those last years in Rome the myth was already beginning to emerge, and a talented dramatist might write an informative, entertaining, ironical play on the theme of a living man helplessly watching his translation into a star in the face of the facts which had reduced him to poverty, exile and defeat.' For my view of Friel's play, see 'Making History: a criticism and a manifesto', *Text and Context*, iv (1990), 61–5.
48 G. A. Hayes-McCoy, *Scots mercenary forces in Ireland, 1565–1603*, Dublin 1937.
49 Idem. 'Strategy and tactics in Irish warfare, 1563–1601', *IHS*, ii (1941), 255–79; 'The army of Ulster, 1593–1601', *Irish Sword*, i (1950), 105–17; and *Irish battles*, London 1969, chs vi–ix.
50 Cyril Falls, *Elizabeth's Irish wars*, London 1950.
51 J. J. Silke, 'The Irish appeal of 1593 to Spain: some light on the genesis of the Nine Years War', *Irish Ecclesiastical Record*, 5th ser, xcii (1959), 279–90, 362–71; idem. *Kinsale*, Liverpool 1970.
52 Nicholas Canny, *The Elizabethan conquest of Ireland: a pattern established, 1565–1576*, Hassocks 1976; Brendan Bradshaw, *The Irish constitutional revolution of sixteenth century*, Cambridge 1979; Steven G. Ellis, *Reform and Revival: English government in Ireland, 1470–1534*, Woodbridge 1986; Ciarán Brady, 'The government of Ireland, c. 1540 to 1583', unpubl. PhD. thesis, Trinity College, Dublin 1981. Brady's thesis is the basis of his forthcoming book, *The chief-governors: the rise and fall of vice-regal government*, Cambridge 1993.

scientific method is increasingly being found wanting and that, if we are being honest, interpretation cannot be value-free. Yet we can still strive towards an objective record of past events, although we will never do better than a rough and ready appproximation. The key factor here is critical judgement; we must interrogate all the primary sources critically both internally and in relation to one another. In this way personal, political and historiographical predilections can be marginalised. In the case of the Nine Years War, there is an additional element; the need to strike a balance between the policies of the crown and the Gaelic lords opposing it. The main source is still the Irish state papers. It is possible to agree with Standish O'Grady that used selectively these papers will suit any argument. But, if used judiciously, they can do the job. This large body of papers consists mainly of letters from officials in Dublin to the privy council in London. The uncritical use of these papers would give us a view of Ireland from the perspective of Dublin Castle. However, this archive also includes the documents which Dublin officials enclosed with their correspondence as well as letters from provincial officials writing directly to London in an attempt to circumvent the jurisdiction of Dublin. It also contains letters of Irish lords petitioning or complaining to London and newsletters from men acting as agents for English privy councillors. Clearly then it is possible to draw out the opinions of Gaelic lords as well as the nuances of government policy from the state papers. Yet it is also valid to say that the opinions of Gaelic lords expressed therein may have been for English consumption and that we should reorientate ourselves by using Gaelic source material as Sylvester O'Hallaron insisted. Unfortunately, this material is small in extent, often difficult to use and no less engaged. There is an extensive body of bardic poetry but it is a highly stylised reflection of the mentality of the Gaelic elite and little help as a guide to the events. We also need to be careful when using the annals. The *Four Masters* was compiled under the direction of Micheál Ó Cléirigh whose family were hereditary historians of the O'Donnell family. The uncritical use of these annals would give a history of Ireland from the perspective of Donegal Castle. Moreover the compilers used Lughaidh Ó Cléirigh's biography of Hugh Roe O'Donnell as their principal source for the Nine Years War but it was a very inaccurate, deliberately propagandistic work. Its object was probably to advance the claims of the O'Donnell family to be equal if not superior to the O'Neill family when both retreated into the self-deluding world of political exile. As a result of the availability of these primary sources an exaggerated view of Hugh O'Donnell's importance has developed over the last century. No poem-books or annals relating to the Tyrone O'Neills have survived to act as a counterbalance. It was once thought that there were vast undiscovered collections of documents in foreign archives which would tell the Irish side of the story. This is not the case but there are key documents which can alter the focus. Even so the opinions expressed therein by Gaelic lords have again to be carefully sifted because they are leavened with the rhetoric of Counter-Reformation Catholicism and a cravenness born out of military weakness. The history which has emerged from the critical interrogation of these sources has been divided into three parts, the first two thematic and the third narrative.

Part one concerns crown policy in the north of Ireland during the deputyships of Sir John Perrot and Sir William Fitzwilliam. The first attempted to rule as a reforming governor but was eventually forced to adopt a minimalist approach; the second began as a minimalist but stumbled into a reform programme. During Perrot's rule, there was an interest in curtailing the authority of provincial officials such as Bingham in Connacht and Bagenal in Ulster. Conversely, in Fitzwilliam's time with central government less active, these individuals had a freer hand and their ambitious activities helped provoke trouble. Fitzwilliam was no more cruel towards the Gaelic Irish than his predecessor. However, it is possible to confirm that he was far more corrupt and that this served to undermine confidence in his rule. Although there was bitter factional rivalry within these administrations and between them culminating in Perrot's trial for treason, this factor concealed continuity of policy. Most of Perrot's grandiose schemes came to nothing, but the process of feudalising land tenure, known to scholars as surrender and regrant, did make a significant comeback in the 1580s. This policy climaxed under Fitzwilliam in the grant of property rights to freeholders in Monaghan in 1591. This settlement became a model for the reorganisation of the other Ulster lordships. The implementation of this policy threatened the militarism which was the controlling mechanism in Gaelic society. However, in attempting the reformation of Ulster on a shoe-string budget, the government in Dublin remained dependent on the goodwill of the dominant O'Neill.

The development of the two principal Ulster lordships, Tyrone and Tirconnell, is the subject of part two. Their internal structures merit examination because of our scant knowledge of Gaelic society. The examination reveals the enduring importance of 'tanistry', the Gaelic mode of political succession and challenges the Victorian conception that Gaelic society was moribund and doomed to destruction. Traditional succession crises in these lordships, in spite of increasing English intrusion, produced energetic leaders in the persons of Hugh O'Neill and Hugh Roe O'Donnell. The role of Hugh O'Neill, the second earl of Tyrone, was pivotal. The state held the mistaken opinion of him as a 'creature' to command. In reality, its relationship with him developed from one of interdependence to reliance. The turning point in this relationship came in 1587 when the crown began to seek means to curtail his power. Thereafter, O'Neill had to resort to bribery of officials to maintain his freedom of action. O'Neill's power was based on a web of personal connections and on the development of demesne agriculture on ecclesiastical lands. His ultimate success lay in the marriage alliance with the ruling sept of Tirconnell. At the start of 1592, he rescued his son-in-law, Hugh Roe O'Donnell, from imprisonment in Dublin Castle. Tirconnell under Hugh Roe recovered from a long period of internal strife and government interference to determine the final destruction of Turlough Luineach, the ageing ruler of Tyrone. With the two Hughs in control, the ancient rivals for power in the North were now allied by mutual interest.

The contingency of events forces the foregoing themes into a narrative format in part three. A structural crisis between the centralising state and the consolidating overlords was triggered by a botched attempt to establish a sheriff in Fermanagh. Afterwards at Dundalk, the Lord Deputy and council examined O'Neill's role in a plot by Catholic bishops to procure Spanish assistance and his part in the ejection of the sheriff from Fermanagh. To extricate himself,

O'Neill was forced to make war on Maguire who as the lord of Fermanagh was his principal dependent. To prevent further encroachment and to wring concessions from the crown, the earl fought proxy wars. With a spurious claim of inability to control his own followers as a smokescreen, he hoped to avoid a complete rupture. He brought a confederacy into existence in which each participant swore a solemn oath on the Gospels not to make peace without the others' consent. He also organised a capable Ulster army and the flexible *buannacht* system of keeping mercenaries facilitated its expansion when new territories were overrun. The Elizabethan regime, racked by factional disputes and committed financially and militarily on the Continent, proved slow to respond to the challenge. The crown eventually proclaimed O'Neill a traitor. However, its war effort, with a divided command and a ramshackle army, was a failure. By this time the confederacy, to prevent English encroachment, had become a vehicle for the expansionism of Tyrone and Tirconnell. In 1596 fears of Spanish invasion forced concessions from the crown in return for an acknowledgement of suzerainty. This peace settlement was aborted by the dramatic intervention of Spanish agents.

The summing-up tackles two points. It assesses the early career of Hugh O'Neill in the light of the foregoing investigation and reaches a conclusion not all that dissimilar from the contemporary ones of Camden and Lombard. It also looks at the Nine Years War in context. It eschews the notion that this conflict was a straightforward 'Tudor rebellion'. Rather, it compares the crisis facing England in Ireland with that facing Spain in the Netherlands. The appendix is last but not least. It contains a document from the Spanish archives which proves the overall argument of the book.

2

Political Background

The Nine Years War was the climax of a period of direct and continuous English involvement in Irish affairs which had begun in the 1530s. In the aftermath of the Kildare rebellion of 1534, it was no longer safe for the Tudors to govern Ireland by a system of aristocratic delegation. Instead, they chose to rule directly through English governors. These men lacked the extensive network of local connections which the earl of Kildare had built up to secure consent outside the Pale. Consequently the English state had to make a sustained effort to develop new approaches to the government of its Irish dependency. In so doing the Tudors sought political reform in Ireland: the actual result of their prolonged endeavours was military conquest.[1]

The principal agents of political reform were the English viceroys, usually holding the title of lord deputy but occasionally bearing the more honorific designation of lord lieutenant. In the first half-century after intervention, three modes of vice-regal government have been distinguished. The first English governors were conservatives whose policies were reactive to local events. The first major reform initiative was launched by St Leger with the support of Anglo-Irish reformers in the 1540s. Its primary objective was attained when Ireland was made a kingdom in 1541. Of more significance was the policy, now known as 'surrender and regrant', under which Gaelic and Gaelicised lords surrendered their lands to secure their titles by regrant from the crown. This policy was an attempt to integrate the Gaelic polities as feudal lordships within a unified kingdom and as such remained basic government policy throughout the century. This reactive approach to government was superseded in the mid-1550s with the appointment of the earl of Sussex, whose radical policies were preconceived in England. As a result, Sussex and his successor, Sir Henry Sidney, have been termed 'programmatic governors'. Their programmes focused on certain nodal problems, notably Shane O'Neill, to which colonisation and provincial presidencies were the declared solutions. A contrasting mode was the minimalist approach of Sir William Fitzwilliam during his deputyship in the early 1570s. Allotted few resources by the crown, he was uninterested in, indeed inimical to, the reform processes in motion in Ulster, Connacht and Munster. Uncontrolled by central authority, these provincial policies only provoked confrontation. Fitzwilliam was replaced by Sidney whose final term in office saw a return to programmatic government. His new policy, known as 'composition', aimed at stabilising relations at all levels within Irish society by commuting arbitrary military exactions into fixed taxes and rents. The

---

[1] Steven Ellis, *Tudor Ireland: crown, community and the conflict of cultures, 1470–1603*, London 1985, ch. v.

Palesmen refused to operate the scheme. However, compositions were established in Connacht and Munster which energised the work of the provincial presidencies.[2]

The difficulties of governing Ireland are evident in an anonymous memorandum of 1588. Everything depended on the governor's authority. Because the rule of law was not universal, disputes were 'redressed most commonly by order and warrant from the governor, whereof some have pleasantly termed it the paper state'. The analyst advised the governor to use the army or to play off the factions against each other to enforce his decisions. He went on to describe a bipolar factional system – the Geraldines and the Butlers – which prevailed throughout the realm, incorporated Gaelic and Anglo-Irish, and penetrated every family. For instance in Ulster 'O'Neill and his followers are naturally Geraldines, O'Donnell and his naturally Butlers'. In this way he provided a complete breakdown of the factions in every province, though he ended up with the admission that the alignments could change as a result of 'marriage or accident'.[3] What was being delineated here was a rudimentary system of national politics which worked on the principle of the enemy of my enemy is my friend. The Geraldines were headed by the earl of Kildare and the Butlers by the earl of Ormond. However, these factions were as much a hinderance as a help to the advance of crown government. Certainly the Geraldine interest never fully recovered from the disastrous rebellion of 1534 in spite of the restoration of the earldom two decades later.[4] But the Butlers could, when pressed, flout governmental authority in Ireland because they had married into the Boleyn family – Queen Elizabeth referred to the tenth earl as 'our cousin of Ormond'.[5]

However, a far greater obstacle to Tudor reform in Ireland than the operation of faction was the existence of Gaelic lordships. These polities represented constitutional anomalies, quite distinct from the Anglo-Irish lordships which had their legal bases in royal grants. The Gaelic lords, when obliged to do so, recognised the suzerainty of the English crown. The principal Gaelic region was a continuum of inter-related lordships which stretched diagonally from Connacht and the Midlands through Ulster and then across the North Channel to include the Western Isles and Highlands of Scotland. Ulster was the strongest component. Indeed it was an accepted principle in government circles that the way to reform Ireland was to begin with Ulster.[6] The northern province had two lordships which competed for regional hegemony. In the west Tirconnell showed its head from time to time but Tyrone, occupying the geographical centre of the province, was undoubtedly the more important. The physical location and exceptional concentration of power made Ulster a veritable fortress. This was well-described by Nicholas Dawtrey in the early 1590s:

---

[2] This is Dr Ciarán Brady's classification of governors with some amplification of my own: Brady, 'Court, castle and country: the framework of government in Tudor Ireland', in Ciarán Brady and Raymond Gillespie (eds), *Natives and newcomers: essays on the making of Irish colonial society, 1534–1641*, Dublin 1986, ch. i.
[3] NRO, Fitzwilliam papers (Ireland), no. 68.
[4] Bagwell, *Ireland under the Tudors*, i. 375, 392–3.
[5] Cyril Falls, 'Black Tom of Ormonde', *Irish Sword*, v (1960–1), 17.
[6] PRO SP 63/111, no. 82; BLO, Perrot 1, fos 34–5.

Ulster hath of long time been and yet is the very fostermother and example of all the rebellions of Ireland. The reasons are because the country is itself large and strong of woods and bog rivers and fresh pools, which maketh that province full of straits and hard passages, having the islands of Scotland at hand to assist them in all their rebellions. And because the chief power of that country is always in the command of some one or two at the most of those barbarous men's hands, who through their greatness of command have puffed themselves up with pride to the great charge of the kings of England, as to late experience was had in Her Majesty's reign of that monster, Shane O'Neill.[7]

The key to Gaelic society was military power.[8] It determined succession to political office and control of land and labour. In relations between lordships, overlords claimed the right to inaugurate the *uirríthe* (literally, sub-kings) in office, to billet mercenaries on their territories and to exact tribute.[9] Failure to pay these exactions could result in the transfer of territory; in this way Oriel had lost lands to Tyrone.[10] Gaelic lordships constituted separate polities and the method of political succession within them was known to English observers as 'tanistry'. Although eligibility was still conditioned by custom, successful election now depended on force. Naturally, this system left many disgruntled claimants in collateral branches of the ruling family. Military power also affected property rights in a lordship and caused downward social pressure. Given favourable conditions, a strong lord could dispossess the chief lord of a locality: in 1593 Hugh O'Neill killed Phelim MacTurlough, chief lord of Killetra, and took over his lands.[11] More generally, the freeholders were oppressed by the arbitrary exactions of the chief lords and inability to pay could lead to the mortgaging of demesne lands. Examples of this can also be cited from Tyrone. Niall Connallach expanded at the expense of his kinsmen, the Sliocht Airt; his son, Turlough Luineach, undertook further demesne expansion.[12] In this way, freeholders might lose their property rights and find their status reduced to tenants-at-will.

The fact that Gaelic society was a series of overarching military despotisms meant the existence of dissident groups which the crown could exploit as collaborators. The small lordships of the *uirríthe* were natural allies of the government against the larger units of the overlords. The crown could also expect assistance from the chief lords, in particular those who as collaterals harboured claims to political succession. Most significantly, the freeholders in each lordship represented a possible 'collaborating class'. At its fullest extent,

---

[7] BL Lansdowne 111, no. 46.
[8] For discussion of Gaelic society see the work of Kenneth Nicholls, *Gaelic and gaelicised Ireland in the later Middle Ages*, Dublin 1972 and *Land, law and society in sixteenth century Ireland*, National University of Ireland, O'Donnell lecture, Dublin 1976. See also Mary O'Dowd, 'Gaelic economy and society', in Brady and Gillespie, *Natives and Newcomers*, ch. v.
[9] 'Ceart Uí Néill', trans. Myles Dillon, *Studia Celtica*, i (1966), 1–18.
[10] *Inquisitionum in officio rotulorum cancellariae Hiberniae asservatarum repertorium*, ed. J. Hardiman, 2 vols, Dublin 1826–9, ii. pp. xxx.
[11] *CSPI*, v. 107–9.
[12] Ibid. iii. 520–2; iv. 487.

the surrender and regrant policy sought to take advantage of all three disaffected groups.[13] This reform strategy was however blunted at its very inception
by increased military capacity on the Gaelic side. In the 1540s came the final
collapse of the Lordship of the Isles as a political entity and in its aftermath
large numbers of Scottish soldiers became available for hire.[14] If anything, the
aggrandisement of the regional overlords began to accelerate. O'Cahan and
O'Doherty, the uirríthe on whose territories the mercenaries were most frequently quartered, suffered a steady degradation in status.[15] Greater military
strength also helped counterpoise the commercial impulse which was the economic concomitant of political reform. In a land where labour was scarce and
mobile because of low population density, force must have assisted the retention of tenantry. Indeed, powerful lords like Hugh O'Neill, who controlled the
means of production in this way, benefitted from commercialisation. Conversely, a weak lord like Shane MacBrian of North Clandeboye was unable to
retain his tenants and found himself in debt to the townsmen of Carrickfergus.[16]
Arguably then, Gaelic society in this period was moving towards the Eastern
European pattern of territorial magnates and serf labour.

In the context of these remarks, it is worthwhile surveying government
policy towards Ulster, in particular towards the lordship of Tyrone. In the
period of the Kildare ascendancy, dynastic marriage alliances had played an
important role in policy-making towards the North.[17] In the 1540s surrender
and regrant offered constitutional integration as an alternative to factional
connection but it was only partially implemented in these years and proved
over-optimistic. With most northern lordships, agreements did not reach beyond the preliminary stage; in the form of a traditional submission, the lords
accepted the king as sovereign lord and head of the church and agreed to
annual rents and military services.[18] Only with Tyrone did the process begin in
earnest. After the appliance of force and the denial of the royal title of earl of
Ulster, Conn O'Neill surrendered his lands and was created earl of Tyrone with
much pomp in London in 1542. The earldom was to descend to Conn's designated heir, Matthew, who was given the title of baron of Dungannon. Conn
himself renounced the use of his surname as a title.[19] Subsequently, both
O'Neill and O'Donnell agreed to give up their claims over the uirríthe.[20] In
practice Conn was unable to pass on his earldom. Matthew, though supported
militarily by the government, was killed by followers of Shane O'Neill, the

---

13 Ellis, Tudor Ireland, 137–8.
14 Donald Gregory, The history of the western highlands and isles of Scotland from A.D. 1493 to
A.D. 1625, 2nd edn, Edinburgh 1881, 173–80; Hayes-McCoy, Scots mercenary forces, ch. ii.
15 BLO, Carte 55, fo 591; NLI MS 669, fos 50–2; PRO SP 63/66, no. 50(2); Nicholas Canny,
'Hugh O'Neill, earl of Tyrone, and the changing face of Gaelic Ulster', Studia Hibernica, x
(1970), 13–5.
16 CSPI, v. 141–2; PRO SP 63/175, no. 35(3).
17 M. Katherine Simms, 'Gaelic lordships in Ulster in the late Middle Ages', unpubl. PhD
thesis, Trinity College, Dublin 1976, 781–5.
18 C, Carew, i. 175–6, 183–4, 186–7. For greater detail see Bradshaw, Irish constitutional revolution, ch. vii.
19 CSPI, i. 63; C, Carew, i. 198–9.
20 Ibid. 205–7.

tánaiste or successor under Gaelic custom.[21] The government's acceptance of a designated heir, whose parentage was dubious and local power limited, had proved a disaster.

That the rise of Shane O'Neill posed a 'problem' to the crown in the 1560s was largely the making of the influential governors, Sussex and Sidney. Shane was portrayed as the centre of a renewed Geraldine conspiracy and therefore his overthrow was consistently shown to be the key to the reformation of Ireland. In fact, it was these attitudes which encouraged Shane, in his pursuit of local power, to seek allies in other provinces and indeed overseas. Furthermore there was little real attempt to reach a compromise with Shane even though a basis for one existed since the legitimacy of Matthew, baron of Dungannon, was questionable.[22] It is clear that Sussex and Sidney were using the war against O'Neill to enhance their own prestige, rather than to attain a peaceful settlement. Indeed, having made the military power of Shane O'Neill a 'crux' issue, Sussex's failure against him contributed greatly to his own downfall and replacement by Sidney.[23] Sidney had more success – he had Shane assassinated by the MacDonalds.[24] The projected policy during this war and its immediate aftermath was the limited colonisation of eastern Ulster, the reduction of O'Neill power in central Ulster and the establishment of a provincial presidency.[25] There was no immediate action on these plans and Sidney on a journey through the North was forced to recognise the *tánaiste* to Shane, Turlough Luineach, as ruler of Tyrone.[26] The government did make some gains by siding with a collateral and two *uirríthe*. In this way, Hugh O'Neill, who succeeded his father and elder brother as baron of Dungannon, was established in lands south of the Blackwater river. Also, O'Connor Sligo and O'Reilly surrendered their lands in the hope of achieving independence from O'Donnell and O'Neill, their respective overlords.[27]

The legacy of this war was the posthumous 'Act for the attainder of Shane O'Neill' passed by the Irish parliament in 1569. This act set out the queen's claim to the province of Ulster. It declared void the title and sovereignty of O'Neill in Ulster, abolished the use of Gaelic exactions and formally annexed Tyrone and other territories in central and eastern Ulster to the crown. The attainder was essentially an enabling act allowing for limited colonisation and the further development of surrender and regrant.[28] As a result of this legislation the most coercive side of the reform policy was launched in the early 1570s. This was the scheme known as the 'Enterprise of Ulster' in which private colonists, by conquering and colonising a large part of the province, were to keep out the Scots and destroy the power of the O'Neills. The principal

21 AFM, v. 1563–5.
22 Brady, 'Government of Ireland', 153–4, 180–5.
23 Ibid. 120–1.
24 This is the implication of idem, 'The killing of Shane O'Neill: some new evidence', *Irish Sword*, xv (1982), 116–23.
25 Idem, 'Government of Ireland, 181–2, 192–3.
26 Henry Sidney, 'Memoir of government in Ireland', *Ulster Journal of Archaeology*, 1st ser. iii (1855), 86–7.
27 *Sidney State papers, 1565–70*, ed. T. Ó Laidhin, Dublin 1962, 84–6; C, *Carew*, i. 378.
28 *Statutes at large*, ed. W. Ball, 21 vols Dublin 1786–1804, i. 322–38.

undertakers were Sir Thomas Smith and the earl of Essex. However, no permanent settlements were made. Fitzwilliam, the lord deputy, who saw the prospective colonists as provoking needless political chaos, gave little assistance. Furthermore, the colonists were badly organised from the outset and the financing of both conquest and colonisation proved beyond their means.[29] The only lasting result was the bridge and fortifications which the earl of Essex built on the Blackwater river on the route into the heart of Tyrone.[30]

For nearly a decade after the 'Enterprise of Ulster' there was little active involvement of the crown in the affairs of the northern province. Nevertheless, important issues of policy were discussed. One of Sidney's proposals after his tour of Ulster in 1575 was the winning over of the *uirríthe* by surrender and regrant; he was particularly keen to see the settlement of Iveagh under the loyal Sir Hugh Magennis.[31] The upshot of this proposal was a debate on Gaelic freeholders. The privy council in London advised the appointment of freeholders in the regrant of the lands.[32] Sidney was agreeable in principle: 'the dissipation of the great lords and their countries by good distribution in many hands is a sound way of proceeding to the perfect reformation of this unhappy and cursed estate'. The lord deputy also made plain that such a policy would disturb the *status quo* and that its implementation would require force.[33] The appointment of freeholders – subinfeudation – was an integral part of the surrender and regrant process and had been envisaged by St Leger in relation to the lordships of O'Reilly and O'Toole.[34] However, no progress was made on this front until Sidney's inclusion of freeholders in his settlement of Longford in 1571. Conditions in the Midlands were uniquely favourable: the O'Farrells had no Gaelic overlord, they were internally divided and were closely linked to the government through galloglass service.[35] Although nothing similar was attempted in Ulster during the 1570s, this was an issue of the utmost importance. It represented plans for social engineering on the part of crown officials. By attacking the class structure of Gaelic society at its weakest point, they hoped to cause the destruction of the lord's authority and the fragmentation of the lordship.

Response to government policy can be gauged from the actions of the lords of Tyrone. Conn held the O'Neillship between 1519 and 1559. The support of the earl of Kildare was vital in the acquisition of this title.[36] However, neither the power of Tyrone nor Conn's position within it were secure during his rule. The dynastic troubles within the O'Neill kindred between the years 1493 and 1509 saw the rise of the O'Donnells to a position of equal power in Ulster.[37] This

[29] Canny, *Elizabethan conquest*, 84–90; Hiram Morgan, 'The colonial venture of Sir Thomas Smith in Ulster, 1571–75', *Historical Journal*, xxviii (1985), 261–78.
[30] C, *Carew*, ii. 9, 12.
[31] *Letters and memorials of state*, ed. Arthur Collins, 2 vols, London 1746, i. 75–80.
[32] PRO SP 63/55, no. 5.
[33] *Letters and memorials*, i. 89–97.
[34] Ellis, *Tudor Ireland*, 138, 143.
[35] C, *Carew*, i. 406–9.
[36] Simms, 'Gaelic lordships', 784.
[37] J. Hogan, 'The Irish law of kingship, with special reference to Ailech and Cenél Eoghain', *PRIA*, xl (1932), sect. C, 232.

power permitted their interference in Tyrone and during Conn's time their strong support for his rival Niall Connallach.[38] However, the establishment of Manus O'Donnell, a previous adherent of Conn as lord of Tirconnell, facilitated the curtailment of Niall Connallach's power and the creation of the Geraldine League. This coalition was supported by most Gaelic and Gaelicised lords in the country as a means of re-establishing the house of Kildare and of opposing royal ecclesiastical supremacy.[39] The league was defeated in 1539. Nonetheless, the temporary Gaelic combination and its embassies to France and the Empire had alarmed crown government and the subsequent initiative of St Leger was as much a result of this immediate circumstance as the theories and plans of the Anglo-Irish reformers.[40] Fear of being isolated might have encouraged Conn's acceptance of surrender and regrant; at any rate his participation made sound political sense. The new settlement permitted Conn to steal a march on his rival Niall Connallach, whom the crown had previously supported. As legitimate ruler of Tyrone, he procured the permanent support of the crown to replace the loss of the Geraldine marriage alliance. The confirmation of lands gave the O'Neills security of tenure instead of an ambiguous, unstable relationship with the crown. Phelim Roe and Niall Connallach had their demesne lands confirmed, but they remained under the government of Conn.[41] In fact, the surrender and regrant settlement had temporarily shored up Conn's rule within Tyrone.

By contrast, the crown derived little benefit from the initiative. The renunciation of the O'Neill title, which signified a loss of sovereignty in theory, did not prevent Conn from asserting authority over the *uirríthe* in practice. This is evident from a council order of June 1549 whereby the crown, following complaints from Farney and Fermanagh, declared those territories exempt from the exactions of O'Neill.[42] The case of Fermanagh is especially interesting. It was formerly within the O'Donnell sphere of influence but now the earl of Tyrone was asserting control there. In 1551 we have evidence of Tyrone attempting to extract rent from the MacCartan clan in eastern Ulster.[43] Furthermore, the acid test of the settlement, the succession of the designated heir, proved a failure. In the years 1552-3 Shane gained effective control of the lordship. His use of Scots mercenaries was probably the decisive factor in the succession dispute with Matthew.[44] It can be no accident that the failure of the first phase of surrender and regrant in the North coincided with the increasing availability of such men. It is hardly surprising then that the state enacted legislation in 1556 to make the hiring of Scots soldiers a capital offence.[45]

Shane O'Neill is regarded as a major figure of continuity in Ulster power

38 Ibid. 232-3.
39 Brendan Bradshaw, 'Manus "the magnificent": O'Donnell as Renaissance Prince', in Art Cosgrave and D. McCartney (eds), *Studies in Irish History, presented to R. Dudley Edwards*, Dublin 1979, 30-2.
40 Hogan, 'The Irish law of kingship', 234; Bradshaw, 'Manus "the magnificent" ', 32.
41 C, *Carew*, i. 188, 208.
42 Ibid. i. 215-20. Farney is now a barony of Co. Monaghan.
43 *CSPI*, i. 113.
44 C, *Carew*, i. 243-5.
45 *Statutes at large*, i. 274.

politics: the ruler of Tyrone ruthlessly seizing power into his own hands by time-proven methods – war against the O'Donnells and shows of strength against wayward vassals. But circumstances had changed; unlike a strong O'Neill of the late Middle Ages, Shane had to reckon with the crown more closely. The need for crown recognition is evident throughout Shane's short, eventful career. After his inauguration as O'Neill in 1559, Shane demanded that the crown recognise him as the legal ruler of Tyrone, both as the nominee of its nobility and as Conn's eldest legitimate son. In so doing, Shane advanced the claim that the late Matthew, baron of Dungannon, was neither an O'Neill nor legitimate being the son of a blacksmith of Dundalk called Kelly and thereby inferred that the claims of Matthew's sons to the earldom were void.[46] These demands were ignored at first but with Sussex's military failures multiplying and Shane's power increasing, his position was eventually recognised. This was achieved in two stages. First came Shane's much publicised visit to London in 1562 and then the agreements of 1563.[47] By the latter Shane was granted the title of O'Neill and the government of the *uiríthe* and pending a successful investigation into Matthew's parentage, he would be made earl of Tyrone. With this remarkable agreement, the crown had recognised O'Neill's local supremacy and he its sovereignty. The grant of the earldom would have bound both closer together within the one system. Shane never became earl of Tyrone although he continued to petition for the title: after his death Hugh O'Neill successfully obtained an exemplification of his grandfather's patent of 1542 to strengthen his claim.[48] Even though Shane may be characterised as the ambitious O'Neill vigorously pursuing supremacy in Ulster by traditional methods, he was fully aware of the realities of the new situation. He wanted government recognition of his regional authority and by the very English method of disproving Matthew's legitimacy tried to obtain the earldom as a means of regularising his relationship with the crown.

Turlough Luineach, the next holder of the O'Neill title, had good access to mercenaries through the agency of his Scottish wife.[49] However, he knew from the overt and covert action taken against Shane that the crown would in turn seek to curtail his power. Moreover, his room for negotiation was lessened, first by the fact that as son of Niall Connallach he had no claim to the earldom and second by the attainder of Shane which had, in theory, abolished the title of O'Neill and annexed Tyrone. The first real test of Turlough's strength came with the 'Enterprise of Ulster': yet it also presented an opportunity. The colonisation scheme highlighted the northern lords' insecurity of tenure and as a result Turlough was able to secure the alliance of O'Donnell and the subservience of the *uiríthe*. These vassal lords, including the normally independent lord of Clandeboye who was directly threatened by plantation, accepted a *buannacht* of Scots mercenaries. Only the baron of Dungannon was willing to support the colonisers.[50] However this coalition under Turlough's leadership

---

[46] C, *Carew*, i. 304–8; Bagwell, *Ireland under the Tudors*, ii. 2–4.
[47] C, *Carew*, i. 312–14, 352–3.
[48] *CSPI*, i. 347.
[49] Hayes-McCoy, *Scots mercenary forces*, ch. iii.
[50] Joseph Costello, 'Turlough Luineach O'Neill, the uiríthe and the government', unpubl. MA thesis, University College, Dublin 1973, 134–5.

evaporated as Essex's plantation attempt collapsed into ruins.[51] In the negotiations which followed both Essex and Turlough were realistic. Peace was agreed on 28 June 1575. Turlough renounced his claims east of the Bann. The treaty gave him the overlordship of MacCann and Maguire and did not deny him the title of O'Neill by omitting to mention it.[52]

Although Turlough emerged well from the 'Enterprise of Ulster' in a largely private agreement with Essex which the crown reluctantly accepted, the episode brought home to him the need for clear recognition of his power and status. Moreover, the Blackwater fort constituted not just a government outpost in his territory but also a bulwark for the baron of Dungannon, based south of the river. Turlough's demand for an aristocratic title and confirmation of his lands must be regarded in this light. In 1578 a patent was drafted and sent over but as a result of Sidney's departure and his own illness at the beginning of 1579, Turlough did not receive the earldom of Clanoneill.[53] Nonetheless in August 1579, he put forward his most ambitious demands. He wished to be created earl of Armagh and have the whole of Tyrone confirmed to him. For an annual rent of £3,000 Irish, he offered to govern the province on behalf of the crown as lord president of Ulster through a composition with the uirríthe.[54] Although this and subsequent proposals were rejected by the government, it did reflect O'Neill's thinking on how his local power might have been reconciled with the sovereignty of the crown. Indeed in this period, O'Neill's pretensions were matched by his actions. The Desmond war gave Turlough the opportunity to increase his authority in Ulster at the expense of outlying uirríthe and to exploit the ideology of the Counter-Reformation for political purposes.[55] After an abortive marriage alliance, war broke out with O'Donnell: Turlough defeated him in 1581 with the assistance of his rival, Conn.[56] However, Turlough's success was short-lived.

This examination of attempted reform in Ulster and indigenous reaction illustrates some general points. Clearly, the different modes of vice-regal government did affect the way in which policy was applied. And, in spite of the coercive interlude, the basic policy remained surrender and regrant. However, it was not implemented in any sustained fashion and was still an unopened bag of tricks. Clearly, time and money were required to bring the reform process to fruition. Whatever the circumstance, the crown had to reckon with the power of the O'Neills. Their power was needed to advance reform as witnessed by the 1542 agreement; equally, in the absence of reform, it was needed to keep the North quiet as revealed in the agreements of 1563 and 1575.[57] For their part,

51 Ibid. 162, 167; Brady, 'Government of Ireland', 376–7.
52 Costello, 'Turlough Luineach', 171–5; C, Carew, ii. 12–13.
53 Costello, 'Turlough Luineach', 190–1. In 1585 Lord Deputy Perrot wrote, 'he did then refuse the same, upon what respects, I know not': BLO, Perrot 1, fos 102–3.
54 PRO SP 63/67, no. 21.
55 The Walsingham letter-book or register of Ireland, May 1578 to December 1579, ed. J. Hogan and N. McNeill O'Farrell, Dublin 1959, 134–5, 224–6; C, Carew, ii. 156.
56 Walsingham letter-book, 238; AFM, v. 1767–9.
57 Brady touches on the government's dilemma in relation to Hugh O'Neill, the baron of Dungannon, but in fact it faced the same problem in its dealings with all the O'Neills: 'Government of Ireland', 418–19.

the O'Neills were fully aware of the new situation resulting from Tudor centralisation. Therefore, they sought – on their own terms whenever possible – to
exchange regional power for devolved government. At times, they managed to
subvert government policy to their own ends: Conn benefited from the piece-
meal attempt at surrender and regrant; Turlough Luineach took advantage of
the colonisation scheme. More generally, the hiring of Scots mercenaries increased their military capability and by 1580 the lordship of Tyrone was
stronger than ever.

PART ONE
CROWN POLICY

3

The Apotheosis of Perrot

Sir John Perrot, reputed by tradition, size and temperament the bastard son of Henry VIII, was lord deputy of Ireland between 1584 and 1588.[1] He died four years later a convicted traitor in the Tower of London. His tarnished image was rescued in the early seventeenth century. Three histories – two of which were written by his own bastard son, Sir James – presented his Irish administration in a positive light. Only one of these studies, by the unidentified E. C. S., appeared in print at the time.[2] Until the recent work of Victor Treadwell and Ciarán Brady, modern scholarship took only a desultory interest in the career of this Tudor politician.[3] As governor of Ireland Perrot's policies were programmatic in method and maximalist in objective. Such a strong reforming tendency threatened many vested interests in government and in the country at large. The outbreak of war with Spain was the most important determinant on the course of Perrot's deputyship. London's reluctant support for a forward policy in Ireland evaporated, resources were diverted to the continent and Perrot was forced to abandon the most adventurous aspects of his programme. He tried to continue his attack on tanistry but the grant of Tyrone to Hugh O'Neill finally caused him to abandon programmatic government in favour of a minimalist style and a day to day policy of containment. The loss of support in London also strengthened the vested interests ranged against him in Ireland. It facilitated a violent and vituperative outburst of factionalism in the Irish council.

Perrot had gained his experience of Ireland as a provincial governor. He was part of Lord Deputy Sidney's experiment to establish the authority of the crown in outlying regions. In the early 1570s he left his Pembrokeshire estates to serve as lord president of Munster during the first Desmond rebellion. Perrot resolved to kill James Fitzmaurice Fitzgerald but after a long campaign he had to settle for a grovelling submission with a token halter round the rebel's neck. Perrot had bested the captain of the Geraldines only to fall foul of the head of the opposing faction, Thomas Butler, the earl of Ormond. He fell out with the earl even though 'they had been sworn brothers ever since the coronation of

---

1   Naunton, *Fragmenta regalia*, 41–4.
2   Richard Rawlinson (ed.), *The life, deedes and death of Sir John Perrot*, London 1727 and James Perrot, *The chronicle of Ireland, 1584–1608*, ed. Herbert Wood, Dublin 1933. These histories have many textual similarities. Wood has established Sir James Perrot's authorship of the unfinished *Chronicle of Ireland*. The fact that neither was published at the time of writing strengthens the contention that both are the work of the same author. E. C. S., *The government of Ireland under Sir John Perrot 1584–1588*, London 1626.
3   David Matthew, *The Celtic peoples and Renaissance Europe*, London 1933, ch. xi, and Pauline Henley, 'The treason of Sir John Perrot', *Studies*, xxi (1932), 404–22. More recently, Victor Treadwell, 'Sir John Perrot and the Irish parliament of 1585–6', *PRIA*, lxxxv (1985), sect. C, 259–308 and Brady, 'Government of Ireland', 352–3, 423–6.

Edward'. He accused Ormond of half-hearted support against the rebels and then antagonised him further with plans to subject his palatinate jurisdiction of Tipperary to presidential authority. This was injudicious because Ormond was the most powerful feudatory in Ireland and one of the great survivors of Elizabethan politics. He and other enemies began to work Perrot's discredit at Court. Fearing the gathering storm, Perrot threw up his office and returned to England without permission. He had been a high-spending military-minded governor actively pursuing reforms which proved largely superficial in the face of vested interests. Perrot's presidency of Munster was a microcosm of his subsequent deputyship of Ireland.[4]

Brady has described Perrot as 'the apotheosis of the programmatic governor'. The term 'programmatic governor' was coined by Brady to denote those governors, such as Sussex, Sidney and Perrot, who presented ambitious programmes to reform Ireland, politically and financially, in a given number of years.[5] Out of government Perrot drew up at least three projects; the first in 1574 for the reformation of Munster and the other two in the early 1580s for the reformation of Ireland. Sir John included many ideas then in vogue as well as pet schemes of his own such as the debasement of the Irish currency and the removal of the seat of government to Athlone. He demanded a governor fully accredited and well financed from England committed to the execution of a single overall plan.[6] When Perrot himself entered into negotiation with the privy council to take over the deputyship in the winter of 1583/4, these plans were whittled down in favour of more practical considerations. His priorities were to be the holding of parliament and the settling of Munster after its devastation in the second Desmond rebellion.[7] In the event the parliament proved a fiasco and the Plantation of Munster was directed from London.

Perrot was given a jubilant welcome in Ireland. He received the respects of the many Irish lords who had converged on Dublin to meet him and found a measure of goodwill amongst his colleagues on the Irish council. Sir Geoffrey Fenton, the secretary of the Irish council, recorded the public address delivered by the new governor on taking up the sword of state on 21 June 1584.[8] He told his Irish listeners that the queen considered them as much her subjects as those of England and that it was the object of his government 'to bring them to the same felicity and quietness which her majesty's subjects in England do live in'. Perrot then consulted the council on the state of the kingdom, despatched Marshal Bagenal with commission to Ulster and departed himself to the West to place Sir Richard Bingham and Sir John Norris in their respective provinces.[9] But Perrot's honeymoon period did not last long. His dispute with Christopher Carleill, a lowly but well-connected army captain, was a taste of things to come. At the end of the year Carleill wrote to his step-father, Sir

---

[4] Rawlinson, *The life of Perrot*, 55–85. For a recent discussion of Ormond's career see Ciarán Brady (ed.), *Worsted in the game: losers in Irish history*, Dublin 1989, ch. iv.

[5] Brady, 'Government of Ireland', chs. iv, v and 423–6.

[6] *The life of Perrot*, 86–101; NRO, Fitzwilliam papers, Ireland, no. 66; BL Add. 48015 (Yelverton MS xvi), fos 309–11.

[7] PRO SP 63/106, no. 43; 108, nos 76–87.

[8] Ibid. 111, nos 1, 16, 31.

[9] Ibid. no. 16.

Francis Walsingham, the principal secretary of the privy council. He told him of Perrot's caustic and insensitive speeches about other political figures. He described the lord deputy as 'being wonderful and furiously opinionative in maintaining his own conceit' and 'so absolute in determining of causes as I dare undertake he shall procure himself more enemies then ever any man that came in this place'. It seems then that Perrot was single-minded enough to make a programmatic governor but lacked the diplomatic skills to pull it off. Carleill also informed Walsingham that 'here it is generally conceived he was preferred hither by your honour's only means'; in other words Perrot was not beyond impeachment because he was not fully backed at Court.[10]

To ascribe the internal divisions which emerged in the Dublin regime to Perrot's abrasive personality alone would be naive. The real irritants were the effects of his patronage and policies on the vested interests of his fellow councillors. It was normal practice for new lord deputies to place their servants and followers in offices in the civil, military and ecclesiastical establishments. Lord deputies also did favours through their influence over commissions which leased lands, collected debts and granted wardships. Perrot readily availed himself of these perquisites of office.[11] Perrot and the rest of the council were in fundamental agreement about the objectives of government policy. However, individual councillors often had country interests which might be adversely affected by the implementation of a particular policy even though they themselves supported its general objective.[12] Likewise, it would be wrong to see the factional divisions as unchanging monolithic blocs devoid of individual antagonisms or as New English versus Anglo-Irish. We should not countenance the jibes of Perrot's opponents that his only allies were Anglo-Irish councillors.[13] Certainly, Sir Lucas Dillon, the chief baron of the exchequer, and Sir Nicholas White, the master of the rolls, were his main political allies. He needed these native councillors to manage the forthcoming parliament and was able to align with them easily because they had been out of the limelight under the previous regime.[14] Even so the lord deputy never indulged these men with material rewards as he did his own followers.[15] Perrot also had the constant backing of two New English councillors, Sir Charles Calthorpe, the attorney-general, and Sir Edward Waterhouse, the chancellor of the exchequer.[16] And for the first half of his deputyship he also had the good offices of Fenton and Wallop.[17] The views expressed by Sir Henry Wallop, who occupied the important offices of vice-treasurer and treasurer-at-wars, are particularly valuable because they are

[10] Ibid. 113, no. 4. For details of Carleill's career see the biography by Rachel Lloyd, *Elizabethan adventurer: a life of Captain Christopher Carleill*, London 1974.
[11] *CPSI*, iii. 65–7; PRO SP 63/131, no. 28.
[12] Ibid. 119, no. 10. This document, in which Perrot defends himself against his critics, is incorrectly placed in the calendar under September 1585; it should be redated 1587 or 1588.
[13] *CPSI*, iii. 210–13.
[14] In fact, Dillon and White found it difficult to manage parliament and Perrot wrote that they had, by their parliamentary activities, 'made themselves less acceptable unto them [the Pale Gentry] than they were': BLO, Perrot 1, fos 102–3.
[15] *CPSI*, iii. 66–7.
[16] Treadwell, 'Sir John Perrot and the Irish parliament', 273; PRO SP 63/117, no. 47; 126, no. 10.
[17] Ibid. 114, no. 47; 115, no. 21.

critical of both alignments. He denounced his fellow councillors, both English and Irish, as dissemblers and self-seekers who would forego a revenue of £5,000 to the queen to make £100 for themselves or their friends.[18]

Perrot's most persistent and visible opponent was Adam Loftus, who occupied a nodal position in church and state. He had been in Ireland since the early 1560s becoming successively archbishop of Armagh, archbishop of Dublin, lord keeper and lord chancellor. Between August 1582 and June 1584 he had acted as lord justice in tandem with Sir Henry Wallop.[19] His fifteen children presented a problem as well as an opportunity. They were at once needy dependents and the building-blocks of an extensive network of marriage alliances with other New English families.[20] Loftus's closest associate was Thomas Jones, whose advancement he secured during his justiceship to the bishopric of Meath and the council board from the deanery of St Patrick's Cathedral.[21] Loftus also had an Anglo-Irish supporter, Sir Robert Dillon, chief justice of the common pleas, whom he had praised for his 'love and zeal of religion'.[22] The clash between Perrot and Loftus was not surprising: the lord deputy had arrived with a warrant to establish a university in Ireland with the livings of St Patrick's which were in the hands of Loftus.[23] The archbishop spurned an offer of compensation and with the assistance of Lord Treasurer Burghley in England managed to obtain a letter from the queen overturning the decision. This reversal only increased Perrot's determination. In June 1585 he sent over Mr Secretary Fenton – 'a man of choice to solicite so bad a cause, having professed hatred against me and my church' – with a letter to Walsingham. Philip Williams, Perrot's private secretary leaked the letter to Loftus in which the lord deputy accused him of corruptly using his offices in church and state to enrich himself and his family. In retaliation Loftus wrote to Burghley 'whom in all my good causes, I have found a special patron and defender' refuting the charges.[24] Loftus had successfully fended off the challenge and was able to maintain his interest at St Patrick's, but Sir Henry Wallop concurred in the charges levelled against him.

> I found when we were last joined [in government], that my colleague chiefly sought his own profit and the pleasuring of his friends in respect of the matches made and to be made with his children. Besides by nature he is and always hath been inconstant and oftentimes passionate and now will happly be higher-minded than formerly in respect of the great countenance he hath had there against the lord deputy; he is a very good preacher and pity he is not employed only therein.[25]

18 Ibid. 116, no. 8(1).
19 Ellis, *Tudor Ireland*, 330, 336.
20 PRO SP 63/117, no. 43; Donald Jackson, *Intermarriage in Ireland, 1550–1650*, Montreal 1970, ch. ii.
21 *CPSI*, ii. 468, 491, 499, 505, 507, 514, 515, 576.
22 Quoted in Treadwell, 'Sir John Perrot and the Irish parliament', 273.
23 PRO SP 63/119, no. 10; 'The Perrot Papers: the letter-book of Lord Deputy Sir John Perrot between 9 July 1584 and 26 May 1586', ed. Charles McNeill, *Analecta Hibernica*, xii (1943), 17–19.
24 Ibid. 23–4; PRO SP 63/117, no. 43; APC, xiv. 55–6, 324.
25 PRO SP 63/116, no. 8(1).

Loftus did not only have Lord Burghley as a backer at Court, he also had 'a great league' with the earl of Ormond who spent most of his time there. Ormond held the nominal posts of treasurer and admiral of Ireland but his real power derived from large estates, palatinate liberties and a bastard feudal connection of kinsmen and clients. Consequently, he cut a figure at Court where he was on good terms with Burghley and had ready access to the queen.[26] He could make or break Irish governments: Wallop said 'My lord of Ormond in all times hath been a cross and a hinderance to such governors as have been here'.[27] In 1584 Ormond did his best to stay friendly with Perrot visiting the newly-appointed lord deputy at Carew castle in Wales and returning temporarily to Ireland with him.[28] Over the next four years the earl used his client Sir Nicholas White as a channel to Perrot as well as a source of information about his activities.[29] Disputes arose nonetheless. There were three principal points of contention. Ormond disliked the operation of the admiralty court in Ireland because of its infringement on the perquisites of his office.[30] He claimed his liberty of Tipperary gave him the right to lands escheated within it and so he held up the Desmond attainder bill in parliament until it was amended in his favour.[31] The issue which involved Perrot most was the execution of law and order in Ormond's home county of Kilkenny. The lord deputy was supporting Francis Lovell as sheriff against followers of Ormond such as Richard Shee.[32] In Kilkenny and Tipperary it was a question of whose writ ran – the queen's or the earl's. Perrot was acting as a good reforming governor by pursuing these issues but in so doing he was activating a far more powerful opponent than Archbishop Loftus.

As a reforming governor, Perrot should have regarded provincial presidencies as vehicles of English law and order. Instead he saw them like palatinate liberties as rival centres of power and patronage communicating with the metropolis over his head. In jurisdictional terms Perrot's most serious disputes were with Sir Richard Bingham, the chief commissioner of Connacht. Ironically, Perrot was a supporter of Bingham's appointment, having knighted him on his arrival in Ireland.[33] By 1586 Perrot was attempting to vilify Bingham by allowing Brian O'Rourke, the lord of West Breifne, and Francis Barkley and Tibbot Dillon, two minor provincial officials, to make allegations against the chief commissioner at the council table.[34] Perrot's biggest policy achievement, the Composition of Connacht negotiated by Sir Nicholas White, can also be seen as an attack on the provincial governor because it advanced the power of the local lords. Sir Henry Wallop assured Lord Burghley that Sir Richard was 'a very sufficient gentleman, and one who would govern that province under his

26 CPSI, ii. 550; iii. 65.
27 PRO SP 63/115, no. 8(1).
28 Rawlinson, The life of Perrot, 141.
29 PRO SP 63/117, no. 47; CPSI, iii. 66–7.
30 John Appleby and Mary O'Dowd, 'The Irish admiralty: its organisation and development, c. 1570–1640', IHS, xxiv (1985), 300–1.
31 Treadwell, 'Sir John Perrot and the Irish parliament', 283, 301.
32 CSPI, ii. 515, 554, 558, 562, 583; iii. 325–30: E. C. S., Gov't of Ire. under Perrot, 108–10.
33 Ibid. 7–8; PRO SP 63/116, no. 3.
34 CPSI, iii. 66.

charge better than he doth, if the lord deputy did not continually cross him almost in everything, even as he doth likewise the other provincial governor [Sir John Norris]'.[35] Bingham eventually became so exasperated with the lord deputy's interference that he retreated to Court and then took service with Leicester in the Low Countries. The more malleable Thomas Le Strange took over his responsibilities. Bingham returned in 1588 only to discover that Perrot had made a new ally in the person of Donough O'Connor Sligo.[36]

Given this attitude, Perrot would not have welcomed the erection of another provincial administration in Ulster where the Bagenals regarded themselves as the chief candidates for office. Sir Nicholas Bagenal was connected to Loftus as Perrot said: 'Mr Marshall married his daughter to the Chancellor's son and therefore is engrafted in the faction'.[37] The Bagenals had been settled in Ulster since the early 1550s when Sir Nicholas was granted extensive lands in and around Newry.[38] After the death of Shane O'Neill, he had consolidated his influence over the neighbouring Gaelic lords, Magennis and O'Hanlon, and started to show a similar interest in the lordship of the MacMahons.[39] However in the 1580s Hugh O'Neill began to reassert traditional claims of overlordship and the position of the Bagenals was strongly challenged.[40] As a result, mutual interest drove the Bagenals into an association with Turlough Luineach O'Neill, even though the Bagenals hated the power of the O'Neills in general.[41] The family also derived revenue and influence from office. Sir Nicholas Bagenal had been Marshal of the Army since 1566 and his son Sir Henry obtained a reversion of then post in 1583.[42] The Bagenals were keen to develop Newry town and in 1577 they put proposals to Lord Deputy Sidney. Although Sidney refused to grant them the extensive immunities they sought, he did formally appoint Sir Nicholas chief commissioner of Ulster, with an annual stipend of £100 and with Henry as one of his assistants. The long-term objective was stated as the creation of a lord presidency in Ulster along the lines of the new structures in Connacht and Munster.[43] In reality, the jurisdiction of the chief commissioner was restricted to the area which the military forces at his disposal could control. Nevertheless, the Bagenals were ambitious to extend their jurisdiction and eager to hold on to what they already possessed. Obviously to avoid disputes with this vested interest, crown policy in Ulster had to agree with the ambitions of the Bagenals.

Perrot had no experience of the North and until the other provinces were settled, he had intended 'for a time to look through my fingers at Ulster as a fit receptacle of all the savage beasts of this land'.[44] However, an opportunity to intervene came within months of his entry into office. First a conspiracy was

---

35 Ibid. 131.
36 PRO SP 63/159, nos 18, 18 (1); CPSI, iii. 519.
37 PRO SP 63/119, no. 10.
38 P. H. Bagenal, Vicissitudes of an Anglo-Irish family, 1530–1800, London 1925, 23.
39 PRO SP 63/129, no. 3. Bagenal, Vicissitudes of an Anglo-Irish family, 49.
40 PRO SP 63/129, no. 3.
41 BL Cotton Titus F v. fos 31–2.
42 Fiants, 11th report, no. 809; 13th report, no. 4195.
43 Letters and memorials, i. 189–91; Fiants, 13th report, no. 3021.
44 PRO SP 63/111, no. 70.

uncovered when a messenger of Turlough Luineach O'Neill was captured at Athlone. The lord of Tyrone was allegedly inciting his counterparts in Connacht and Munster to take up arms against the crown in anticipation of military support from Scotland and Spain. But his messenger had received short shrift because potential supporters had been frightened off by the arrival of a military man as governor. Then the situation changed suddenly and with it the government's attitude to Turlough Luineach. Large contingents of Scots mercenaries had landed in Lough Foyle, not as at first suspected to support Turlough's nationwide revolt, but actually to depose him from the lordship of Tyrone in favour of the sons of Shane O'Neill. As a result, Perrot decided immediately to march into Ulster with all available forces.[45] It later transpired that the majority of the council opposed this expedition even though Marshal Bagenal had encouraged it, no doubt to prop up Turlough Luineach.[46] The plan was to blockade the Scots in Lough Foyle with ships and then to hunt them down with the army. In the event the mercenaries had fled back to their homeland before the ships sent from Dublin reached the lough. So Perrot and his army had no military objective when they eventually reached the North. Unperturbed, Perrot declared war on the Scots resident in Ulster. The lord deputy took Dunluce, the stronghold of Sorley Boye MacDonald, and set about garrisoning the north Antrim coast against the further ingress of Scots. He rounded off his tour by concluding a series of agreements with the lords of the Irishry aimed at the complete reformation of the province.[47]

In October 1584 Perrot sent Sir Lucas Dillon – 'a special good member of his country' – to London with the reformation proposals. Since Dillon was also seeking approval of the projected legislation for the forthcoming parliament, the plans for Ulster can be seen as part of a nationwide attempt at reform. Even so the Ulster programme was strikingly unoriginal and was largely the promotion of existing policies on a more general basis. To lobby the privy council, Perrot wrote individually to its members extolling his intervention in the North and his plans for its reformation.[48] Indeed, the manner in which Perrot glorified the general agreement he had made with the Ulster lords, hailing it as a step towards making Ireland financially self-sufficient, was all in the familiar mode of programmatic government. According to Walsingham, there was reluctance in London to support the scheme since 'other projects heretofore laid for like purposes, carrying at first sight great show and appearance of good success, had not proved so happy in execution'.[49] The main obstacle was the queen herself who was annoyed that the lord deputy had committed her finances to plans she had not approved. However, Burghley and Walsingham dissuaded her from total rejection since such a response would have compromised Perrot at the very start of his rule.[50] The main broker here was Walsingham; he was encouraging and supporting Perrot because he had long

[45] Ibid. nos 39, 43, 70.
[46] Ibid. 114, no. 42; Lambeth, Carew 619, fo. 14.
[47] PRO SP 63/111, no. 88; 112, no. 41; BLO, Perrot 1, fos 29–30
[48] Ibid. fos 45–8; Treadwell, 'Sir John Perrot and the Irish parliament', 270.
[49] PRO SP 63/113, no. 39.
[50] BLO, Perrot 1, fos 144–57.

regarded the settlement of Ulster as the key to the reformation of Ireland.[51] Consequently, the queen's letter of 20 January 1585 signalled a limited acceptance of the programme.[52]

The queen had vetoed the most ambitious feature of Perrot's 1584 scheme – his plans for the construction of seven towns, seven bridges and seven forts throughout the country. Perrot reckoned the construction project together with the upkeep of a trained garrison of 2,000 footmen and 400 cavalry would cost £50,000 over the next three years. The lord deputy's earlier proposals had all included plans for fortification in one form or another and this feature of the 1584 programme was strongly reminiscent of the proposals of Sidney and Essex in the mid-1570s.[53] A building programme of this nature was necessary and this was recognised by Wallop and the Bagenals as well as the lord deputy. However, Perrot's plans were clearly undercosted and short on timescale.[54] That the fortification plan had fallen at the first hurdle should not have surprised Perrot because, before his departure to Ireland, he had been told that the crown would only provide funds towards construction projects to which the local inhabitants made substantial contributions.[55] Undaunted by the queen's refusal, Perrot took the unprecedented step of soliciting the financial support of the English parliament, which was then in session, for the reformation of Ireland.[56] The Irish council agreed to back the lord deputy's request.[57] Nevertheless, Burghley and Walsingham suppressed Perrot's letter to parliament. Walsingham told Perrot that it would have further annoyed the queen since all public motions to parliament had to proceed from her. Furthermore, the queen had to be well-furnished with treasure because of the current state of affairs in the Low Countries 'either to maintain a war, if she take upon her the protecting of the said countries or to withstand the malice of Spain if he go through with his conquest'. Therefore the queen wanted Ireland governed as quietly as possible without wastage of men and money which might be needed elsewhere.[58]

Given the international climate, the queen was surely less than happy about Perrot's unprovoked attack on Scottish immigrants. Her lord deputy regarded the Scots as a priority and he extended the conventional analysis to include them: 'to keep out the Scot is to suppress Ulster and to suppress Ulster is to reform Ireland'.[59] Perrot was taking a major gamble because previous attempts to evict the Scots by Croft, Sussex, Sidney and Essex had failed.[60] The role of the Scots was twofold: as mercenary soldiers in the service of the Gaelic lords and, in the case of the MacDonalds, as claimants to the Glens in north Antrim. The threat they posed was wildly exaggerated and more often than not a convenient pretext for intervention in the North. Perrot's problems with the

51 CPSI, ii. 272.
52 CPCRI, ii. 92–5.
53 BL Add. 48015 (Yelverton MS xvi), fos 313–18; PRO SP 63/153, no. 67.
54 Ibid. 123, no. 52; 127, no. 35.
55 Ibid. 108, no. 79.
56 BLO, Perrot 1, fos 67–9; E. C. S., Gov't of Ire. under Perrot, 43–58.
57 BLO, Perrot 1, fos 67–9.
58 PRO SP 63/114, no. 59.
59 Ibid. 112, no. 72.
60 George Hill, An historical account of the MacDonnells of Antrim, Belfast 1873, chs iii, iv.

Scots were largely of his own creation. Having missed his original objective – the mercenaries of Clan MacLean – he decided to attack Sorley Boye MacDonald, as he himself acknowledged, in order to avoid wasting expenditure already incurred.[61] This lord enjoyed a peaceful occupation of the Glens and he had a signed agreement with Lord Deputy Sidney to prove his claim.[62] It was indeed foolhardy to attempt to evict Sorley Boye from such a difficult and exposed region.[63] The forces Perrot left behind in Antrim proved incapable of wiping out the remaining Scots let alone interdicting their reinforcements. As early as November 1584, Sir Henry Bagenal, colonel of the forces there, met the first of a number of near disasters when he was ambushed in a narrow defile and forced to beat a hasty retreat.[64] When Sorley Boye returned with new forces in January 1585, the garrisons could not cope. The lord deputy had to be dissuaded from mounting another costly expedition to the North; instead Captain Edward Barkley was dispatched with 300 infantry and 150 cavalry.[65] Unable to encounter the combatants, the garrison turned in frustration to massacring Sorley Boye's tenantry and 'houghing' those cattle and horses they could not drive away.[66] The campaign was unwinnable. Even the divide and rule tactics whereby Perrot tried to obtain the support first of Donnell Gorm and then of Angus against their uncle Sorley proved fruitless.[67] It was also difficult to supply the garrisons. The victualling had to be done by ship which was a perilous business especially in wintertime because of the lack of suitable harbourage and the extreme turbulence of the waters where the Atlantic Ocean meets the Irish Sea.[68] Perrot's impotence was clear in June 1585 when he sent Captain Nicholas Dawtrey, the Seneschal of Clandeboye, 'to move the king of Scots to restrain the Irish Scots from disturbing Her majesty's subjects here'.[69]

Like Perrot's local war against the Scots, the queen had to accept his composition with the Ulster lords as un fait accompli. In fact, she had unwittingly encouraged it and her principal secretary had directly promoted it. In common parlance a composition meant simply an agreement. To policy-makers, and more especially the scholar who has interpreted them, it increasingly meant the conversion of the cess, the burdensome royal prerogative which permitted the billeting of troops on the populace, into regular cash revenue. Such compositions were in force elsewhere in Ireland.[70] Perrot's agreement in the North was really the establishment of a cess rather than the commutation of pre-existing one into taxation. Even then, the soldiers thus maintained were to be under the command of the Gaelic lords rather than part of the military establishment. In

61 PRO SP 63/111, nos 70, 88.
62 Letters and memorials, i. 75–80; PRO SP 63/114, no. 67.
63 For a general account of the military campaign against Sorley Boye see Hill, MacDonnells of Antrim, 159–81.
64 PRO SP 63/113, no. 5(1).
65 Ibid. 114, nos 47, 62; BLO, Perrot 1, fos 67–9.
66 PRO SP 63/114, no. 82.
67 'Calendar of the Irish council book: 1 March 1581 to 1 July 1586, made by John P. Prender-gast between 1867 and 1869', ed. D.B. Quinn, Analecta Hibernica, xxiv (1967), 159, no. 284; PRO SP 63/112, no. 41; 113, no. 7; BLO, Perrot 1, fos 144–57, 189–93.
68 PRO SP 63/113, no. 39.
69 'Calendar of the Irish council book', 164–5, no. 311.
70 Brady, 'Government of Ireland', ch. vii.

fact, the Ulster composition was the extension of an expedient which had grown up during the Desmond War and its immediate aftermath. In the West O'Donnell and O'Connor Sligo had, for a time, maintained English troops.[71] In the East the lords of Clandeboye and the Route had agreed to keep English soldiers to defend themselves from marauding Scots islanders.[72] In addition to these precedents, Perrot received encouragement from London. The queen's instructions of January 1584 had drawn to Perrot's attention the case of Carberry, county Cork, in which the lord had contributed to the upkeep of soldiers.[73] Finally, in August 1584 Walsingham instructed Perrot to reach agreements with the Ulster lords so that they would contribute to the maintenance of troops.[74]

The Ulster composition was agreed upon in September and October 1584 during Perrot's military expedition to the North. The object of the composition was the upkeep of 1,100 English soldiers whose function was to keep the indigenous population in obedience and to interdict the frequent incursions of the Scots. The Gaelic lords and the crown would provide victuals for the soldiers' maintenance, worth £13,000 and £2,750 per annum respectively. In time, Perrot claimed, the allowance from the Gaelic lords could be converted into ordinary revenue.[75] Perrot summarised the policy in glowing terms: 'hereby the Irish man is bridled for his own good, the Scot is shut out, the Englishman received in his place and Her Majesties forces increased'.[76] The English soldiers were to replace the Scots mercenaries employed by the Ulster lords, but the fact that they were to be under the command of the lords themselves and were to collect their own allowances from the country were potential sources of trouble.[77] Sir John Norris, who accompanied the lord deputy on his northern journey, expressed misgivings at the scheme's inception. He believed that the maintenance of the soldiers would put too great a burden on the country. It was also clear to Norris that Turlough wanted troops only to stem his declining influence within Tyrone.[78] By early 1585 the composition forces had victualling problems. In the Route Sir William Stanley complained of 'small help of the country' while Beverley, the crown victualler, reported friction between the soldiers and country people over provisioning.[79] Such problems were bound to arise in the wintertime. Unlike the Scots mercenaries whom the lords employed for the summer months only, the English troops expected larger rations and needed victualling all year round.[80] In May Wallop echoed Norris's misgivings, stating that the composition troops would be used, like the Scots, in wars between the lords themselves and discarded when unnecessary. He also

71 PRO SP 63/94, no. 20; 101, no. 43.
72 BL Cotton Titus F v. fos 4–5: PRO SP 63/85, no. 7; 101, no. 43.
73 Rawlinson, *The life of Perrot*, 301; *CPSI*, ii. 463.
74 PRO SP 63/111, no. 82. This letter, in draft form, is from Walsingham to Perrot, not from the privy council as stated in the calendar.
75 Ibid. 112, nos 23, 41.
76 Ibid. no. 22.
77 Ibid. 111, no. 70.
78 Ibid. 112, no. 11.
79 Ibid. 114, no. 29(2); 116, no. 7(1).
80 BLO, MS 30237, fo. 51.

indicated that the object of the composition in keeping out the Scots had already failed, since the composition troops were ill-prepared and dispersed when the Scots had raided in January and that they had needed the support of ordinary garrison soldiers.[81] It is apparent from these defects that the queen's rejection of the fortification plan had been a body-blow to the composition at the outset because without a proper military infrastructure the success of the scheme depended wholly on the co-operation of the lords.

The absence of actual military control by the crown was reflected in Perrot's decision in October 1584 to divide the greater part of Ulster into three lieutenancies. The two eastern counties of the province were placed under the rule of Sir Nicholas Bagenal; the baron of Dungannon, Hugh O'Neill, was given command of the area covered by the modern counties of Armagh and Monaghan; Turlough Luineach was to rule the territories shired the following year as Tyrone, Fermanagh and Coleraine.[82] The establishment of these lieutenancies was an expedient means of keeping Ulster quiet at a time when the government was powerless to interfere with the *status quo*. This is reflected in the indentured agreement with Turlough Luineach. It began by declaring abolished his claims over the *uirríthe* and then went on to state 'we ourselves being far occupied in other services, must commit the trust of well ordering and governing them to some meet for that purpose'.[83] In other words the *status quo* would remain for the present. Hugh O'Neill was given a distinct area to control instead of an earlier and vaguer commission for the defence of the Pale; his indenture maintained the polite fiction that he had possessed no subject lords in the first instance.[84] Marshal Bagenal was quite right in his subsequent claim that the *uirríthe* 'were otherwise converted by authority to such as claim them by usurpation'.[85]

In fact the main objective of the lieutenancies was the demarcation of spheres of influence, in particular between the baron of Dungannon and Marshal Bagenal. There were two areas of contention between them. In 1583 the marshal complained about the baron usurping control of the *uirríthe* south of the Blackwater river. In fact the marshal wanted to control them himself.[86] For his part, Hugh O'Neill fiercely resented the official authority which government commissions gave the marshal in Ulster. This was evident during the abortive Scottish invasion of Ulster in August 1584. Hugh O'Neill proved an embarrassment to the marshal when he tried to take charge in the crisis. 'He refused to yield to my commission in the presence of the Lord of Louth, Sir Hugh Magennis and others wishing me to put my commission in my pocket and that he would not be commanded by any but Her Majesty and her deputy.'[87] Perrot did not not favour the marshal over the baron when subsequently establishing the lieutenacies. Indeed when Perrot notified the privy council about the new arrangements, he implied that Bagenal was just another Ulster

---

81 PRO SP 63/116, no. 46.
82 Hatfield House, Cecil 163, fos 48–9.
83 Ibid. fo. 48.
84 Ibid. fo. 49: Fiants, 13th Report, no. 4054: PRO SP 63/104, no. 28; 105, nos 87–9.
85 CPSI, iii. 50.
86 PRO SP 63/105, no. 85.
87 Lambeth, Carew 619, fo. 14.

power-broker.[88] However, he did compensate the marshal by extending his jurisdiction northwards into an area where his influence was previously slight. Furthermore, Bagenal's sons benefitted from the lord deputy's intervention in Ulster. Sir Henry became colonel of the forces stationed at Carrickfergus and Dudley became captain of the band of composition soldiers cessed in South Clandeboye.[89] That the Bagenals were jealous of their authority is plain from their disputes with other Englishmen. When Sir William Stanley and Sir Henry Bagenal disagreed over a commission in February 1585, 'Captain Dudley Bagenal borrowed a round blow on the ear of Sir William Stanley'.[90] And Captain Nicholas Dawtrey was so resentful of the interference of the Bagenals that he resigned his position as seneschal of the rival jurisdiction of Clandeboye.[91] So Marshal Bagenal did gain from Perrot's arrangements. However, he was no nearer making his empty title of chief commissioner of Ulster a reality, the more so because Hugh O'Neill's power was steadily increasing.

The fact that the lieutenancies merely concealed rather than actually abolished the claims of overlordship seriously flawed Perrot's other plans to establish local government and English inheritance in Ulster. There was no royal opposition to the shiring of the Gaelic areas of Ulster. Shiring would see the completion of a process begun by Sidney.[92] By this means, six new counties were delimited in Ulster in the late summer of 1585. With the conversion of West Breifne in north-east Connacht into the county of Leitrim, Perrot saw the process of shiring completed throughout the realm.[93] However this was cosmetic and declaratory. English local government did not follow automatically in the wake of shiring. This is neatly illustrated by the case of Captain Mostian appointed sheriff of Donegal and ejected by O'Donnell.[94] The author of A treatise of Ireland, an important gazetteer of 1586, demanded these counties 'as well brought to the nature as to the name of shires'. He wanted the appointment of 'sheriffs of English education' and the introduction of common law procedures.[95] Perrot also claimed to have shired the O'Reilly lordship as the county of Cavan. In fact this had been accomplished in 1579, though he did make it effectual with the appointment of a sheriff and other law enforcement officers.[96] Archbishop Long of Armagh, one of the first commissioners to hold court sessions in the county, was heartened by the inhabitants' enthusiasm for English law.[97]

The queen approved Perrot's plan that surrender and regrant should once

88 PRO SP 63/112, no. 41.
89 Ibid; PRO Audit Office 1/284/1074 (I owe this reference to Anthony Sheehan).
90 PRO SP 63/114, no. 62.
91 BL Cotton Titus B xii. fos 284–5.
92 Statutes at large, i. 347–9; PRO SP 63/31, no. 33.
93 Inquisitionum in officio rotulorum cancellariae Hiberniae, ii. pp. xiv–xix; NLI MS 669, fos 41–2.
94 CPSI, iii. 513–14.
95 NLI MS 669, fo. 61. Prototypes of A treatise of Ireland executed in the 1570s: PRO SP 63/56, nos 62–3. Waterhouse's copy: BLO, MS 30237. Standard copies with maps: NLI MS 669; Trinity College Dublin, MS 473; Northumberland Papers, Alnwick MS 476. Bagenal's edited extract under the title The description and present state of Ulster: PRO SP 63/127, no. 35.
96 CPSI, iv. 82.
97 PRO SP 63/117, no. 7.

again be promoted on a general basis.[98] This did not mark a dramatic return to the policy of St Leger since it had continued fitfully under Sidney and the lords justice.[99] In 1583 Marshal Bagenal had delivered a petition to Court from the minor Ulster lords in which they requested detachment from the rule of O'Neill by means of surrender and regrant. A warrant to implement these requests had been considered at the time but the enfeoffment of Iveagh, the lordship of Magennis, was the only successful result of the marshal's initiative.[100] After his first visit to Ulster, Perrot declared that the Irish custom of tanistry was 'the root of all the barbarity and disorder of this land' and that the only solution was the establishment of an English system of inheritance.[101] Nevertheless Perrot did seek common ground with the Gaelic lords by modifying the government's traditional approach to the problem of inheritance. When negotiating with the O'Reillys, Perrot requested a royal warrant to grant 'states in fee simple to them and their heirs general since they and all others do utterly refuse to accept any states male'. He hoped that this departure from primogeniture in making re-grants would induce 'all the lords of the North' to come to similar arrangements.[102] The enabling instrument was drafted by Walsingham and corrected by Burghley in London at the end of December 1584.[103] Perrot explained his policy at greater length in a treatise written after his deputyship. He believed that tanistry caused wasteful succession struggles between competitors and that it led to the militarisation and impoverishment of the lordship. This system was also a source of instability to its neighbours and in the case of the Pale, which bordered many Gaelic lordships, a crippling burden in the upkeep of soldiers. Perrot saw surrender and regrant as a promising alternative. It would encourage a stable system of inheritance and the peaceful development of the lordship. Feudal dues, in the form of rents and military services, would be paid. If the lord committed treasonable acts, his lands could be escheated to the crown. In the course of his government Perrot supervised surrender and regrant settlements in most of the territories which had hitherto gone unaffected by the policy. These comprised large sectors of the north Midlands, Connacht and Ulster in which the only major lords who lacked letters patent or the less formal indentures at the end of his deputyship were O'Donnell, O'Cahan and O'Rourke.[104] Perrot was free with the truth in claiming North Clandeboye, Sligo and West Breifne amongst his successes.[105] Perrot reckoned that in his deputyship the policy had brought an increase in rents of £3,000 *per annum*.[106] The fact that most rents remained unpaid at the end of Perrot's deputyship shows the declaratory nature of the policy.[107]

---

[98] CPCRI, ii. 92–5.
[99] *Statutes at large*, i. 367–8.
[100] BL Cotton Titus F v. fos 31–2; Fiants, 13th report, nos 4218, 4327.
[101] PRO SP 63/112, no. 45.
[102] Ibid. 113, no. 9.
[103] Ibid. no. 40 (draft warrant).
[104] Ibid. 156, no. 51.
[105] BL Cotton Titus F v. fos 90–1; PRO SP 63/112, no. 41; C, *Carew*, ii. 393–4; BLO, Perrot 1, fos 62–3; PRO SP 63/146, no. 60.
[106] PRO SP 63/156, no. 51.
[107] Ibid. 135, no. 47.

The queen also praised Perrot's decision to divide up the lordship of the O'Reillys. This was another major modification of the surrender and regrant policy which signalled an end to its declaratory phase. The intention was to undermine the tanist system by breaking up the Gaelic lordships. The assault was two-pronged. Perrot's deputyship saw an attack on the political structure of the lordship with the division of East Breifne amongst its chief lords. A tract presented to Lord Burghley in 1585 by Nicholas Taaffe, an Anglo-Irishman linked to the Bagenal interest, indicates that the idea found acceptance amongst the political community of the Pale. Not only did Taaffe back the completion of surrender and regrant but he also argued for the division of Tyrone, Tirconnell and Armagh to eliminate the power of the Macs and Oes.[108] The second prong was socio-economic. Perrot's inaugural address contained a social message which echoed around the kingdom, to the consternation of the lords and to the elation of the lower classes.

> He wished to be suppressed and abolished throughout the realm the name of churl and the crushing of a churl, affirming that howsoever the former barbarous times had devised it and nourished it yet he held it tyrannous both in the name and manner, and would therefore extirp it and breed in the place of it the titles used in England, namely husbandmen, franklins or yeomen.[109]

In fact Perrot never achieved this aim and it was left to his successor Fitzwilliam to commence an attack on the social and economic structure of the Gaelic lordship with the appointment of freeholders as private landowners in Monaghan. These elements were always latent in the surrender and regrant process. The early policy-makers had been over-optimistic in expecting sub-infeudation to take place naturally. By the 1580s these measures had become necessary because it was plain that the Gaelic lords were using their letters patent to usurp the customary rights of other inhabitants by claiming ownership of whole lordships.

The settlement of East Breifne, the territory of the O'Reillys, at the end of 1584 was accomplished only by indenture, not the more formal letters patent; nonetheless it was one of the most significant developments of Perrot's government.[110] In a hard piece of negotiating, Perrot achieved the division of the territory into four parts.[111] Each part was given to a chief lord of the O'Reillys to be held as a separate entity from the crown. From the existing divisions, seven baronies were created; four of these were allotted to Sir John, whom the crown had made O'Reilly in 1583.[112] Most significantly, Sir John lost the rights and dues owed to him out of the other three baronies.[113] The other baronies were now to pay rents and military services direct to the crown. The fact that these rents were actually paid to the crown during the period of Perrot's deputyship

---

108 Ibid. 116, no. 31.
109 Ibid. 111, no. 16.
110 BLO, Perrot 1, fos 65–7.
111 PRO SP 63/113, no. 10.
112 Ibid; C, *Carew*, ii. 391–2; Fiants, 13th report, no. 4197.
113 Lambeth, Carew 614, fo. 162.

demonstrates two points.[114] First, it shows that Sir John was unable to continue to assert his old rights and hence that the lordship was effectively broken up and that tanistry was in abeyance. Furthermore, this situation contrasts dramatically with the territories where simple surrender and regrant settlements were undertaken from which no rents were forthcoming. The reorganisation of the O'Reilly lordship succeeded because of the dependence of Sir John O'Reilly on the state and the growing influence of powerful Palesmen such as Sir Lucas Dillon over their Gaelic neighbours. The settlement was also assisted by the imprisonment of Philip O'Reilly who was a threat to the policy's implementation and by the confusion of the O'Neills and their inability to interfere in a territory where their claim to overlordship was slight. Indeed Philip O'Reilly was imprisoned on a technicality and it was widely acknowledged that keeping him in Dublin Castle was the key to the settlement.[115] Ironically, the settlement was never perfected. The only adequate explanation is the involvement of the O'Reillys as MPs at the 1585 session of parliament. The rumours spread by the Anglo-Irish opposition apparently made the Gaelic lords 'less forward' in embracing the lord deputy's policies.[116] Later in 1587 Perrot proposed 'to make a composition between the gentlemen of the Brenny and their freeholders'.[117] This did not take place either.[118] Nevertheless, the O'Reillys had become 'harmless neighbours' to the Pale where not long before they had been persistent marauders.[119]

The difficulties facing Perrot's programme in Ireland were compounded by the gradual loss of support from the privy council in London. Perrot's English adversaries capitalised on his failures in Ireland and made the most of visits to Court by Ormond, Norris and Fenton.[120] Fenton's visit was crucial: having been sent by Perrot to embarrass Loftus and to conduct parliamentary business, the Irish Secretary saw which way the wind was blowing and promptly changed tack. This *volte face* was caused by changes in English foreign policy. Anglo-Scottish relations entered a new and more amicable phase with the draft treaty of Berwick and an English pension for King James in the summer of 1585. The assurance of Scottish neutrality opened the way for an even more significant agreement. The Treaty of Nonsuch, which provided aid for the United Provinces, entailed a final break with Spain and diverted funds from Ireland.[121] The change of opinion within the privy council is obvious in the letters of Walsingham. In April 1585 with the opposition of the other councillors increasing, Walsingham was still advocating Perrot's cause.[122] By December he was writing to Archbishop Long that Perrot should have lived in 'the time of Henry the Eighth, when princes were resolute to persist in honourable attempts'.[123] By

[114] PRO SP 63/135, no. 47.
[115] BLO, MS 30237, fo. 59.
[116] BLO, Perrot 1, fos 99–102; PRO SP 63/117, no. 62.
[117] CPSI, iii. 338–9.
[118] HMC Salisbury MSS, iii. 284–5.
[119] BLO, MS 30237, fo. 59.
[120] Cal S.P. Ire., ii. 565, 576–7; BLO, Perrot 1, fos 78–80; Brady, 'Government of Ireland', 424.
[121] Treadwell, 'Sir John Perrot and the Irish parliament', 290–3.
[122] PRO SP 63/116, no. 13.
[123] CPSI, ii. 588.

February 1586 Walsingham was instructing the lord deputy to pursue peaceful policies since it was now 'impossible to draw Her Majesty into any further charge, having many necessary occasions to use the money elsewhere'.[124]

It was the dispatch which Fenton brought from Court in March 1586 which effectively ended the first phase of Perrot's government. In a letter to Perrot, the queen told the lord deputy to abandon his coveted policies without further expostulation.[125] Fenton also carried 'A letter written to the lord chancellor and others of the council which was the cause that bred all the broil'. The queen was troubled by the excessive expenditure of the Irish government 'which hath chiefly proceeded through the attempt in Ulster for the expulsion of the Scots: a thing, as we are informed, only prosecuted by the Deputy contrary to the opinion of the better sort of you of our council in that Realm'. Therefore she ordered the lord chancellor and the other councillors that no important policy decisions were to be made without the consent of the majority of their number and if the deputy proceeded contrary to their opinions they were to inform on him. As a body they were to ensure that the lord deputy reached 'some reasonable composition with Angus MacDonald, Sorley and the rest of the Principal Persons of that Province' and in particular the lord chancellor was to ensure that no unwarranted grants, such as the recent one to Sir Edward Waterhouse, passed his seal.[126] Perrot complained that Fenton's dispatch compromised him in the vital areas of policy, patronage and income. His capacity for independent action was now circumscribed because 'a kind of superintendency of this council' had been set over him. He was now 'made unable to pleasure friend or servant, so as I shall have no man of value to tarry with me or depend on me' because the chancellor's possession of the seal prevented him from passing grants. Furthermore his household revenues would be reduced because of the privy council's willingness to strike a deal with the Palesmen rather than force an agreement on them in parliament.[127]

The queen's letter brought on a bitter faction-fight in the Irish council, the cause of which was vested interest rather than policy. Perrot later wrote: 'Our disagreement had not his beginning of any controversy for causes in council but for private and particular griefs, although now by reason of those particular causes they both combine and oppose themselves as well in matters of council as otherwise, taking hold of Your Majesty's letter brought by Mr. Fenton.' Perrot held Fenton responsible for the letter and accused him of 'double-dealing'.[128] The secretary reported his banishment from the lord deputy's chamber and his exclusion from 'consultations of importance' which he attributed to his 'bringing the late dispatch from the council and modestly maintaining some points thereof'.[129] As a result of this antagonism, Fenton was forced into the arms of the Loftus faction.[130] The phrase in the queen's letter relating to 'the better sort of you of our council' was regarded as a reference not to the wisest or most

[124] PRO SP 63/122, no. 94.
[125] BL Cotton Titus F v. fos 198–9.
[126] PRO SP 63/122, no. 94.
[127] CPSI, iii. 44.
[128] PRO SP 63/119, no. 10.
[129] CPSI, iii. 151–2.
[130] PRO SP 63/119, no. 10.

experienced but to the councillors of English birth. This was divisive and gave Perrot's opponents more ammunition to fire at him. Furthermore the queen sent over new appointees to the council at this juncture; Roger Wilbraham became solicitor-general and Robert Gardiner lord chief justice of the king's bench. Gardiner was to examine all the proceedings of the courts of the common pleas and the exchequer for the purposes of administrative reform.[131] Gardiner's appointment was a snub to Perrot; it was not that he disagreed with the principle of reform so much as that the candidates he had proposed to execute it, first Shuttleworth and then Walshe, had been overlooked; as a result he was in no hurry to sign the new councillor's patent of office.[132]

At Easter 1586 Perrot and Loftus took communion together.[133] But the beneficial effects of this public reconciliation did not last longer than the start of December when Chancellor Loftus, Secretary Fenton, Chief Justice Gardiner and Marshal Bagenal sent Bishop Jones to Burghley. Although they wrote separate letters, they were mounting a co-ordinated attack on the lord deputy. They emphasised Perrot's contempt and abusive treatment of his fellow councillors, which they claimed was directed at the New English members. They alleged that he was using the Castle Chamber, the Irish equivalent of the Star Chamber, to remove cases from Loftus' jurisdiction in chancery and Gardiner's in king's bench. Gardiner claimed Perrot was obstructing his reforms of the exchequer, in particular of the commissions which leased crown lands. They also accused Perrot of ignoring the advice of the law officers in the appointment of sheriffs, justices of the peace and justices of assize.[134] A partial explanation for the timing of this attack was the decision by Calthorpe and Wilbraham to sue Loftus, Jones and other clergymen for large sums in unpaid first fruits.[135] It is interesting that Wallop, the New English treasurer, held himself aloft from this business even though he concurred with Gardiner about the lord deputy's excessive control over leases. He condemned unreservedly 'the continual jarring and mislike between the lord deputy and lord chancellor' as a hindrance to royal service.[136] Perrot's chosen method of crushing dissent was imprisonment. On 6 December he imprisoned Thomas Colclough and his wife, one of Loftus's daughters, after the husband had uttered contemptuous speeches against the deputy and the wife had tried to prevent his arrest.[137] Shortly afterwards Philip Williams began a longer stint in prison when his master, the lord deputy, finally discovered his treacherous dealings with the opposing faction.[138] In January 1587 Perrot took revenge on Fenton by publicly humiliating him. With the help of Robert Dillon, Fenton's enemy at the court of common pleas, he put the Irish Secretary in the Marshalsea jail for failing to repay him a debt of £70.[139] Patrick O'Cullen, a client of the Bagenals, who had carried a letter from

---

[131] CPCRI, ii. 107.
[132] PRO SP 63/112, no. 45; CPSI, iii. 67.
[133] Ibid. 49.
[134] Ibid. 210–14, 218–20.
[135] Ibid. 221.
[136] Ibid. 226–7.
[137] Ibid. 220.
[138] Ibid. 350.
[139] PRO SP 63/119, no. 10; CPSI, iii. 247–8, 255–7.

Turlough Luineach to the queen the previous summer, was also imprisoned by the lord deputy at this time. Perrot alleged that he had been defamed by the letter which he claimed had been forged 'by means of Sir Henry Bagenal and other of that Machiavellian device'.[140] This led to a famous incident in the council Chamber in May 1587 when the marshal demanded that the lord deputy clear his son's name. We have two accounts. Sir Nicholas White insisted that Perrot only touched the seventy-nine year old Sir Nicholas on the cheek before he went to the floor in an exchange in which both men accused each other of being liars, drunkards and doubtless much else besides. The marshal insisted that 'He arose from his seat, struck me with his hand and beat me to the ground, and had not Mr Justice Gardiner and Mr Secretary Fenton been there, God knoweth how it had further fared with me.' We must incline to the marshal's version because White subsequently tore up the joint account of Fenton and Gardiner.[141]

The conciliar strife in Dublin had been intensified by the prolonged presence of Sir Henry Bagenal at Court to further the interests of his family and faction. In May 1586 the marshal had alleged that the lord deputy was consistently refusing his advice on the North. Therefore he was sending his son to England 'to the end he may make true report'.[142] Sir Henry went to England with a number of references, including a letter of 'singular commendation' which Loftus had induced many of his fellow councillors to sign. Loftus wanted him to succeed his aged and impotent father as marshal of the army without further ado.[143] Wallop, on the other hand, dismissed Sir Henry as a military incompetent who deserved no praise for his recent actions in the North and who had never shed a drop of his blood in the queen's service as the letters alleged.[144] In England Sir Henry presented a number of petitions to Lord Burghley which demanded changes in government policy in Ulster. One of his petitions, *The description and present state of Ulster*, was in fact an edited extract from *A treatise of Ireland*. The probable author of this national gazetteer was Sir Edward Waterhouse, who was both a supporter of the lord deputy and a friend of the Bagenals. Sir Henry inserted prejudicial remarks into his edited extract about the policy of the lord deputy and the activities of the earl of Tyrone. However, the very fact that he utilised a gazetteer which praised the settlement of East Breifne shows that he was only at variance with Perrot's general approach when the interests of his family were at stake.[145]

Most of Bagenal's proposed changes to policy were for his own benefit. He condemned Perrot's composition for impoverishing the country and inciting

---

[140] Ibid. 277.
[141] Ibid. 353–61. The hostility between Bagenal and Perrot had intensified in the run-up to the council chamber incident following the death of Captain Dudley Bagenal in action in Co. Carlow and the refusal of Perrot to grant the Marshal wardship of his grandson: ibid. 287. The wardship was finally granted to the Marshal in December 1587: Fiants, 16th report, no. 5094.
[142] CPSI, iii. 50.
[143] PRO SP 63/124, no. 14.
[144] Ibid; CPSI, iii. 65–6.
[145] PRO SP 63/127, no. 35; NLI MS 669. For Waterhouse's connections see: PRO SP 63/129, no. 20; DNB, xx. 899–901.

rebellion. He favoured a rent in cattle instead.[146] This condemnation masked self-interest. The composition had curtailed the military role of the marshal and his son by placing the soldiers under the lords themselves and had since become a burden to the Magennises, their Gaelic clients.[147] Sir Henry requested a peaceful resolution with the MacDonalds omitting to mention his own inept campaigns against them. On the contrary, he made it plain that the real problem was the Scots mercenaries brought over by Irish lords such as the O'Neills. He demanded a reduction in the power of the O'Neills by the permanent division of Tyrone and the liberation of the *uirríthe*. The tussle with Hugh O'Neill was especially evident with Sir Henry claiming that his rival was now asserting control over the petty lords in county Down as well. Sir Henry wanted a lord president in Ulster. Such an official would have the benefit of a shire hall and jailhouse to make crown government effective in the province. In Bagenal's view the enforcement of English law in Ulster was being undermined. Commissions enjoining his father, himself and others to dispense 'Justice' in the province had not been renewed under the Perrot regime.[148] Sir Henry made another application to develop Newry. By taxing the local lords, he planned to build a town wall and, this time, a college. The educational facility was of course a civilised method of keeping the sons of Ulster lords as hostages. Most significantly, the Bagenals requested a commission similar to that possessed by Sir Richard Bingham in the provincial presidency of Connacht.[149]

A letter from the queen to the lord deputy shows that she had endorsed Sir Henry Bagenal's plans for the development of Newry and the grant of a commission to himself and his father, similar to that enjoyed by Bingham in Connacht. However, this letter of April 1587, extant in draft form only, was never enrolled as a patent in the Irish Chancery.[150] How can we explain the sudden rebuff? First, the dispute over the alleged forgery of O'Cullen's letter was an embarrassment to Sir Henry Bagenal. Secondly, Hugh O'Neill arrived at Court and petitioned the queen for the exemption of his lordship from any future provincial government 'whereby the obedience and attendance due to Your Highness shall no way be delayed and many inconveniences avoided by provincial governors many times proffered'.[151] He clearly feared the interference of a provincial governor and the likelihood that Sir Henry Bagenal would fulfil that role. Furthermore there was the presence of Captain Nicholas Dawtrey. He had been given the task of evaluating Waterhouse's plans for Ulster and took the opportunity to launch a bitter attack on the Bagenals. He blamed their hatred of Hugh O'Neill on 'ambition or covetousness in the marshal'. 'Mr Marshal', he said reflecting on his own experience, 'hath neither agreed with English or Irish that hath had as much or more discretion in governing of Ulster than himself and that hath been known by his good agreement with all the seneschals of Clandeboye in his time; as also with any commissioners that hath

---

[146] PRO SP 63/124, no. 66; 128, no. 75.
[147] Ibid. 124, no. 17.
[148] Ibid. no. 66; 127, no. 35; 128, no. 75.
[149] Bagenal, *Vicissitudes of an Anglo-Irish family*, 48–50.
[150] PRO SP 63/129, no. 46.
[151] *CPSI*, iii. 290–1.

been employed in that province, except his sons.'[152] However, Sir Henry Bagenal's mission was not a complete failure. In September 1587 he was sent back to Ireland to deputise for his father 'in all the services of Her Majesty appertaining to his charge' and Perrot was ordered to permit him to do so 'without any trouble, molestation or impeachment'.[153]

In the second half of his deputyship, Perrot was forced into policy changes. These changes reflected the exigencies of the international situation more than the pressure of factional opponents in Ireland or the activities of Sir Henry Bagenal in London. In the first instance, he was forced to give up his obsessive struggle against Sorley Boye MacDonald which, like his earlier one against James Fitzmaurice Fitzgerald, had become *une idée fixe*. In September 1585, Lord Burghley had urged Perrot to come to terms with the MacDonalds and 'so close up the Scottish wars'.[154] The events of the following winter forced Perrot's hand. Dunluce fell to Sorley Boye.[155] Then came the order from the queen obliging the lord deputy to abide by the majority decisions of the Irish council. Sorley Boye's position also suffered when his son Alexander was killed leading a mercenary contingent in Inishowen.[156] Sorley agreed to come to Dublin after a parley with Captain Warren, Loftus's son-in-law. This taken together with a statement from Fenton that the lord deputy was inwardly opposed to a pacification suggests that the settlement was forced upon Perrot by the council.[157] Perrot did not forsake the divide and rule tactic because in May 1586 Angus MacDonald was alloted the Glens.[158] Sorley Boye submitted in June. He became a naturalised subject and was allotted part of the Route and granted the constableship of Dunluce. At the time Perrot tried to produce evidence in an attempt to justify his original attack on Sorley Boye.[159] Obviously, this was a huge embarrassment to Perrot in the summer of 1586 but after his deputyship he glorified his acceptance of Sorley Boye's submission: 'I compelled the said Sorley Boye MacDonald to come to Dublin to submit himself there upon his knees; confessing his folly and his faults, as appears by his submission.'[160] Perrot had failed to make Sorley Boye a victim of his programmatic style of government and with the settlement of 1586, the MacDonalds ceased to be a headache to the Government, although problems posed by Scots mercenaries did not.

Perrot's Ulster composition also collapsed. In November 1585, the Irish council had agreed with Hugh O'Neill, negotiating on behalf of the other Lords, that the number of composition troops should be reduced to 550 and be placed in garrison rather than be dispersed throughout the country.[161] By January 1586 there was trouble between the MacSweenys and the composition

152 PRO SP 63/129, nos 3, 20.
153 APC, xv. 169–70, 226–7.
154 BLO, Perrot 1, fos 144–57.
155 PRO SP 63/112, no. 11; BLO, Perrot 1, fos 177–8.
156 PRO SP 63/123, no. 20.
157 CPSI, iii. 48–9; PRO SP 63/123, 46.
158 Ibid. 124, no. 29.
159 Ibid. nos 6, 77, 83–5.
160 CPSI, iv. 85.
161 'Calendar of the Irish council book', 175, no. 356.

troops in Tirconnell.[162] In March the composition forces scored their only notable success when they defeated a band of incoming Scots and killed its leader Alexander MacSorley MacDonald.[163] By April O'Donnell, Maguire and O'Cahan had ejected the troops placed upon them, but the composition was still in force in Tyrone and Clandeboye.[164] Wallop said that the burden of bearing the soldiers had been exacerbated 'by an extreme year of dearth and death of cattle'; Loftus announced gleefully that the expelled companies now had to be cessed on the Pale.[165] It is significant in terms of overall Tudor policy that many rejected composition soldiers were now transferred to the Netherlands.[166] Most of these troops were Irish, the original English ones having been gradually displaced because they could not bear the discomforts of Ulster and the diet of butter and oatmeal.[167] Hopes were now centred on a general conversion of composition allowances into rent in cattle. This had been part of Perrot's original plan.[168] It was rumoured that the lords were willing to pay high rents to the crown to be rid of the troops, and this plan was supported by White and Dillon on the one hand and the Bagenals on the other.[169] O'Donnell was the first lord to agree to these new arrangements. On a visit to Dublin in July 1586 he agreed to pay a fine of 700 cattle and an annual rent of the same number to the crown in lieu of maintaining troops.[170] According to Fitzwilliam, who marched into Tirconnell after the shipwreck of the Armada, neither the fine imposed at the time nor the two subsequent annual rents were ever paid.[171] At some point, the compositions with the minor lords were also converted into rent in cattle; at the end of Perrot's government none of these rents had been paid.[172] Meanwhile English captains, such as Merryman, petitioned in vain for assistance. He claimed that he and his company received only a quarter of their pay from Turlough Luineach and that he was still owed over £1,200.[173] Perrot maintained that his composition was still in force when the Armada arrived; this claim was refuted by Fitzwilliam.[174] Long after it had evidently failed, he was still defending the operation of a policy on which he had staked his credibility. Consequently the composition was rightly condemned, though not always for reasons of policy.

In spite of these setbacks, Perrot did continue his attack on tanistry by attempting to divide up the lordships of Lower Macwilliam Bourke in Mayo and O'Neill in Tyrone. The Composition of Connacht in 1585 theoretically

162 BLO, Perrot 1, fos 189–93.
163 PRO SP 63/123, no. 20.
164 Ibid. no. 52; BLO, Perrot 1, fos 237–8.
165 PRO SP 63/123, no. 52; CPSI, iii. 48–9.
166 BLO, MS 30237, fo. 51.
167 PRO SP 63/112, no. 41(2); 113, no. 71; 119, no. 10.
168 Ibid. 112, no. 41.
169 Ibid. 116, no. 7(1); 123, no. 31; PRONI Ellis papers, D683 no. 2.
170 PRO SP 63/125, no. 14.
171 CPSI, iv. 94–5.
172 PRO SP 63/135, no. 47.
173 Ibid. 128, no. 72; CPCRI, ii. 153; CPSI, iii. 469–70.
174 Ibid., iv. 81–2, 96–7.

abolished Gaelic titles and jurisdictions.[175] The Lower MacWilliam died in the winter of 1585/6 and Perrot planned a division of the lordship along the lines of his settlement in East Breifne.[176] In May 1586 he declared the title abolished and divided the lordship between the six main competitors.[177] The household lands were allotted and later granted to William Bourke, son of the late Mac-William. This left the *tanáiste* and other principal men discontented.[178] There-fore it was the abolition of the Lower MacWilliamship and the subsequent land division by Perrot, not arbitrary government by Bingham which drove the Bourkes and their following septs into revolt.[179] The same degree of success was not forthcoming in Mayo as had been achieved in Cavan. Unlike the O'Reillys, the Lower Macwilliam Bourkes were overlords in their own right and were less subject to anglicisation. When this attack on tanistry amongst the Lower MacWilliams is considered in the context of the Composition of Connacht, then it becomes clear that the agreement did not have the same stabilising effect in Mayo as in Thomond and Clanrickard where earlier surrender and regrant arrangements had acquired a degree of permanence.[180] Moreover, the abolition of the Lower MacWilliamship is important to the later outbreak of the Nine Years War because thereafter the Bourkes were in a continuous state of insurrection against the crown.[181]

An opportunity for the division of Tyrone and the reduction of its power seemed to present itself in Perrot's deputyship. Both Sidney and Essex had proposed dividing up the lordship. In 1583 when Turlough Luineach's death seemed imminent, the privy council had hoped that the lordship would be 'rather divided into the hands of many than come to the possession of one'. Perrot hoped to settle Tyrone along the lines of East Breifne and in this he had the backing of all sectors of the Irish council.[182] At parliament in 1585, Hugh, baron of Dungannon, demanded the title and lands of his grandfather, Conn O'Neill. He was duly admitted to the title of earl, but was asked to petition the crown for the estates because the attainder of Shane O'Neill had, since Conn's time, annexed Tyrone to the crown.[183] A petition was subsequently sent to Court but the decision was postponed for further deliberation.[184] It was not until the spring of 1587 that Hugh O'Neill was able to travel to London to conclude the issue; in the interim he had greatly strengthened his position by occupying the central third of Tyrone.[185] At the same time Irish council

[175] Bernadette Cunningham, 'The composition of Connacht in the lordships of Clanricard and Thomond, 1577–1641', *IHS*, xxiv (1984), 4.
[176] BLO, Perrot 1, fos 189–93.
[177] 'The Perrot Papers, 62–3.
[178] *CPSI*, iii. 198–204. Fiants, 16th report, no. 4978.
[179] *CPSI*, iii. 198–204.
[180] Cunningham, 'Composition of Connacht', 5–8.
[181] The activities of the Bourkes of Mayo in this period are well summarised in Anne Chambers, *Chieftain to knight: Tibbot Bourke, 1567–1629, first viscount Mayo*, Dublin 1983, chs iv, v.
[182] BL Add. 48015 (Yelverton MS xvi), fos 313–18; *Letters and memorials*, i. 89–97: PRO SP 63/102, no. 74; 130, no. 27.
[183] Ibid. 117, no. 52.
[184] Ibid. no. 53; Lambeth, Carew 632, fos 82, 84.
[185] PRO SP 62/118, no. 59.

members lobbied vigorously for a settlement by the division of Tyrone. Arch-bishop Long of Armagh wanted to apply the model of East Breifne. He pro-posed that those septs who opposed Hugh O'Neill's primacy within the lordship should be granted their lands to hold directly from the crown rather than under the subjection of the earl.[186] Sir Henry Bagenal echoed this demand on his visit to London.[187] At the start of 1587, aware that the earl soon intended to travel to Court, Loftus, Marshal Bagenal and Bingham wrote a joint letter to the privy council warning of his ambition to be supreme in Ulster.[188] On the eve of Hugh O'Neill's departure, Perrot wanted Turlough Luineach made earl of Omagh and the lordship divided up. In this way, he hoped to extinguish the title of O'Neill and to obtain a revenue for the crown out of the territory.[189]

At the negotiations in London in April and May 1587, the privy council, and Walsingham in particular, wished to endorse Perrot's proposals. The earl of Tyrone was adamant in his refusal, resting his case as a legitimate heir to his grandfather's estate and as a constant and faithful servitor, which could not be claimed for Turlough.[190] The privy council eventually yielded to the earl's demands for a patent in line with his grandfather's (the Blackwater fort exempted). All Turlough received was the captaincy of Tyrone for life.[191] The crown was forced to yield to Hugh O'Neill for three reasons. Tyrone's legitimate claim was undeniable and, as upholders of the English law, the crown had little option. Also, by making a division and antagonising Hugh O'Neill, the crown risked turning him into a malcontent at a time when fear of Spanish invasion was increasing. But how did O'Neill pull off this success in the face of such overwhelming opposition? He had clearly exploited his contacts; as Sir James Perrot later wrote 'by applying himself to those that were greatest in authority, he got grace at Court'.[192] Here the key broker on O'Neill's behalf must surely have been the earl of Ormond. He was at odds with Perrot, friends with Burghley, had access to the queen and wanted to contain Geraldine influence in Ulster.[193] Not surprisingly, Perrot was furious that the settlement was made in Tyrone's favour; White later wrote that the patent given to the earl was 'more bountiful than beneficial for the state of that Province'.[194]

The letter, in which Perrot condemned the arrangements of May 1587, also provides a neat summary of his northern policy. He wrote of how the plans for fortification had been rejected and how the composition had collapsed. None-theless the policy of surrender and regrant and the division of the lordships seemed to have been proceeding well. However, with the failure to divide up Tyrone, he was sure that similar settlements elsewhere in Ulster were now impossible. Moreover after Turlough's death the earl would control the area between Dundalk and Strabane. Perrot saw only one result: 'I cannot imagine

---

186 Ibid. no. 79.
187 Ibid. 127, no. 35.
188 CPSI, iii. 248–9.
189 Ibid. 277.
190 PRO SP 63/129, nos 58–9.
191 CPCRI, ii. 123, 126–7.
192 PRO SP 63/129, no. 92; 132, no. 31; Perrot, The Chronicle of Ireland, 54.
193 Brady, Worsted in the game, 57–8.
194 PRO SP 63/130, no. 27; 131, no. 16.

of any third course to be taken other than to maintain the quiet of that province by the sword and by continual charge'.[195] Consequently, in the final year of his deputyship, Perrot was forced to switch to a policy of containment. He used two tactics in an attempt to curb the power of the earl of Tyrone. The surrender and regrant of the lordships of MacMahon and O'Hanlon was rushed through by him in the hope of freeing them from Tyrone's control.[196] A more significant move by Perrot was his kidnapping and imprisonment of Tyrone's prospective son-in-law, Hugh Roe O'Donnell.[197]

All governors were concerned as much with patronage and profit as they were with policy. Loftus complained of Perrot's appointment 'even of his own servants and followers' as sheriffs and other law enforcement officers.[198] Sir Henry Duke and Captain William Mostian represent two such appointments. Duke was, in his own words, 'by his lordship's commandment and direction employed as sheriff of the Brenny' while Perrot described Mostian who was sent as sheriff into O'Donnell's country as 'my man'.[199] In this light the extension of crown authority into Gaelic areas must be seen as an enlargement of the patronage at the disposal of the chief governor. Furthermore, friction between Perrot and regional power-brokers such as Bagenal, Bingham and Ormond reflects conflict between central and local patronage systems. The Tudor administration of Ireland, in common with other early modern states, had an acceptable level of constitutional corruption. Charges of financial corruption were levelled against Perrot. Fenton and Gardiner complained that many of the composition beeves due to Her Majesty from Gaelic lords – Maguire was cited as an example – were not unpaid but in fact had been taken up by the lord deputy instead.[200] Wallop, who had earlier defended the lord deputy against allegations of negligent overpayment, claimed that Perrot was falsifying his household accounts by rating all his expenses by the two dearest weeks of the year.[201] All that can be said in mitigation is that in the second half of Perrot's government the revenue due the deputy may have suffered through the change-over in the Pale from cess to composition.[202]

Finally, part and parcel of Perrot's deputyship, like those of Sussex and Sidney before him, was a thinly disguised propaganda campaign. Sir John promoted the idea that he enjoyed good relations with the Gaelic lords and that they were conformable to his will. He emphasised how the Irish lords had donned English dress for the state opening of parliament and how Turlough Luineach had 'carried Her Majesty's sword before me (being but Her Majesty's shadow) when before he had held his sword many times against Her Majesty's

[195] Ibid. 130, no. 27. Perrot had plans to divide up North Clandeboye at the time of his departure: ibid. 156, no. 52.
[196] Fiants, 16th Report, nos 4985, 4991, 5041, 5091.
[197] HMC, Salisbury MSS, iii. 285–6.
[198] CPSI, iii. 211–13.
[199] Ibid. 264–5, 513–14.
[200] Ibid. 142–3, 409.
[201] PRO SP 63/119, no. 10; CPSI, iii. 97, 284–5.
[202] PRO SP 63/119, no. 10.

forces'.[203] Certainly, the Gaelic lords welcomed his speeding up of the surrender and regrant policy but Perrot was neither pro-Gaelic nor were his policies born out of simple altruism.[204] To facilitate the government settlement of East Breifne, Philip O'Reilly was imprisoned for not bringing in Maguire's hostage for whom he acted as surety.[205] Hugh Roe O'Donnell and three other leading men of Tirconnell were captured by stratagem and shipped off to languish in Dublin Castle.[206] In Connacht Perrot supported Sir Brian O'Rourke and Donough O'Connor Sligo as part of the conflict between himself and Bingham.[207] The emotional send-off given to Perrot by the Gaelic lords, with Turlough Luineach in tears, would appear to have been a propaganda stunt for which purpose he kept the lords six weeks in Dublin.[208] The lords mentioned at the farewell were those who had proved troublesome under previous administrations; nor is there any contemporary evidence of Turlough Luineach shedding tears. Bingham writes that Perrot was casting around generally at his departure for attestations of his good government.[209] On his departure Perrot presented the City of Dublin with a silver bowl inscribed *reliquo in pace*. White composed this eulogy: *Subjugavit Ultoniam, pacificavit Conaciam, relaxavit Mediam, ligavit Mononiam, fregit Lageniam, extirpavit Scotos, refraenavit Anglos, et hiis omnibus per aeque vertigal acquisivit Reginae.*[210]

That Lord Deputy Perrot was ill-tempered in humour and authoritarian in method is not surprising. If anything he was an unusually energetic reforming minister whose goals were frustrated by the meanness of a conservative monarch and the inadequacies of the early modern administrative machine. Taking Dawtrey's mission to the Scottish king and the suppressed application to the English parliament as examples, it is obvious that Perrot regarded himself as a viceroy rather than as a mere lord deputy. Because of his presence in central government, subordinate palatinate and provincial jurisdictions suffered a diminution in authority. We can safely conclude that there was no substantive linkage between faction and policy. The image of Perrot and his supporters pursuing a conciliatory approach towards the Gaelic Irish and the Loftus-Bagenal nexus advocating aggressive forward measures must be discarded. The control of patronage rather than the orientation of policy was the essential cause of the bitter factional clashes which characterised Perrot's administration. This is not to say that factional rivalry precluded policy considerations. The shortcomings of Perrot's policies were frequently used to condemn him personally and developments in the North were often a cause of friction with the Bagenals whose private interests were at stake. Perrot's obsession with the Scottish threat was a costly mistake but previous governors had engaged in similar simplicities. In spite of this, there was consensus between Perrot and his

---

[203] BLO, Perrot 1, fos 99–102. Quoted in Treadwell, 'Sir John Perrot and the Irish parliament', 281.
[204] BLO, Perrot 1, fos 99–102.
[205] CPSI, iv. 82; 'Calendar of the Irish council book', 174, no. 351.
[206] PRO SP 63/177, no. 48(1).
[207] Northumberland Papers, Syon House MS Y III 1(4), unfoliated; CPSI, iii. 519.
[208] Rawlinson, The life of Perrot, 289; CPSI, iv. 82.
[209] CPSI, iii. 470–1, 519.
[210] Rawlinson, The life of Perrot, 286.

fellow councillors on the ends and means of crown policy in the North. Perrot's programme of 1584, intended to reform Ulster, proved a failure; nevertheless, an attack on tanistry, aimed at the division of the Gaelic polity, began to develop during his deputyship which was important for the future. Perrot handed over a generally peaceful kingdom to his successor-in-office, Sir William Fitzwilliam. This was a deceptive state of affairs. Policy by 1588 was reduced to a minimalist holding operation. The diversion of Tudor attention to continental Europe and the superficial nature of their power in Ireland had permitted Hugh O'Neill to begin consolidating his authority within Tyrone, the most powerful Ulster lordship.

4

The Nemesis of Fitzwilliam

Sir William Fitzwilliam, who succeeded Perrot as lord deputy, has been regarded historically as the corrupt and cruel governor who caused the Nine Years War. This lacklustre figure was Elizabeth's most experienced Irish administrator. He had been lord deputy in the early 1570s and before that had served fifteen years in the exchequer. The early phase of Fitzwilliam's second deputyship saw a recrudescence of factionalism which climaxed in the trial of Perrot for treason in Westminster Hall. The eclipse of Perrot did not signify the emergence of an aggressive forward policy in Ireland, rather it gave Fitzwilliam greater freedom to pursue his own personal enrichment. Sir William's style of government was minimalist. With central authority less active, provincial officials such as Bingham and Bagenal were let off the leash. Fitzwilliam needed a policy success and the opportunity came in Monaghan. For the first time under the surrender and regrant policy, Gaelic freeholders were granted property rights. In achieving this radical departure, the influence of the Irish solicitor-general and the English privy council was probably more determinant than that of Fitzwilliam himself. With the policy breakthrough in Monaghan, the minimalist governor had stumbled by chance into a programme.

Fitzwilliam was acutely aware of how Sidney, his predecessor as lord deputy in the 1570s, had used his influence at Court to criticise, interfere and eventually replace him.[1] He now feared Perrot would do likewise. On the other hand, he knew that retiring lord deputies were vulnerable – allegations made by Fitzwilliam himself had contributed to the downfall of St Leger in the mid-1550s.[2] Perrot became a member of the privy council in February 1589. It was soon obvious that he would remain influential in directing Irish affairs as revealed by the council book entry: 'Lord of Buckhurst, Sir John Perrot, Mr. Fortescue did sit to hear Irish causes.'[3] Almost immediately allegations and counter-allegations were exchanged between Fitzwilliam and Perrot.[4] In his opening salvo, Perrot complained about a purge of officials appointed by him.[5] It is not clear to what extent Perrot's appointees were displaced. In June 1589 Perrot secured a privy council letter demanding the reinstatement of Seager to his post as constable of Dublin Castle.[6] Sir Henry Duke protested about his harsh treatment at the hands of the lord deputy. As a result he had lost the daily allowance and thirty soldiers pertaining to the office of seneschal of Cavan

---

1 Brady, 'Government of Ireland', 220.
2 Ibid. 105.
3 APC, xviii. 76, 133.
4 CSPI, iv. 161–7.
5 Ibid. 165.
6 APC, xviii. 254–5.

which he had received from Perrot.[7] Fitzwilliam conducted a smear campaign against him. He alleged that Duke was ineffectual as a military commander and that the seneschal had attempted to bribe him in order to obtain a wider command in South Ulster.[8] In the case of councillors like Sir Lucas Dillon and Sir Nicholas White, who were adherents of Perrot, the change of governor meant that their role as advisors was diminished.[9] Immediately after the new appointment to the privy council, Fitzwilliam requested Burghley's assistance to prevent Perrot mounting an attack on Archbishop Loftus, his earlier opponent.[10]

On his part, Perrot used his influence to have Sir Edward Moore nominated to the Irish council and later recommended to command a company of fifty horsemen.[11] The extent to which Perrot was prepared to exert influence is demonstrated in a suggestion by him that his son should be made chief commissioner of Connacht when the death of Sir Richard Bingham was rumoured.[12] Perrot maintained contact with Gaelic lords such as Turlough Luineach O'Neill and Brian O'Rourke. Although the letters from the privy councillor were encouragements to support the lord deputy, they were also intended to increase reliance on Perrot himself.[13] Not surprisingly, Fitzwilliam regarded such correspondence as interference in his right to govern.[14] Fitzwilliam's exasperation with Perrot increased markedly as a result of Sir Thomas Cecil's visit to Ireland in September and October 1589. Fitzwilliam claimed that letters from Perrot to major figures in all sectors of Irish society had caused them to regard Sir Thomas rather than himself as governor.[15] Cecil was clearly being used by the enemies of Fitzwilliam. Sir Nicholas White claimed that 'the coming hither of Sir Thomas . . . hath altered the minds of the people and greatly abated his [Fitzwilliam's] credit'.[16] The lord deputy learnt from Burghley that 'Sir John Perrot doth not allow of my form of proceedings' and consequently he felt that 'my credit and service is already in the balance and cannot long stand unoverthrown'.[17] However, Fitzwilliam's greatest fear was that he was merely a caretaker for the absent Perrot.[18]

In February 1590 Fitzwilliam set in train the conspiracy which was to bring down not only Perrot but also his allies in the Irish government. In attacking Perrot the initiating and leading role was taken by Fitzwilliam; former rivals, like Loftus, played only walk-on parts. In carrying forward the plot, Fitzwilliam's principal assistant was the most frequent recipient of his letters – Lord Burghley. Fitzwilliam alleged that Sir Denis O'Roughan, a priest and prisoner in

7 PRO SP 63/149, no. 51.
8 Ibid. 154, nos 24, 40.
9 Ibid. 143, no. 7.
10 Ibid. no. 12.
11 Ibid. 146, nos 62–3; APC, xix. 24.
12 PRO SP 63/151, no. 66.
13 CSPI, iv. 234–6.
14 PRO SP 63/144, nos 61, 63.
15 Ibid. 147, no. 35.
16 Ibid. no. 49.
17 Ibid. no. 35.
18 Alnwick, Northumberland MS vi., no. 15, fo. 27.

Dublin Castle, had brought him a letter written by Sir John Perrot in 1585 to Philip II. In this Perrot offered the Spanish king his assistance in return for a hereditary grant of Wales. O'Roughan also alleged that Perrot had heard mass and received the sacrament from him. Fitzwilliam informed Burghley of this and sent him a copy of the incriminating letter which he had transcribed himself. Fitzwilliam's son was sent to the queen bearing the original letter.[19] Bishop Meredith of Leighlin (formerly Perrot's chaplain), Sir Lucas Dillon and Sir Nicholas White learned of the affair and moved to forewarn Sir John.[20] As a consequence of these allegations, the privy council appointed a commission to interrogate Denis O'Roughan and Henry Bird, who had previously been con-victed with O'Roughan for counterfeiting Perrot's signature. With the excep-tion of Bishop Jones of Meath, the composition of the commission favoured Perrot having Meredith, Lucas Dillon, White, Moore, Waterhouse, Walshe and Calthorpe as its other members.[21] In Ireland Perrot's cause was extremely popu-lar if the assertion of his partisan, Lord Slane, is any guide:

> Your honour is much beholding to God, for every man that openeth his mouth within this land (as well the rich as the poor) do cry out against the vipers that so villainously have conspired against you. I could make a long discourse of the miserable state of this poor Realm, but I will not trouble your honour otherwise than to desire you to be a mean to Her Majesty to have a better exchange of governor who I pray God may be yourself. For this lord deputy maketh no accompt of no nobleman nor any other within this Realm, but only of his son John, his son[-in-law] Dyer, and of his daughter the Lady Dyer; they ruleth the roost as pleaseth them with the help of their mother Lady Fitzwilliams; these be his chief councillors. As for Sir Lucas Dillon, Sir Edward Waterhouse and Sir Edward Moore, they have no credit with him, and as for myself, since your departure hence I never had credit nor counten-ance of him, and for no cause but for that I do lament to see the state of this Realm miserably altered since your government.[22]

It was only after the death of Walsingham, his ally and patron at Court, in April 1590 that the tide turned against Perrot. Burghley and Hatton, an old enemy, were now able to take a tougher line. It must be be emphasised that Perrot's fall was due to the strength of his opponents in England rather than the insubstantial allegations made against him in Ireland. Perrot wrote to the queen for an audience but it was not granted: 'If Your Majesty this last year had not often commanded me to be ready to serve Your Majesty there (which was known to many) Your Highness had never heard of this Machiavellian strate-gem devised as a stop of that your purpose without any matter at all as will appear in the end and hath been nourished here as I guess for some respects I will disclose to Your Majesty.'[23] The findings of the commission had been favourable to Perrot and the probity of O'Roughan and Bird was further

---

19 PRO SP 63/150, nos 44, 44(1).
20 Ibid. no. 71.
21 APC, xviii. 424–6.
22 Alnwick, Northumberland MS vi., no. 25, fo. 51.
23 Ibid. no. 15, fo. 27.

questioned.[24] However, O'Roughan's stories received more credence on his arrival in England. Furthermore, Sir Denis alleged mental and physical torture by members of the Irish investigating commission. Consequently, the bishop of Leighlin and Sir Nicholas White were ordered to London for questioning. The priest also levelled accusations against Moore and probably against Attorney-General Calthorpe.[25] At the same time, Rice Ap Hugh, the provost-marshal and a supporter of Perrot, was summoned to London and Stephen Seager, whom Fitzwilliam had refused to reinstate as constable of Dublin Castle, was sent over as a prisoner.[26] Meanwhile Sir Henry Duke was imprisoned in Dublin Castle for offences perpetrated by the soldiers under him.[27] It was Burghley and Hatton who had the most frequent dealings with O'Roughan and Fitzwilliam in building up the case against Perrot; Secretary Fenton, seconded from Ireland, assisted with the investigations.[28] Finally in December 1590, articles were drawn up against Perrot on which he was examined and charged.[29] Subsequently, Perrot, Meredith and White were imprisoned in the Tower of London.[30]

It was not until April 1592 that Perrot was tried for treason in Westminster Hall. He was charged on four counts: that his intemperate speeches showed an evil disposition towards the sovereign; that he had maintained traitors, namely Catholic priests and Irish rhymers; that he had conspired with foreign enemies against the state and that he had supported Irish rebels such as Brian O'Rourke. Perrot refuted these charges and claimed that O'Roughan, the main prosecution witness, was completely untrustworthy, having changed his religion at least five times and having been convicted for counterfeiting his signature. Such protestations were to no avail and Perrot was pronounced guilty. Two months later he was sentenced to death; but the sentence was never carried out and he died in the Tower in September 1592.[31] Subsequently Meredith and White were tried in Star Chamber. The bishop was released after paying a fine of £2,000 and resumed his office. White died later in the Tower.[32] The trials of Moore and Calthorpe never took place.[33] Following the death of Sir Lucas Dillon in February 1591, the rump of Perrot's party now exercised little or no influence on government in Ireland.[34] On the other hand, Fitzwilliam's position was immeasurably strengthened: in fact this had been the case since mid-1590 when Perrot's influence as privy councillor was eclipsed.

The factional struggle between Perrot and Fitzwilliam did not lead to the

[24] CSPI, iv. 342–3.
[25] Ibid. 350; CSPD, ii. 672, 677.
[26] CSPI, iv. 344, 350.
[27] Ibid. 355.
[28] CSPD, ii. 694; CSPI, iv. 355, 357–8; APC, xix. 420.
[29] CSPD, ii. 704–5; APC, xx. 103.
[30] During his imprisonment Perrot drew up a long paper entitled 'Most certain reasons to prove that I am a true man to my Queen and country and neither Papist or in confederacy with the king of Spain, the only enemy of God's word and to these parts of Christendom and that Sir Denis is the most wickedest and falsest man in the world': Alnwick, Northumberland MS vi., no. 1.
[31] BLO, Willis MS 58, fos 245–9, 263–305; Camden, History of Elizabeth, 462–3.
[32] APC, xxiv. 44, 135.
[33] CSPI, iv. 485.
[34] Ibid. 462.

emergence of a new forward policy in the North; that was already evident in Perrot's approach. The removal of Perrot did however give Fitzwilliam the freedom to turn his deputyship into a vast money-making exercise. Fitzwilliam was in fact a liability to the crown even before he entered the government of Ireland in the summer of 1588. Earlier, when his treasury account was audited in 1571, a serious shortfall had been discovered. Obviously, this irregularity was attributed to negligence rather than corruption because Fitzwilliam remained a trusted servant. Nevertheless, he was held personally responsible for a debt of £3,964 and although the queen remitted £1,000 in 1572, he still owed £1,778 in 1588. When he took on his second deputyship the same year, he was allotted a higher stipend because he was 'not so well furnished in his patrimony as other deputies'. Fitzwilliam was lumbered with debts and still in the process of estate building whereas Perrot had a mature estate of fifteen well-stocked manors from the rents of which he was able to raise £1,500 for his trial.[35] Fitzwilliam's financial straits were doubtless exacerbated by the switch from purveyance to composition in the upkeep of the deputy's household, a point about which Perrot had already been complaining.

Fitzwilliam was strongly backed by Lord Burghley. Significantly, his re-appointment coincided with a vigorous campaign for concealed lands in Ireland which Burghley directed from England. Aimed at boosting crown revenues, this prying into land titles by rapacious adventurers involved such financial corruption and legal chicanery that it caused serious discontent in Connacht and Munster.[36] For the corruptions attributable to Fitzwilliam himself the principal source is a document presented to Lord Burghley by Robert Legg in April 1593.[37] Legg had a grudge against Fitzwilliam but his allegations are detailed and convincing. Although difficult to verify, Legg was uniquely placed as deputy remembrancer to obtain such data. He maintained that Fitzwilliam's allies, Bishop Loftus of Dublin, Bishop Jones of Meath and Sir Roger Wilbraham, abetted his corruption. The monies which Fitzwilliam had illicitly obtained were not received directly but through proxies, either relatives such as his daughter, Lady Dyer, or minor officials. Legg claimed that Fitzwilliam as head of the commission on leases, wards and liveries retained the fines for himself. Crown rents and payments for pardons were pocketed by the lord deputy rather than lodged in the treasury. Likewise, 'there never was such a mart in Ireland for selling of sheriff's offices as hath been since his time'. Spiritual livings were also up for sale. Fitzwilliam's interference in the grant of export licences and his abuse of the courts, especially the exchequer, were noted. Legg claimed that the lord deputy's main policy success – the Monaghan settlement – was riddled with corrupt dealings. Fitzwilliam's only desire was apparently 'to fill his own bags daily and hourly' and according to Legg's calculations, by 1593 he had obtained

[35] M. E. Finch, *The wealth of five Northamptonshire families, 1540–1640*, Northampton 1956, 105–11; P. W. Hasler, *The Commons, 1558–1603*, 3 vols, London 1981, iii. 207.
[36] T. O. Ranger, 'Richard Boyle and the making of an Irish fortune, 1588–1614', *IHS*, x (1957), 258–64.
[37] PRO SP 63/169, nos 2, 3. At the same time, Legg also presented a list of sinecures in the Irish administration and a note on the corrupt dealings of Sir Roger Wilbraham, the solicitor-general. These documents (PRO SP 63/201, nos 153, 4) have been incorrectly placed in the calendar under 1597.

at least £9,600 by illicit means.[38] A second source of information is a document addressed to Queen Elizabeth by Captain Thomas Lee. Lee was stationed in Leinster and held lands there. However, he had also seen service in the North and was an acquaintance of Hugh O'Neill. Lee went so far as to claim that Fitzwilliam had seized 'poor men's goods, for the satisfaction of his own old debts grown in his latter time of government'. Yet his allegations are valuable in that they verify the existence of corruption in instances where otherwise there would only be circumstantial evidence.[39] The implication of these documents must be that Fitzwilliam's administration was far more corrupt than Perrot's and in dealing with policy we must attempt to judge to what extent this corruption impinged on its development and implementation.

Fitzwilliam did not have a ready-made programme when he arrived in Ireland in 1588 nor was he soon to adopt one. As an administrator, Fitzwilliam was essentially a pragmatist working from day to day. To some extent, his instructions on this occasion were similar to the objectives of his previous government, to cut costs and, where possible, increase revenue.[40] War with Spain inevitably consigned Ireland to the bottom of the budgetary list. In the changed international situation, a number of instructions concerned the fear of an impending Spanish invasion and the precautionary measures to be taken. The instructions indicate a holding operation rather than a radical departure in relations with the Gaelic Irish.[41] The dispute between Fitzwilliam and Perrot had also involved their contrasting styles of government. Perrot backed Sir Edward Moore in his offer to collect the cattle to which the Ulster composition had been commuted.[42] Fitzwilliam saw this plan as just as unworkable as the original composition and called for more pragmatic and less declaratory measures.[43] Contrarily, White blamed the northern disorders in early 1589 on the lack of energetic government by the lord deputy.[44] Another feature of Fitzwilliam's minimalist style of government was the lack of control over provincial officials. Bingham had a freer hand in policy-making than under Perrot, although jurisdictional disputes continued with his successor.[45] Using the strategic pretext that neighbouring Gaelic lords threatened areas already reduced, Bingham conquered Mayo and Leitrim and took over Sligo Castle.[46] He then began to take an interest in West Ulster which he claimed was a destabilising influence on newly-established North Connacht.[47] The other exemplar is Sir Henry Bagenal, who pursued his ambitions in Ulster with the active cooperation of Fitzwilliam. The uncontrolled activities of regional commanders inevitably provoked trouble. These may be taken to include sheriffs who had purchased their offices from the lord deputy.

38 Ibid. 169, no. 3.
39 BL Harleian 35, fos 258–65; DNB, xxxii. 380–2.
40 CSPI, iii. 455–62; Brady, 'Government of Ireland', 219.
41 CSPI, iii. 455–62.
42 PRO SP 63/146, no. 19; 147, no. 11.
43 Ibid. 151, no. 93.
44 Ibid. 147, no. 7.
45 Ibid. 146, no. 64.
46 Ibid. 135, no. 26; 145, nos 6, 61, 85: CSPI, iv. 8–9.
47 Ibid. 544–6; v. 34–40.

However, Fitzwilliam did take the opportunity to resume Perrot's attack on tanistry in Oriel, the lordship of the MacMahons, which had been shired in 1585 as the county of Monaghan.[48] In 1587 Sir Ross MacMahon had surrendered his lands and obtained a regrant under letters patent. Tanistry was, nominally, abolished and the territory was remaindered to his brothers.[49] MacMahon, *urrí* by tradition and son-in-law by contract, was one of the earl of Tyrone's main dependents. The grant of letters patent had encouraged him in a vain attempt to break free of Tyrone's overlordship.[50] Afterwards, the earl increased MacMahon's reliance on him by acting as surety for the debts which the latter owed in Drogheda.[51] Early in his deputyship Fitzwilliam attempted to impose sheriffs upon the border counties of Leitrim, Donegal, Fermanagh and Monaghan.[52] Sir Ross refused to admit a sheriff apparently on the orders of the earl of Tyrone.[53] Only after his lordship was invaded by a force led by Sir Henry Bagenal, did MacMahon agree to accept the local government official.[54]

In the summer of 1589 Sir Ross MacMahon died. His brother, Hugh Roe, came to Dublin to seek confirmation of the letters patent. The lord deputy invited three other contenders for the lordship to Dublin and tried to browbeat them into accepting a division of the territory. Fitzwilliam and the Irish council threatened Hugh Roe with charges of treason but he and the other MacMahons proved obstinate. It was therefore decided to establish Hugh Roe in the lordship. This entailed deposing Brian MacHugh óg who meanwhile 'had made himself MacMahon by the custom of the country' with the backing of his cousin, the earl of Tyrone.[55] The force dispatched to establish Hugh Roe was beaten by Brian MacHugh óg on the borders of Fermanagh and subsequently it withdrew to the Pale.[56] The first indication we have of Hugh Roe's imprisonment in Dublin Castle is the privy council letter of November 1589 complaining about his detention for 'march' offences and implying that the lord deputy had switched his support to Brian MacHugh óg.[57] These accusations were procured by Perrot; but it is strange that there are no extant letters from Fitzwilliam himself reporting the retreat from Monaghan nor any at all reporting Hugh Roe's imprisonment. This must lead us to suspect that Fitzwilliam was displeased at the failure of the military campaign and that the subsequent rumours of bribery by Brian MacHugh óg contain a grain of truth.

In March 1590 Fitzwilliam made specific proposals for the future of Hugh Roe and the MacMahon lordship. Fitzwilliam recited the offences committed by Hugh Roe. He was accused of subverting the sheriff's authority, maintaining

---

[48] *Inquisitionum in officio rotulorum cancellariae Hiberniae*, ii. pp. xv–xviii.
[49] Fiants, 16th Report, nos 4989, 4991.
[50] PRO SP 63/130, no. 63(2); 133, no. 10.
[51] APC, xix. 306–7.
[52] PRO SP 63/142, nos 57(1), 61; *CSPI*, iv. 94–5.
[53] PRO SP 63/143, no. 7.
[54] Ibid. 142, no. 57(1). It is not without significance that the invading force was led by Sir Henry, the earl's rival. Amongst Bagenal's assistants, on this occasion, were O'Hanlon and Magennis whose overlordship the two men contested. The activities in Monaghan were, in some ways, an extension of the theatre of rivalry.
[55] Ibid. 146, no. 5.
[56] Ibid. 142, no. 12.
[57] APC, xviii. 231–2.

Scots mercenaries and levying exactions from his neighbours by force.[58] The lord deputy considered these actions to be treasonous rather than simply 'march' offences. Since the territory was now a feudal fiefdom, its holder could be executed and his lands escheated to the crown.[59] This concurred with the views expressed in the treatise subsequently written by Perrot on the subject.[60] By the execution of Hugh Roe MacMahon, Fitzwilliam intended to set an example to other wayward Ulster lords. The lordship could then be divided between the competitors; at first Fitzwilliam suggested a partition between three of them, later he added two more names. He also planned a new composition to increase the rents due to the crown.[61] During 1590 the situation in Monaghan improved in the government's favour, though correspondence intercepted from the MacMahons suggests that this was obtained by military repression.[62] In the spring, court sessions were held in the county. Brian MacHugh óg was now prepared to abandon the armed struggle and accept a partitioned settlement.[63] Fitzwilliam rejected the allegation that he had been bribed, by way of a gift of cattle to Lady Dyer, to prefer Brian MacHugh óg for the MacMahonship.[64] In a memoir written after his deputyship, Fitzwilliam said that he had refused large offers of cattle to make a new MacMahon.[65] Fitzwilliam contrasted his approach with that of Perrot: 'I like better of somewhat in substance and so likely to continue, such as I am persuaded may be had of the MacMahons by division of that territory than a great deal in show.'[66] The allegations of Perrot and more generally the factional complications between the privy councillor and the lord deputy delayed a privy council decision on Monaghan. However, it is clear from Perrot's views and his own settlement of East Breifne, which Fitzwilliam's plans closely resembled, that there were no policy differences between the two men on this issue. At the end of June 1590, Fitzwilliam renewed his request for a decision in the case of Hugh Roe and sent over a more extensive list of charges against him.[67]

The circumstances surrounding the trial and execution of Hugh Roe MacMahon are unclear.[68] With Perrot removed from the political scene, the privy council gave the go-ahead for MacMahon's trial in August 1590.[69] He was to be tried by process of the common law as was the normal procedure in treason cases. Attainder by statute, used against Shane O'Neill and the earl of Desmond, was only necessary when individuals were absent or dead and to specify forfeitures of land.[70] It is unfortunate that no contemporary account of

58 PRO SP 63/151, nos 2(1, 2).
59 Ibid. no. 2.
60 Ibid. 156, no. 51.
61 Ibid. 151, no. 2.
62 Ibid. 153, no. 32.
63 Ibid. 151, nos 7, 93.
64 Ibid. no. 93; 153, no. 24.
65 BL Add. 12,503, fo. 390.
66 PRO SP 63/151, no. 93.
67 Ibid. 153, nos 23, 24(4).
68 A good account of this episode is provided by Peader MacDuinnshleibhe, 'The legal murder of Aodh Rua MacMahon, 1590', Clogher Record, i (1955), 39–52.
69 APC, xix. 374–6.
70 Penry Williams, The Tudor regime, London 1979, 378–9.

MacMahon's indictment, trial and execution exists in the state papers. Fitzwilliam informed the privy council on the 10 September 1590 that he was sending the chief justice, Sir Robert Dillon, and the solicitor-general, Sir Roger Wilbraham, to verify the evidence against MacMahon. The commission given to Dillon and Wilbraham concerned other matters so that if the accusers retracted their evidence, 'the purpose against MacMahon may be clean suppressed'. If, on the other hand, the evidence held good, Fitzwilliam himself would proceed to the sessions at Monaghan.[71] The next piece of information which we possess, dated 21 September, was that Fitzwilliam planned to take 300 soldiers with him for his twelve day stay in Monaghan.[72] By the time Monaghan was next mentioned in October, Hugh Roe had been executed. Fitzwilliam simply stated that MacMahon had been 'by course of Her Majesty's laws executed to the great contentment of the country'. Wilbraham was more informative; Hugh Roe had been found guilty of levying exactions from Ever Mac Con Uladh MacMahon by force and of freeing the MacArdles from the sheriff's custody but he had been acquitted of keeping Scots mercenaries and the other charges had not been required.[73]

The evidence for a miscarriage of justice comes from three later sources. None of these deponents was well-disposed towards Fitzwilliam. In 1593 Robert Legg alleged that Hugh Roe MacMahon had outbid the other competitors by offering Fitzwilliam 800 head of cattle as a bribe. In the event, Hugh Roe had been unable to gather this number and was imprisoned. Afterwards, Fitzwilliam had brought Hugh Roe to Monaghan, promising to place him in his inheritance, but instead had him tried and executed. The prisoner had been indicted for old offences and the jealousy of his competitors was utilised against him. Legg saw MacMahon's execution as an example of how Fitzwilliam hoped to benefit himself by 'seeking the blood of Her Majesty's subjects in tyrannical manner without fear of God'. He also believed that 'the putting away of that man in such sort will be remembered hereafter'.[74] A most prophetic statement as it turned out. Further allegations were made by the MacMahons during the 1596 negotiations. Ever Mac Con Uladh confirmed the incidence of bribery and mentioned the same number of cattle. At the same time Brian MacHugh óg made specific allegations about the conduct of the trial. First, where MacMahon had been indicted for taking a 'distress' according to the custom of the country for duties owed to him, MacHugh claimed that this had been done with the approval of the state and the assistance of the companies of Captains Willis and Plunkett. Secondly, he alleged that the grand jury, which drew up the indictment, was composed of soldiers rather than freeholders of the country. Finally, the trial had a jury of four soldiers and nine gentlemen. The soldiers were allowed to come and go as they pleased. The countrymen were kept under duress, separately and without food, for twenty-four hours until eventually they pronounced MacMahon guilty.[75] Brian MacHugh óg's claims were more specific

71 PRO SP 63/154, no. 22.
72 *CSPI*, iv. 365.
73 PRO SP 63/155, nos 8, 19.
74 Ibid. 169, no. 3.
75 ULC Kk 1 15 no. 63, fos 158–9.

than those of Legg but they were made five years after the event when he was in arms against the crown. In 1596 he claimed to be lord of Oriel by Gaelic custom, but in 1591/2 he had acquiesced in the land settlement which followed the execution.[76] Fitzwilliam in his memoir answered these allegations obliquely: 'for avoiding the scandal of justice with severity, he had the favour to be tried in his own country, and by a jury of the best gentlemen of his own name and blood'.[77]

Although no contemporary account of the proceedings at Monaghan in September–October 1590 exists, it is clear that the surviving evidence does not warrant a blackening of Fitzwilliam's name. If success was to be achieved, secrecy was necessary in the commission sent down beforehand and in Hugh Roe's delivery to Monaghan. The three hundred soldiers who accompanied Fitzwilliam may, indeed, have helped the jury reach the requisite decision but it was not unusual for soldiers to travel with the lord deputy for purposes of prestige and protection. Furthermore, this was a journey into a border county with a political objective. Since the crown was introducing English law into Gaelic areas, it is probable that the legal procedures were conducted properly. In addition, the principal lords would have been glad to sit on a jury to dispose of a competitor. The ideology of Gaelic lordship had long since been divested of its sacred quality; and anyhow it was Brian, not Hugh Roe, who had been elected by the country.[78] In this light, the issues of morality and politics diverge; the real question becomes not whether the trial was partial or impartial but what effect the judgement had as a legal precedent.

The execution of MacMahon showed Gaelic lords the potential consequences of refusal to implement the terms of the surrender and regrant agreements which they had made. Most Ulster lords had accepted surrender and regrant in order to secure titles to their lordship from the crown, to ensure inheritance to designated heirs and to obtain protection against regional overlords. Under these settlements, customary duties, pertaining to Gaelic lords, were abolished; yet in reality the levying of these duties continued. The collection of such duties entailed violence and the use of force against crown subjects could be construed as treason. By surrender and regrant the lord had recognised crown sovereignty and therefore he could be tried for treason and his lands confiscated. Brian MacHugh óg in his grievances of 1596 alleged that the whole surrender and regrant policy was designed deliberately with this end in mind: 'which allowance of succession was granted to the said Hugh purposely to draw an interest onto him and his heirs contrary to the custom of the country and then by his execution to draw the country into Her Majesty's hands as the sequel showeth'.[79] This goes too far; the Gaelic lords had knowingly entered into the surrender and regrant process to benefit from it, while continuing to take advantage of their old political system. Now they would have to bear the consequences of their actions. Henceforth, the maintenance of Gaelic practices of lordship would permit no middle way which the surrender and regrant policy

[76] BL Harleian 3292, fo. 32.
[77] BL Add. 12,503, fo. 390.
[78] Simms, 'Gaelic lordships', ch. i.
[79] ULC Kk 1 15 no. 63, fo. 158.

in its earlier declaratory phase had facilitated. Later in 1594 Thomas Lee expressed the view that the execution of MacMahon 'hath bred a terror in other great lords of like measure, as maketh them stand upon those terms which they now do'.[80]

The subsequent land settlement of Monaghan was no less momentous than the legal decision. The division of the territory amongst the chief lords and the appointment of freeholders constituted a major assault on the class structure of Gaelic society. The settlement was complicated by the outstanding land claims of the second earl of Essex to one of the county's five baronies. It is not surprising to find that the main victims of the settlement Brian MacHugh óg, the Gaelic lord, and Ever Mac Con Uladh, to whose land Essex possessed legal title, were both in revolt five years later. The MacMahon lordship was a dependency of the O'Neills and therefore the settlement must be regarded as an indirect attack on the earl of Tyrone. Moreover, the crown saw the Monaghan settlement as a prototype for the reduction of the other lordships in the North to civil government.

In December 1590, the five principal lords of Monaghan came to Dublin for negotiations with the Irish council. However the queen's warrant and a resolution on the Essex claim was required. Therefore, the solicitor-general, Sir Roger Wilbraham, was sent to Court to settle matters.[81] Wilbraham was employed for the greater part of the winter on this business; he was paid £62 maintenance money for his 124 days away.[82] His influence on the subsequent settlement was probably more profound than actually suggested by the surviving evidence. As we shall see, Wilbraham, in seeking a settlement in the North favourable to the crown, employed similar methods to those used after the war by his successor-in-office, Sir John Davies.[83] Before Wilbraham's visit to Court, no significant mention had been made of freeholders in the projected settlement of Monaghan.[84] Here it should be recollected that when the Magennis lordship was discussed in the 1570s, it was the privy council which had been the major proponent for the establishment of freeholders. Ironically the issue seems to have been raised at this time by the imprisoned Sir John Perrot in a memorandum to Burghley. In relation to Monaghan and Leitrim, he opined that 'if it be well looked into there may be gotten to Her Majesty's use yearly from the freeholders and tenants of those lordships or countries above a £1,000 with good contentment, for their lords spent a great deal more upon them'.[85] In January 1590 the queen's permission was given to allot lands unto both chief lords and freeholders following a survey by commissioners.[86] The commission, which was eventually established in September 1591, included Bagenal and

[80] Lee, 'Brief Declaration', 96.
[81] PRO SP 63/156, no. 1; APC, xx. 239–40.
[82] PRO Audit Office 1/285/1077 m.62d. I owe this reference to Anthony Sheehan.
[83] Nicholas Canny, 'The government reorganisation of Ulster, 1603–7', unpubl. MA thesis, University College, Galway 1967, chs vii, viii; Hans Pawlisch, *Sir John Davies and the conquest of Ireland: a study in legal imperialism*, Cambridge 1985, 67–71.
[84] PRO SP 63/156, no. 1.
[85] Ibid. no. 52.
[86] CPCRI, ii. 215–16.

Wilbraham.[87] The resulting survey of Monaghan was made by inquisition. It appointed seven chief lords. They were given twenty-eight ballybetaghs of land in demesne for which rent and military services were due. 287 inferior free-holders were appointed. They were to pay rents to both their chief lords and the crown but were to hold their lands in fee simple. The termon (ecclesiastical) lands were granted to various outsiders. Bagenal received the largest grant; most of the other grantees were Palesmen. This did not amount to confiscation because the termon lands constituted a small part of Monaghan's total land area and had been, nominally, outside the control of the MacMahons.[88] On Fitzwilliam's recommendation, the composition, a hang-over from Perrot's time, was phased out and Captain Henshaw was made seneschal of Monaghan with a band of 100 footmen paid out of the rental.[89] Henshaw was later given a twenty-one year lease of the mensal lands – *lucht tighe* – of MacMahon in the vicinity of Monaghan town.[90] All these grants, including those made to the freeholders, were confirmed by letters patent.[91] The total annual rent revenue to the crown out of the county was £570 and the first instalment was expected in Michaelmas 1592.[92]

The allegations of Robert Legg at the start of 1593 cast a different light on the land settlement in Monaghan and especially on Fitzwilliam's role in estab-lishing it. First, Legg was of the opinion that the settlement would not have taken place had MacMahon paid Fitzwilliam the promised 800 cattle. Further-more, he asserted that Fitzwilliam's 'service therein all men know to be very chargeable to her Majesty, but beneficial to himself'. For instance, the lord deputy had sold the seneschalship of Monaghan to Captain Henshaw for £500.[93] Also, Wilbraham, the solicitor-general, had drawn 'Mr Marshal's grant of lands in Monaghan larger and more effectual than the rest'. Subsequent claims by the MacMahons confirm Legg's allegation that Wilbraham received part of these lands.[94] Although at the time the cost of establishing the settle-ment was put at £128, Legg later insisted that at least £2,000 had been ex-pended from government coffers to obtain the desired results.[95] Finally, Legg asserted that the first half-yearly instalment of rent had brought in only £60. In order to collect the arrears, Fitzwilliam had ordered 'the seneschal to levy the rents by distresses.' If this proved unsuccessful, Legg was certain that Fitzwilliam would be prepared to pay the rents himself since he had staked his credibility on the Monaghan settlement.[96] The fact that Fitzwilliam increased the number of chief lords from three to five and then to seven may also point to bribery. It is

---

87 Fiants, 16th Report, no. 5582.
88 *Inquisitionum in officio rotulorum cancellariae Hiberniae*, ii. pp. xxi–xxx. A good article on this subject is P. J. Duffy, 'The territorial organisation of Gaelic landownership and its transforma-tion in county Monaghan, 1591–1640', *Irish Geography*, xiv (1981), 1–26.
89 PRO SP 63/160, no. 43; Fiants, 16th Report, no. 5690.
90 Ibid. no. 5705.
91 Ibid. nos 5621–80, 5705, 5719–22, 5736, 5760.
92 NRO Fitzwilliam papers, Ireland, no. 65; PRO SP 63/160, no. 43.
93 Ibid. 169, no. 3. Tom Lee also alleged that Fitzwilliam had sold the seneschalship to the highest bidder: BL Harleian 35, fos 258–65.
94 PRO SP 63/201, no. 154; ULC Kk 1. 15 no. 63, fo. 158.
95 NRO Fitzwilliam papers, Ireland, no. 65: PRO SP 63/169, no. 3.
96 Ibid. no. 3. These allegations make an interesting comparison with Bingham's views on the

also paradoxical that Cú Uladh MacArdle received a land grant.[97] The liberation of this 'traitor' from prison was one of the crimes for which Hugh Roe MacMahon had been executed.[98] The malpractices involved in the establishment of the land settlement in no way lessened its impact on Gaelic society.

The land settlement was a devastating attack on the social structure of a Gaelic lordship. The chief lords now had legal title to their land which they held separately from the crown rather than paying duties to the MacMahon. Therefore, the Gaelic mode of lordship was in abeyance and it is not surprising that Brian MacHugh óg, its last representative, later took up arms. This aspect of the settlement, although subdivision was greater in Monaghan, resembles the settlement made by Perrot in county Cavan. The appointment of freeholders was even more radical. Freeholders had been included in the Composition of Connacht in 1585 solely for the purpose of taxation.[99] Now, while still under chief lords, the freeholders, possessed of letters patent, had legal ownership of the land which they occupied. The annual rent which they now paid to the chief lords was, according to the lord deputy, less than a tenth of the old imposition.[100] Therefore, Fitzwilliam could report that 'the inferior sort of freeholders most greatly rejoice in their happy estates, as men delivered from tyranny and intolerable exactions to have property in their own'.[101] Ironically, Brian MacHugh óg had paid for the issue of letters patent to the freeholders within his own barony of Dartry – we know this because the council signed an order permitting him to take a once and for all distress of 305 beeves to pay off these and other debts which he had incurred during the settlement of Monaghan.[102]

Dispensing with the organic structure of the Gaelic polity, the settlement now created a county of property-holders, great and small. The most important feature of this development was the halting of downward social pressure; the families of chief lords could no longer expand at the expense of the weaker freeholders. Partible inheritance amongst the freeholders and heavy exactions by lords leading to indebtedness had favoured this process. The traditional pledge (or mortgage) had been the usual means by which the land of the freeholders was taken over by the families of the chief lords.[103] Duffy's study of county Monaghan has shown that no redistribution of land took place between the surveys of 1591 and 1606. This testifies to the stability of the settlement in spite of the disruptions of the Nine Years War.[104] This piece of social engineering was a great success for the crown. Henceforth, social and economic change would be governed by the cash nexus rather than military oppression. Indeed, the commercialisation of land ownership may already have been underway in

Monaghan settlement. He made no charges against Fitzwilliam, but questioned the financial viability of his settlement and thought it had been 'painfully' effected: *CSPI*, iv. 468.

97 Fiants, 16th Report, no. 5652.
98 PRO SP 63/153, no. 24(4); 155, no. 19.
99 Cunningham, 'Composition of Connacht', 2–5, 11–13.
100 PRO SP 63/160, no. 43.
101 Ibid. 161, no. 44.
102 BL Harleian 3292, no. 5, fo. 32.
103 Nicholls, *Gaelic and gaelicised Ireland*, 38–9, 65–7.
104 Duffy, 'Gaelic landownership', 10–12.

the lordship and as such the settlement would merely have accelerated the process. The 1591 survey shows that there were already some Palesmen, including a Newry merchant called Christopher Fleming, holding lands near Monaghan town.[105] In his grievances, Brian MacHugh óg claimed erroneously that the lordship had been divided between Henshaw and the grantees of termon land 'so that the native country people [are] for the most part disinherited'. The Palesmen who owned land in the county and the grantees of termon land were, however, the forerunners of the land speculators of the seventeenth century.[106]

Unlike the greater part of the county, no settlement was reached in the barony of Donamayne which belonged to the earl of Essex. In 1576, with the Attainder of Shane O'Neill as an enabling act, the first earl of Essex had been granted the territory of Farney, but neither he nor his son ever occupied the area or received any rents from its inhabitants.[107] When the MacMahon lordship had been shired the territory became the barony of Donamayne comprising Farney, possessed by Ever Mac Con Uladh, and Clancarvell, possessed by the MacCollas.[108] After the execution of Hugh Roe, Fitzwilliam requested that Essex surrender his title to the barony – a fifth part of the county – and be given compensation so that a full division of Monaghan might ensue.[109] The earl of Essex, whose finances were in a parlous state, refused the recompense offered, estimating his lands instead at £300 per annum.[110] The privy council believed that Essex had been 'informed by some without any good ground for intent secretly to disappoint the establishing of this county in good English government'.[111] Here it is possible to point the finger at Hugh O'Neill because at this time he forced Ever Mac Con Uladh to pay £200 in rent to an agent of the earl of Essex.[112] When the land settlement was made at the end of 1591, the barony belonging to Essex was exempted and Ever Mac Con Uladh and the MacCollas were granted lands in the neighbouring barony of Cremorne.[113]

The land settlement activated Essex's interest in his Irish claims and at the end of 1592 a commission was established to survey his lands in county Monaghan and at Islandmagee in county Antrim.[114] Fitzwilliam still wanted a settlement favourable to the indigenous landholders. The Irish council wrote on behalf of Ever Mac Con Uladh who had travelled to Court, stating that the neighbouring barony in which Ever and his sons had been allotted lands was waste and that he was of proven loyalty and service.[115] Ever Mac Con Uladh spent six months petitioning for his lands at Court which proved a costly and

---

105 Inquisitionum in officio rotulorum cancellariae Hiberniae, ii. p. xxiii.
106 Duffy, 'Gaelic landownership', 14–18.
107 CPRE, vii. 185; PRO SP 63/167, no. 32.
108 Inquisitionum in officio rotulorum cancellariae Hiberniae, ii. pp. xvii–xviii.
109 PRO SP 63/156, no. 6.
110 Howell A. Lloyd, 'The Essex inheritance', Welsh Historical Review, vii (1974), 30–6; APC, xx. 239–40.
111 Ibid.
112 ULC Kk 1 15 no. 63, fo. 158.
113 Inquisitionum in officio rotulorum cancellariae Hiberniae, ii, pp. xxv–xxvii.
114 Fiants, 16th Report, no. 5763.
115 PRO SP 63/168, no. 2.

fruitless procedure.[116] In England Ever offered the earl £300 *per annum* but Essex refused this and instead leased the barony to one John Talbott at the annual rent of £250.[117] Fitzwilliam had already rejected Talbott's application for the sheriffalty of Monaghan, dismissing him as an avaricious and unreliable Palesman, whose presence would only endanger the settlement.[118] In 1593 Talbott expelled Ever Mac Con Uladh from his patrimony and destroyed his property.[119] However, the following year Ever's sons together with the MacCollas were back in Donamayne and Talbott was virtually under siege.[120] In this light, it is not surprising to find Ever Mac Con Uladh in the O'Neill entourage presenting his grievances along with Brian MacHugh óg in 1596. Nonetheless, had Essex been willing to surrender his title or to compromise, then Ever Mac Con Uladh would have remained loyal. Unlike Brian MacHugh óg, Ever was not the object of a concentrated attack on the socio-political structure of a Gaelic polity, but the belated victim of an earlier policy of confiscation.

Hugh O'Neill, the earl of Tyrone, was adversely affected by the Monaghan settlement. In the first place, he lost the military services, which the MacMahons owed to him as their Gaelic overlord.[121] The 1591 survey of Monaghan found the earl in possession of the ballybetagh of Porterlare in the Barony of Trough; 'he and his ancestors seem to have held it long in mortgage from some of the MacMahons'. The principal gentlemen of Monaghan declared the ballybetagh to be within their county. Therefore, the land could not be claimed under the earl's patent for Tyrone and consequently it was granted to John Connalan, a clergyman from the Pale.[122] Most significantly, Hugh O'Neill lost control of the termon lands of Muckno to his rival, Sir Henry Bagenal. O'Neill had developed demesne agriculture in this territory even though he had no legal right to do so. Now Fitzwilliam, without mentioning the identity of the occupier, granted the three ballybetaghs of land 'being upon a most dangerous border' to the marshal.[123] Although smarting at the effects of this settlement, the earl could only react subtly and indirectly because of the essential illegality of his position.

During his visit to London in 1590, O'Neill tried to pre-empt the developments impending in Monaghan. He demanded the grant of a third of the lordship to his daughter in repayment for the dowry which she had brought to the late Sir Ross MacMahon. The earl himself wanted reimbursement for the debts of Sir Ross, which he had been forced to pay off. The privy council referred these requests to its Irish counterpart but they were ignored.[124] Tyrone adopted a more forceful approach after the land settlement. In July 1592 court sessions at Monaghan were adjourned because of a raid by Conn O'Neill, the

---

[116] Ibid. no. 72.
[117] Ibid. 167, no. 32; *CSPI*, v. 81: E. P. Shirley, *Some account of the territory or dominion of Farney*, London 1845, 102–3.
[118] PRO SP 63/161, no. 12.
[119] ULC Kk 1 15 no. 63, fos 158–9.
[120] HMC *Bath MSS*, v. 257–8.
[121] Perrot, *Chronicle of Ireland*, 69.
[122] *Inquisitionum in officio rotulorum cancellariae Hiberniae*, ii. pp. xxx.
[123] Ibid; NLI MS 669, fos 52–3.
[124] APC, xix. 306–7.

earl's bastard son, into the barony of Trough.[125] Fitzwilliam saw the raid as an attempt by Tyrone 'to subvert the young and weak planted good estate of the county of Monaghan'.[126] The attack earned the earl of Tyrone a caustic letter from the queen.[127] Conn Mac an Íarla presented himself before the lord deputy at Dundalk and gave a rather facile account of the event. The earl himself renewed his claims on the estate of Sir Ross MacMahon while expressing a willingness to defend the settlement of Monaghan with the same resolve as his own property.[128] Already in his reaction to the Monaghan settlement, Tyrone's devious and indirect method of dealing with the advance of crown government was evident. Later, when the earl of Tyrone presented a list of grievances to the crown in March 1594, two of the seventeen articles related to Monaghan. Hugh Roe MacMahon had, he asserted, been executed unjustly for levying customary duties. 'And when the country was divided, every peddling merchant and other men of no account or desert had a stake thereof. And the Marshal (who never took pains in bringing that country to subjection) had a great part of it, almost within some part of the earl's inhabitance, and the earl himself, neither for payment of the said debts or for service done in that country, had any part thereof, neither had any gentlemen or others that belonged to him.'[129] Indeed, raiders out of Tyrone were at this time paying special attention to Eoin O'Duffy, the marshal's tenant at Muckno, who was 'the first that brought in the new establishment in Monaghan and so that country drawn from the earl'.[130]

The reorganisation of Monaghan was generally regarded in government circles as a prototype for future settlements in the North. Sir George Carew, the master of the ordnance, believed that the execution of Hugh Roe and the division of his lordship was 'the soundest and surest way to bring Ireland to due obedience' and a practical alternative to wasteful military expeditions into the interior in pursuit of rebels.[131] Wilbraham saw the settlement as part of a developing policy: 'the good establishment of the counties of Longford, the Cavan and this last and best of Monaghan are great encouragements'.[132] Fitzwilliam saw Monaghan as a model: 'hereby an entry is made and a good foundation laid to reduce Tyrone and all the North parts of this realm to like conformity'.[133] The archbishop of Cashel, a native of Termon Magrath on the western borders of Ulster, also saw the importance of the policy. He wanted Monaghan's new order established in every Ulster lordship and to this end he furnished the crown with details of the internecine conflicts of each lordship.[134] Amongst the most eager proponents of this policy were the queen and the privy council who, no doubt, saw its application as an opportunity to boost Irish revenues.[135] The

---

125 *CSPI*, iv. 539–40.
126 PRO SP 63/166, no. 4.
127 HMC *Salisbury* MSS, iv. 218–19.
128 *CSPI*, iv. 566–7.
129 Lambeth, Carew 617, fos 208–9.
130 PRO SP 63/173, no. 64(11).
131 Lambeth, Carew 618, fo. 46.
132 Ibid; *CSPI*, iv. 441–2.
133 PRO SP 63/160, no. 43.
134 *CSPI*, iv. 489–502.
135 Here a useful comparison can be made with the contemporary search for concealed lands in

queen instructed the Irish council to establish freeholders in the division of North Clandeboye between Shane MacBrian and Niall MacHugh.[136] According to Fitzwilliam, Marshal Bagenal had already divided the country and tenants between the two contenders in accordance with the Monaghan settlement.[137] However, the issue of letters patent was suspended pending further inquiries after objections were made against Shane MacBrian's land claims in London.[138] Although the Nine Years War intervened and Scots and English colonists began to arrive, the Monaghan pattern was followed in making settlements with the indigenous landholders of Clandeboye.[139] The more immediate attempt to apply the example of Monaghan came in West Breifne, the lordship of O'Rourke. The different outcome in this Connacht lordship points up the radical nature of the Monaghan settlement.

O'Rourke's lordship of West Breifne had been shired as county Leitrim by Perrot. Sir Brian O'Rourke was described in *A treatise of Ireland* as 'being somewhat learned but of an insolent and proud nature and is no farther obedient than he is constrained by Her Majesty's forces'.[140] In the 1580s, O'Rourke enjoyed a semi-independent position of an ill-defined nature. In June 1585, he surrendered his lands whilst attending parliament at Dublin but no regrant of his lordship was ever made.[141] Later the same year, Leitrim was included in the Composition of Connacht.[142] However, it is clear that shire government was never effective in Leitrim and that its composition rents were paid only intermittently.[143] O'Rourke's autonomy endured until the spring of 1590 when his lordship was invaded and occupied.[144] In February 1591, O'Rourke arrived in Scotland, ostensibly seeking the protection of James VI, but with the actual object of recruiting mercenaries.[145] A request from Queen Elizabeth secured Sir Brian's arrest and delivery into England.[146] This was achieved in April 1591 and the captive was brought to London where he was placed in the Tower.[147] In November 1591, O'Rourke was tried for treason in Westminster Hall, on charges of denying the queen's sovereignty, assisting the survivors of the Spanish Armada and attacking his neighbours. After refusing to stand trial, O'Rourke was convicted solely on the charges contained in his indictment. He was hanged at Tyburn.[148]

Ireland. Burghley encouraged this to boost crown revenues; Fitzwilliam probably regarded it as another means of personal enrichment: Ranger, 'Richard Boyle', 257–97.

[136] *CPCRI*, ii. 235–7.

[137] *CSPI*, iv. 443–5.

[138] Ibid. v. 61–2, 68–70; *APC*, xxii. 219–20.

[139] Timothy McCall, 'The Gaelic background to the settlement of Antrim and Down, 1580–1641', unpubl. MA thesis, Queen's University, Belfast 1983, ch. iii.

[140] NLI MS 669, fos 41–2.

[141] Fiants, 15th Report, no. 4683.

[142] *The compossicion book of Conought*, ed. A. M. Freeman, Dublin 1936, 143–51.

[143] PRO SP 63/143, no. 5.

[144] Ibid. 151, no. 57.

[145] *CSP, Sp.* iv. 610; *CSP, Scot.* x. 470–1.

[146] Ibid. 470–1, 480–1.

[147] Ibid. 495–6, 514; *APC*, xxi. 114.

[148] For a full account of the trial of O'Rourke and its implications for that of Perrot, see Hiram Morgan, 'Extradition and treason-trial of a Gaelic lord: the case of Brian O'Rourke', *Irish Jurist*, xxii (1987), 285–301.

In the immediate aftermath of O'Rourke's expulsion from his lordship, his lands had been divided provisionally between the chief lords, and composition arrears and rents had been paid. Bingham was convinced that the inhabitants were pleased with the new situation: 'for his country for the most part doth mortally hate him, his tyrannies are so intolerable'.[149] Now after O'Rourke's attainder and execution for treason, the queen and privy council saw his lands as being at the disposal of the crown. On the other hand, Bingham's reaction to O'Rourke's execution was simply to request a general survey of West Breifne for the purpose of establishing a proper composition rent since Sir Brian had concealed much from the 1585 commission.[150] John Merbury, one of the Commissioners of Connacht, and Sir Geoffrey Fenton, the Irish secretary, both of whom were visiting London, provided more radical suggestions. Merbury, in a somewhat rambling discourse, condemned the shortcomings of the 1585 Composition of Connacht which had only increased the power of the lords. In the case of West Breifne, he wanted tanistry and the onerous exactions, which it entailed, abolished through a proper division of land leading to ownership by lords and freeholders alike. Such a settlement 'shall be indeed pleasing [to] God, highly profitable to the queen, and the precedent of it a light and candle to their neighbours of the North to find out speedily the way to wealth, civility and obedience'.[151] Fenton's views were more radical. He wanted the annexation of not only O'Rourke's demesne lands but also the lands of the chief lords and freeholders, since they had been implicated in his rebellion. He provided two options – either a division amongst the chief lords after the example of Longford, Cavan and Monaghan or plantation by English and Anglo-Irish colonists.[152] In the light of the success of the Monaghan settlement, these more radical solutions attracted the attention of the queen and Burghley as a means of increasing revenue.[153]

Nevertheless, Fitzwilliam left the settlement of West Breifne to Bingham's consideration.[154] The chief commissioner wanted to keep the territory within his provincial jurisdiction and did not want a radical departure there to unsettle the province generally. Bingham maintained that only O'Rourke's demesne lands and the termon land could be annexed to the crown. Moreover, 'the chief of the sept of the O'Rourkes do look to have O'Rourke's seignory divided amongst themselves, taking their example from the Bourkes in Mayo, where MacWilliam's seignory, after his death was divided amongst five competitors of the best of the sept by Sir John Perrot, the lord deputy at that time; and so is continued to them in perpetuity'. The queen had every right to be pleased with the Monaghan settlement, but its large rents would be absorbed by its government. Leitrim, he emphasised, was part of Connacht and an alteration in its composition would entail a new composition for the whole province. Any

149 PRO SP 63/151, no. 57.
150 Ibid. 161, no. 36(1).
151 Ibid. 146, no. 60. This document is incorrectly placed in the state papers at 27 Sept. 1589; in fact it should be dated to the early months of 1592.
152 Ibid. 161, no. 44.
153 Ibid. 164, no. 33(3).
154 CSPI, iv. 443–5.

attempt to modify the composition in the crown's favour would only provoke insurrection.[155] After Bingham's remarks, there is no further mention of the reorganisation of West Breifne in the state papers of the period. No doubt, Bingham had to back up his arguments with cash to win Fitzwilliam's acquiescence. Logically then, Bingham's informal settlement of the territory followed the O'Reilly–MacWilliam Bourke format with a division amongst the chief lords rather than the more radical type of reorganisation which took place in the MacMahon lordship. Furthermore a revived medieval claim to part of the O'Rourke lordship by Lord Gormanston was passed over unlike the more recent one of the influential earl of Essex in Monaghan.[156] Nonetheless the Gaelic mode of lordship was once more the loser, symbolised in this case by Brian óg O'Rourke. In 1592 his request for appointment to his father's office was ignored.[157]

Despite the initiation of reform in the minor Gaelic polities, the lordship of Tyrone remained a central concern. As before, the crown required the assistance of the leading O'Neill to pursue reform there. This posed a dilemma. Hugh O'Neill, long regarded as the best hope for internal reform, was now too powerful and was himself a target for the reformers. The attitude of Fitzwilliam and the Dublin administration towards the earl of Tyrone was remarkably conciliatory in the period before the Monaghan land settlement. There were at least three occasions – Turlough Luineach's demand for the early return of central Tyrone, the earl's employment of Scots mercenaries and his hanging of Hugh Gavelach MacShane – when the crown might have attempted to curb his power. The stated reasons for the government's relative indifference were the fear of the MacShanes, the instability they might cause in the North and the expenditure which their overthrow might entail. In fact, the earl was using bribery to win Fitzwilliam's acquiesence.

By indentured agreement in 1585, Turlough Luineach had leased central Tyrone to the earl for a period of seven years. The lease gave Turlough the option to demand the return of the lands after three years.[158] Turlough did this in the autumn of 1588 and the privy council wrote to the earl ordering him to comply with Turlough's wishes.[159] On his northern journey after the shipwreck of the Armada, Fitzwilliam visited both Turlough and the earl. Hugh O'Neill promised to surrender the lands the following May and therefore the lord deputy suppressed the imperative letter from the privy council.[160] At this time, Fitzwilliam had a good opinion of the earl's loyalty and believed erroneously that the queen had made O'Neill powerful and could, if she wished, humble him. He also hoped to play Turlough off against the earl.[161]

This even-handed approach changed in the early months of 1589. In February 1589, Hugh Gavelach MacShane arrived from Scotland; later he proceeded to Dublin where he made allegations against the earl which the lord

155 Ibid. 467–71.
156 PRO SP 63/166, no. 64; 167, nos 3, 3(1).
157 Ibid. 163, no. 48.
158 Ibid. 118, no. 59.
159 CSPI, iv. 66; APC, xvi. 337–8.
160 CSPI, iv. 95.
161 PRO SP 63/136, no. 26; 140, no. 1.

deputy saw as 'a mere practice proceeding from the great and inveterate malice which Sir Turlough Luineach and the sons of Shane O'Neill and that race have ever borne against the honour and well-being of the earl'.[162] Fitzwilliam feared that the MacShanes, who were well-connected in the Scottish highlands and islands, would succeed Turlough and thereby cause great disturbances in the North.[163] Consequently the lord deputy and council inclined towards the earl in his plea for retention of the leased land when the parties met at Dundalk in May. The earl of Tyrone contended that under the Act for the Attainder of Shane O'Neill, the lease could not have been made in the first place since the land was in the queen's possession and that only his letters patent were valid. Turlough, on the other hand, argued along the lines of the 1585 lease agreement. A compromise was reached whereby the earl agreed to pay a larger rent.[164] The Irish council favoured this line through fear that the revocation of the lease might benefit the MacShanes and thereby provoke 'a war no less offensive, and chargeable to the crown, than that of their said father Shane O'Neill'.[165]

Peaceful coexistence did not last in Tyrone; the MacShanes, supported by Turlough Luineach, and the earl were soon at loggerheads. Both sides levied mercenaries: the MacShanes brought in the MacLeans while the earl employed the MacDonalds from North Antrim and some of their Scottish relatives.[166] Following a complaint from Turlough that the earl had recruited Scots mercenaries, the lord deputy and council met both men at Newry in October 1589. Turlough agreed to answer for the actions of the MacShanes; the earl was ordered to Dublin to explain his use of Scots before the council.[167] The earl explained to the council that he was unaware that a number of men hired by him were foreigners since they were all under the command of MacSorley. Furthermore, he had been forced to use mercenaries because his life and country were endangered by the MacShanes. Since the earl wished to visit Court and submit himself to the queen's judgement, the council referred the matter.[168] Fitzwilliam was even more amenable to Tyrone. He blamed Turlough and the MacShanes and was willing to act as the earl's intermediary with Burghley.[169] In the opinion of Sir Nicholas White, however, the council should have taken the opportunity of the earl's treasonous hiring of Scots to recommend the reduction in the extent of his land grant. He also claimed that the council had reneged on its resolution to fine the earl and that the final draft of its letter appeared to accept his excuses. As a result, White had refused to sign the council's letter.[170] The fear of the MacShanes was cited as the reason for the leniency shown to the earl, but the fact that he was not even fined suggests

---

[162] Ibid. 141, no. 22; 143, no. 46.
[163] Ibid. 142, no. 12.
[164] Ibid. 144, no. 34(5).
[165] Ibid. no. 38.
[166] Ibid. 146, no. 12; 148, no. 10(1).
[167] Ibid. 147, no. 34.
[168] Ibid. 148, no. 10(1).
[169] Ibid. no. 10.
[170] Ibid. no. 13.

ingredients other than policy. This is a possible case of bribery. Also, Fitzwilliam was willing to support Tyrone because White and Perrot were backing the claims of Turlough. At this time, the manipulation of the visit of Sir Thomas Cecil by his opponents was a personal affront to Fitzwilliam and an attack on his authority as lord deputy.[171]

In 1590 the crown was presented with another opportunity to curb the power of Hugh O'Neill. In January 1590, the earl executed Hugh Gavelach Mac-Shane. It was alleged that he had hanged MacShane with his own hands and contrary to the express command of the lord deputy and council.[172] The evidence that O'Neill used bribery to extricate himself in this instance is not just circumstantial. Thomas Lee alleged that Fitzwilliam 'most unconscionably in respect of a great bribe hath pardoned the heinous offence and thereby kept Your Majesty from your right and benefit in no small value'.[173] So the Irish council baulked at arresting the earl but its English counterpart had no such qualms in doing so on his subsequent arrival at Court.[174] On 19 March the earl managed answers to four charges levelled against him by the privy council.[175] During this time, the lord deputy remained favourably disposed towards O'Neill. Fitzwilliam admitted to Walsingham that the earl's hiring of Scots mercenaries and his hanging of Hugh Gavelach were grounds for suspicion. Nonetheless, he commended his good government of Tyrone which had brought quiet to the borders of the Pale.[176] Again following a request from Burghley for advice on whether to detain Tyrone in England or permit his return home, Fitzwilliam, Loftus and two other councillors gave a reply beneficial to the earl. Tyrone might become a threat after Turlough's death 'when he is absolute and hath no competitors' but for the time being his presence was very necessary to defend the North against the MacShanes and the Scots mercenaries whom they recruited.[177] In short, the Dublin government depended on the earl of Tyrone to control the North.

The privy council in London was more anxious to take advantage of Tyrone's discomfiture than the Irish council. Under the instructions of Burghley, a number of memoranda were drawn up at the end of May. Wallop and Gardiner presented a piece on the reformation of Ulster. They wanted a lord president placed at Armagh, the appointment of sheriffs, the introduction of common law processes, the establishment of a composition and a scheme of fortification. A well-financed programme, they argued, would be more worthwhile in the long run than a divide and rule policy which might change for the worse after the death of Turlough Luineach.[178] Three memoranda were then drawn up by Perrot, Fenton and Wallop and Gardiner respectively dealing with the earl of Tyrone. All three memoranda wanted an end to his control of the *uirríthe*, his employment of Scots mercenaries and the use of Gaelic customary law. They

[171] Ibid. 147, no. 49.
[172] Ibid. 150, nos 21, 27.
[173] BL Harleian 35, fos 258–65.
[174] PRO SP 63/150, no. 75; 151, no. 5: BL Add. 19,837, fo. 876.
[175] CSPI, iv. 319–21.
[176] PRO SP 63/151, no. 39.
[177] Ibid. 152, no. 4.
[178] Ibid. no. 39.

wanted the introduction of sheriffs and the establishment of a composition after the Connacht model.[179] Fenton was particularly concerned with the O'Neillship and the earl's claim to the Blackwater fort.[180] Wallop and Gardiner were pessimistic about the prospects of success: 'in our opinions we see no great appearance or means to have it performed: or being at the beginning performed, no likelihood to be continued, either to the benefit of Her Majesty or the peace of the country'.[181] The earl then presented his offers on the basis of the memoranda; in these, his diffidence was patently obvious. He was willing to give sureties in the English Pale but no hostages out of Tyrone. He claimed that O'Cahan was not one of the *uirríthe* but an inhabitant of his lordship. His agreement to a composition was partial and he cited a number of caveats. He requested the use of martial law for the time being.[182] In Perrot's view, the earl 'answereth part and overstepeth the rest'; moreover, 'he will have as many evasions as possible and will promise much and perform little'.[183] It is evident that Tyrone disliked the proposals but in the circumstances he had little choice. Therefore, on 17 June 1590 he submitted to an agreement of twenty-five articles which combined all the proposals put forward in the memoranda.[184] Six years later, the earl complained that these articles had been 'wrested upon him through Sir John Perrot's means'.[185]

The privy council regarded this plan for the reduction of Tyrone as a blueprint for a wider reformation of Ulster. It requested the Irish council to obtain Tyrone's resubmission to the agreement in Dublin and then for the establishment of similar agreements with other northern lords.[186] Accordingly, Tyrone reacknowledged the agreement before the Irish council on his return.[187] However, Fitzwilliam would have preferred a privy council resolution on the case of Hugh Roe MacMahon. He obviously regarded the articles to which the earl had submitted as yet another paper programme.[188] Indeed, the earl had little intention of carrying out proposals designed to curb his power to which he had consented under duress. The only result of this agreement was cosmetic. In the summer of 1591 the county of Tyrone was delimited, divided into eight baronies and Dungannon was appointed the county town. The significant inclusion of O'Cahan's country prevented earlier plans for its separate creation as the county of Coleraine.[189] However, the successful imposition of a settlement in Monaghan transformed the Dublin administration's attitude to the possibilities of reforming Ulster. Not long after the completion of business there, negotiations began in secret to promote a similar settlement in Tyrone. The proponents were Fitzwilliam, who provided the initiative, and Bagenal and

[179] Ibid. no. 38, 41(1); ULC Kk 1 15 no. 3, fos 9–10.
[180] PRO SP 63/152, no. 41(1).
[181] ULC Kk 1 15 no. 3, fos 9–10.
[182] Ibid. no. 4, fos 11–13.
[183] PRO SP 63/153, no. 1.
[184] ULC Kk 1 15 no. 5, fos 16–17.
[185] Ibid. no. 63, fo. 167.
[186] APC, xix. 244–5.
[187] PRO SP 63/154, no. 16.
[188] Ibid. no. 9.
[189] *Inquisitionum in officio rotulorum cancellariae Hiberniae*, ii. pp. xvi, xix–xx; NLI MS 669, fos 51–2.

Wilbraham, who did the paperwork. By searching for loopholes in the indentured agreements and letters patent between the O'Neills and the crown since the days of Conn O'Neill, it was hoped to provide a means to force the earl to accept a government-imposed settlement when the seven year land lease from Turlough expired in August 1592. This method of examination into prior agreements presaged the activities of Chichester and Davies when they sought to reduce the earl's power after the Treaty of Mellifont. However, in 1592 the earl's position was powerful enough to render the plans of the government still-born.

Following a conference with Fitzwilliam, Bagenal sent Burghley a detailed analysis of the present situation which provided a line of action to be followed with the earl of Tyrone. 'The chiefest, or rather only means to reduce these barbarous people to obedience is so to disunite them as all may be enforced to depend of the queen.' The way to achieve this was to establish freeholders in line with the Monaghan settlement. Previously, the surrender and regrant policy had been declaratory, if not regressive. This policy had enabled private individuals to gain title to large stretches of country without the nomination of any freeholders; indeed, Bagenal claimed that it had entailed the enslavement of the old freeholders. In replicating the Monaghan model elsewhere in Ulster, the major obstacle was the lordship of Tyrone where the earl, by his control of judicial and law enforcement functions, had 'the very marks and signs of sovereignty'. To secure the captaincy after Turlough's death, the earl had taken up a lease of the most fertile part of Tyrone; now Turlough was demanding its return on 10 August. Sir Henry believed that the earl would submit to a review of his patent to ensure the inheritance of his posterity. Therefore, this opportunity should be taken to reduce the size of his estate, to divide the remainder between the freeholders and to replace the intolerable exactions of the Gaelic lords by an equitable composition to the crown. The reform of Tyrone in this way would force the *uirríthe* to follow suit and hence enough revenue would be generated to establish civil government in the province. Its establishment would facilitate the settlement of disputes by peaceful means and as a result the employment of Scots mercenaries by the lords would be unnecessary.[190]

After Bagenal's contribution, the onus of promoting a settlement in Tyrone fell upon the shoulders of the solicitor-general, Sir Roger Wilbraham. Wilbraham felt that the earl of Tyrone possessed enough land for three English earls and in March 1592 he endorsed Bagenal's proposals for a division and composition of Tyrone when Turlough demanded the return of his lands in August.[191] The hand of the state was strengthened in the spring of 1592 when Turlough's son, Sir Art O'Neill, requested assurance of the lands of his grandfather, Niall Connallach. As a result, Wilbraham made an investigation of the various indentures and letters patent concerning Tyrone. His considered opinion was that the letters patent of May 1587 granted the earl of Tyrone only the demesne lands and chiefs rents of the lordship as had been the case with his grandfather Conn. Niall Connallach had possessed a freehold under Conn,

---

[190] PRO SP 63/163, no. 29. Ironically, this plan to take advantage of the expiry of the land lease was in line with the earlier demands of Perrot and White.
[191] *CSPI*, iv. 441–2; PRO SP 63/163, no. 46.

therefore the crown could now make a grant to Art MacTurlough. Since the earl would desire continued possession of central Tyrone after August 1592, it was assumed that he would concur with this decision.[192] In July, with the termination of the lease approaching, Wilbraham was asked to draw up another memorandum, this time based on an exemplification of indentured agreements and letters patent made to Turlough Luineach in the late 1570s. Sir Roger concluded that 'the meaning is plain, and the words sufficient to pass an actual freehold to Sir Turlough'. If this was so – and Wilbraham admitted a different interpretation was possible – the letters patent made to the earl were void.[193] Subsequently, Edward Coke, the English solicitor-general, examined the same information. He concluded that the agreements of the late 1570s were not sufficient to give Turlough legal title to any lands. Moreover, the grant of the earldom of Clanoneill, which Turlough never actually received, was purely honorific. Nevertheless, Coke believed that the earl could be held to the covenant, made after the grant of his letters patent, in which he promised to assure lands to Turlough and his heirs in the north-west of his lordship.[194] The investigations into prior agreements, therefore, produced three different interpretations, although all concluded that Turlough Luineach possessed some sort of claim to the lands which he occupied. These methods closely resembled those employed by Sir John Davies to free Henry óg and Turlough MacArt from the jurisdiction of the earl in the aftermath of the Nine Years War. And like their predecessors in 1592, Chichester and Davies were planning to establish a composition between the earl and freeholders of Tyrone.[195]

The secret scheme for the reformation of Tyrone promoted by Fitzwilliam, Bagenal and Wilbraham had no effect. Although we lack evidence, we must assume that Burghley and the privy council refused to consent to its attempted implementation. The privy council letters of September 1592 display a conciliatory attitude towards the earl.[196] The three Irish officials were, in fact, naive in the extreme to assert that since the earl of Tyrone had been established with the queen's assistance, her disfavour might pull him down. They overestimated the power of Turlough Luineach, who was in his final years, and the influence of his son, Sir Art. Most importantly, they had not reckoned on the escape of Hugh Roe O'Donnell, the earl's son-in-law, and the rapid regeneration of Tirconnell, which left Turlough Luineach hemmed in on two sides and the earl's hand greatly strengthened.[197] The window of opportunity to promote reform, which may have existed when the MacShanes were strong and the earl in trouble with the government but not undertaken for fear of chaos in the North, was now firmly shut. No government action was taken over the expiry of the lease;

[192] *CSPI*, iv. 486–8. Wilbraham also maintained in this analysis that the earl, by means of 1587 patent, had usurped the whole of Tyrone as demesne land and reduced all the other inhabitants to tenants-at-will.
[193] Ibid. 552–4.
[194] Ibid. 572–3.
[195] Canny, 'The government reorganisation of Ulster, 1603–7', chs. vii, viii.
[196] *APC*, xxiii, 170–3.
[197] PRO SP 63/163, no. 36; 165, no. 6(1): *CSPI*, iv. 520–2.

Turlough and the earl themselves appointed two gentlemen of Tyrone and two Pale lawyers to settle their differences.[198] This period also saw two connected administrative developments in the North. Both signify the advance of crown government there. The first threatened the authority of the Gaelic lords in general and the second the earl of Tyrone in particular. At the end of the 1580s a northern assize circuit was created. Initially it covered only the counties of Louth and Cavan; by 1593 it also encompassed Down, Antrim and Monaghan. This development brought royal justice into the localities on a regular basis for the first time.[199] The rulings made at the assizes required enforcement and in June 1591 a commission was established to do this in Ulster with the assize judges named amongst the assistant commissioners. More significantly, Sir Henry Bagenal was named as chief commissioner.[200] The previous year the queen had appointed Sir Henry to his father's office of marshal of the army and to his seat on the Irish council.[201] Although Sir Henry held a reversionary interest in his father's military command, he had no particular right to the position of chief commissioner which his father had formerly exercised in Ulster.[202] This was clearly a case of Fitzwilliam using his authority over commissions to advance the ambitions of Bagenal. At this time Hugh O'Neill asked Sir Henry for the hand of his sister, Mabel, in what was obviously an attempt to neutralise the marshal's growing power. When the marshal refused, the earl married Mabel secretly as his third wife in August.[203] Afterwards, Bagenal had Armagh diocesan officials brought before the lord deputy, who was settling the county of Monaghan, in a vain attempt to prove that the earl was not properly divorced from his first wife. O'Neill ended a detailed relation of these events to the privy council with a complaint about the commission: 'The Marshal hath procured an authority under the great seal of this Realm, to have a kind of superiority over all Ulster (the county of Louth excepted) and to deal in all causes as largely as either the president of Munster or Connacht doth, by force whereof he reigneth as a little king and seeks to have authority over myself and my people, which I can hardly endure, considering he is my malicious enemy.'[204] Significantly, the privy council chose to regard the commission (about which it had no previous knowledge) as the root cause of the whole dispute. In order to prevent any trouble between the rivals, it demanded that the earl's country be exempted from the commission's jurisdiction.[205] The provincial commission was ineffectual anyhow without an adequate financial base. The need to generate such a revenue explains Bagenal's interest in reforming Ulster.

It is a difficult task to generalise about Fitzwilliam's erratic performance in government. His struggle with Perrot concerned patronage not policy. Their

---

198 Ibid. 568–9.
199 NLI MS 669, fo. 21; BL Add. 5754, fo. 104; *CSPI*, iv. 566–7; v. 141–2.
200 Fiants, 16th Report, no. 5552.
201 C, *Carew*, iii. 41; PRO SP 63/154, no. 38.
202 Fiants, 13th Report, no. 3021; CPCRI, ii. 47.
203 Professor Canny pointed out the significance of this abortive marriage alliance in ch. v of his recent study, *From Reformation to Restoration: Ireland, 1534–1660*, Dublin 1987.
204 PRO SP 63/160, no. 58.
205 APC, xxii. 105–7.

contrasting styles reflected different attitudes to the role of private interest in the administration of public affairs. The combination of circumstantial evidence and allegations from different sources do point to increased corruption under Fitzwilliam. The lord deputy's willingness to accept bribes does appear to have been a factor in developments at Monaghan. By the same token, the earl of Tyrone used bribery to forestall government moves against him in the early years of Fitzwilliam's adminstration. Thomas Lee provided an explanation of why this situation changed:

> Sir Henry Bagenal, Your Majesty's marshal (than whom never a prince of Your Highness' worthiness had a worse), hath been called by Sir William Fitzwilliam in the hearing of many of great credit 'coward' with other vile terms of great disgrace; Sir Henry knowing himself to be justly charged with these imperfections sought by large bribes of plate, and other things to purchase Sir William's favour. And now he accompts him as tall a gentleman as is in Ireland. The virtue of this plate will cause cowards to be accompted tall men.
> The earl of Tyrone so long as he fed Sir William Fitzwilliam with one rich jewel or another was accompted of him the honourablest gentleman in the world, but when he left off his liberality, then did he accompt him the notablest traitor living, and was ready to hear anything, that might tend to the dishonour of the earl, though never so true.[206]

This argument would relate the incidence of bribery to the general drift of policy. This is much too simplistic because in all cases the earl was rich enough to outbid Bagenal. It is much more plausible to argue that Fitzwilliam made a conscious decision to take Bagenal's bribes and to refuse O'Neill's. In this light the importance of bribery can be negated – Fitzwilliam had found an additional source of income. During his re-organisation of Monaghan he discovered that reforming the North could be a more profitable business than temporising with its Gaelic rulers. As a result he decided to back Bagenal's ambitions in Ulster which coincided with the policy shift. It was not for nothing then that Nicholas Dawtrey later cited Bagenal's desire to be lord president of Ulster as a principal cause of Tyrone's going to war.[207]

The Monaghan settlement was the most important policy development during Fitzwilliam's deputyship. The execution of MacMahon ended the earlier declaratory phase of the surrender and regrant policy. The passing of that phase meant that Gaelic lords would eventually have to choose between retaining their own political system or accepting full English sovereignty. The division of Monaghan must be regarded as an extension of earlier settlements made by Perrot in Cavan and Mayo, but it was more radical still. The appointment of freeholders there constituted an assault on the fluid class structure of a Gaelic lordship. The land grants, made to freeholders and passable by primogeniture, halted traditional means of downward social mobility. This opened the way for the commercialisation of landownership in Gaelic areas. The Dublin adminis-

---

206 BL Harleian 35, fos 258–65.
207 PRO SP 63/174, no. 62(1).

tration had found allies in the freeholders, a disaffected group which constituted the Achilles' heel of Gaelic society. The Monaghan settlement also affected Hugh O'Neill more profoundly than hitherto recognised. Fitzwilliam's successor was undoubtedly correct in regarding it in 1596 as 'the very seed of all these troubles'.[208]

The reorganisation of Monaghan was a success for the government and it became a prototype for further settlements in the North. The execution of Brian O'Rourke for treason was similar in many respects to that of Hugh Roe MacMahon. The privy council wanted a Monaghan-style settlement in West Breifne but fear of upsetting the *status quo* in Connacht prevented the appointment of freeholders there. However, the attack on tanistry in Monaghan and West Breifne left two disaffected members in the persons of Brian MacHugh óg MacMahon and Brian óg O'Rourke. Plans were also afoot in government circles to establish freeholders in the fragmented lordship of Clandeboye but this did not take place until after the war. Nevertheless, civil government had made a solid advance in Ulster; the establishment of a northern assize circuit, which encompassed Cavan, Monaghan, Louth, Down and Antrim by 1593, shows that English sovereignty was functional in a large part of the province.

The regional overlords of the North, the O'Neills of Tyrone and the O'Donnells of Tirconnell, had always been the major obstacles to the extension of crown government. Early in Fitzwilliam's deputyship, a number of opportunities had presented themselves to deal with the earl of Tyrone's increasing power. Due to fear of the MacShanes and the instability which they might provoke, no moves were made against the earl. After the reorganisation of Monaghan, plans were set in motion to produce a similar settlement in Tyrone by methods eventually taken up by Chichester and Davies after the war. However, the escape of Hugh Roe O'Donnell, which led to the re-emergence of Tirconnell from internal shambles to regional power, greatly strengthened the position of his father-in-law, the earl of Tyrone. As a result, the plans for Tyrone were quietly dropped. Henceforth, the replication of the Monaghan model by the crown elsewhere in the North would require force of arms.

[208] Ibid. 189, no. 46(12).

PART TWO

ULSTER OVERLORDS

5

The Rise of Hugh O'Neill

At the onset of hostilities in the mid-1590s, Queen Elizabeth described Hugh O'Neill as 'a creature of our own' whom her Irish government had suffered to come to power 'by receiving excuses and subterfuges'.[1] In 1597, when government negotiators reminded O'Neill of how beholden he was to the queen, 'he answered most ungratefully that Her Majesty owed him nothing but what belonged to him and that he rather ascribed the things he had gotten to his own scratching in the world than Her Majesty's goodness'.[2] In fact the viewpoints of both protagonists were mistaken and self-deceiving. The relationship was more complex; it had changed over time from mutual interdependence to reliance upon O'Neill in the North. This relationship soured after 1587 when the crown began to seek means of curbing his power. Thereafter, Hugh O'Neill had to resort to bribing government officials to maintain his freedom of action. His ultimate success rested not on government support but on the demesne agriculture which he developed and the web of personal connections which he constructed. The marriage alliance with the ruling sept of Tirconnell was especially important in this regard. These strengths brought Hugh O'Neill to power in what manifested itself as a traditional struggle for political succession in a Gaelic lordship. In this light, Hugh O'Neill's rise can best be seen within the context of the politics and structures of Tyrone and the resources at the disposal of himself and his rivals.

The O'Neill lordship of Tyrone was the most powerful Gaelic polity in Ireland. It was a sovereign entity. The rights claimed by O'Neill over other Ulster lordships and over his own subjects within Tyrone are outlined in the *Ceart Uí Néill*. This document was compiled at different stages in the late medieval and early modern periods. Although it contains many anachronisms and details of claims which had become inoperative, the fact that it was reworked during the rule of Turlough Luineach (1567–95) shows the continuing validity of the document and the claims it encompassed.[3] The exercise of authority alone does not create a sovereign entity. Two other features must be taken into account. First, Gaelic lords were inaugurated. 'The O'Neill' was inaugurated at Tullaghoge seated on a stone chair in an elaborate ceremony which dated back into antiquity. The investiture was performed by O'Cahan, the principal *urrí*, and O'Hagan, the principal follower. As suzerain, O'Neill had the right to inaugurate *uirríthe* in their offices. In the late Middle Ages, the

[1] ULC Kk 1 15 no. 31, fos 87–8.
[2] *CSPI*, vi. 484.
[3] 'Ceart Uí Néill', trans. Myles Dillon, *Studia Celtica*, i (1966), 1–18; 'Ceart Uí Néill', trans. Eamon Ó Doibhlin, *Seanchas Ard Mhacha*, v (1970), 324–59. Dillon's translation of this document is the more reliable. However Ó Doibhlin's piece includes a commentary.

THE O'NEILLS OF TYRONE

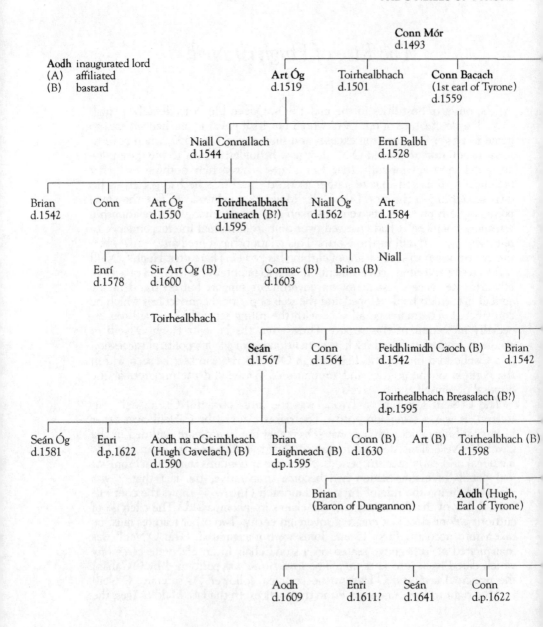

86

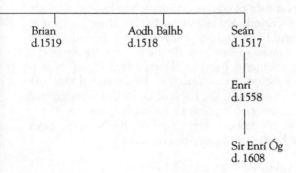

Brian
d.1519

Aodh Balbh
d.1518

Seán
d.1517

Enrí
d.1558

Sir Enrí Óg
d. 1608

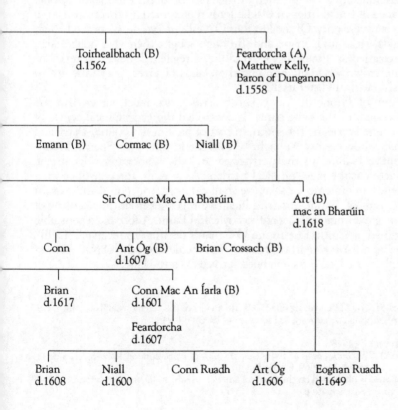

Toirhealbhach (B)
d.1562

Feardorcha (A)
(Matthew Kelly,
Baron of Dungannon)
d.1558

Emann (B)

Cormac (B)

Niall (B)

Sir Cormac Mac An Bharúin

Art (B)
mac an Bharúin
d.1618

Conn

Ant Óg (B)
d.1607

Brian Crossach (B)

Brian
d.1617

Conn Mac An Íarla (B)
d.1601

Feardorcha
d.1607

Brian
d.1608

Niall
d.1600

Conn Ruadh

Art Óg
d.1606

Eoghan Ruadh
d.1649

87

archbishop of Armagh had attended the ceremony at Tullaghoge. Towards the close of the Nine Years War, Lord Deputy Mountjoy made a symbolic point of breaking up the inaugural stone chair and destroying the Tullaghoge site.[4] Miler Magrath, the archbishop of Cashel, was an informed commentator on Gaelic society. He indicated the importance of the investiture when he stated 'if any should undertake the name of O'Neill not appointed by O'Cahan, the people will think themselves not bound in conscience to obey him'.[5] Secondly, there was recognition of O'Neill's claim to sovereignty. By the Act for the Attainder of Shane O'Neill, the Irish parliament theoretically abolished O'Neill sovereignty and asserted crown rights; yet in so doing, it demonstrated that the sovereignty did exist.[6] On the Gaelic side, the O'Neill lordship was recognised precisely for its claims of sovereignty. In a poem to Turlough Luineach, Tadhg Dall Ó Huiginn showed O'Neill's descent from Niall of the Nine Hostages through the prestigious line of Eoghan and described him as:

> A king who never allowed the men of Ireland to
> outdo the Ulstermen in anything, the king proven to be
> best, surpassing all Ireland.[7]

Therefore the O'Neill lordship of Tyrone was recognised by English and Irish alike as the most powerful Gaelic sovereign entity in the country. This picture of the O'Neill lordship is complicated by the creation of the earldom of Tyrone. The acceptance of feudal titles by Gaelic lords represented, in theory at least, a degradation of sovereignty. Of the last four O'Neills of Tyrone, Conn and Hugh obtained feudal titles and Shane and Turlough sought them. No doubt, such titles were regarded as a means of establishing a regulated, devolved relationship with the crown while maintaining the claims of sovereignty inherent in the O'Neillship within Ulster itself.

The lordship of Tyrone in the sixteenth century was much larger than the present day county of the same name. It controlled the geographical centre of the province, encompassing the southern part of present day county Derry and much of what is now county Armagh. Within the lordship, the Sperrin Mountains and Slieve Gallion in the north-west and the Blackwater river in the South-East acted as the main physical barriers. As a result, three distinct areas existed which, for convenience sake, we shall call western, central and eastern Tyrone. The lords of Tyrone obtained lucrative revenues from the licensing of fishing on the great salmon rivers of the Foyle and Bann. A fort and a constable were maintained at Castle Roe inside O'Cahan's territory to receive O'Neill's share of the Bann fishery.[8] Although a fish was included on the O'Neill coat of arms, the bulk of the lordship's revenues derived from the land.[9]

---

[4] G. A. Hayes-McCoy, 'The making of an O'Neill: a view of the ceremony at Tullaghoge, Co. Tyrone', *Ulster Journal of Archaeology*, 3rd ser. xxxiii (1970), 89–94.
[5] *CSPI*, iv. 500.
[6] *Statutes at large*, i. 322–38.
[7] E. Knott (ed.), *The bardic poems of Tadhg Dall Ó Huiginn*, 2 pts, London 1922–6, ii. 28–33.
[8] *C, Carew*, ii. 12–14; NLI MS 669, fos 51–2.
[9] The coat of arms is illustrated on the cover of Micheline Walsh, *'Destruction by peace': Hugh O'Neill after Kinsale*, Armagh 1986.

There were six categories of land within Tyrone which owed various rights to the O'Neill. Ecclesiastical land of three types – bishop's demesne land, termon and erenagh land, and abbey land – was theoretically independent of secular jurisdiction but since the late Middle Ages it had been increasingly subject to the physical and fiscal encroachment of the O'Neills.[10] The lands of the subject families, such as those of the O'Mellan family or of minor branches of the O'Neill family itself, owed 'bonnaght, rising out, cutting and spending' to O'Neill. On the other hand, there were 'certain chief lords of his surname, who paid only bonnaght and rising out'.[11] The *lucht tighe Uí Néill* means literally 'the people of O'Neill's household'. These lands held by the household families were referred to as mensal lands by English commentators and were situated in the district surrounding O'Neill's main seat at Dungannon. This territory was free from bonnaght; part of the territory provided O'Neill with rent in money and goods while the rest was the freehold land of the four main household families: O'Devlin, O'Donnelly, O'Hagan and O'Quinn.[12] By tradition, the O'Devlins were one of the three families of *fircheitheam* whose duties were to take and guard hostages and to collect fines for robbery, bloodshed and the breaking of ancient customs for which they received a commission.[13] However, no evidence survives on the role which this family played in the affairs of the late sixteenth-century lordship. The O'Donnellys, as the hereditary marshals of O'Neill, were responsible for organising his armies. The *Ceart Uí Néill* describes the O'Quinns and O'Hagans as 'the high stewards and chief administrators of O'Neill in the province of Ulster'. According to this document, the O'Quinns received two-thirds of the profits of their office and the O'Hagans one-third.[14] In spite of this division of rewards, the O'Hagans were the more dominant family as evidenced by their custodianship of the inaugural site at Tullaghoge. In the late sixteenth century these two families still provided the civil servants of the lordship.[15] 'Seneschal O'Hagan' was Hugh O'Neill's chief administrative officer within Tyrone.[16] The O'Quinns provided the law enforcement agents. In 1590 Hugh O'Neill had 'appointed a kerne of his called Cahil O'Quinn to be in place of sheriff of Tyrone who did use all disorders by executing such as pleased the earl'.[17] In view of their respective positions, it is not surprising to find that 'a mortal hatred' existed between the O'Hagans and O'Quinns.[18] Closely associated with the mensal lands were the galloglass lands at Ballygawley, ten miles south-west of Dungannon. These lands were held by MacDonnell Galloglass.[19]

---

[10] Philip Robinson, *The plantation of Ulster*, Dublin 1984, 69–72; M. Katherine Simms, 'The archbishops of Armagh and the O'Neills, 1347–1471', *IHS*, xix (1974), 41, 50, 52.
[11] PRO SP 63/129, no. 49.
[12] Dillon, 'Ceart Uí Néill', 10–13; Nicholls, *Gaelic and gaelicised Ireland*, 36–7; BLO, Carte 55 no. 309.
[13] Dillon, 'Ceart Uí Néill', 10–11.
[14] Ibid. 12–13.
[15] Eamon Ó Doibhlin, 'O'Neill's "own country" and its families', *Seanchas Ard Mhacha*, vi (1971), 7–16, 21–3.
[16] PRO SP 63/170, no. 23(8).
[17] Perrot, *Chronicle of Ireland*, 66.
[18] BL Cotton Titus B xii. fos 269–70.
[19] BLO, Carte 55 no. 309.

This tenure was freehold in return for military service.[20] By the 1580s there was also galloglass land south of the Blackwater river with 'Clancarne pertaining to MacDonnell for service'.[21] In 1575 it was estimated that Art MacDonnell and his brethren supplied O'Neill with twenty horsemen and 300 galloglasses.[22] The final category of land was the demesne land at Dungannon itself which was attached to the office of O'Neill; this land would have been worked by 'churls' directly under O'Neill's control.[23]

In the 1570s and 1580s the politico-military complex of Tyrone was headed by Turlough Luineach. Modern historians have generally regarded him as an ineffectual ruler.[24] Colourful accounts such as that given by Sidney in his *Memoir* have been partly responsible for this view.[25] Turlough was, undoubtedly, a heavy drinker and excessive drinking bouts contributed to two of his three major illnesses.[26] However, it is unclear to what extent this reduced his effectiveness as a politician. As late as the 1590s opinion was divided. Fitzwilliam stated that 'Sir Turlough is very old and what with decay of nature through his age and overrun with drink which daily he is in, he is utterly past government.'[27] Another report said that 'although this Sir Turlough seem old and impotent, yet he is able to ride thirty Irish miles a day; being longer than forty English miles and by his devices and policy can more prevail than any of that land'.[28] It must be noted that Turlough's rule represented a break with tradition since he came from a subordinate branch of the O'Neills and from the less favoured western area. Miler Magrath declared that Turlough Luineach was a member of the sept of Art óg, 'who heretofore have not had the principal name nor government in their hands by many descents till this O'Neill, which was admitted to the same, rather by strength and policy, than by right course according to the observations and customs of that country'.[29] Furthermore, the Four Masters point out that it was unusual for an O'Neill to reside at Strabane as Turlough did.[30] Indeed, Turlough Luineach, it could be said, only gained the O'Neillship through the premature death of Shane and the youthfulness of his competitors. One contemporary geneaolgy cited Turlough as a bastard – if correct, this would make his success all the more remarkable.[31]

The power base of Turlough Luineach was western Tyrone. The demesne lands of his father, Niall Connallach, and his grandfather, Art óg, were in the country of Slewisse.[32] Turlough himself originally held the upland territory of

[20] Hayes-McCoy, *Scots mercenary forces*, ch. ii.
[21] PRO SP 63/129, no. 60.
[22] C, *Carew*, ii. 8–9.
[23] Nicholls, *Gaelic and gaelicised Ireland*, 36–7.
[24] Nicholas Canny, 'Hugh O'Neill, earl of Tyrone, and the changing face of Gaelic Ulster', *Studia Hibernica*, x (1970), 20–5; Hayes-McCoy, *Scots mercenary forces*, 77–9.
[25] Sidney, 'Memoir' (1857), 309–10; (1860), 187–8.
[26] PRO SP 63/65, no. 4; 102, no. 30(2); BLO, Perrot 1, fos 67–9.
[27] PRO SP 63/161, no. 44.
[28] Ibid. 170, no. 11. The author's name is not given on this document, but internal evidence points to Miler Magrath.
[29] *CSPI*, iv. 497.
[30] *AFM*, vi. 1929.
[31] PRO SP 63/56, no. 64.
[32] *CSPI*, iii. 333, 520–2.

Muintir Luinigh and later expanded down towards Strabane and constructed a castle there.[33] In time the castle of Strabane provided the nucleus of a small town.[34] Turlough's principal supporters in the north and west of Tyrone were Niall MacArt MacHenry O'Neill, 'a man of great force' and Hugh MacNeill MacCoyne O'Neill, 'lord of the Omagh'.[35] As O'Neill, Turlough Luineach also possessed lands and services pertaining to his office in the Dungannon area. Turlough's cognomen shows that he was fostered amongst the Muintir Luinigh, a family of such obscurity that it must be taken as another intimation of illegitimacy.[36] However, it is also probable that Turlough was fostered by the Flemings on the northern borders of the Pale, since he maintained close connections with them throughout his life.[37] In 1569, he married Agnes Campbell, the lady of Kintyre. The relationship was to prove a stormy one and the marriage did not always bring the political advantages which Turlough intended. Through his wife's influence in Scotland, Turlough hoped to obtain a constant supply of mercenaries; these were not always forthcoming. Agnes Campbell was more concerned to establish her sons, Angus and Donald Gorm MacDonald, in the Glens of Antrim. This made it difficult for Turlough to maintain Sorley Boye, their uncle and rival, as a dependant.[38] Turlough had one son Henry killed by the O'Gallaghers in 1578 but he was outlived by two other sons, Art and Cormac, both of whom were illegitimate.[39] Turlough petitioned the crown for Art's legitimatisation and wanted him to succeed to the demesne lands of the sept of Art óg and to Strabane.[40] He never entertained any hope of his son attaining the O'Neillship. Art was frequently at loggerheads with his father, probably over Turlough's continued control of the demesne lands into his old age; as a result he sometimes sided with Hugh O'Neill.[41]

Except in times of government crisis, Turlough Luineach possessed little influence east of the river Blackwater and lacked the ability to threaten the Pale. For this reason, many English contemporaries and consequently modern scholars saw Turlough as a weakling. On the other hand, it must be emphasised that Turlough Luineach had more continuous influence in Tirconnell and greater authority over Maguire, than any other O'Neill in the sixteenth century.[42] This was primarily because Turlough was based at Strabane and not at Dungannon. However, all the competitors seeking to succeed Turlough came from the Dungannon branch of the family which he had outflanked in 1567.

Turlough Breasalach, as the son of the eldest son of Conn O'Neill, was the best qualified candidate under Gaelic custom.[43] His seniority was itself a drawback; the Lords Justice dismissed him in 1583 as 'old, senseless and without

---

33 BLO, Carte 55 no. 309; *CSPI*, iv. 487.
34 BL Add. 31878, fo. 12.
35 PRO SP 63/145, no. 16.
36 Ibid. 56, nos 62–3.
37 Costello, 'Turlough Luineach', 50–1; *APC*, xvii. 382.
38 Hayes-McCoy, *Scots mercenary forces*, 100–8.
39 AFM, v. 1701: Fiants, 16th Report, no. 5213; PRO SP 63/129, no. 52.
40 *The Tanner letters*, ed. Charles McNeill, Dublin 1943, 32; *CSPI*, iii. 375–6.
41 PRO SP 63/153, no. 1; 169, no. 41.
42 Costello, 'Turlough Luineach', 4; PRO SP 63/94, no. 20; 101, no. 16(1); *CSPI*, iii. 464–5.
43 Sidney, 'Memoir' (1855), 93; PRO SP 63/170, no. 11.

credit in the country'.[44] The sons of Shane O'Neill sought to regain the position of their father and therefore the Dublin government regarded them as a major threat to the stability of the North. The MacShanes were to adopt Shakespeare's expression a 'hydra-headed faction'. Shane O'Neill had at least eight sons by various women.[45] Shane óg and Henry, the sons of Catherine MacDonald, were legitimate.[46] Catherine MacLean, the wife of Calvach O'Donnell, bore Shane two sons, Hugh Gavelach and Art. Conn MacShane was the result of Shane's liaison with the daughter of Shane óg Maguire.[47] Miler Magrath mentions three other sons, Brian, Edmond and Turlough, but they seem to have played less prominent political roles. Magrath also records that 'the said sons of Shane O'Neill are taken amongst the Irishry to have more right than any other to the principality in that country, for that they have descended by the right line from the O'Neill's principal house by many descents, and so they think no right against themselves'.[48] Here it must be noted that Miler Magrath had been patronised by Shane O'Neill and continued as a partisan of his sons.[49] Nevertheless, it was a reflection of the prominence accorded the MacShanes within Tyrone that Turlough Luineach appointed Shane óg *tánaiste* during his first illness in the winter of 1578/9. This aspirant was killed leading a raid into Breifne O'Reilly in 1581.[50] The main obstacle to the ambitions of the MacShanes was Hugh O'Neill. In 1592 Magrath stated that 'the said earl of Tyrone is thought by the Irishry to have his nomination and authority, rather by English government than by any right to the principality after the manner of that country'.[51] In fact, Hugh's relationship with the state was more complex than that suggested by the archbishop.

One of the most persistent myths about Hugh O'Neill, most recently retold by Sean O'Faolain, was his supposed upbringing in the Sidney household in England. However there is no evidence to substantiate this claim. O'Faolain himself could not find any evidence for O'Neill's departure to England in 1562. Instead of rejecting the claim out of hand, he suggests that Hugh left Ireland with Sidney in 1559, thereby giving him nine rather than six years in England.[52] The main evidence for Hugh O'Neill's presence in England is Gainsford's mention that 'in his younger time he trooped in the streets of London, with sufficient equipage and orderly respect'. Yet this is surely a reference to a visit to Court by a number of Irish lords, including the baron of Dungannon,

---

44 Ibid. 102, no. 29.
45 The number of MacShanes can be increased to ten if Niall and Cormac named in the seventeenth-century genealogy in the Carew MS are included: *Facsimiles of the national manuscripts of Ireland*, ed. J. T. Gilbert, 4 vols, Dublin 1874–84, VI/i. 125–6.
46 PRO SP 63/56, no. 64.
47 Hayes-McCoy, *Scots mercenary forces*, 149–52.
48 CSPI, iv. 497.
49 Robert Wyse Jackson, *Archbishop Magrath: the scoundrel of Cashel*, Dublin 1974, 12–14.
50 PRO SP 63/65, no. 4(2); Lambeth, Carew 619, fo. 52.
51 CSPI, iv. 497.
52 O'Faolain, *The Great O'Neill*, 34–44. The English version of Lombard's *Commentary* also gives the impression that Hugh O'Neill was brought up at court. However, an examination of the Latin text reveals Byrne's translation to be incorrect, indeed historiographically determined: Byrne, *The Irish war of defence*, 28–9, 34–5.

which Sidney organised in 1567/8.[53] The other evidence has been misconstrued. Sidney in his bombastic *Memoir* of 1583 refers to 'the young baron of Dungannon, Shane's eldest brother's son, whom I had bred in my house from a little boy, then very poor of goods and full feebly friended' and Hugh O'Neill himself states that he was a 'ward of Your Majesty' and mentions his 'education amongst the English'.[54] Yet in the 1560s Sidney spent most of his time in Ireland and it is notable that Hugh refers to his education amongst the English rather than in England itself. In fact, Hugh O'Neill was a ward of Giles Hovenden, an English settler in Laois. Under this arrangement, Hovenden had farmed the property granted to Conn O'Neill at Balgriffen, near Dublin.[55] Hovenden's sons were frequently termed Hugh's fosterbrothers whose 'mother brought up the baron from a child'.[56]

In 1567 Hugh sued out his livery, though it is clear from records of arrears compiled in 1585 that he never paid the full fine.[57] After his return to Ulster in the late 1560s, the baron relied on subventions from Dublin. The government's assistance reflected its need for a dependable O'Neill to counteract the regeneration of Tyrone under Turlough Luineach. The crown paid the baron for the maintenance of a cavalry detachment and 'for his diets attending parliament at Dublin where his expenses exceeded his ability'.[58] Between September 1573 and September 1575 Hugh fought for the earl of Essex in Ulster and was paid £2,786 7s 6d for the upkeep of himself and his soldiers.[59] But Hugh O'Neill was 'his own man' and the first cracks in the reciprocal relationship with the crown showed at the end of the 1570s. When Turlough waxed strong in 1579, the baron of Dungannon sent Siobhán O'Donnell back to her father and was preparing to marry a daughter of Turlough.[60] The baron accompanied Turlough on his various 'hostings' to awe the *uirríthe* into submission and was accepted as *tánaiste* of Tyrone.[61] The Irish council gave a caustic denunciation of this alliance: 'we understand of the proud speeches and actions of Turlough Luineach, and the deep dissimulation of the baron of Dungannon, the one in his drunkeness giving out words that if we were overthrown he would be king of Ireland, the other playing the hypocrite both in his letters to us and the lord chancellor, when indeed he is the very original of Turlough's outrage to open a

---

[53] Gainsford, *The history of the earle of Tyrone*, 14; Sidney, 'Memoir' (1855), 94. Even a close reading of the *Memoir* shows that Hugh O'Neill travelled to England with Sidney in 1567. It may have been the publication of Sidney's memoir in the 1850s which gave rise to this whole misconception.

[54] Ibid. 92; *CSPI*, iii. 290–1; iv. 321.

[55] College of Arms, Betham papers, 'Repertory to records of the Exchequer: Philip & Mary to James I', p. 99; *Fitzwilliam accounts, 1560–65*, ed. Ada Longfield, Dublin 1960, 8, 16, 31; Fiants, 7th Report, no. 436.

[56] PRO SP 63/104, no. 28.

[57] Fiants, 11th report, no. 1201; PRO SP 63/121, no. 75.

[58] Ibid. 65 no. 7, fos 22, 29.

[59] Ibid. no. 8, fo. 37.

[60] Ibid. 63/65, no. 44; 66, no. 14. At this stage in their marriage, Siobhán had not as yet produced a male heir for Hugh.

[61] *Walsingham letter-book*, 115, 135, 189: C, *Carew*, i. 171–2.

way to his own ambition, that is assured to be his successor'.[62] In any case, Turlough and Hugh soon fell out and the marriage alliance was called off.

At the end of 1579 Hugh O'Neill reached a new accommodation with the crown which lasted until 1587. When informing Lord Justice Pelham about his difficulties with Turlough Luineach, Hugh made much of his dependency on the state, being 'raised from nothing by Her Majesty'.[63] Nevertheless, when he received '25 horsemen in pay', he was 'promising service upon certain conditions'. In other words, the crown was buying the baron's support to defend the Pale against the depredations of his fellow Ulstermen.[64] The following autumn, when the baron was again hard pressed by Turlough, he left Ulster to serve briefly in Munster.[65] During the Munster campaign the baron's horseband was increased to fifty men and in December 1580 Lord Deputy Grey commended him as 'the only Irish nobleman that hath done any service and drawn blood since my coming'.[66] More generally, the Desmond war gave Hugh a free hand on the Ulster borders and the opportunity to interfere in Louth and Clandeboye.[67] In December 1582 Hugh O'Neill was given a commission to defend the northern borders of the Pale between Kells and Dundalk and the temporary use of government footsoldiers in addition to his own horseband.[68] He used these troops and his influence over the neighbouring Irish lords to such effect that the border was rendered virtually free of trouble. The following year the Pale gentry, in spite of their dislike of the baron, saw the necessity of his retention at the post and the crown, because the arrangement had proved economical, was anxious for its continuance.[69] It is clear that the government quickly became dependent on the baron's defence of the Pale. Indeed, Hugh O'Neill used the situation to demand a 'liberal commission over the Irish' and the permission to cess troops upon them; in other words, recognition of his political and military authority over them.[70] These demands were eventually satisfied in 1584 with the grant of the lieutenancy and the right to cess 200 soldiers.[71] Thereafter, Hugh had only a horseband of fifty men paid directly out of the Exchequer.[72] In 1587 the payments towards the upkeep of this horseband were transferred to Turlough Luineach.[73] In effect, the crown had switched its support to Turlough. It is only fair to say that government backing was important during the crucial early period of Hugh O'Neill's career. However, a successful bid for the O'Neill-ship depended on control of land and use of personal connections.

Turlough Breasalach and the MacShanes had only limited access to land.

---

62 *Walsingham letter-book*, 172–4.
63 Ibid. 252. This was echoed in a later statement by the queen that O'Neill was an ungrateful wretch whom 'we have raised from the dust': ULC Kk 1 15 no. 62, fos 128–9.
64 *Walsingham letter-book*, 252.
65 PRO SP 63/76, nos 6, 7; 77, no. 60(5); 78, no. 4. Hugh O'Neill had left Munster before the massacre at Smerwick took place.
66 Ibid. 79, no. 5.
67 Ibid. 72, no. 74; 80, no. 67.
68 Fiants, 13th Report, no. 4054; PRO SP 63/104, no. 28; 105, no. 87.
69 Ibid. nos 28, 87.
70 Ibid.
71 Hatfield House, Cecil 163, fo. 49; PRO SP 63/112, no. 23.
72 Ibid. 105, nos 87–9; 117, no. 54.
73 APC, xv. 74–5; Fiants, 16th Report, no. 5013.

After the death of Shane O'Neill, Turlough Breasalach had been alloted the territory of Clanbrassilagh by Sir Henry Sidney.[74] Turlough's cognomen suggests that he was fostered in this territory which formed part of the lordship of MacCann, a minor *urrí* of O'Neill, on the southern shores of Lough Neagh.[75] It is more significant in political terms that we later find Turlough Breasalach and his sons occupying Glenaule for which they paid rent and service to Hugh O'Neill.[76] The MacShanes were unable to control the lands they once held. They were prevented from doing so by frequent spells of imprisonment and exile and by opposition from rival O'Neills and from the government. Hugh and Art MacShane complained that Turlough had banished them as children to a foreign country and in their absence he had given part of their lands to men fit only to be their followers while the rest went to ruin.[77] In the late 1560s the baron of Dungannon was placed in Oneilland by the lord deputy. This territory had been previously held by Shane O'Neill and was described by Sidney as 'the very first and most ancient possession of the O'Neills'.[78] Not content with this, Hugh also took over neighbouring lands. By 1586, he had annexed Tiranny (part of Henry óg's country) and Muckno (a termon land) which were situated on the border with Oriel. Hugh developed demesne agriculture in these territories by placing 'there certain of his own waged followers which yield him rent and service'. By the same date, he also controlled Glenaule, the rightful possession of the archbishop of Armagh.[79] The O'Neills had been intruding into these and other ecclesiastical lands since the fourteenth century.[80] The Reformation witnessed an attempt on the part of the archbishops and the crown to regain control. Lord Deputy Sidney had specifically exempted the archbishop's lands from the interference of the baron of Dungannon.[81] This did not discourage Hugh O'Neill; in 1590 his meddling was prohibited by the privy council but two years later Archbishop Garvey was again complaining about his usurpations and exactions.[82]

More important than the control of land was the net of personal connections at the disposal of each competitor. In Gaelic society, the most important bonds were formed by consanguinity, marriage and the custom of fosterage by which political figures committed the upbringing of their children to others. Such connections with the household families and the ruling families of other Ulster lordships provided the competitors with political and military support in the contest for supremacy in Tyrone. Turlough Breasalach had the backing of the MacCanns, his fosterers. In 1575 the government estimated their combined strength at forty horsemen and 200 footmen.[83] Hugh Gavelach and Art MacShane could call upon considerable military support, in the form of Scots

---

74 Sidney, 'Memoir' (1855), 93.
75 Dillon, 'Ceart Uí Néill', 8–9; NLI MS 669, fos 52–3.
76 Ibid.
77 PRO SP 63/112, no. 25.
78 BLO, Carte 55 no. 309: Sidney, 'Memoir' (1855), 93.
79 NLI MS 669, fos 52–3.
80 Simms, 'Archbishops of Armagh', 41, 50, 52; BLO, Carte 55 no. 309.
81 Sidney, 'Memoir' (1855), 93.
82 ULC Kk 1 15 no. 15, fos 16–17; PRO SP 63/163, no. 28.
83 C, *Carew*, ii. 8–9.

mercenaries, from their cousin Lachlan MacLean of Duart.[84] This Scottish lord provided them with a place of refuge in times of danger and after their deaths he was sheltering two of their sons.[85] All the MacShanes were fostered by the O'Donnellys, the marshals of Tyrone and fosterers of their father.[86] Perrot found James Carragh, the head of the O'Donnellys, 'most devoted to Shane O'Neill's house'.[87] Henry MacShane had also been fostered by O'Cahan and by the household family of O'Quinn and possibly MacDonnell Galloglass as well. Conn MacShane had also been fostered by the O'Hagans and was connected with the strongest *urrí* in Ulster since his mother was a Maguire and he was married to a daughter of Maguire.[88] Yet Turlough Breasalach and the Mac-Shanes could not match the connections of Hugh O'Neill.

During his infancy, Hugh O'Neill had been fostered by the O'Hagans and O'Quinns.[89] It was said that 'the O'Hagans be a sept whom the earl greatly loveth and trusteth'.[90] Hugh's control of land enabled him to reward these families with leases in the territory of Oneilland.[91] The most comprehensive account of Hugh O'Neill's connections with other Irish lords was given in 1589 by the aging Marshal Bagenal. At that time O'Neill was described 'as so allied by kindred in blood and affinity as also by marriages and fosters and other friendships as if he should be ill-disposed might hap put the crown of England to more charges than the purchase of Ulster should be worth'.[92] Turlough MacHenry O'Neill, captain of the Fews, was his half-brother. Sir Eoin O'Gallagher was his stepfather. Maguire was his uncle, whose son was later to marry one of O'Neill's daughters. O'Neill himself was married to Siobhán, a daughter of O'Donnell, and in turn a daughter, presumably from O'Neill's first marriage, was to marry Hugh Roe O'Donnell. This alliance with the ruling sept of the O'Donnells was to prove crucial in Hugh O'Neill's rise to power in Tyrone. Hugh O'Neill had first cousins in Brian MacHugh óg MacMahon, the captain of Dartry, in Connor Roe Maguire, the third most powerful man in Fermanagh, in O'Doherty, the lord of Inishowen, and in Niall MacArt MacHenry O'Neill who was under Turlough Luineach. O'Hanlon's wife was Hugh's sister and in 1579 MacMahon married one of Hugh's daughters. Hugh's sons were being fostered by Ever Mac Con Uladh MacMahon, the O'Reillys and MacQuillan amongst others. Meanwhile the sons of O'Cahan and Sorley Boye MacDonald were being brought up in the household of Hugh O'Neill.[93] During his life O'Neill was to contract four marriages, three of which produced children, which in turn permitted the establishment of a wide net of marriage alliances.[94] By the 1580s, it was clear that Hugh O'Neill was at the centre of a

84 PRO SP 63/111, no. 39(3).
85 *CSP, Scot.* xi. 558, 649.
86 PRO SP 63/102, no. 72.
87 BLO, Perrot 1, fos 126–9.
88 PRO SP 63/170, no. 11; BL Cotton Titus B xii fos 269–70.
89 PRO SP 63/127, no. 35.
90 CSPI, v. 99.
91 NLI MS 669, fos 52–3.
92 PRO SP 63/145, no. 16.
93 Ibid; Paul Walsh, *The will and family of Hugh O'Neill, earl of Tyrone*, Dublin 1930, 7, 22, 33.
94 Ibid. 16–31.

matrix of connections in Ulster. Of course it must be noted that the individuals connected to him had their own intrinsic interests and were not automatically loyal to his cause.

The competitors also needed connections with the English establishment in order to retain the good offices of the state. In the first place, links with the Geraldine and Butler factions could be utilised.[95] The MacShanes had kinship with the earl of Kildare while Hugh O'Neill had 'dependency in friendship' with the earl of Ormond.[96] In 1600 O'Neill acknowledged Ormond's 'goodwill and good turns shewed to me before the wars'.[97] Hugh O'Neill had additional connections – with English settlers in Ireland and with political leaders in England. As a youth, Hugh had been fostered by the Hovendens of county Laois. His fosterbrothers became his most trusted servants. Henry and on one occasion Walter Hovenden acted as agents for O'Neill in Dublin and London.[98] Three of the brothers – Henry, Richard and Piers – commanded companies of troops which the crown permitted Hugh O'Neill to cess on the areas he controlled.[99] Fosterage in the Pale by a settler family and subsequent involvement in the defence of its northern frontier allowed O'Neill to make contacts with other New Englishmen. These contacts provided a lobby which could influence decisions in his favour and assist him in times of trouble. In 1590 Hugh listed Sir Henry Harrington, Sir Edward Moore and his eldest son Henry, Warham St Leger, Robert Harpole and Henry Warren as 'men of good credit and living' in the Pale willing to enter into bonds on his behalf.[100] In particular, O'Neill developed 'a strong link of amity' with Sir Edward Moore of Mellifont, county Louth.[101] Another important New English acquaintance of O'Neill's was Captain Thomas Lee, who served the first two earls of Essex.[102] On the highest political level, Sir Henry Sidney acted as a suitor on Hugh O'Neill's behalf on at least one occasion.[103] The visits which Hugh made to Court in 1567/8, 1587 and 1590 permitted the establishment of links with the earl of Leicester (Sidney's brother-in-law) and then with his political successor, the second earl of Essex.[104] Another connection at Court is suggested by the fact that O'Neill wore armour given to him by Sir Christopher Hatton, the lord chancellor, at the battle of Clontibret.[105] These connections with the English establishment in both Ireland and England were to stand Hugh O'Neill in good stead throughout his long and eventful career.

Speculation about Turlough's Luineach's likely successor began at the time of

---

[95] For a factional breakdown of Irish politics in the 1580s see NRO Fitzwilliam papers, Ireland, no. 68.
[96] PRO SP 63/152, no. 54; 176, no. 15.
[97] CSPI, ix. 187.
[98] PRO SP 63/102, no. 30; 105, nos 87–8; 117, nos 53–4: CSPI, iii. 481–2.
[99] Ibid. 40–1.
[100] ULC Kk 1 15 no. 4, fos 11–3.
[101] PRO SP 63/153, no. 53. Moore was also stepfather to the Warrens, Henry and William.
[102] For information on the career of Thomas Lee see: Brian de Breffny, 'An Elizabethan political painting', Irish Arts Review, i (1984), 39–41.
[103] PRO SP 63/102, no. 73.
[104] Lambeth, Carew 619, fos 7, 10; PRO SP 63/132, no. 31; 141, no. 10; 170, no. 16.
[105] Ibid. 180, no. 23.

his first illness in the winter of 1578/9.[106] However, Turlough remained supreme in the North until 1583 and only after his illness of that year did his grip on the reins of power begin to loosen. The subsequent power struggle went through various phases: the growth in Hugh O'Neill's power between 1583 and 1587; the counter-attack by Turlough and the MacShanes in 1588–91 and Hugh O'Neill's final assumption of full control of the lordship between 1592 and 1593. Three points can be noted in regard to this struggle. First, such power struggles within lordships were normal as the ruling lords entered old age; for instance the conflict between Shane and Matthew in Conn O'Neill's final years. Secondly, the crown was unable to affect the eventual outcome of the struggle in spite of the military forces at its disposal, the hostages it took, the commissions it set up or the truces it arranged. However, two government interventions – the containment of the MacShanes and their Scottish allies in 1584 and the capture of Hugh Roe O'Donnell in 1587 – did prolong the struggle. Thirdly, the alliance between Hugh O'Neill and the ruling sept of the O'Donnells in Tirconnell was crucial in determining the outcome of the conflict.

The first phase in the power struggle saw dramatic changes in Tyrone. At first, Turlough Luineach was under pressure from the allied threat of Hugh O'Donnell and Hugh O'Neill. Then, in 1584, his fortunes plummeted with the intervention of the MacShanes. The crown attempted to shore up Turlough's authority and to contain the MacShanes, but was only marginally successful. The main beneficiary of the situation was Hugh O'Neill who by mid-1585 was in control of two-thirds of Tyrone. Hugh O'Neill's new power received official recognition when the government created him earl of Tyrone and granted him letters patent. Turlough Luineach suffered a major setback in March 1583 with the death of his ally, Conn O'Donnell. Turlough razed Conn's castle of Lifford and filled in its ditches to prevent it being used against him because his own stronghold of Strabane was 'within a flight-shot' on the opposite bank of the Foyle.[107] This proved futile. Without Conn's presence as a buffer, western Tyrone was exposed to direct attack from Hugh O'Donnell, the lord of Tirconnell.[108] Soon afterwards Hugh O'Neill made his first bid for power. In May the death of Turlough was reported. Henry MacShane, with Scottish support, was a strong candidate for the O'Neillship.[109] Nevertheless, Hugh O'Neill quickly mustered a large force and marched on the inaugural stone at Tullaghoge. Turlough Breasalach was already in occupation but he bowed to Hugh's superior force and announced that he had come 'to give voice to the baron'. These manoeuvres proved abortive when news arrived of Turlough's recovery from a drink-induced coma which had lasted twenty-four hours.[110] During this crisis the government regarded Hugh O'Neill as the lesser of two evils and had considered backing his claim militarily. Yet, it must have been alarmed by his subsequent demands. Hugh's initial request was for the possession of the

---

[106] Ibid. 65, nos 4, 4(2), 12.
[107] Ibid. 84, no. 24; 102, no. 4(1).
[108] AFM, v. 1793, 1811–13.
[109] PRO SP 63/102, no. 29.
[110] Ibid. no. 30.

Blackwater fort.[111] The Lords Justice referred the case to the privy council since the fort was not in their gift. Moreover they were very uncertain about the baron's future disposition since once in charge of Tyrone he would be 'the greatest subject of form that hath been in this realm of long time . . . able to command all Ulster even to the town of Dundalk'.[112] The privy council would give O'Neill only restricted access to the fort: 'for avoiding of danger of surprising the said fort' his company was to be limited to three persons during any visit.[113] Later in the year a more extensive list of the baron's demands was presented to the queen.[114] Even at this stage in his career, Hugh O'Neill's ambitious nature was evident. Playing on the fear of the MacShanes and exaggerating the military support which they could obtain from the O'Donnellys, he again requested possession of the Blackwater fort. He demanded letters patent for Tyrone. Nor were his ambitions limited to central Ulster. He requested letters patent for the territories of Moira, Killultragh and Kilwarlin in the Lagan Valley, ostensibly to keep out the Scots. He asked for a forty-one year lease of the ecclesiastical lands in Lecale 'for the better maintenance of his lordship's houses'. Finally, he wanted the grant of the castle of Belfast; the strategic position of this castle between North and South Clandeboye would have given him control of the region.[115]

The reassertion of O'Donnell's power in the West and the growing power of Hugh O'Neill in the East were not isolated, individual actions but a concerted effort between father-in-law and son-in-law. By the autumn of 1583 the allies equalled Turlough in strength and their activities had initiated an attempt by Agnes Campbell to recruit Scots mercenaries to assist her husband's cause.[116] In October 1583 government commissioners managed to negotiate a truce between the three parties which was to last until St Patrick's Day the following year.[117] Therefore the developments of 1583 had seen the decline in the supremacy of Turlough and the rise of Hugh O'Donnell and Hugh O'Neill to equal prominence within Ulster. Hugh O'Neill's influence within Tyrone was now substantial and although the crown was willing to renew his commission for the defence of the Pale, he was now a man to be feared.[118] Sir Nicholas White believed that the crown should switch its support from Hugh O'Neill to Turlough Luineach to maintain the balance of power in the North. Marshal Bagenal asserted that the *uirríthe*, far from being freed from the oppression of the O'Neills, were merely passing out of the control of Turlough Luineach into the authority of Hugh O'Neill.[119] By the spring of 1584, the worst fears of the government seem to have been realised: 'they are suddenly grown into a very firm league of amity and friendship, in so much as in confirmation thereof Turlough (as we hear) hath in secret sort made the baron tanist or secondary of

[111] Ibid. nos 71(1–2).
[112] Ibid. no. 71.
[113] Ibid. no. 74.
[114] Ibid. no. 72; 105, nos 87–9.
[115] Ibid. 102, no. 72.
[116] BL Cotton Titus F v. fos 93–4.
[117] 'Calendar of the Irish Council Book', 151, no. 251.
[118] PRO SP 63/104, nos 28, 76.
[119] Ibid. 105, nos 20, 85.

his country, and the baron embracing that offer keepeth the matter as secret as he may for he knoweth it be against Her Majesty's laws'. The lords justice feared a general combination amongst the leading men of the North. To all these developments the officials in Dublin were 'mere strangers'.[120]

The MacShanes made a push for power in the summer of 1584 and their actions precipitated the temporary collapse of Turlough's authority. Hugh Gavelach and Art MacShane had spent two years in Scotland soliciting the aid of their kinsman, Lachlan MacLean.[121] In August 3,000 Scots led by MacLean landed in Lough Foyle. Their purpose was to free Henry and Conn MacShane from Turlough's custody and then to establish the MacShanes in power.[122] Although Henry and Conn remained in Turlough's hands, the O'Donnellys and O'Cahans at once defected to the invaders.[123] As Turlough retreated towards the Blackwater, Hugh O'Neill took advantage of the situation to attack him and draw off his herds of cattle and his followers.[124] In desperation, Turlough was forced to fall back on the crown for assistance. On meeting Lord Deputy Perrot, he handed over his son, Art, as a hostage; later he also surrendered custody of Henry MacShane.[125] According to Sir John Norris, Turlough had 'waited upon my lord very slenderly accompanied' and afterwards he confessed that his followers had deserted him.[126]

The sudden crisis gave Lord Deputy Perrot an opportunity to intervene in Ulster. Although the subsequent composition was primarily intended to extend crown authority, it was also a means of strengthening Turlough Luineach. Three hundred troops were appointed to his use. The articles of agreement, by which Turlough undertook these troops, demonstrate his lack of support within Tyrone. The troops were 'to be disposed and directed by O'Neill both for his defence and surety and to be employed in the gathering up his rents and duties due upon his followers'.[127] In spite of this, Turlough's circumstances remained difficult for some time. In October 1584 the MacShanes were describing themselves as now 'in better sort' and using the capture of Oliver Lambert, a gentleman-soldier, to make overtures to the government.[128] Lambert himself indicated that the MacShanes still had the support of O'Cahan and that Hugh Gavelach 'is far better beloved in the country than O'Neill is and commands all at his pleasure'. As a result Turlough was forced to make an accommodation of an unspecified nature with this MacShane.[129] During the winter, Turlough fell gravely ill once more and a succession crisis similar to that of the previous year occurred with the government again backing the baron of Dungannon.[130] About this time the government returned Art to his father in exchange for four

---

[120] Ibid. 108, no. 56.
[121] Ibid. 112, no. 11.
[122] Lambeth, Carew 619, fo. 14.
[123] PRO SP 63/111, no. 70.
[124] Lambeth, Carew 619, fo. 14.
[125] PRO SP 63/111, no. 88; 112, no. 41.
[126] Ibid. 111, no. 12.
[127] Ibid. 112, no. 41(2).
[128] Ibid. no. 25.
[129] Ibid. no. 33.
[130] BLO, Perrot 1, fos 67–9.

leading men of the country.[131] By the early months of 1585 Turlough and Art with the support of the composition forces seem to have established some semblance of control in Tyrone west of the Blackwater.[132]

Between the summer of 1585 and the summer of 1587 Hugh O'Neill achieved control over two-thirds of the Tyrone lordship and by the assumption of the title, earl of Tyrone, and the grant of letters patent, he gained the recognition of the crown for his new position. The rapid extension of Hugh O'Neill's power resulted from a coup which he engineered in the summer of 1585. The MacShanes were once more gaining in strength: 'Shane O'Neill's sons called Hugh, Art and Brian aspiring to the insolency of their father being greatly followed by the people of the country and their mother a Scot, committed divers robberies and spoils which T. Luineach was unable to suppress.'[133] To prevent any further aggrandisement by the MacShanes, Hugh O'Neill and Turlough's son, Art, took charge in central Tyrone. Offical agreements, ratified after the event, attempted to put a veneer of government authority on a situation over which it exercised no control. Indeed, an act of the Irish council contained the admission that the government had been compelled 'to frame our purposes and counsels to the times and occasions'.[134] An indenture was drawn up at the behest of the government in which Hugh O'Neill and Art MacTurlough agreed to pay Turlough 1,000 marks *per annum* for a seven year lease of the territory.[135] In this instance Hugh O'Neill had clearly used Art MacTurlough against his father. Although Art was a party to the agreement, he played no subsequent role in the government of the territory handed over. Under the agreement, Hugh O'Neill achieved control in central Tyrone and acquired the overlordship of MacCann; Turlough remained O'Neill and retained western Tyrone and overlordship of Maguire and O'Cahan.[136] One distinct advantage which this territorial expansion gave Hugh over his competitors was control of 'the place and chair of election' at Tullaghoge.[137]

Conversely, the fortunes of Turlough Luineach and the MacShanes were at a low ebb. In this period, Turlough Luineach was largely dependent on the crown.[138] In 1585 he was unable to maintain the 300 composition soldiers whom he had undertaken and, as a result, they 'endured great want and misery'.[139] Nonetheless, he had no option but to retain these troops whose numbers were reduced to 200 the following year.[140] The MacShanes also suffered setbacks. Lord Deputy Perrot, on a tour of the North in 1585, took Art MacShane captive and imprisoned him in Dublin Castle along with his brother, Henry. Moreover, Perrot permitted Hugh O'Neill and Turlough Luineach to spoil the territory of James Carragh O'Donnelly, the main supporter of the MacShanes

---

[131] Ibid.
[132] Ibid. fos 76–7; HMC, *Rutland* MSS, i. 171–2.
[133] PRONI, Ellis Papers, D682 no. 2.
[134] PRO SP 63/118, no. 59.
[135] 'Calendar of the Irish Council Book', 169–70, no. 333.
[136] Ibid; PRO SP 63/129, no. 51.
[137] BLO, MS 30237, fo. 51.
[138] PRO SP 63/123, no. 52.
[139] Ibid. 118, no. 59.
[140] BLO, Perrot 1, fos 238–9.

within the lordship.[141] In spite of these developments, there remained a ground-swell of support for the MacShanes in central and eastern Tyrone.[142]

During the same period, the crown recognised the power which Hugh O'Neill had attained within Tyrone by his further ennoblement and the grant of his grandfather's lands. On the other hand, the decline in Turlough's power prevented him from attaining such status. The first stage in this process of recognition came at the parliament of 1585. A meeting of seventy lords and councillors decided to give Hugh O'Neill 'the name, dignity and place of earl of Tyrone, according to his creation'.[143] In the spring of 1587 the earl of Tyrone travelled to Court to negotiate a final settlement. At this time his position in Tyrone was unchallenged and this was translated into a strong negotiating stance. In his petition to the queen, he reminded her that he had already 'recovered and repossessed some part of his patrimony and inheritance, with adventure of his life'.[144] Furthermore, Hugh was determined to make no concessions to Turlough Luineach whom he claimed to be a usurper of the rights granted to his grandfather.[145] Indeed, with the queen's permission, Hugh offered to evict Turlough altogether without cost to the crown or harm to the subjects of the Pale.[146]

The subsequent settlement with the crown reflected the *status quo* in Tyrone and secured Hugh O'Neill's future position there after Turlough's death. Hugh O'Neill was to inherit all the lands and services of his grandfather, Conn O'Neill. A commission was to be established to determine the lands and services which Conn had held. Turlough's son, Art, was to be given the lands of his grandfather, Niall, and he was to pay services to the earl of Tyrone as his grandfather had done. Hugh O'Neill promised to prevent the inhabitants of Tyrone from raiding the Pale, to renounce his claims to the fort of the Black-water and its hinterland and to release neighbouring territories from his over-lordship.[147] O'Neill's considerable charm had impressed the queen – a lease of lands was obtained for Piers Hovenden at the request of the earl of Tyrone 'to whom Her Majesty would not willing deny any favour, knowing his devotion to her'.[148] The findings of the land commission, which operated in the autumn of 1587, also favoured the earl. It concluded that the territory ruled by O'Cahan was part of the lordship of Tyrone. Although O'Cahan's country constituted a separate lordship under Irish law, the inclusion of this area within Tyrone under English law permitted Hugh O'Neill to retain control of the most important *urrí* in Ulster, the one with the right to inaugurate 'the O'Neill'. Moreover, the Fews, inhabited by one of the most independent O'Neill septs, was included within the lordship.[149] Another part of the commission's brief was to determine the portion of lands to which Turlough Luineach and Art MacTurlough were

---

[141] PRO SP 63/118, no. 78(1); BLO, Perrot 1, fos 126–9.
[142] NRO, Fitzwilliam Papers, Ireland, no. 68.
[143] PRO SP 63/117, no. 52.
[144] *CSPI*, iii. 290–1.
[145] Ibid. 335–6.
[146] Ibid. 334–5.
[147] PRO SP 63/129, no. 79.
[148] *CPCRI*, ii. 125.
[149] Fiants, 16th Report, no. 5031; *CSPI*, iii. 332–4, 520–2.

entitled and there were subsequent allegations that one of the principal commissioners, Chief Justice Dillon, had been bribed by Hugh O'Neill. As a result,
Dillon had allegedly influenced the jury, which reviewed the extent of the
lordship, to reduce by half the amount of land alloted to Turlough and his
son.[150]

In 1578 a patent for the ennoblement of Turlough Luineach had been drawn
up but never conferred and as a result in 1585 'being here at parliament he took
some disgrace to himself that he could not have place in the house as other
noblemen had'.[151] Unlike Hugh O'Neill, Turlough now renewed his interest in
obtaining a title not as a means of recognition of power but as a means of
reasserting some semblance of his old authority with government help. Indeed
during the negotiations at Court, Hugh O'Neill inferred as much: 'the said earl
humbly informeth that the said nobilitation of the father and the son is sought
and intended by them only to abate and diminish the countenance of the said
earl wherewith they are much aggrieved'.[152] Turlough petitioned that he should
be created earl of Omagh and that his son, Art, should be legitimated and made
baron of Strabane, holding western Tyrone as a perpetual inheritance.[153]
Turlough's case at Court was seriously weakened following a dispute between
his secretary and agent, Solomon Fernan, and Sir Henry Bagenal over the
forgery of some letters.[154] The upshot was that the settlement in London simply
reflected the arrangements made in 1585. Turlough remained captain of Tyrone
for life with Maguire and O'Cahan as *uirríthe*. The most significant change was
that he now received the government's allowance for Hugh O'Neill's horseband
because of the latter's refusal to pay the rents agreed in the 1585 lease.[155]

When Hugh O'Neill returned to Ireland at the end of May 1587, he probably
believed that his position in Tyrone was now secure and that he would soon be
supreme in Ulster.[156] If so, he was mistaken. Perrot and others in Dublin had
begun to work against him and they were to make some timely and strategic
interventions that delayed his accession to power in the North. Over the next
four years Turlough Luineach and the MacShanes took advantage of the situation not just to halt the earl's aggrandisement but actually to retard it. Because
of these difficulties, Hugh O'Neill was now forced to justify his actions before
crown officials. He had to resort to bribery in order to maintain the acquiescence of the Dublin administration. There is corroboration from the Gaelic side
in a statement of Lughaidh Ó Cléirigh: 'Aodh Ó Néill had many friends too
among the English, for he gave them large presents and stipends of gold and
silver for supporting him and speaking on his behalf in the council.'[157] Nicholas
Dawtrey later referred to Richard Weston, one of the earl's principal officers, as
'the manager of his bribes also, which I think is very great'.[158] Moreover we

150 PRO SP 63/148, no. 31.
151 BLO, Perrot 1, fos 101–3.
152 CSPI, iii. 335–6.
153 PRO SP 63/130, no. 28.
154 CSPI, iii. 284–6, 349–50; APC, xv. 9–10.
155 CPCRI, ii. 126–7.
156 PRO SP 63/129, no. 92.
157 Life, i. 27.
158 CSPI, ix. 414.

know from O'Neill himself that he tried to use bribery when faced with similar difficulties after the Nine Years War.[159] In Hugh O'Neill's absence, Perrot had arranged for Sir Ross MacMahon, the lord of Oriel, to surrender his lands and to obtain them as a feudal fiefdom from the crown.[160] Later in the year, Perrot organised the surrender and regrant of the lands of Sir Oghy O'Hanlon, lord of Orior.[161] The earl complained to the queen that 'MacMahon and O'Hanlon who were the best helps I had next unto your Highness' had been taken from him.[162] At the same time the earl was protesting about a far more serious development, namely the detention of Hugh Roe O'Donnell, his son-in-law, in Dublin which 'is the most prejudice that might happen unto me'.[163] In reporting the capture of Hugh Roe O'Donnell to the queen, Perrot claimed that it had been undertaken primarily because his father was unwilling to give hostages to the crown. However, he ended by stating: 'the having of Mr. Hugh Roe O'Donnell, in respect he is come of the Scots, and matched in marriage with the greatest in Ulster, will serve you to good purpose'.[164] The Four Masters echoed this view when they later claimed that the English had captured Hugh Roe because they feared an alliance between O'Donnell and the earl of Tyrone.[165] With Tirconnell neutralised, Turlough and his followers were able to turn their undivided attention onto the earl, who was forced to construct a fort in Termonmagurk to guard the pass below Slieve Gallion.[166]

In spite of these adverse developments, Hugh O'Neill remained determined to achieve supremacy in Ulster by whatever means possible. During 1587 he entered into a mutual alliance with Angus MacDonald of Dunyveg, lord of Clandonald South in Scotland.[167] In the summer of that year, he freely admitted to the lord deputy: 'I have sent Nyse McJames [Angus MacDonald] forty shot to help him against McEulane [MacLean], in hope to get the like of him.'[168] Doubtless, the earl saw this as a way to keep the MacLeans busy at home and to prevent them giving assistance to the MacShanes. This alliance gave him the opportunity to recruit Scottish troops during the winter and spring of 1588 for an attempt to reduce the *uirríthe* and Turlough Luineach.[169] Hugh also took advantage of the news of Perrot's imminent departure. Sir Henry Duke warned Perrot, 'the earl's men do openly say that whatsoever they shall do in your lordship's time that the next deputy will forgive them'.[170]

In January 1588 MacMahon was again under the control of the earl, and Maguire was under pressure from MacMahon on the one side and O'Donnell on

[159] M. Walsh, *'Destruction by peace'*, 30.
[160] Fiants, 16th Report, nos 4989, 4991.
[161] Ibid. nos 5041, 5091.
[162] PRO SP 63/132, no. 30.
[163] Ibid. no. 31.
[164] HMC *Salisbury* MSS, iii. 285-6.
[165] AFM, v. 1859-65.
[166] CSPI, iii. 464-7.
[167] Ibid. 396-7, 450-1; PRO SP 63/145, no. 16; Hayes-McCoy, *Scots mercenary forces*, 87, 183.
[168] CSPI, iii. 397-8; *Criminal trials and other proceedings before the High Court of Justiciary in Scotland*, ed. Robert Pitcairn, 3 vols, Edinburgh 1833, i. 226-9.
[169] CSPI, iii. 466-7; BL Add. 19,837, fos 46-7.
[170] CSPI, iii. 455, 466-7.

the other 'to be at the earl's commandment'.[171] In April the earl mounted an attack aimed at joining up with O'Donnell, taking Strabane and then reducing O'Cahan and MacQuillan.[172] The lord deputy sent a pursuivant to demand a truce. Hugh O'Neill not only disobeyed this instruction but also used the pursuivant in an attempt to gain advantage over Turlough.[173] The earl effected the rendezvous with O'Donnell but was subsequently defeated at Carricklea by Turlough's forces.[174] Perrot was delighted at the outcome: 'the overthrow given the earl by Turlough O'Neill's small company hath done much good in the North as anything that happened these nine years, for it hath abated the earl's edge much'.[175] Hugh O'Neill subsequently wrote to the earl of Leicester and the queen in a feeble attempt to allay suspicion. He said that he and his tenants had suffered much from the incursions of Turlough's sons, Art and Cormac, and that the action should 'be construed as a necessary mean used for my safeguard and the defence of the subject and not to the end I may by strength become great among the Irishry in these parts as hath been spoken'.[176] Hugh O'Neill's reduced circumstances are reflected in the recognisance of £1,000 which he was forced to make with the crown in July 1588. By this he promised to submit his disputes with Turlough to the arbitration of commissioners, not to recruit Scots mercenaries nor to interfere with 'O'Hanlon, MacMahon or any of Her Majesty's urriaghs'.[177] However, the earl still had cards to play and Perrot feared that in the future his colleagues would 'be corrupted, as the earl hath cunning enough in that faculty'.[178] Perrot's fears were not groundless: the recognisance was later marked 'cancelled for that condition was observed' by Chancellor Loftus.[179]

Following the shipwreck of the Spanish Armada, the struggle for supremacy in Tyrone continued, although it did not go unaffected by the dramatic events. Rumours that both Hugh O'Neill and Turlough Luineach had joined up with the Spaniards against the crown were wild and wholly unsubstantiated.[180] The fears of the government echoed the fact that it had less than 1,000 soldiers stationed in the realm whereas the number of Spanish survivors landing in north-west Ulster was reported to be twice that number.[181] In fact the competitors in Tyrone were exploiting the novel situation for their own ends rather than acting jointly against the crown. It is probable that Turlough Luineach was trying to recruit the Spanish survivors as soldiers to fight against the earl of Tyrone.[182] It was also rumoured that one of the MacShanes in the Western Isles of Scotland was trying to draw over Spaniards to build up an army there to stage

171 Ibid. 466–7.
172 Ibid. 516–17.
173 Ibid. 514–16.
174 Ibid; AFM, v. 1867–9.
175 CSPI, iii. 513–14.
176 Lambeth, Carew 619, fos 7–8.
177 BL Add. 19,837, fos 46–7.
178 CSPI, iii. 513–14.
179 BL Add. 19,837, fos 46–7.
180 PRO SP 63/137, nos 10(4–7).
181 Ibid. 136, no. 36; 137, nos 10(1, 8): CSPI, iv. 64.
182 PRO SP 63/137, nos 10(1, 14, 18); Costello, 'Turlough Luineach', 276.

a recovery against the earl in Ulster.[183] All this neatly paralleled the situation in Scotland itself where Lachlan MacLean used shipwrecked Armada sailors in his feud against Clandonald and its ally, Clan Ian.[184] Most Spaniards preferred to leave Ulster rather than fight in the internecine quarrels of its inhabitants. The majority of them died in attempting to do so when the *Girona* crashed into rocks on the north Antrim coast.[185]

The earl utilised the situation in a different way. He sent his composition-mercenary forces under Richard and Henry Hovenden to Inishowen where they put a large number of Spaniards to the sword. Although Lord Deputy Fitzwilliam refused to believe this news and was suspicious of the earl's activities, the massacre is confirmed in the report of a Spanish escapee.[186] In a move to exploit the government's fears, the earl requested 'a commission to myself to serve not only against the Spaniards, but also against all those that taketh their parts; and to take victuals where I can during the time of my abode in that service'. Fitzwilliam rejected this as a transparent attempt by the earl to obtain official sanction for an attack on Turlough.[187] And Hugh O'Neill may have been playing a double-game. We know from the examinations of Don Alonso de Luzon and Don Baltasar Lopez del Árbol that O'Neill sheltered three noblemen and a number of commoners who were sick.[188] We know that one of the latter, Pedro Blanco, entered the earl's service.[189] We also know that he helped one of the noblemen, Don Antonio Manrique, escape because the MacShanes intercepted a messenger of his in Scotland, bringing a letter of thanks to the earl. As a result, the MacShanes alleged that the earl was practising with Spain.[190] However, when Hugh Gavelach MacShane produced the letter and messenger as proof, Fitzwilliam dismissed the evidence as insufficient grounds to indicate an actual conspiracy.[191] Of course, an overture to Spain by Hugh O'Neill would have been sensible at this juncture because the crown had begun to take measures to curb his power the previous year but there is no evidence of one in the Spanish records.

The latter part of 1588 and the early months of 1589 were a period of continued success for Turlough Luineach. At this time, he had hired English mercenaries, commanded by Captains Mostian and Merryman, who were cessed on his part of Tyrone.[192] In October 1588 Captain Mostian's company was used to reassert control over Maguire who had been lost to Hugh O'Neill earlier in the year.[193] Solomon Fernan's statement of February 1589 that 'Maguire and O'Neill are agreed' demonstrates the re-establishment of the traditional bonds

183 *CSPI*, iv. 65.
184 Hayes-McCoy, *Scots mercenary forces*, 190.
185 *CSPI*, iv. 64, 92–3; Niall Fallon, *The Armada in Ireland*, London 1978, ch. vi.
186 PRO SP 63/136 nos 36(2, 4), 43(12); 137, no. 10(2, 8): *CSP, Sp.* iv. 506–10.
187 PRO SP 63/137, no. 10(8).
188 Ibid. nos 15, 16.
189 M. Walsh, *'Destruction by peace'*, 369–70; *CSP, Sp.* iv. 642.
190 PRO SP 63/142, nos 12, 12(3); *CSP, Scot.* xi. 558; Perrot, *Chronicle of Ireland*, 65.
191 PRO SP 63/143, no. 46; 144, no. 38.
192 *CSPI*, iv. 51, 113; PRO SP 63/140, no. 51.
193 *CSPI*, iv. 51.

of overlordship.[194] Turlough Luineach continued to have considerable success in Tirconnell where he supported Hugh O'Gallagher and then Niall Garbh.[195] Later Turlough married one of his daughters to Donnell O'Donnell, who had usurped much of his father's power in the country.[196] At this time, Turlough was also demanding the return of the lands let to the earl, the lease of which was revocable after three years. A privy council letter to the earl ordered the return of the lands.[197] However, the latter was suppressed after an extremely amicable meeting between Fitzwilliam and Hugh O'Neill at Dungannon. This situation contrasted starkly with the aspersions Fitzwilliam cast on the earl's loyalty at the time of the Armada crisis.[198] This is an obvious case of bribery.

In 1589 Turlough Luineach established an alliance with the MacShanes. In February Hugh Gavelach returned to Ulster after one and a half years in Scotland and, at his request, Turlough released Conn MacShane from imprisonment.[199] Sir Nicholas White reported the sequel. Turlough disavowed Sir Art as his son for marrying a daughter of Hugh O'Neill and for plotting his father's death. Next he adopted Conn as his son and tánaiste. Consequently, 'many of the earl's people that be greatly addicted to Shane O'Neill's sons (especially the Hagans) are gone with their cattle to him'.[200] In attempting to crush the earl, Turlough Luineach and the MacShanes first tried diplomatic channels. However, Fitzwilliam rejected both Turlough's application for the return of the lands leased to the earl and Hugh Gavelach's allegations about the earl's collusion with the Spaniards.[201] Afterwards military means were essayed and both sides employed Scots mercenaries. Sorley Boye MacDonald fore-warned Hugh O'Neill that the MacLeans were preparing to sail for Lough Foyle and subsequently he supplied him with troops under the command of his son, James.[202] In the ensuing conflict, Hugh O'Neill found himself at first under considerable pressure.[203] Then at harvest time, Richard Hovenden mounted a counter-attack on western Tyrone with a large force of Scots galloglasses and English soldiers. This force burned a number of fortifications, including the castle of Dunnalong, and wreaked havoc in the countryside.[204] Nevertheless, the result of the conflict was uncertain stalemate.

In the first days of 1590, the earl of Tyrone scored a major success: he executed Hugh Gavelach MacShane. Hugh Gavelach had been captured by one of the Maguires who then sold him to the earl.[205] The O'Donnellys, who were subject to the government of the earl 'only by pledges and constraint',

[194] PRO SP 63/142, no. 12(2).
[195] W. M. Hennessy (ed.), The Annals of Loch Cé: a chronicle of Irish affairs, 1014–1590, 2 vols, London 1871, ii. 487–91; AFM, v. 1875; CSPI, iv. 113.
[196] PRO SP 63/150, no. 27; AFM, vi. 1891–3.
[197] APC, xvi. 337–8.
[198] CSPI, iv. 95; PRO SP 63/137, no. 10(1–3, 8–9).
[199] PRO SP 63/142, no. 12(2); 141, no. 22.
[200] Ibid. 143, no. 7.
[201] Ibid. 144, no. 34, 38.
[202] Ibid. 146, no. 6(5); 148, nos 9, 10(1).
[203] Lambeth, Carew 618, fo. 23.
[204] PRO SP 63/151, no. 43.
[205] Ibid. 150, no. 71.

offered large ransoms for their fosterbrother.[206] Letters from the lord deputy and the lord chancellor commanded the earl to forebear from taking any action against the captive.[207] Nevertheless, Hugh O'Neill proceeded and hanged Mac-Shane, allegedly from a thorn tree with his own hands.[208] Years later, it was claimed that Captain William Warren had advised Tyrone to hang Hugh Gavelach because he knew 'both their secrets' – presumably a reference to the Armada survivors.[209] Fitzwilliam's reaction was noted by Owen Wood, a correspondent of Perrot: 'the deputy storms at it, but as your honour knoweth his counsels will be swallowed'.[210] The Irish council compelled the earl to enter into a £2,000 recognisance with Henry Harrington and Henry Warren acting as sureties.[211] Although O'Neill had to go to Court to justify himself, he had letters supporting him from Fitzwilliam and Loftus, the very persons whose orders he had supposedly disobeyed. Both mitigated his execution of MacShane; indeed Loftus applauded the act.[212]

Hugh O'Neill soon found himself under house arrest at Sir Henry Wallop's London residence.[213] Yet, he was in no sense repentant when he came before the privy council to defend himself. In reply to charges of illegally killing Hugh Gavelach, he stood by his actions. He held that Hugh Gavelach had been guilty of many murders and depredations in his part of Tyrone. It also became clear that Hugh Gavelach's execution had not been a foregone conclusion but rather it had been subject to negotation between the earl and the MacShanes. The earl offered to spare Hugh's life if Hugh and Conn submitted to his government as their brother, Brian, had done, with each of them acting as pledge in turn for the good behaviour of the other two. Conn MacShane was given fourteen days to ratify the agreement but failed to do so. After the expiration of that time, Hugh Gavelach was executed by Melaughlin and Cormac MacMurrehy in the presence of the leading nobles of Tyrone. In authorising the execution, the earl asserted that he was Her Majesty's lieutenant in the region and that, by equity, the use of Brehon law was valid.

> I humbly desire that consideration may be had to the place where this fact was done, and to the person a notable murderer, and to the ancient form of government amongst us in Ulster where there is neither magistrate, judge, sheriff nor course of laws of this realm, but certain customs by which O'Neill and I and others of our sort do govern our followers.[214]

After a period, Hugh O'Neill was released on the recommendation of Fitzwilliam and other Irish councillors.[215]

Not surprisingly, Hugh O'Neill's adversaries in Tyrone attempted to take

---

[206] Ibid. 152, no. 4; 150, no. 27.
[207] Ibid.
[208] Ibid. no. 21.
[209] Ibid. 203, no. 58.
[210] Ibid.
[211] BL Add. 19,837, fo. 87; PRO SP 63/150, no. 75.
[212] Ibid. nos 78, 80.
[213] Ibid. 151, no. 52.
[214] Ibid. no. 20.
[215] Ibid. nos 39, 93; 152, no. 4.

advantage of his difficulties at Court. To this end, Conn MacShane travelled to London. Unlike the earl, he had no letters of approbation from Fitzwilliam and Loftus, but instead carried letters in his favour from Turlough Luineach, the earl of Kildare and the lord of Delvin.[216] When Conn MacShane reached the Court, the earl had already departed but much to the latter's chagrin, an order was secured for his return.[217] Conn MacShane presented a long list of accusations against Hugh O'Neill. He cited the earl's marriage alliances and fosterings by which he intended 'to make himself great in Ulster'. Hugh O'Neill's dealings with foreigners were noted: his reciprocal alliance with Angus MacDonald and his assistance to Don Antonio Manrique, a survivor of the Armada. It was alleged that the earl had plotted the escape of Hugh Roe O'Donnell from Dublin Castle. Hugh O'Neill had imposed bonnaght on Orior and had interfered in Oriel, even though both were now held directly off the crown. Furthermore, Hugh O'Neill refused sheriffs any jurisdiction in his territory and forced his neighbours to do likewise. Last but not least he had hanged two of Conn MacShane's brothers, Edmond and Hugh Gavelach. Hugh O'Neill made evasive answers and alleged that the only cause of these complaints was his opposition to the pursuit of the O'Neillship by the MacShanes. Eventually, the earl won the day and since no witnesses were to be had in England, the case was referred to the investigation of the Irish council.[218] However, no subsequent action was taken against the earl in Ireland. The fears expressed by Conn MacShane at Court were fully justified: 'if the earl were permitted to pass without trial in England upon proof made in Ireland, his friends were there so many and his forces so great that none durst aver any matter against him in that country whilst he were there'.[219]

When the earl presented himself before the Irish council on his return home, he requested assurance of the O'Neill title, ostensibly to prevent the Mac-Shanes gaining it. This demand was particularly ironic after the agreement which he had signed in London for the establishment of civil government in Tyrone. Fitzwilliam refused the request.[220] In 1591 the struggle for supremacy reverted from diplomatic to military means. The early summer saw both sides raiding each other's territories. In one fray, Turlough Luineach 'was shot through the shoulder with a bullet and strucken with a horseman's staff in the small of his back' but he made a good recovery.[221] Once again government commissioners tried to pacify the situation and once again Hugh O'Neill's actions were excused.[222] In December 1591 the territory of Hugh O'Neill was again subject to the murder and devastation of the followers of Conn Mac-Shane. A pursuivant was dispatched from Dublin and a truce was patched up until St Patrick's Day. However, this was almost immediately broken and a second pursuivant had to be sent.[223] At the same time as these attacks on the

---

[216] Ibid. 151, no. 74; 152, nos 30, 54.
[217] Ibid. 153, no. 60.
[218] Perrot, *Chronicle of Ireland*, 65–7; APC, xix. 361–2.
[219] Perrot, *Chronicle of Ireland*, 67.
[220] BL Add. 12503, fo. 396; ULC Kk 1 15 no. 5, fos 16–17.
[221] PRO SP 63/158, no. 47.
[222] Lambeth, Carew 605, fo. 178.
[223] PRO SP 63/161, no. 44.

earl, an important event took place which caused the struggle for power in Tyrone to enter its third and final phase. This phase saw the re-emergence of Tirconnell under the leadership of Hugh Roe O'Donnell. Turlough Luineach was now hemmed in and at the mercy of his opponents. Eventually in May 1593 Turlough Luineach was forced into an agreement, whereby he was 'pensioned off'.

Hugh Roe O'Donnell escaped from Dublin Castle at the beginning of 1592, ironically in the company of Henry and Art MacShane. O'Donnell returned safely to Tirconnell with assistance from Feagh MacHugh O'Byrne and then Hugh O'Neill. The MacShanes were not so lucky. Art died in Glenmalure. The standard Gaelic source recorded the cause of his death as exposure but his cousin, Lachlan MacLean, claimed that he had been murdered. Henry managed to return to Ulster, only to be imprisoned by Hugh O'Neill for the duration of the Nine Years War.[224] In Tirconnell, Hugh Roe took the O'Donnell title and asserted control over much of the lordship. Turlough Luineach responded by recruiting two companies of English mercenaries from the Pale for his defence. Subsequently, Hugh Roe mounted a series of raids on western Tyrone. In his biography of Hugh Roe, Ó Cléirigh relates that on one such expedition O'Donnell burned the town of Strabane and besieged Turlough and his mercenaries in the castle. On the other hand, Fitzwilliam asserted that the raids were relatively harmless and that Hugh Roe was not always victorious.[225] Turlough Luineach was also attacked from the East by Hugh O'Neill and complained to the lord deputy of 'far greater preys and spoils taken from him by the earl than heretofore has been on either side'.[226] In July the government was trying to pacify the quarrel between Turlough Luineach and Hugh O'Neill but it is interesting to note that on this occasion a truce was arranged by 'commissioners specially chosen by themselves' with each party represented by a principal follower and a lawyer from the Pale.[227]

To believe Lughaidh Ó Cléirigh would be to assert that Hugh Roe O'Donnell was solely responsible for the reduction of Turlough Luineach. It is more reasonable to say that his power was the deciding factor. In the second half of 1592, O'Donnell gained control of the dissidents in Tirconnell who had previously been allied with Turlough. Then in January 1593 O'Donnell began attacking Turlough from his base at Lifford. Ó Cléirigh claims that this onslaught forced Turlough to surrender the O'Neill title to the earl. In actual fact Hugh did not acquire the title until Turlough's death in 1595.[228] Ó Cléirigh's propaganda is balanced by the information which government papers provide on Hugh O'Neill's role in Turlough's downfall. In the early months of 1593, the earl also mounted attacks on western Tyrone.[229] By this stage he had won over O'Cahan and Maguire, Turlough's *uirríthe*, and the Sliocht Art within western Tyrone itself.[230] Crucially, Art MacTurlough defected from his father and entered into

[224] CSPI, iv. 518; *Life*, i. 13–33; *CSP. Scot.* xi. 558; C, *Carew*, iii. 94.
[225] *Life*, i. 39–49: CSPI, iv. 518.
[226] CSPI, iv. 522.
[227] PRO SP 63/166, no. 32: CSPI, iv. 568–9.
[228] *Life*, i. 53–9.
[229] APC, xxiv. 190.
[230] PRO SP 63/170, nos 11, 23(18).

an agreement with Hugh O'Neill, which presumably related to demesne lands. Pending negotiations, a truce came into operation under which Turlough agreed to disband his two companies of mercenaries.[231] Finally at the start of May 1593 an agreement was reached whereby Turlough surrendered the government of the whole lordship to Hugh in exchange for an annual pension of £2,000.[232]

On 28 June a further agreement between the earl of Tyrone and Turlough Luineach was made before the lord deputy and council. This was surely a ratification of the treaty already made between the parties to provide the window-dressing of government consent. Indeed, the earl had already dismissed the lord deputy and councillors as 'intermeddlers' in their wish to investigate the circumstances of the agreement.[233] The formal ratification has, however, preserved the agreement for posterity. Under its terms, Turlough was alloted a pension of £2,000 *per annum*, made up of the government allowance for the earl's horseband, the rents and duties of Maguire and the rest in cattle. Turlough was granted the town of Strabane and the surrounding district, and the tribute of O'Doherty. Arbitrators were appointed to examine Turlough's demand for a larger pension and to resolve the land disputes between himself and his son, Art. Hugh O'Neill offered to protect Turlough from the ravages of O'Donnell and to obtain the restitution of any goods stolen by him. Turlough was to receive rent arrears out of the lands of the Sliocht Art and out of Fermanagh and Oidhneacht-Uí-Chatháin. Finally, Turlough surrendered all outstanding claims to the lordship of Tyrone, holding only his demesne lands which henceforth were to contribute *pro rata* as other territories in the lordship to Hugh O'Neill.[234] This was a solemn agreement, but in the light of the interim settlement of 1585 which Hugh O'Neill failed to honour, it is questionable whether Turlough ever received the pension due to him.

In summary, the rise of Hugh O'Neill was not exceptional. The succession crisis which convulsed Tyrone in these years was a normative process in the politics of a Gaelic lordship. The limits of eligibility were set by tradition but success was determined by the power of connection. In spite of the seniority of Turlough Breasalach and the popularity of the MacShanes, Hugh O'Neill was always the prime candidate. The connections of various sorts which he had established with Irish and English alike were unmatched by his rivals. Such connections brought influence, military support and ultimately power. Hugh used this power in a ruthless fashion to remove his competitors and opponents within the lordship. Certainly, the backing of the government helped Hugh establish a base for himself in eastern Tyrone, but this support decreased over the years and ceased altogether in 1587. Government intervention – by the containment of the MacShanes and the confinement of Hugh Roe O'Donnell – delayed but could not prevent the final outcome. However much the crown wished to prevent the paramountcy of Hugh O'Neill, it could not bring itself to accord any support to the MacShanes who were regarded as atavistic and

---

[231] Ibid. 169, no. 23(18).
[232] Ibid. no. 49(1); 170, no. 23(19).
[233] *CSPI*, v. 100.
[234] C, *Carew*, iii. 74–5.

unmanageable. Furthermore, its officials were susceptible to bribery. In fact, the political situation in Tirconnell was a more important determinant in the outcome of the succession crisis than the actions of the crown. Finally, although Hugh O'Neill was anxious to obtain the status of earl, it must be seen in terms of government recognition. Actual power within Tyrone rested with Gaelic institutions which Irish and English alike regarded as sovereign and which Hugh O'Neill was equally anxious to maintain.

6

The Realignment of Tirconnell

In the last two decades of the sixteenth century a profound change took place in Ulster politics. For generations the lordship of Tirconnell, ruled by the O'Donnell family, had opposed the hegemony of the O'Neills. In this situation, the O'Donnells were the natural allies of the Dublin government in the North. This alliance remained a basic fact of Irish political life for most of the sixteenth century. The only aberration from the pattern had been the brief existence of the Geraldine League under Manus O'Donnell in the late 1530s. However, in the Nine Years War the O'Donnells were aligned on a permanent basis with the O'Neills, their traditional enemies, against the state. Two reasons can be given for this development. The high level of government interference, in the form of spasmodic military incursions, onerous exactions and unprovoked kidnappings, served to alienate the O'Donnells from their natural ally. Furthermore, a dynastic marriage alliance of seminal importance was arranged between the ruling branch of the O'Donnells and the earl of Tyrone. These novel developments formed a backdrop to a more normal preoccupation for Tirconnell's nobility – a struggle for succession within their ranks. In this, Hugh Roe came to power in spite of the political interference of the state.[1]

Tirconnell, situated on the north-western seaboard of Ireland, was the second most powerful lordship in Ulster. Although the Laggan district on the banks of the Foyle contained some of the most fertile land in Ireland, the lordship consisted largely of mountainous terrain.[2] The long coastline more than compensated for this rocky land-mass and made possible strong trading links with Britain and the Continent.[3] In 1560 O'Donnell was described as 'the best lord of fish in Ireland, and he exchangeth fish always with foreign merchants for wine by which [he] is called in other countries the king of fish'.[4] Contemporary Irish writers divided Tirconnell into two geographical regions. Barnesmore was the dividing point: references were made to places situated east or west of this mountain.[5] To the modern scholar a more obvious division would be the upland region of the western seaboard, occupied in the sixteenth century by the Mac-Sweenys, O'Boyles and the O'Freels, and the lowland districts, occupied by the O'Donnells. Given the paucity of primary source material, it is a difficult task to obtain a clear picture of the internal organisation of Tirconnell.

---

1 M. Walsh, 'Destruction by peace', 208; Bradshaw, 'Manus "the magnificent" ', 30–2; PRO SP 63/177, no. 48(1).
2 An excellent guide to the topography of the region is provided by Brian Lacy et al., Archaeological survey of county Donegal, Lifford 1983.
3 PRO SP 63/41, no. 86; 166, no. 20(1). R. J. Hunter of the University of Ulster is currently working on the trade links between Tirconnell and Bristol.
4 C, Carew, i. 308.
5 LCS, pp. xxxiii: AFM, vi. 1927–9.

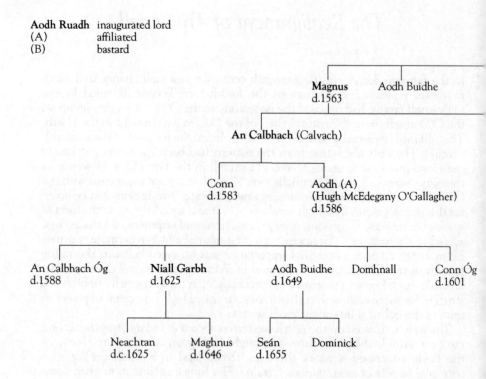

Aodh Ruadh inaugurated lord
(A) affiliated
(B) bastard

Magnus   Aodh Buidhe
d.1563

An Calbhach (Calvach)

Conn   Aodh (A)
d.1583   (Hugh McEdegany O'Gallagher)
d.1586

An Calbhach Óg   **Niall Garbh**   Aodh Buidhe   Domhnall   Conn Óg
d.1588   d.1625   d.1649   d.1601

Neachtan   Maghnus   Seán   Dominick
d.c.1625   d.1646   d.1655

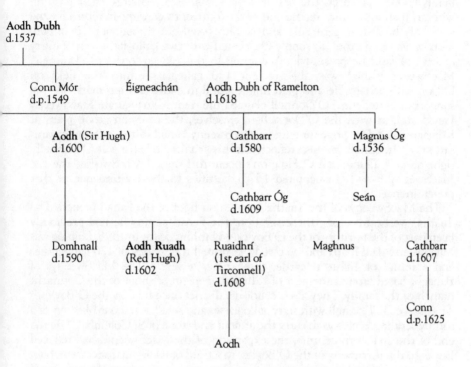

Aodh Dubh
d.1537

Conn Mór
d.p.1549

Éigneachán

Aodh Dubh of Ramelton
d.1618

Aodh (Sir Hugh)
d.1600

Cathbarr
d.1580

Magnus Óg
d.1536

Cathbarr Óg
d.1609

Seán

Domhnall
d.1590

Aodh Ruadh
(Red Hugh)
d.1602

Ruaidhrí
(1st earl of
Tirconnell)
d.1608

Maghnus

Cathbarr
d.1607

Conn
d.p.1625

Aodh

The galloglass family, the MacSweenys, played a more independent and far more influential role in Tirconnell than their equivalents in other Gaelic lordships. The MacSweenys of Fanad represented the senior branch of the family.[6] They had been the first galloglass family to regularise their position with an Irish lord. Towards the end of the fourteenth century, in return for the grant of the Fanad peninsula and certain privileges throughout Tirconnell, MacSweeny undertook to supply O'Donnell with two galloglasses out of every quarter of land he possessed.[7] According to the 'old customs of O'Donnell', MacSweeny Fanad was able to put 120 galloglasses into the field on O'Donnell's behalf. He also paid him a rental in cattle and ten marks for the support of bonnaghts.[8] O'Donnell claimed the right to inaugurate MacSweeny Fanad and, as with the O'Donnells themselves, the ceremony took place at Kilmacrenan.[9] The pre-eminence of MacSweeny Fanad in the internal organisation of Tirconnell was also reflected in his privilege of sitting at O'Donnell's right hand.[10] Tadhg Dall Ó Huiginn's poem to Donnell MacSweeny, the last MacSweeny Fanad (inaugurated 1570), testifies to the continuance of that pre-eminence.[11]

The MacSweenys of the Tuatha were an offshoot of the Fanad branch. The Tuatha, westwards along the coast from the Fanad peninsula, had previously been part of the territory of the O'Boyles.[12] Until his death in 1596, Éoin óg was MacSweeny na dTuath and he owed O'Donnell the service of 120 galloglasses and a rental of eighteen cattle, three times a year.[13] The MacSweenys of Banagh, based around the port of Killibegs, were an offshoot of the Connacht branch of the family. They also occupied a district once held by the O'Boyles.[14] They served O'Donnell with sixty galloglasses and acted as standard-bearers of a sort by sending 'a person to carry the armour and stone of St Columba'.[15] By the end of the sixteenth century, the expansion of the MacSweenys had reduced Boylagh, the patrimony of the O'Boyles, to a third of its original size; to such an extent that O'Donnell now received an exiguous revenue from the territory.[16] The MacSweenys, on account of their military strength, had a strong voice in the succession to the O'Donnell title. Factions within the various branches tended to support different contenders. One faction of the MacSweenys of Fanad supported the descendants of Calvach O'Donnell and as a result they no longer resided in the peninsula but along the margins of Lough Foyle.[17] The

---

6 LCS, pp. xx–xxi.
7 Ibid. 43–5; Hayes-McCoy, Scots mercenary forces, 32.
8 RIA, Miscellaneous O'Donovan MS, labelled 'Ordnance Survey, Ireland', 14/B/7 (strongroom). This is John O'Donovan's translation of an Irish document now held as ULC, Add. 2766 (20) (7), fos 4–8, which is itself a later copy of an early seventeenth-century manuscript.
9 LCS, 51.
10 Ibid. 43–5.
11 Ibid. pp. xxx–xxxi; Knott, The bardic poems of Tadhg Dall Ó Huiginn, i. 130–4.
12 LCS, p. xxxiii.
13 Ibid. p. xxxv; RIA, Miscellaneous O'Donovan MS, 14/B/7.
14 LCS, pp. xxxvii–xl.
15 RIA, Miscellaneous O'Donovan MS, 14/B/7. St Columba or Columcille (c. 521–97) was patron saint of the O'Donnells.
16 Ibid.
17 AFM, v. 1767; vi. 1929.

MacSweenys of Banagh provide another example. In 1588 Donough Mac-Sweeny returned from exile under Turlough Luineach O'Neill. He defeated and killed MacSweeny Banagh in battle and acquired the title himself. This represented a victory for the opponents of the ruling O'Donnell.[18]

The church occupied an anomalous position in the political structure of Tirconnell. Manus (O'Donnell 1537–63) was the first lord to impose bonnaght and other exactions on churchlands.[19] However, the bishops of Raphoe retained considerable independence, especially under Calvach (O'Donnell 1563–66) and his brother Hugh (O'Donnell 1566–92) who were relatively weak lords. Art MacPhelim O'Gallagher as bishop of Raphoe had his own horse company and actually fought battles against Calvach. His successor, Donnell MacGonigle, obtained a letter from Lord Deputy Sidney in the hope of making the lands of his bishopric immune from secular encroachment and taxation.[20] This may have been the result of the dispute between Hugh O'Donnell and the church in 1577 over the levying of tribute payable to the crown.[21] The bishops of Raphoe were also important brokers in any succession crisis as witnessed by Art's warlike stance and the mention of bishops at the election of Hugh O'Donnell in 1567.[22] By contrast, termon and erenagh lands were firmly under secular control. These territories were usually situated where land was of marginal value or where buffer zones were required with other lordships. According to the recollections of Hugh Roe's steward in 1620, the termon of Kilmacrenan gave O'Donnell twenty-four measures of butter and forty measures of meal four times a year whilst the Termon of Derry paid eighteen cattle.[23] The O'Freels, as erenaghs of Kilmacrenan, performed the inauguration of O'Donnell.[24]

The subdivisions of Tirconnell under the direct control of the O'Donnells and the rents due from them were detailed by Donnell O'Gallagher and Tadhg MacLinchy in the 1620s. The land in each territory was divided into quarters and out of each a number of garments were paid. For instance, Tirenda provided forty-two coats out of each of its thirty quarters. Unlike the other districts, Tir Breasil paid a mark per quarter. In addition, O'Donnell received from each quarter of land two measures of butter in peacetime and three in wartime.[25] The items rendered in kind would have been either consumed by O'Donnell's household and army or would have been used as commodities to exchange for foreign luxuries.

No evidence exists to determine the location of the mensal lands of O'Donnell. However, since Tirhugh is not mentioned as paying rents to O'Donnell and Donegal town was described by Lord Deputy Fitzwilliam as 'the ancient and chief house of the O'Donnells', the *Lucht Tighe Uí Dhomhnaill* must

18 Ibid. v. 1865–7.
19 Hayes-McCoy, *Irish battles*, London 1969, 86.
20 BL Add. 4797, fos 39–40; Aubrey Gwynn, *The medieval province of Armagh*, Dundalk 1946, 206–9.
21 PRO SP 63/79, no. 4.
22 Sidney, 'Memoir' (1855), 93.
23 RIA, Miscellaneous O'Donovan MS, 14/B/7.
24 AFM, vi. 1929.
25 RIA, Miscellaneous O'Donovan MS, 14/B/7.

have been located in this area.[26] Moreover, although the Laggan district was the most fertile part of the lordship, it was continually subject to the attacks and ravages of the O'Neills.[27] Little is known about the household families of the O'Donnells. Tadhg MacLinchy served as Hugh Roe's steward and it can be assumed that his family possessed a hereditary right to the post.[28] The O'Gallaghers were another household family. They lived in the southern part of Tirhugh and had Ballyshannon as their 'chief house'.[29] During the rule of Hugh O'Donnell, the head of the family was Eoin. He was granted a pension in 1574 and knighted in 1581; facts which testify to his good relationship with the Dublin government.[30] Sir Eoin's influence on the direction of affairs in Tirconnell is evidenced by his description in 1579 as O'Donnell's 'word and deed'.[31] He had married the widow of Matthew O'Neill and was therefore the stepfather of the second earl of Tyrone.[32] The O'Gallaghers had strong ecclesiastical connections. The family dominated the diocese of Raphoe, supplying many of its bishops and deans. Likewise, Redmond O'Gallagher, apparently unrelated to the senior sept, served as bishop of Derry between 1569 and 1601.[33] A reference to 'Seneschal McGonnell' in a 1601 document suggests that the MacGonigle family also performed both household and ecclesiastical functions within the lordship.[34] The Mac an Bhaird and Ó Cléirigh families held household lands in return for service. In their respective roles as poets and historians, they supplied propaganda to support the claims of the ruling sept of the O'Donnell family.[35]

Our knowledge of Tirconnell's internal structure is scanty in comparsion to information detailing its relations with neighbouring lordships. The O'Neills claimed suzerainty over Tirconnell but their claims were only occasionally effective in the Elizabethan period.[36] During his imprisonment of Calvach O'Donnell, Shane O'Neill held Tirconnell in subjection.[37] In 1579 Turlough Luineach O'Neill and his allies invaded Tirconnell and made the extraordinary demand upon O'Donnell that 'I should forsake my prince and help defend Ireland against Englishmen'. Hugh O'Donnell ignored this rhetoric and secured a six week truce by giving a 'buying' of 800 marks rather than enter into a

---

26 CSPI, iv. 94.

27 NLI MS 669, fos 50–1.

28 RIA, Miscellaneous O'Donovan MS, 14/B/7.

29 PRO SP 63/205, no. 31.

30 Paul Walsh, 'The septs of Muintear Ghallchubhair', Irish Book Lover, xxvii (1940), 194. In his capacity as governor of Ulster, the first earl of Essex had granted O'Gallagher a daily pension of 5s Irish. When he demanded payment in 1581, he received £420 7s 6d sterling. The treasury did not have the requisite amount, therefore a merchant was detailed to pay Sir Eoin and then sent to London with the bill: PRO SP 63/85, no. 64.

31 Walsingham letter-book, 223.

32 PRO SP 63/145, no. 16.

33 Gwynn, The medieval province of Armagh, 197–209; Walsh, 'Septs of Muintear Ghallchubhair', 197–200.

34 CSPI, x. 278; AFM, vi. 1879.

35 Fiants, 18th report, no. 6761; Life, ii. 4; Colm Ó Lochlainn (ed.), Irish chiefs and leaders: studies by Father Paul Walsh, Dublin 1960, ch. xi.

36 Ó Doibhlin, 'Ceart Ui Neill', 327–8.

37 AFM, v. 1587.

dependent relationship with the traditional enemy.[38] In 1555 and again in 1560 Calvach O'Donnell had voluntarily subjected Tirconnell to the overlordship of MacCailin Mór, the earl of Argyll. However, this seems to have been a temporary arrangement by which Calvach obtained military aid initially against his father, Manus, and later against Shane O'Neill.[39] In its own right, Tirconnell claimed overlordship in Ulster and Connacht.[40] Although the prosperous period in Tirconnell's history at turn of the fifteenth century lent some credibility to these claims, during the rules of Calvach and Hugh they were largely chimerical.[41]

In the time of Hugh O'Donnell, Tirconnell exerted influence over two other Ulster lordships. In 1589 Hugh Maguire not only received military support from Hugh's son, Donnell O'Donnell, but was actually inaugurated as lord of Fermanagh by him.[42] The right of inauguration was one of the most important aspects of overlordship and in this case it renewed O'Donnell interest in Fermanagh which had been lost to the O'Neills since the early 1560s. Yet, this account from the Four Masters conveniently ignores the important role played by Hugh O'Neill in setting up the new Maguire for which evidence exists in the state papers.[43] Whilst O'Donnell power in Fermanagh was marginal, in Inishowen it was paramount. This peninsula, originally the home of the O'Neills, had been taken over by the O'Dohertys in the course of the Late Middle Ages after they themselves had lost out to the O'Donnells in the contest for the control of Tirconnell.[44] A *treatise of Ireland* recorded that: 'it is governed by a captain named O'Doherty who being not able to defend himself is forced to contribute to O'Donnell and O'Neill *alterius vicibus*. His country lying upon the sea near the Isles Islay and Jura of Scotland is continually invaded from thence and he thereby forced to be at their pleasure'.[45] The O'Neills disputed O'Donnell claims to overlordship in the area. However, the state-sponsored agreement between them in 1544, which was renewed forty years later, had placed Inishowen within the orbit of Tirconnell.[46] An arrangement existed whereby O'Doherty paid O'Donnell a rent of 120 cows a year and O'Neill sixty.[47] In wartime, the peninsula provided O'Donnell's army with sixty horsemen and 120 footsoldiers and 'entertained his bonnaghts be they ever so numerous for the space of nine nights'.[48] It is also evident from the archives of the duke of Argyll that O'Doherty had an agreement with MacCailin Mór in the 1570s, whereby he received his protection against the depredations of the

[38] PRO SP 63/66, no. 50(2).
[39] *Highland papers*, ed. J. R. N. MacPhail, 4 vols, Edinburgh 1914–34, iv. 212–16.
[40] Ó Doibhlin, 'Ceart Uí Néill', 331–5; 'Agreement between Ó Domhnaill and Tadhg Ó Conchobhair concerning Sligo Castle (23 June 1539)', trans. Maura Carney, *IHS*, iii (1943), 282–96.
[41] Simms, 'Gaelic lordships', 609–21.
[42] AFM, vi. 1875–7.
[43] PRO SP 63/170, no. 11.
[44] Simms, 'Gaelic lordships', 501, 577.
[45] NLI MS 669, fos 50–1.
[46] 'Calendar of the Irish council book', 154–6, no. 273.
[47] RIA, Miscellaneous O'Donovan MS, 14/B/7; C, *Carew*, iii. 74.
[48] RIA, Miscellaneous O'Donovan MS, 14/B/7.

MacLeans and possibly other Scots Islanders.[49] A discourse of 1600 went so far as to describe O'Doherty as depending 'upon the Scots of Argyle'.[50]

In Connacht O'Donnell most frequently claimed authority over O'Connor Sligo. Sligo town was strategically placed – in Bingham's words, 'the key and door of Connacht' – and its continental trade meant that its customs duties were a major source of revenue.[51] The O'Donnell claim to overlordship at its fullest extent was represented by the agreement between O'Donnell and Tadhg O'Connor in 1539. According to this treaty, Sligo Castle was to be surrendered to O'Donnell on demand and it could be demolished by him if he saw fit. Tadhg O'Connor was to help O'Donnell to impose his lordship throughout Lower Connacht and was to maintain his bonnaghts when necessary. The lord of Sligo was to render to O'Donnell the king's cocket of his town and the quitrents of his country and was only to make war and peace with the permission of his overlord.[52] After this high point, the O'Donnells were unable to enforce their claims of overlordship on a regular basis. The annals of Loch Cé record raids into Connacht in 1561, 1571 and 1577, the last being a counterattack by O'Donnell after an attempt by O'Connor and MacDermot to capture the frontier stronghold of Bundrowes.[53] At the time of the Desmond war, we find O'Connor Sligo paying O'Donnell 300 head of cattle in 1579 and the overlord invading the area the following year when the agreement had presumably broken down.[54] Two poems by Tadhg Ó Huiginn show that Hugh O'Donnell did make expeditions into Connacht, but the first of these clearly reproaches him for his failure to subjugate the province.[55] During the succession crisis at the end of his lordship, Hugh O'Donnell did not interfere in the affairs of Connacht, although one of his opponents did. In 1582 Conn O'Donnell marched into the western province with a large force of Scots mercenaries and Irish kerne.[56] Conn's objectives were traditional though somewhat ambitious. Before he was forced to retreat to Ulster he reportedly told Robert Dillon that 'his predecessors had a tribute out of Connacht and he would not lose it, and that before his departure out of the province he would have all the pledges between Sligo and Limerick'.[57] Tirconnell's demands on Sligo over the years and the failure of the O'Connors to pay up led to the transfer of lands between the two lordships. In 1585 the survey for the establishment of the composition of Connacht found Cowrin Moygeny in the barony of Carbury 'now in the possession of O'Donnell'.[58]

Tirconnell had its most important external relationship with the Dublin

49 HMC 6th Report, 630.
50 CSPI, ix. 119.
51 Quoted in T. O'Rorke, The history of Sligo, town and county, 2 vols, Dublin 1889, i. 132.
52 'Agreement between Ó Domhnaill and Tadhg Ó Conchobhair', 282–92.
53 Hennessy, Annals of Loch Cé, ii. 381, 413, 415–19.
54 Walsingham letter-book, 225; Lambeth, Carew 619, fo. 46.
55 Knott, The bardic poems of Tadhg Dall O Huiginn, i. 7–18.
56 PRO SP 63/94, nos 15(2), 20.
57 Ibid. 94, no. 20. There is evidence to suggest that the Scots invasion of Connacht to support the Burkes in 1586 was also an attempt to collect O'Donnell's rents in the province: CSPI, iii. 161–2.
58 The compossicion booke of Conought, 126: CPCRI, ii. 127.

government. This old alliance had begun to assume a constitutional dimension in the early 1540s when Manus O'Donnell responded favourably to the 'surrender and regrant' initiative. However, these negotiations did not progress beyond the preliminary stage and the process of feudalisation was not finalised until the opening years of the seventeenth century.[59] In the interim, the parties occupied the respective positions of suzerain and vassal, formalised by an indentured agreement between Lord Deputy Sidney and Calvach O'Donnell in 1566. Under this, Calvach acknowledged the sovereignty of Queen Elizabeth and promised to pay her rents and risings-out.[60] Calvach died the same year after falling from his horse, without receiving letters patent which had been drawn up to make him earl of Tirconnell and baron of Lifford.[61] The following year the indentured agreement of 1566 was renewed when the government recognised the election of Hugh O'Donnell by appointing him captain of Tirconnell.[62] The crown had discovered a faithful servant in Sir Hugh O'Donnell. In 1567 he overthrew Shane O'Neill at the battle of Farsetmore; later he resisted the blandishments and threats of Turlough Luineach to join him in support of the earl of Desmond. It was Hugh Roe who later reminded the state of these actions on its behalf. It seemed to him that his father's services had been ignored and that the only repayment had been interference and devastation.[63] He submitted a full account of this interference in the document entitled *A note of such oppressions and indirect courses as hath been held in Tirconnell and other places.*[64]

The early 'oppressions' cannot in fairness be considered as such. In 1577 Tirconnell was forced to honour its agreement with the government by paying rent arrears. The assessment was undertaken by the earl of Tyrone and the collection by Thomas Fleming with the tacit agreement of Sir Hugh O'Donnell. Lord Deputy Sidney put the amount levied at £1,200. The O'Donnells later complained that the sum totalled £3,200; clearly those involved had taken hefty commissions.[65] Later at the start of the 1580s when Turlough Luineach was strong and inflicting heavy losses on Tirconnell, Sir Hugh procured the services of Captain Mince and two hundred troops from the government. However, the upkeep of the soldiers and the cattle raids, which they carried out in Inishowen, caused great hardship. After an appeal to Lord Deputy Grey, the contingent was withdrawn.[66] By contrast, the subsequent interventions took place without the co-operation of O'Donnell and on a far grander scale.

Between 1584 and 1592 Tirconnell found itself a microcosm for two conflicting modes of government. Perrot's approach was public-spirited but frequently

[59] Bradshaw, 'Manus "the magnificent" ', 32–3; *Irish patent rolls of James I: a facsimile of the Irish Record Commissioners' calendar prepared prior to 1830*, intro. M. C. Griffith, Dublin 1966, 13. In 1603/4 James I granted Rory O'Donnell the earldom of Tirconnell and letters patent to the lordship.
[60] C, *Carew*, i. 373–5.
[61] PRO SP 63/20, no. 13; Ulster Museum, acc. no. 282 1913 (Charter creating Calvach O'Donnell earl of Tirconnell and baron of Lifford).
[62] Fiants, 11th Report, no. 1021.
[63] ULC Kk 1 15 no. 63, fos 152–3.
[64] PRO SP 63/177, no. 48(1).
[65] Ibid. 79, no. 4; 177, no. 48(1); Sidney, 'Memoir' (1854), 40.
[66] PRO SP 63/101, no. 43; 177, no. 48(1).

ill-conceived; Fitzwilliam's was short-term with an eye to profit. Both proved counter-productive. The garrisons, which they placed in Tirconnell with quite distinct objectives, became freebooting operations under the respective captains. In 1584, Hugh O'Donnell agreed, against his will, to take two hundred troops under Perrot's composition scheme which was intended 'for the maintenance of both lords and people in awe to be obedient to this government and for defence against the invasion of Scots'.[67] The composition force, commanded by Captain Bowen, took hostages to force the local population to pay for its upkeep. It plundered the countryside with the assistance of Turlough Luineach O'Neill and captured and ransomed a number of important individuals.[68] The MacSweenys and Manus óg O'Donnell opposed these depredations. Eventually, the earl of Tyrone and Sir Edward Moore negotiated the payment and withdrawal of the troops.[69] In 1588 Perrot appointed William Mostian as sheriff of Tirconnell. In a short space, Mostian and his brother, Hugh, carried out eight cattle raids. More significantly, they were responsible for the ransacking of the Donegal Abbey and the murder of its guardian, Brother Tadhg O'Boyle.[70] Next on the list of government-backed desperadoes was John Connill. He had allegedly given Fitzwilliam a bribe of two gold chains salvaged from the Armada to obtain the rank of captain and charge of Tirconnell. This captain assisted the opponents of O'Donnell within the lordship and ravaged the countryside. By offering to pay his maintenance, O'Donnell tried to win over Connill but the accommodation was short-lived. Connill was then joined by Captain Humphrey Willis and a force of two hundred soldiers sent by Fitzwilliam. The O'Donnells recalled that no sooner had Willis entered Tirconnell than 'he took upon him the whole rule thereof, banished O'Donnell, took his followers and did what he pleased, so as in very short space, by preying and spoiling the same, that he damaged it to the value of four thousand pounds sterling'.[71] Not surprisingly, these indiscriminate attacks by English soldiery made the prospect of royal government unpopular in Tirconnell.

Further meddling was evident in the government's attempt to detach the lords whom O'Donnell claimed as *uirríthe*. In 1568 O'Connor Sligo surrendered his lands to the queen.[72] Almost immediately O'Donnell lodged an objection to this development because it entailed the loss of his rents out of the territory.[73] In 1576 Lord Deputy Sidney examined the case. He found that O'Donnell and 'his ancestors have had a rent of 300 marks yearly out of O'Connor Sligo's country fabulously challenged to have been paid since St. Patrick's days, but probably averred on both sides, that it has been taken these four or five descents by the O'Donnells, but never without violence alleged O'Connor, and so think I'. The lord deputy forced O'Donnell to suspend his exactions pending a

[67] Ibid. 112, nos 11, 23, 41(3).
[68] Ibid. 177, no. 48(1); BLO, Perrot 1, fos 193–4.
[69] PRO SP 63/123, no. 52; 177, no. 48(1); BLO, Perrot 1, fos 189–94; ibid. MS 30237, fo. 49.
[70] CSPI, iii. 513–14; PRO SP 63/177, no. 48(1): Donatus Moneyus, 'De Provincia Hiberniae S. Francisci', ed. Brendan Jennings, *Analecta Hibernica*, vi (1934), 48.
[71] Ibid. 177, no. 48(1).
[72] C, Carew, i. 375–6. The regrant of the lands was not finalised until 1584: Fiants, 15th Report, no. 4560.
[73] PRO SP 63/24, no. 9(5).

commission of inquiry, but in all likelihood this never sat. Here Sidney's intention was to free O'Connor from O'Donnell's control so that the state itself could extract a larger rent from Sligo.[74] O'Donnell's claims in Inishowen came under scrutiny the following decade. Sir Hugh had pointed out in 1579 that 'the revenue of O'Doherty was more to me than all the rest of Tirconnell' and six years later Inishowen was incorporated in the county of Donegal.[75] Then, on a visit to Dublin in 1588 Sir John O'Doherty surrendered his lordship and received a regrant of the territory. He agreed to the abolition of his Gaelic title and the payment of rents and services directly to the crown.[76] However, Inishowen's remoteness from the seat of government ensured O'Doherty's continuance as an *urrí* of O'Donnell and his participation in the succession crisis in the final years of Hugh O'Donnell's lordship.

The government interference in Tirconnell was facilitated by the feeble rule of Hugh O'Donnell and then exacerbated by the dissension within the ruling family during his old age. This dissension was caused by the intense rivalry between the contenders for Hugh O'Donnell's position as lord of Tirconnell. Each believed that he possessed 'the best right to the superiority of that country'. The competing parties were the sons of Hugh O'Donnell, the descendants of his predecessor and brother, Calvach, and Hugh Dubh O'Donnell, the uncle of the incumbent lord.[77] The title of O'Donnell remained the subject of awe and focus of authority within the lordship despite the frequent interventions of the state and its agents. When at one point O'Donnell was held captive by Captain Connill, it was Niall Garbh, one of his opponents, who rescued him.[78] Moreover, when Hugh Roe eventually attained his father's title, he informed the lord deputy that it was impossible to command the allegiance of the nobles of Tirconnell 'without the title of O'Donnell'.[79] Successful election to this title depended on the connections which the rival candidates possessed or could establish. The most important political connections – those formed by blood, fosterage and marriage – were with the household families and with the ruling families of other Gaelic lordships. The background to this succession struggle must be gleaned with care from a number of sources. We have the annalists of the early seventeenth century strongly favouring the incumbent sept. Of these annalists the most biased account is Lughaidh Ó Cleirigh's eulogistic biography known as *The Life of Aodh Ruadh Ó Domhnaill*. On the other hand, some of the most interesting insights are provided by Miler Magrath, who favoured the opponents of the leading sept. The rest of our information comes from scattered references in government papers.

Donnell O'Donnell was Sir Hugh's eldest son by his first wife.[80] The Four Masters praise his military skill but misrepresent his claim to the lordship: 'although this Donnell was not the rightful heir to his father, it would have

---

[74] Ibid. 55, no. 58.
[75] Ibid. 66, no. 50(7); *Inquisitionum in officio rotulorum cancellariae Hiberniae*, ii. p. xvii.
[76] Fiants, 16th Report, nos 5190, 5207.
[77] CSPI, iv. 498.
[78] PRO SP 63/177, no. 48(1).
[79] Ibid. 165, no. 6(2).
[80] CSPI, iv. 457.

been no disgrace to Tirconnell to have elected him as its chief'.[81] Donnell's powerbase was in Tirhugh in the southern part of the lordship and he was supported by O'Boyle and MacSweeny Banagh.[82] Lacking the support of his father, he was forced to rely upon the crown and Turlough Luineach O'Neill.[83] It was assumed in government circles that Donnell could command popular support in the country because he was the son of a local woman, whereas Hugh Roe, his half-brother, was the son of a foreigner, Ineen Dubh.

Ineen Dubh was the nickname of Finola, the daughter of James MacDonald and Agnes Campbell. She married Hugh O'Donnell in 1569 at the same time as her mother married Turlough Luineach O'Neill.[84] These two women, brought up at the court of the Stuarts, recruited most of the Scots mercenaries who served in Ireland.[85] O'Donnell gave his wife lands on the banks of Lough Foyle and fortified houses at Mongavlin and Carrigans.[86] Residence in this part of the lordship allowed her to retain close contact with her homeland. Therefore it is no surprise when the Four Masters inform us that Ineen Dubh maintained a bodyguard of Scottish auxiliaries.[87] This Scottish military presence and the reinforcements which she could call from Scotland more than compensated for any supposed lack of support in the country. Ineen Dubh bore Sir Hugh O'Donnell four male children.[88] It was the political acumen and powerful connections of Ineen Dubh that were to ensure the succession of Hugh Roe, her eldest son. She was able to play an increasingly important role in Tirconnell's affairs as the authority of her husband began to falter. In 1593 Miler Magrath gave a scathing description of her personality and political methods: 'a cruel bloody woman who has committed sundry murders'.[89]

Hugh Roe, the chosen heir of the incumbent lord, was born in 1572.[90] In an attempt to promote his cause, he had been fostered amongst the leading families not only of Tirconnell itself but also of neighbouring lordships. His biography provides the names of at least four fosterfathers; two potential supporters, O'Cahan and MacSweeny na dTuath, and two potential opponents, Conn MacCalvach O'Donnell and Hugh Dubh O'Donnell.[91] Hugh Roe had an important adherent in Sir Eoin O'Gallagher, his father's adviser.[92] Crucially, Hugh Roe had marriage connections with the most powerful contender for the lordship of Tyrone. By 1587 he was married or at least betrothed to Rose, the daughter of Hugh O'Neill, who had already Hugh Roe's half sister as his second wife.[93] Hugh's succession was also the subject of a old and popular prophecy.

81 AFM, iv. 1891–3.
82 Ibid. 1891.
83 CSPI, iv. 94–5; PRO SP 63/150, no. 27.
84 Hayes-McCoy, Scots mercenary forces, 106.
85 PRO SP 63/28, no. 10.
86 Ibid. 177, no. 48(1); CSPI, x. 278.
87 AFM, v. 1873.
88 Life, ii. 25–6.
89 PRO SP 63/170, no. 11.
90 BLO, MS 30237, fo. 51; Life, ii. 25–6.
91 Ibid. i. 3; ii. 215.
92 CSPI, iv. 93–4.
93 HMC Salisbury MSS, iii. 286; PRO SP 63/145, no. 16: Walsh, The will and family of Hugh O'Neill, 7–8, 36–7.

This foretold that if 'two Hughes lawfully, lineally and immediately succeed each other as O'Donnells, being formally and ceremoniously created, according to the country's custom, the last Hugh shall (forsooth) be a monarch in Ireland and quite banish thence all foreign nations and conquerors'.[94] It is probable that this prophecy attracted more attention after Hugh Roe's succession than before. In any case, Hugh was confronted by some resourceful and well-connected competitors from other septs of the O'Donnell family.

On the issue of succession the ruling sept was strongly opposed by the descendants of Calvach O'Donnell, lord of Tirconnell between 1563 and 1566. His eldest son, Conn, had been a hostage in the English Pale and needed 'no interpreter by reason of his good bringing up with that worthy knight Sir Thomas Cusake'.[95] Because of his civil education, the government in the early 1560s had held high hopes of his future loyalty.[96] However, the attitude of the government to the election of Calvach's brother, Hugh, drove Conn into the hands of Turlough Luineach O'Neill. Lord Deputy Sidney described the election and claimed to have promoted the settlement himself: 'this Conn looked to be captain of the country, but the bishops and other landlords of the same elected Sir Hugh to be O'Donnell. Whereupon there was great likelihood of great wars, which I quieted, establishing Hugh in the place of O'Donnell and gave unto Conn the castles of Lifford and Finn, and all the countries belonging to the same, being a good third part of all Tirconnell'.[97] On the other hand, Miler Magrath claimed that, since Calvach O'Donnell had been granted Tirconnell by letters patent, his descendants should have their benefit.[98] As a consequence of his failure to obtain the lordship, Conn was afterwards constantly at loggerheads with Hugh O'Donnell and frequently at war with him in alliance with Turlough O'Neill.[99] Conn O'Donnell had a number of sons, the most prominent of whom was Niall Garbh (born 1569).[100] In 1599 the sons of Conn still occupied the lands between the river Finn and Lough Swilly where their military capability was assessed at 150 footmen and thirty horsemen.[101]

Another competitor closely aligned with this sept was not an O'Donnell at all. This was Hugh O'Gallagher, son of the dean of Raphoe. At some point he had changed his patronymic, perhaps as a result of fosterage, to MacCalvach and had thereby become a competitor for the title of O'Donnell.[102] Nicholls has shown that the adoption of new surnames in this way was not an unusual practice.[103] Rather than follow Sir Eoin in supporting the ruling sept of the O'Donnells, a large faction of the O'Gallagher family backed the candidature of

---

94 PRO SP 63/170, no. 11; *Life*, i. 3–5.
95 'Calendar of the Irish council book', 154–6, no. 273; PRO SP 63/41, no. 86.
96 *CSPI*, i. 206.
97 Sidney, 'Memoir' (1855), 93.
98 *CSPI*, iv. 498.
99 PRO SP 63/48, no. 3; 79, no. 4: *CSPI*, ii. 167.
100 *Life*, ii. 23; *CPCRI*, ii. 584.
101 PRO SP 63/205, no. 31.
102 NLI MS 669 fos 50–1; AFM, v. 1869. This contender is also referred to as Hugh MacEdegany (Aodh Mac an Deagonaigh).
103 Nicholls, *Gaelic and gaelicised Ireland*, 77–9.

the dean's son.[104] In the late 1570s he was patronised by the crown and received the lease of church lands in Connacht.[105] After the death of Conn O'Donnell, Hugh was able to assume his political mantle and circle of support.[106]

Hugh Dubh O'Donnell possessed the longest-standing claim to the O'Donnell title. He was brother to Manus, who had been lord of Tirconnell in the middle decades of the sixteenth century, and uncle to his successors, Calvach and Hugh. He had in turn contested the election of each of these lords.[107] Miler Magrath was a staunch advocate of this claimant. He asserted that Hugh Dubh possessed the best right to the lordship, according to Brehon law, on account of his seniority within the family.[108] Hugh Dubh was based in the north of the lordship between the rivers Leannan and Swilly.[109] He held two castles at Cahir Anuske and Ramelton and lands in the territories of Gleann Eile and Tier McGuerin.[110] On the eve of the Plantation of Ulster, he still held twelve or thirteen quarters of Gleann Eile as demesne land and drew rents from the rest of the territory.[111] In 1593 Miler Magrath described Hugh Dubh as 'the most valiant and politic man in all that country' and showed that he had retained his position in spite of the attacks of Hugh O'Donnell. Hugh Dubh had, he asserted, never received the support which he deserved from the crown and was not likely to trust the government because of past deceptions.[112] Magrath claimed that Hugh Dubh was the most popular of the competitors for the lordship but other evidence indicates that the vital O'Gallagher family was accounted amongst his enemies.[113] In short, Hugh Dubh may have been a popular nobleman and the best qualified candidate in terms of Brehon law, but he lacked powerful connections in the lordship and beyond and the concomitant military backing to make a success of his candidature.

The succession crisis in Tirconnell lasted thirteen years. It went through a number of phases in which the fortunes of the various contenders fluctuated dramatically. The outcome of the struggle in Tirconnell, in comparison with the simultaneous one in Tyrone, was far more uncertain. Hugh Roe O'Donnell had considerable support within the lordship but the degree of external interference was very great. The lordship was subject to two sudden and effective interventions by crown government and the frequent presence of government troops. Turlough Luineach O'Neill, based nearby at Strabane, possessed great influence in Tirconnell and provided continual military support to the opponents of Hugh Roe. In spite of this heightened level of intervention, especially on the part of the crown, the conflict manifested itself as a normal Gaelic power-struggle which was settled by traditional means – main force.

The death of Cathbarr MacManus O'Donnell, *tánaiste* of Tirconnell and

---

104 AFM, vi. 1929.
105 Fiants, 13th Report, nos 3160, 3279.
106 AFM, v. 1873.
107 *Life*, ii. 197.
108 CSPI, iv. 498.
109 LCS, 126.
110 C, Carew, i. 375; CSPI, x. 277.
111 LCS, 126; CSPI, xiii. 342.
112 PRO SP 63/170, no. 11.
113 Ibid; C, *Carew*, i. 375.

brother of the ruling lord, in October 1580 signalled the beginning of the succession crisis.[114] Conn O'Donnell, well established in north-eastern Tirconnell, was now the principal contender to succeed Hugh O'Donnell. The Four Masters speak of 'great dissensions' between Conn and his uncle which led to Conn's defection to Turlough Luineach O'Neill and an end to the uneasy alliance between Tyrone and Tirconnell. As a result Conn and a dissident faction of Clann Sweeny of Fanad helped O'Neill inflict a major defeat on O'Donnell in the summer of 1581.[115] Afterwards the Irish council wrote that Conn O'Donnell 'is and hath ever been a dependent upon Turlough and in this last action was the only cause of the quarrel'.[116] In difficult straits, O'Donnell requested and received the support of the crown.[117] Malby marched into Tirconnell from Connacht and demolished Conn O'Donnell's castle at Lifford.[118] O'Donnell was given the assistance of 200 government soldiers.[119] These measures brought only a temporary respite. The next year Malby reported that 'Turlough Luineach hath utterly undone O'Donnell' and that there was no prospect of government aid on this occasion.[120] As a consequence, Conn O'Donnell was able to march the length of Tirconnell and mount a large-scale raid on north Connacht. A pledge and a promise of rent from O'Connor Sligo was adjudged insufficient and as a result Conn burned Sligo town and surrounding countryside before returning to Ulster.[121] According to Malby 'his men do call him no other than O'Donnell at every word and he said to Dillon that he would be O'Donnell in spite of all the World'.[122] Luckily for the ruling sept of the O'Donnells, Conn died in March the following year.[123]

The position of Hugh O'Donnell and his chosen successor, Hugh Roe, improved in the two years after Conn O'Donnell's death. Some military success was achieved against Turlough Luineach.[124] In 1584 Hugh Roe undertook his first military action at the age of twelve years when he participated with O'Gallagher in an attack on Breiffny O'Rourke.[125] This stability was soon upset by the arrival of the composition troops under Captain Bowen. O'Donnell placed these troops in the castles of Derry, Finn and Mongavlin so that they could take up their supplies from the surrounding countryside. However, Bowen intrigued with Turlough Luineach and then handed the castles over to Hugh O'Gallagher. The dean's son was now a serious challenger for the O'Donnell title.[126] Furthermore, Sir John O'Doherty was in opposition to O'Donnell, no

---

114 AFM, v. 1725.
115 Ibid. 1767–9.
116 PRO SP 63/85, no. 7.
117 Lambeth, Carew 619, fo. 40.
118 Hennessy, Annals of Loch Cé, ii. 441.
119 PRO SP 63/177, no. 48(1).
120 Ibid. 94, no. 20.
121 Ibid. nos 15(2), 20.
122 Ibid. no. 20.
123 AFM, v. 1793.
124 Ibid. 1811–13.
125 Hennessy, Annals of Loch Cé, ii. 459. Waterhouse's copy of A Treatise of Ireland (BLO, MS 30237, fo. 51) stated in 1586 that Hugh Roe was 'able to carry weapon'.
126 BLO, MS 30237, fos 50–1; ULC Kk 1 15 no. 63, fos 152–3.

doubt in an attempt to free himself from th overlordship of Tirconnell.[127] Only the expulsion of the composition troops and the support of Scots mercenaries permitted O'Donnell to move against this opposition in 1586.[128] To rid himself of the composition troops permanently, O'Donnell promised the government that he would pay annual rents and give Rory, brother to Hugh Roe, and the eldest sons of MacSweenys Fanad and na dTuath as pledges.[129] At the same time, the position of Hugh Roe was consolidated by matching him in marriage to a daughter of Hugh O'Neill, the earl of Tyrone. Hugh Roe had clearly become a focus of authority within Tirconnell; Hugh O'Neill described him as 'the stay that his father had for the quieting of his inhabitance'.[130] The government in Dublin now saw the situation in Tirconnell as a danger to its entire Ulster policy. Waterhouse's copy of *A treatise of Ireland* warned that the state must not permit Hugh Roe to succeed his father; that instead it should ensure the succession of 'Hugh Dubh O'Donnell or some of that name of known loyalty'.[131]

In September 1587 Hugh Roe O'Donnell was imprisoned in Dublin Castle along with the eldest sons of MacSweenys Fanad and na dTuath and a son of O'Gallagher. Lord Deputy Perrot had sent a ship from Dublin to Rathmullan where Hugh Roe and his companions had been lured on board to drink wine.[132] This mission had been planned some months beforehand and had been executed whilst Sir Hugh O'Donnell was in conference with the lord deputy.[133] The operation was carried out by Nicholas Barnes, captain of the *Matthew* of Dublin, who received a reward of £100 sterling for 'his industry and policy'.[134] The lord deputy had ordered the action because of O'Donnell's reluctance to give the promised rents and pledges and because of his encouragement of the activities of the Scots and the MacSweenys. More importantly, Perrot regarded the marriage alliance between the ruling sept of the O'Donnells and the earl of Tyrone as detrimental to crown policy in the North.[135] Clearly this action was motivated *raison d'état*. The complaints of Hugh Roe O'Donnell and Hugh O'Neill on this issue received a sharp rebuttal from the peace commissioners in 1596: 'yet all princes in policy may and do use to take their subjects in pledge for the good peace of their countries and you both do use the like and therefore should less dislike that course'.[136]

---

[127] PRO SP 63/124, no. 14.
[128] Ibid; BLO, Perrot 1, fos 237–8.
[129] PRO SP 63/125, no. 14.
[130] Ibid. 132, no. 30.
[131] BLO, MS 30237 fo. 51.
[132] HMC *Salisbury* MSS, iii. 285–6; Hennessy, *Annals of Loch Cé*, ii. 483. In July 1594 Hugh Roe O'Donnell, Hugh Maguire and Brian óg O'Rourke were carousing on board two ships (one from Bristol and one from Dundalk) anchored at Ballyshannon. Sir George Bingham sailed up from Connacht and demanded that the captains hand over their guests but the request was refused. After the stratagem of 1587, one might have expected the abandonment of this practice by the Gaelic lords, especially O'Donnell: PRO SP 63/175, no. 35(8).
[133] CSPI, iii. 338–9; PRO SP 63/177, no. 48(1).
[134] 'Reports on manuscripts in the Bodleian Library, Oxford', ed. Charles McNeill, *Analecta Hibernica*, i (1930), 97.
[135] HMC *Salisbury* MSS, iii. 285–6.
[136] ULC Kk 1 15 no. 63 fo. 140.

The kidnapping of Hugh Roe O'Donnell was a disaster for his parents and their supporters. Ó Cléirigh insists that O'Donnell lost all control over developments within his lordship: 'there had sprung up fierce disputes and discords among themselves, so that they were not submissive to their prince as they should be, for he was an aged man then, and he was not able to unite his people or to secure their hostages or pledges since he [Hugh Roe] had been captured, and moreover age lay heavy upon him before he was still old'.[137] A poem by Maolmuire Mac Con Uladh Mheic an Bhaird addressed to Hugh Roe in captivity is particularly instructive. A deep sense of betrayal has been provoked by the high-handed action of the Dublin government: 'More so than any of the noble hound-loving race of Criomhthann, the descendants of Connall have ever refrained from casting even a shot at an Englishman.' Although the poet hopes that imprisonment is having a moderating effect on Hugh Roe's youthful arrogance, Tirconnell nevertheless stands in dire need of his leadership. It has been consumed by war and strife; learned men have been evicted from their inheritances; retainers have been scattered throughout Ireland; all classes have suffered.[138] It is quite clear that there had been a breakdown of seigneurial control in Tirconnell – in the mid-1590s Hugh Roe was still trying to secure the return of the many tenants who had fled into Connacht.[139]

The first beneficiary of the new situation was Hugh O'Gallagher, alias Hugh MacCalvach. In 1586 he had assisted in the killing of Alexander MacSorley MacDonald and it was probably as a consequence of this that he received a pension from the crown.[140] In the spring of 1587 he travelled to Court where he won the commendation of the crown not only for himself but also for his allies, Sir John O'Doherty and Donough MacSweeny.[141] In addition to the indulgence of the crown, Hugh O'Gallagher had the support of Turlough Luineach and the sons of Conn O'Donnell.[142] On the other hand, Hugh O'Neill regarded the dean's son as an imposter in the succession dispute because he had changed his surname.[143] After the capture of Hugh Roe, Hugh O'Gallagher enjoyed considerable success. The earl of Tyrone claimed: 'as for O'Donnell, he is almost driven out of his country, the same made waste by Hugh McEdegany [O'Gallagher] having the aid of Turlough's people and soldiers'.[144] With the assistance of Art MacTurlough O'Neill, O'Gallagher raided the Tirhugh district; about the same time his ally Donough MacSweeny established himself in Banagh.[145] In April 1588 O'Gallagher led the forces of Turlough Luineach and his allies to victory over the earl of Tyrone at Carricklea.[146] However, this

---

[137] Life, i. 33.
[138] Padraig Breatnach (ed.), 'Select document xl: an address to Aodh Ruadh Ó Domhnaill in captivity, 1590', IHS, xxv (1986), 198–213.
[139] PRO SP 63/178, no. 36(4).
[140] Walsh, 'Septs of Muintear Ghallchubhair', 199.
[141] APC, xv. 20–1.
[142] AFM, v. 1873.
[143] PRO SP 63/132, no. 30.
[144] CSPI, iii. 464–5.
[145] Hennessy, Annals of Loch Cé, ii. 489; AFM, v. 1865–7.
[146] Ibid. 1867–9.

competitor was assassinated soon afterwards. He foolishly went to Mongavlin where Ineen Dubh incited her Scottish bodyguard to murder him.[147]

Donnell O'Donnell was the next contender for the lordship. Although as a member of the ruling sept he was a better qualified candidate than Hugh O'Gallagher, he lacked the nomination of his father. Interestingly, it was in alliance with 'the posterity of Hugh O'Gallagher' that Donnell undertook his first action. This was an attack on the the sons of Conn O'Donnell, in which Calvach óg was slain.[148] In addition to considerable internal support, Donnell also received assistance from outside the lordship. On a tour of Ulster after the shipwreck of the Armada, Fitzwilliam appointed Donnell sheriff of Donegal. More importantly, Fitzwilliam took Sir Eoin O'Gallagher captive. This was done ostensibly to force Tirconnell to pay its arrears of rent but in all likelihood the object was political since Fitzwilliam regarded O'Gallagher as 'a great favourer of the Scottish woman, O'Donnell's wife, her race and her children'.[149] Afterwards, O'Gallagher's wife accused Donnell O'Donnell of seizing her husband's lands and chattels.[150] He also received assistance from Captain Connell who had been sent into the lordship by Fitzwilliam in 1589.[151] Within a short time, Donnell had assumed control of Tirconnell west of the Gap of Barnesmore; in other words Tirhugh, Boylagh and Banagh.[152] In 1589 his strength was such that he was able to establish Hugh Maguire as lord of Fermanagh in preference to the challenger, Connor Roe.[153] By the beginning of 1590 Turlough Luineach had clearly switched his support from the sons of Conn O'Donnell since it was reported that he 'hath lately strengthened himself by marrying of his daughter to O'Donnell's son who leads all the MacSweenys and all Tirconnell at his pleasure'.[154] Fitzwilliam noted the rise of Donnell O'Donnell 'by the Irish manner'.[155] At this stage, Ineen Dubh acted decisively fearing that Donnell might attain leadership of the family in preference to her imprisoned son, Hugh Roe. With the support of Scots mercenaries and the lords obedient to her husband – O'Doherty, MacSweeny Fanad and Mac-Sweeny na dTuath – she defeated and killed Donnell at Doire Leathan on the western extremity of Tirconnell on 3 September 1590.[156] The chaos which ensued in the lordship after Donnell's death was exploited by Captain Connill and by Captain Willis, the newly appointed sheriff of Donegal.[157] Based at the abbey of Donegal, these captains took control of much of western Tirconnell and made raids into the eastern part of the lordship.[158]

[147] Ibid. 1873.
[148] Hennessy, Annals of Loch Cé, ii. 487.
[149] CSPI, iv. 94–5. Despite lobbying at court by his wife, Siobhán, and his stepson, Hugh O'Neill, O'Gallagher remained in captivity until 1594: APC, xviii. 177–8; xix. 306–7; Walsh, 'Septs of Muintear Ghallchubhair', 197–8.
[150] APC, xviii. 177–8.
[151] PRO SP 63/177, no. 48(1).
[152] AFM, vi. 1891.
[153] Ibid. 1875–7.
[154] PRO SP 63/150, no. 27.
[155] Ibid. 153, no. 24.
[156] AFM, vi. 1891.
[157] CSPI, vi. 518; PRO SP 63/177, no. 48(1).
[158] AFM, vi. 1925–7.

Whilst Tirconnell witnessed the infighting of claimants and the ravages of freebooters, the supporters of Hugh Roe were using every means at their disposal to have him released from Dublin Castle. In the two years following his capture, his father-in-law, Hugh O'Neill wrote at least five letters to Court on his behalf.[159] The earl of Tyrone informed the queen that he was willing to act as a surety for Hugh Roe's good behaviour and that O'Donnell would give other hostages, including Rory O'Donnell, in exchange for his release.[160] Diplomacy was not the only means. By the spring of 1588 Ineen Dubh was offering Perrot a bribe of £2,000 in addition to sureties and hostages.[161] O'Donnell and his wife tried to take advantage of the Armada shipwreck. In Inishowen they negotiated the surrender of the principal men off *La Trinidad Valencera* on condition that they go to the lord deputy.[162] As a result old O'Donnell was able to bring in thirty Spanish prisoners and to request his son's release in consideration of his service against the enemy.[163] Fitzwilliam also reported that O'Donnell, in lobbying for the release of his son, had offered an inducement of £1,000 and £300 'to some near about me to labour it'. However, Fitzwilliam was completely against the idea of releasing Hugh Roe and referred to 'the dangers that might grow unto this miserable realm by letting loose the reins unto so harebrain and ingracious an imp as O'Donnell's son'.[164]

By the time of Hugh O'Neill's planned visit to England, a 'sea-change' had taken place in Fitzwilliam's opinion. The latter was now willing to accept the sureties and pledges offered and believed that the rent arrears from the lordship would be duly paid. He asserted that Hugh Roe's 'liberty would be better service to Her Majesty than his imprisonment'. Moreover, he stated and later reiterated that Hugh Roe's release would prevent the rise of Donnell O'Donnell. This was in spite of the fact that Donnell had been supported by Fitzwilliam in the first instance and that his succession would have ensured a balance of power in the North more favourable to the crown. Although Fitzwilliam made the excuse: 'upon my duty, no reward maketh me write thus much', his *volte-face* on the issue must point to bribery.[165] The privy council indicated its suspicions about the employment of 'indirect means' in the matter. Nevertheless, as a result of Hugh O'Neill's visit to Court in 1590, it asked Fitzwilliam to review the question of Hugh Roe's captivity.[166] This privy council letter did not lead to the release of Hugh Roe; nor did the lobbying of the English ambassador in Scotland by the laird of Calder the following year.[167] More dramatic events were required to secure the liberty of O'Donnell.

The escape of Hugh Roe O'Donnell from Dublin Castle ranks as one of the great epics in Irish history, whether it is read in the original 'faith and father-

---

159 PRO SP 63/132, no. 30 (to the queen); 132, no. 31; 141, no. 10; *CSPI*, iii. 481–2 (to Walsingham); Lambeth, Carew 619 fo. 10 (to Leicester).
160 PRO SP 63/132, no. 30.
161 *CSPI*, iii. 498–9.
162 PRO SP 63/137, no. 16.
163 *CSPI*, iv. 43–4.
164 PRO SP 63/136, no. 54.
165 Ibid. 148, no. 24; 153, no. 24.
166 *APC*, xix. 306–7.
167 *CSP, Scot.* x. 518.

land' account of Lughaidh Ó Cléirigh or in its retelling by Standish O'Grady, the late nineteenth-century scholar. At Christmas time in 1591 Hugh Roe O'Donnell and Henry and Art MacShane O'Neill escaped through the privies and down the curtain wall of the castle. A servant who had visited them as a horseboy in the castle was waiting to act as a guide. Henry MacShane parted company with the rest in Dublin. The main group headed south but were stranded in Glenmalure. Art MacShane, as the story goes, died of exposure and Hugh Roe suffered frostbite which eventually necessitated the amputation of his big toes. O'Donnell was rescued by a search party sent out by Feagh MacHugh O'Byrne, the lord of Colranell in Leinster. In January he returned to Ulster by a route which included a number of precautionary detours.[168] Behind the drama of these events, we must assess the role of Hugh O'Neill and the possibility of corruption in the Castle.

In the summer of 1590, Conn MacShane O'Neill had alleged at Court 'that the earl [of Tyrone] did lay down a plot and practised the escape of Hugh Roe O'Donnell out of Her Majesty's castle of Dublin and for that purpose furnished him with store of sarsenet in that place and sent horses to receive him and carry him away thence'.[169] While this was clearly a reference to an earlier incident, it turned out to be an accurate forecast of Hugh Roe's subsequent escape attempts.[170] A deposition by Eoin MacHugh MacNeill Mór O'Neill in 1600 implicates Richard Weston, one of Tyrone's men, for bringing O'Donnell 'certain silk called sarsnet, to make him a line to slide down by and break prison, whereby he, the said O'Donnell did escape'. This deponent goes on to confirm in summary form the account later given by Ó Cléirigh.[171] Likewise, confessions extracted by the government in 1595 from James and Walter Fitzgerald, comrades-in-arms of O'Byrne, confirm Ó Cléirigh's claim that Turlough Boye O'Hagan was sent by the earl to escort O'Donnell to Ulster. Furthermore, Walter divulged that the earl had an arrangement with the Warrens and other friends in the Pale to supply horses for an escape attempt. Although this was not activated in the end, we know from Ó Cléirigh that O'Donnell was entertained on his journey northwards by Sir Edward Moore's son, Garrett, who was 'much attached to Aodh Ó Néill'. It is also interesting that Ó Cléirigh should note Hugh O'Neill's payment of stipends to government officials at this point in his narrative.[172] Oddly, the state papers contain no reference to Hugh Roe's attempted escape of January 1591 and no mention of his successful escape of Christmas 1591 until his safe return to Ulster.[173] This lack of documentation would seem to point to corruption; equally however it may reflect government embarrassment at the incident, or simply that the relevant papers have been lost in the passage of time. In June 1592, Fitzwilliam thanked Burghley for his action in assuaging the queen's wrath over the escape. He told his patron that he had sacked Maplesden, the constable of the Castle, and had imprisoned the

168 *Life*, i. 19–33; O'Grady, *Red Hugh's captivity*, 244–75 and more expansively in *The flight of the eagle*, London 1897, chs xxix–xlvi.
169 Perrot, *Chronicle of Ireland*, 65.
170 *Life*, i. 13–27; C, *Carew*, iii. 48.
171 *CSPI*, xi. 310.
172 PRO SP 63/178, no. 53(4); 179, nos 23(3, 4); *Life*, 26–29.
173 PRO SP 63/163, no. 36.

chief gaoler under him. He felt that Maplesden had been too trusting in the choice of servants.[174] In his *Memoir*, written years later, Fitzwilliam mentioned the guide of the escapees as one such servant. By this stage, Fitzwilliam himself was being blamed. In mitigation, he referred to a letter (no longer extant) which he had written to Hugh O'Neill asking for his assistance in the recapture of O'Donnell.[175] Fitzwilliam's detractors asserted that he had deliberately replaced Seager, who held the constableship of the Castle as a patentee, with Maplesden, a man susceptible to bribery, who then permitted the escape to take place.[176] Without better documentary evidence, these allegations made directly against Castle officials and indirectly against Fitzwilliam must remain unproven. Whereas Fitzwilliam may have been willing to take money to recommend O'Donnell's release to the privy council, it would have been quite a different matter to connive at his actual escape.

Soon after his return to Tirconnell, Hugh Roe expelled the English forces under Captains Willis and Connill from the lordship.[177] In April 1592, the ruling sept of the O'Donnells and their supporters, the three MacSweenys and O'Boyle, assembled at Kilmacrenan. Hugh O'Donnell resigned his title and this was conferred upon his son, Hugh Roe, by O'Freel in the traditional manner.[178] The resignation of O'Donnell was apparently voluntary and taken with the agreement of the nobility.[179] Hugh Roe informed the Irish council: 'I have received my father's room and his name upon the whole country by his own will and consent and the best of his chief followers, without persuasion of myself'.[180] Ó Cléirigh however emphasises the role of Ineen Dubh: 'it was an advantage that she came to the gathering, for she was the head of the advice and counsel of the Cenel Conaill . . . she had many troops from Scotland, and some of the Irish at her disposal and under her control and in her hire and pay constantly'.[181] Clearly the appointment of Hugh Roe was in no sense a free election by the nobility of Tirconnell but a stage-managed affair in which the influence of his mother was paramount.

Moreover, a number of important nobles – the chief *urrí*, O'Doherty and the other contenders, Niall Garbh and Hugh Dubh – did not attend the election.[182] Hugh Roe had to use force to crush these opponents. The overlordship of Hugh Roe was only acknowledged by O'Doherty after he was captured at a parley and imprisoned.[183] At the time of Hugh Roe's election, Niall Garbh was in Dublin seeking government support but was afterwards forced to submit 'wholly through fear'.[184] Ó Cléirigh claims that Hugh Dubh O'Donnell, the eldest and

---

[174] *CSPI*, iv. 518–19.
[175] BL Add. 12503 fo. 392.
[176] Sir William Russell (Fitzwilliam's successor as lord deputy), PRO SP 63/179, no. 6; Sir Henry Wallop (Irish vice-treasurer), BL Cotton Titus C vii fo. 158; Perrot, *Chronicle of Ireland*, 70–1, 590–4.
[177] *Life*, i. 37; PRO SP 63/163, no. 36.
[178] *Life*, i. 39–41.
[179] Ibid. 41.
[180] PRO SP 63/165, no. 6(1).
[181] *Life*, i. 39.
[182] Ibid. 41.
[183] Ibid. 55–7.
[184] PRO SP 63/165, no. 6(1); *Life*, i. 55.

best qualified candidate, willingly submitted to the election of Hugh Roe. However, the state papers indicate that he was only brought to book early in 1593.[185] Hugh Roe gained control of his great uncle's last stronghold at Beleek and beheaded sixteen of his principal followers 'by train of a feigned treaty of friendship, mediated by Maguire'.[186] Immediately after his election, the new O'Donnell had mounted raids on the territory of Turlough Luineach O'Neill. Besides Hugh Roe's desire for revenge and the need to assist his father-in-law, Ó Cléirigh inserts another reason: 'for the Cenel Éoghain was a wood of refuge and a bush of shelter at all times for every one of the Cenel Conaill itself who opposed and resisted their own true prince'.[187] In June 1592 Hugh Roe had rekindled O'Donnell interest in Connacht by supporting a revolt amongst the Lower MacWilliam Burkes. Bingham claimed that two newly-arrived Catholic prelates, Niall O'Boyle, the bishop of Raphoe, and Dr James O'Hely, the archbishop of Tuam, were inciting the outbreak or at least mediating between the parties involved.[188]

The government in Dublin was displeased that Hugh Roe 'had taken upon him the name of O'Donnell without Her Majesty's direction or consent of the state here, and had preyed, burned and spoiled Sir Tirlough O'Neill's country'. Although the government threatened to use armed force against him, it probably lacked the capability to do so. Instead to encourage him to submit, the Irish council granted protections to O'Donnell and his followers and promised a loan of £200 to cover expenses.[189] At the end of July 1592, the earl of Tyrone escorted his son-in-law, Hugh Roe O'Donnell, from Donegal to Dundalk where on 2 August he submitted to the lord deputy.[190] According to Thomas Lee, a bribe of £500 to Fitzwilliam facilitated this meeting and the articled agreement which was subsequently drawn up between him and O'Donnell. In return for recognition of his captaincy of Tirconnell, Hugh Roe promised to remain loyal, to treat O'Doherty, Hugh Dubh and Niall Garbh fairly and to pay the rents due from his lordship. Although Hugh did not keep an article to banish Catholic priests and bishops, he did abandon his support for the Burkes after the agreement.[191]

A number of general observations can be drawn from this succession struggle. The idea of 'the eldest and the best' having a paramount right to succession was a legal fiction. This is transparent in an exchange between the government commissioners and O'Donnell at the 1596 peace negotiations: 'If custom, said we, should prevail neither O'Reilly in the Brenny [Breifne] nor yourself have any interest in Tirconnell. So we perceive you now do not stand upon your own customs, unto he answered not but smiled.'[192] Clearly the function of custom was to determine the limits of eligibility. On the other hand, the key to successful election was the application of military power. This rested on the net

185 Ibid. i. 53; ii. 88.
186 *CSPI*, v. 86.
187 *Life*, i. 43.
188 PRO SP 63/165, nos 24, 24(1); *CSPI*, iv. 544–6, 570, 590–4.
189 *CSPI*, iv. 521.
190 AFM, vi. 1933; PRO SP 63/166, no. 44(1).
191 BL Harleian 35, fo. 263; PRO SP 63/166, no. 44(2); *CSPI*, iv. 570, 590–4.
192 ULC Kk 1 15 no. 63, fo. 141.

of connections which the competitor established through kinship, marriage, fosterage and dependence. Nomination by the incumbent lord and the use of the force and influence at his disposal could also be decisive. In this case, on account of her husband's senility, Ineen Dubh played a central role. A woman could exercise authority in the warrior society of Gaelic Ireland just as in the very different societies of contemporary England or France. The interference of the crown was very great during the period of the succession dispute in Tirconnell but this was mitigated by the negligence and probable corruption of its officialdom. It is important to note that the nobility of Tirconnell, despite the almost continual presence of freebooting government troops, remained concerned, indeed obsessed, with the dynastic struggle taking place. The rapid regeneration of Tirconnell from internal chaos in Hugh Roe's first year in office is also noteworthy. It demonstrates the importance of a strong and active military leader and by extension the central position occupied by the institution of lordship in Gaelic politics. The whole episode underscores the continuity and persistence of Gaelic political modes in the closing decades of the sixteenth century.

The succession crisis in Tirconnell also saw a dramatic shift in Ulster power-politics. The havoc wrought and the killings perpetrated by government troops made Tirconnell wary of closer relations with the crown. The attempt to interfere with the succession itself by kidnapping the chosen heir of a proven loyalist was the cause of even greater resentment. The state had of course resorted to this tactic to prevent the realignment of Ulster's ruling families in the double marriage alliance between the O'Neills and O'Donnells. This succeeded as long as Hugh Roe remained a prisoner. The importance of the marriage alliance is outlined in a memorial presented by the earls of Tyrone and Tirconnell to the king of Spain in 1608. For seven hundred years their two families had been embroiled in continuous conflict and the English had eagerly exploited their enmity. The situation was changed in 1574 when Hugh O'Neill married Siobhán, the daughter of Sir Hugh O'Donnell. In the middle years of the 1580s she had borne him two sons, Hugh and Henry, the heirs to the earldom of Tyrone.[193] The memorial did not mention the marriage of Rose O'Neill to Hugh Roe O'Donnell. Although it proved barren, it did underwrite the new dynastic relationship which cut across the traditional pattern of Ulster politics.[194] This alliance, aimed initially against Turlough Luineach in Tyrone and his allies in Tirconnell, became the cornerstone of a Gaelic confederacy against the English crown.

---

[193] M. Walsh, 'Destruction by peace', 98–9, 113, 208; CPCRI, ii. 123; BLO, MS 30237, fo. 51.
[194] Life, ii. 36.

PART THREE

STRUCTURAL CRISIS

7

Conspiracy and Crisis in Ulster

The drift to war in Ulster during 1593 and 1594 is one of the most complex and baffling episodes in Irish history. Its analysis has presented contemporary and modern historians with evidential and interpretative problems. Ó Cléirigh, in his biography of Hugh Roe O'Donnell, casts his hero as the organiser of Gaelic resistance against English encroachment.[1] Recently, Silke has examined Ó Cléirigh's claims about the leading role of O'Donnell and has shifted the emphasis to the plots being hatched by the Catholic bishops of the North.[2] Nevertheless, both Ó Cléirigh and Silke do acknowledge Hugh O'Neill as an influential, albeit indirect, player in the unfolding events.[3] In fact, the need to explain the actions of O'Neill is central to the debate. The Gaelic historians of the early seventeenth century – Ó Cléirigh, O'Sullevan Beare, and the Four Masters – were at a loss to explain satisfactorily why the earl at first sided with the English against his future allies.[4] The contemporary English historians – Camden, Moryson and Perrot – who had access to official documentation concluded that O'Neill was simply playing for time and had long since determined to make war on the crown.[5] The same issue was tackled by Graham, O'Faolain and Falls in the middle of this century with the assistance of the calendars of state papers. Their picture of O'Neill in this period is that of a vacillating politician eventually forced to assume the leadership of a Gaelic coalition.[6]

The first step towards explaining the onset of the crisis in the spring of 1593 is to realise that it took place at a crucial juncture in Ulster politics. With the connivance of Maguire, Hugh Roe O'Donnell was stamping out the last ember of resistance from his competitor, Hugh Dubh.[7] More importantly, the earl of Tyrone, with the assistance of his sons-in-law, O'Donnell and Maguire, was finally pensioning off Turlough Luineach.[8] The interests and therefore the fortunes of O'Neill, O'Donnell and Maguire were inextricably linked. O'Neill

---

[1] *Life*, i. 59–61.
[2] Silke, 'The Irish appeal of 1593', 279–90, 362–71.
[3] *Life*, i. 67; Silke, 'The Irish appeal of 1593', 286.
[4] *Life*, i. 65; M. J. Byrne (trans.), *The history of Ireland under Elizabeth . . . being a portion of the history of Catholic Ireland by Don Philip O'Sullevan Beare*, Dublin 1903, 69–86; AFM, vi. 1941, 1945.
[5] Camden, *History of Elizabeth*, 446; Moryson, *An itinerary*, I/i. 12–13; Perrot, *Chronicle of Ireland*, 7–8, 72–4.
[6] Graham, 'An historical study of the career of Hugh O'Neill', chs vi, vii; O'Faolain, *The Great O'Neill*, 122–42; Cyril Falls, 'Hugh O'Neill the great', *Irish Sword*, vi (1963), 94–102; idem. *Elizabeth's Irish wars*, 174–83.
[7] CSPI, v. 86.
[8] PRO SP 63/170, no. 23(17).

was *primus inter pares*. The central position and strength of his lordship and the multiplicity of his dynastic alliances gave him hegemony in Ulster. This situation left government policy in tatters and its implementation wholly dependent on the goodwill of the earl. Yet, O'Neill's position was equally fraught. He had faced government-backed opposition to his control of Tyrone and supremacy in Ulster since 1587. Now, he must have feared the possibility of a government refusal to recognise his new-won position or at least its demand for his submission to a reform package.[9] This eventuality would render the prize worthless and hand it on a plate to his rival, Sir Henry Bagenal. His employment as chief commissioner of Ulster posed a threat to the earl. In a similar fashion, the ambitions of Sir Richard Bingham in western Ulster threatened the security of his allies, O'Donnell and Maguire. Therefore, O'Neill wanted not only the recognition of his own power but also the abandonment of government reform and the neutralisation of Bagenal and Bingham, its agents and beneficiaries. In pursuit of these objectives, O'Neill did not hesitate to intrigue with Spain. As the tension mounted, he showed himself to be a shrewd and dissembling politician and a clever manipulator of men.

Silke was wrong to assume that the earl was not involved in the bishops' conspiracy. This view can be controverted by looking at the activities of Edmund óg MacDonnell. This man from the galloglass family of Tyrone was the first Counter-reformation dean of Armagh in opposition to the queen's Welsh appointee, Owen Wood.[10] We do not know when he first went to the continent at the behest of the earl but a possible date is 1589 – O'Neill told Philip II in a letter of October 1596 that he had been seeking aid from Spain for the past seven years.[11] In January 1592 Turlough O'Kenny, a priest captured in France and turned over to the English authorities, confessed *inter alia* that Edmund óg MacDonnell was in receipt of a pension from the king of Spain.[12] O'Kenny's confession was distributed to English officials in Ireland and, on receiving it, Sir Richard Bingham was able to report that MacDonnell had recently landed in the North in the company of Dr James O'Hely.[13] O'Hely, the new archbishop of Tuam, was an inveterate conspirator in the Catholic interest.[14] The next development – missed by Silke – highlights the role of Hugh O'Neill. The evidence comes from a debriefing in London of William Pittes, an English sailor who had been imprisoned in Spain. He reported that on 18 August 1592 'One Sourlye, kinsman of the Teron came over messenger in an Irish ship and put into Porto Nuevo, who came presently to the Groyne and rode post haste to Madrid'.[15] This can be none other than Edmund óg MacDonnell who was one of the Clann Éoin Meic Somhairle although it is more likely that he was a foster-

---

9 Various sources alleged that the earl of Tyrone was prepared to use force to secure recognition of his position: PRO SP 63/169, no. 23(5); 170, no. 23(3, 8).
10 J. B. Leslie, *Armagh clergy and parishes*, Dundalk 1911, 11–12.
11 *CSP, Sp.* iv. 642.
12 *CSPI*, iv. 453.
13 PRO SP 63/164, no. 7.
14 AGS Estado 839, fo. 65.
15 HMC *Salisbury* MSS, iv. 258–9. The government's failure to follow up this singular piece of intelligence was to have grave consequences to say the least.

brother than an actual kinsman of the earls.[16] The object or at least the result of the dean's mission is obvious – namely the return of Edmund MacGauran, the titular archbishop of Armagh and Catholic primate of Ireland. MacDonnell was later described as 'a man specially trusted' who had been *camerado* to Mac-Gauran.[17]

Edmund MacGauran was the leading figure in a community of *émigrés* in the dominions of Philip II who were plotting a Catholic recovery in Ireland. His activities were already known to the English authorities because one of their agents on the continent had intercepted his communications in 1591.[18] Prompted no doubt by MacDonnell's arrival in Spain, the primate met with King Philip in Burgos in September 1592. As a result MacGauran's return to Ireland was officially sanctioned – he was supplied and financed out of the royal coffers and sent home on an Irish ship commandeered in the port of Bilbao.[19] MacGauran's appearance in Ireland was registered by James O'Crean, a spy of the Binghams, when the primate held a conference of seven northern bishops in Tirconnell at the end of December 1592.[20] Three months later MacGauran wrote to Juan de Idiáquez, 'chief councillor to the king to whom all English and Irish matters are committed', informing him that all the hereditary lords of Ireland promised to support a Spanish invasion amongst whom were O'Don-nell, the Bourkes and O'Rourke.[21] MacGauran's letter prefaced one from O'Donnell to the Spanish king. O'Donnell said that he had learned from the primate that Philip was willing to help if the Catholic nobles of Ireland took action against the crown. He wanted to be a partaker in this scheme and sought to establish his credentials by mentioning his escape from prison and the retaking of his own country. O'Donnell offered himself as facilitator and wanted no special recognition for his action. He asserted that it was a propitious time for Philip to invade Ireland because it could be conquered at little cost and be used to divert the English from interfering in the affairs of France and Flanders.[22] O'Donnell's letter was seconded a month later by one from Hugh Maguire countersigned by the Bourkes, O'Rourke and the bishops. This empha-sised the oppressions of the lord deputy and wanted an invasion force of 8,000–10,000 men to arrive, as the other letters had requested, by the feast of the nativity of the Blessed Virgin.[23] O'Donnell also took the opportunity to write to Irish noblemen exiled in Spain requesting their furtherance of the project and 'to beg you all to come and help us to fight God's battle and win back our lands'.[24] The conveyance of these letters and the presentation of the Irish cause at the Spanish court was entrusted to the archbishop of Tuam.

16 Donald Schlegal, 'The MacDonnells of Tyrone and Armagh: a genealogical study', *Seanchas Ard Mhacha*, x (1980–1), 207–10.
17 PRO SP 63/196, no. 31(3).
18 HMC *Salisbury MSS*, iv. 117–18.
19 Micheline Walsh, 'Archbishop Magauran and his return to Ireland, October 1592', *Seanchas Ard Mhacha*, xiv (1990), 68–79.
20 *CPSI*, v. 71–2.
21 PRO SP 63/196, no. 30(3); AGS Estado 839, fo. 67.
22 Ibid. 2604 unfoliated.
23 Ibid.
24 *CSP, Sp*. iv. 599.

O'Donnell was the leading light in backing O'Hely's embassy to Spain and the bishops clearly regarded him as their main hope at this point. O'Neill stayed in the background of the conspiracy. It was implicit in the letters written to Spain that the project had other backers who had not declared themselves. A subsequent memorandum written by Idiáquez for Philip II is important in this respect:

> the Irish archbishop of Tuam says that it will be of great importance for the success of the confederacy of Irish Catholics, that Your Majesty should write very affectionately to the earl of Tyrone, whose name is O'Neill to induce him to enter into the confederacy openly. He already belongs to it secretly, and he should be assured that your Majesty's aid shall not fail them.[25]

The Irish government on its part was becoming suspicious of the earl. In February 1592 the privy council in London, acting on intelligence sent to it by Bingham, despatched instructions for the apprehension of the Papist bishops lurking in Fermanagh and Tirconnell.[26] Since the bishops had their most frequent abode under O'Donnell, the Irish council gave the task of arresting them to O'Neill 'who for alliance and other respects of friendship hath no small interest in O'Donnell and by reason thereof, we thought him the fittest instrument to deal with him in this matter or any other the like weighty services for Her Majesty'.[27] A month later the lord deputy had to admit that the earl, despite promises to the contrary, had done nothing to arrest the bishops.[28] Indeed by this stage Fitzwilliam had received a deposition given by Patrick MacArt Moile MacMahon at Monaghan on 11 April which alleged that Archbishop MacGauran had promised foreign aid by mid-May and that as a result O'Neill, O'Donnell, Maguire and other prominent Ulstermen had combined to support such an invasion.[29]

The bishops' conspiracy certainly provided the enemies of O'Neill with plenty of ammunition to fire at him but any idea that it sparked off the Nine Years War must be resolutely opposed. In the first place, the embassy to the Spanish court proved a failure. With so many demands on his resources, Philip II decided against the immediate despatch of military aid. Instead, he sent a ship on a fact-finding assignment to Ireland but it sank in the Bay of Biscay. With it to the bottom of the sea went O'Hely, many returning noblemen and the prospect of prompt Spanish assistance.[30] Secondly, if the bishops intended to act as *agents provocateurs*, the political effectiveness of their propaganda is open to

[25] Ibid. 611.
[26] APC, xxiv. 60.
[27] PRO SP 63/168, no. 68.
[28] Ibid. 169, no. 20.
[29] Ibid. no. 23(3).
[30] Silke, 'The Irish Appeal of 1593', 362–71; Micheline Walsh, 'The military order of St Patrick, 1593', *Seanchas Ard Mhacha*, ix (1979), 274–85. In Madrid, O'Hely faced opposition from Richard Stanihurst, the Anglo-Irish chronicler and alchemist, who was then in the king's service: PRO SP 63/177, no. 9(1); Colm Lennon, *Richard Stanihurst: the Dubliner, 1547–1618*, Dublin 1981, 46–51. The Irish project had similarities with the contemporary plot being hatched by the Catholic nobility of Scotland. However, they represented distinct interests bidding for the same Spanish aid: 'The Spanish blanks and the Catholic earls' in *The collected*

serious doubt. For instance, Miler Magrath informs us that they were propagating the prophecy that O'Donnell would be a monarch in Ireland in an attempt 'to further their intended invasion'.[31] This prophecy must have been widely disseminated because in November 1593 Nicholas Whyte, a Kildare man, was hauled before the Castle Chamber and condemned to be pilloried, whipped and imprisoned for repeating it.[32] Yet, whereas the bishops may have succeeded in raising popular consciousness, Hugh Roe himself did not enter into military action until mid-1594. Most importantly, the first blow was struck by an officer of the crown in Fermanagh. Captain Humphrey Willis invaded Maguire's country 'afore Easter', which in 1593 fell on April 15.[33] Since O'Hely carried letters from O'Donnell and MacGauran dating from the end of March and one from Maguire written at the end of April, he clearly did not depart until after the attack on Fermanagh.[34] The departure of the mission to Spain was not a signal for offensive action on the part of the lords, rather such action only followed that taken by a government agent in Fermanagh!

The crisis was sparked off by Willis's attempt to establish himself as sheriff of Fermanagh. A year later, the earl of Tyrone referred to it as the event 'whereof all the stirs in the North hath grown'.[35] After succeeding his father as lord of Fermanagh, Hugh Maguire came to Dublin in the summer of 1590 and there the lord deputy apparently found him willing to accept a sheriff 'chosen of his own name'.[36] However, in October the following year Maguire bribed Fitzwilliam and Bagenal to postpone the appointment of local government officers.[37] Eventually in the spring of 1593 Captain Willis was commissioned as sheriff and arrived in Fermanagh with a military force, estimated at 300 men or more by Hugh O'Neill and at 100 men and 160 camp-followers by Sir Henry Wallop.[38] Strange as it might seem, Willis was not despatched to Fermanagh to arrest the Papist bishops, at least there was never any justification given for his actions in these terms. Willis went not as a law enforcer but as a freebooter, overrunning and spoiling the country in what was a blatant move to control a lordship straddling the southern borders of Ulster and to tie down a principal dependent of the earl at the point when the latter was achieving undisputed supremacy in Ulster. The best account of the ensuing events comes from the deposition of Moris O'Scanlon who was with Maguire at the time of Willis's irruption. With only his own troops, Maguire found himself hard-pressed until the arrival of reinforcements from Tyrone and Tirconnell. First on the scene was Cormac MacBaron, the earl's brother, with a mixed band of horse and foot;

---

essays and reviews of Thomas Graves Law, ed. Peter Hume Brown, Edinburgh 1904, 244–76; CSP, Sp. iv. 603–8, 613–16.
[31] PRO SP 63/170, no. 11.
[32] HMC Egmont MSS, i. 25. A variation of the Columcille prophecy was again used to fire the popular imagination at the beginning of the 1641 rising in Ulster: R. Gillespie, 'Ulster and the 1641 rising' in Brady and Gillespie, Natives and newcomers, 210.
[33] PRO SP 63/170, no. 23(7).
[34] AGS Estado 2604 unfoliated; ibid. 839, fo. 67.
[35] Lambeth, Carew 617, fos 209–10.
[36] BL Add. 12,503, fo. 391; ULC Kk 1 15 no. 63, fos 156–7.
[37] PRO SP 63/160, no. 28; 174, no. 2(1); ULC Kk 1 15 no. 63, fos 156–7.
[38] PRO SP 63/170, no. 23(7); Lambeth, Carew 617, fos 209–10; BL Cotton Titus C vii fos 156–61.

later Donough and Donnell O'Hagan, the earl's fosterbrothers, arrived with 120 shot. Maguire was also succoured by a hundred galloglasses from Tirconnell under the leadership of Alexander MacDonnell óg MacSweeny. Willis and his men took refuge in a church for a week until the earl of Tyrone arranged a safe-conduct for their departure out of the lordship. Afterwards, the forces of O'Hagan and MacSweeny remained at *buannacht* in Fermanagh.[39]

The forces gathered in Fermanagh facilitated further actions by Maguire in Connacht. Here, an intercepted letter which survives in contemporary English translation is of vital importance. At the end of May 1593 a large force under the leadership of some of the principal Maguires invaded Sligo and attacked Ballimote, the base of George Bingham. As a result, the town and district of Ballimote were burned.[40] In July Maguire informed the lord deputy that his letters of complaint about the attacks of the Binghams had long since been ignored and that he had been forced to take action on his own behalf.[41] Later, in his grievances of 1596, he detailed at least three attacks by the Binghams since his election as lord of Fermanagh in addition to attacks by government officials from the neighbouring counties of Monaghan and Cavan.[42] Maguire's original complaints against the Binghams are no longer extant and in July 1593 the Irish council dismissed the allegations as 'frivolous'.[43] Yet, the intercepted letter from Maguire to Hugh O'Neill states 'the Binghams have done hurt or wrong to us continually'. Since this letter was not intended for English eyes, it must confirm the veracity of Maguire's allegations against the Binghams.[44] Other evidence points to the same conclusion. For some time, Sir Richard Bingham had been demanding the right of 'hot pursuit' into Tirconnell and Fermanagh to apprehend political refugees from Connacht and the Papist bishops domiciled there.[45] Moreover, since the beginning of 1593 Bingham had been backing the suit of his friend, Sir Ralph Lane, for the government of Tirconnell and Fermanagh and for the possession of certain strategic forts.[46] Fitzwilliam refused Bingham permission to apprehend the bishops and later sought to prevent him taking retaliation in western Ulster after Maguire's attacks on Connacht. He did this on the grounds that from Bingham's 'pursuit for cows under colour of service, might grow needless stirs', but his real reason was that he did not want the chief commissioner of Connacht extending his jurisdiction any further north.[47] There was a more immediate reason for the attack on Sligo. The Four Masters relate how a dispute arose in May between George Bingham and O'Rourke over the amount of composition money to be paid which led to the use of armed force by Bingham.[48] Consequently, the

[39] PRO SP 63/170, no. 23(13).
[40] Ibid. no. 5(1); *CSPI*, v. 105–6.
[41] PRO SP 63/170, no. 44(1).
[42] ULC Kk 1 15 no. 63, fos 156–7.
[43] PRO SP 63/170, no. 38.
[44] Ibid. no. 23(15).
[45] *CSPI*, iv. 590–4, v. 34–40.
[46] PRO SP 63/168, no. 57; 169, no. 16.
[47] BL Add. 12,503, fo. 391; PRO SP 63/170, no. 58.
[48] *AFM*, vi. 1935–7; *CSPI*, v. 105–6; PRO SP 63/170, no. 23(15).

declared objective of Maguire's attack was 'to set forth Brian O'Rourke's son, so long as we are displeased ourselves'.[49]

It is necessary to determine to what extent Maguire's activities were directed by other leading Ulstermen. Certain officials, especially Sir Richard Bingham, considered that Primate MacGauran was the promoter of the attacks on Connacht, indeed the chief instigator of the Gaelic revolt.[50] The fact that Mac-Gauran fell in battle attests to his overt political stance, yet the available evidence portrays him as a dependent of Maguire and a mediator between the Gaelic lords. A deposition given by Tadhg O'Nolan, a pursuivant, reveals that Maguire and the primate worked together to reconcile Brian óg and Hugh Galt O'Rourke over the disputed supremacy of West Breifne.[51] An intercepted letter from MacGauran to Hugh Galt, perhaps taken from the archbishop's corpse, states that he had been appointed by Maguire to find an agreement between the O'Rourkes.[52] Here we find Maguire giving directions to MacGauran who came from a small territory situated between Fermanagh and Breifne O'Rourke. Clearly, Bingham had exaggerated the influence of MacGauran merely to further his own ambitions in western Ulster. It is clear, the more so because MacGauran's death did not prevent further attacks by Maguire into neighbouring territories, that the direction of events must be settled upon the Gaelic lords rather than the religious leaders. In this light, if there was a key figure, it was surely Hugh O'Neill.

Donnell Albanagh, a captive taken during the attack on Ballimote, revealed that the O'Hagans had participated with their company of shot. It is highly unlikely that the earl's fosterbrothers would have taken part in such an action without his permission. The captive also confessed that Maguire had been in conference with O'Neill earlier the same month. A subsequent deposition from two disaffected O'Neills confirmed that Maguire and the earl had held talks at Toome on the Bann.[53] The intercepted letter from Maguire to the earl is crucial. Its concluding sentences suggest a wider strategy and implicate O'Neill: 'And we know that we shall have great trouble from this side downwards. And entertain you those bonies [mercenaries], as you promised to Cormac [Mac-Baron]. And send William MacCroddan [a brehon of the earls] from the East without stay, about the business that you know yourself. No more but send all your counsel that you can, and all new news that you have'.[54] The propaganda of clerics and the evidence of the embassy to Spain would seem to confer the leading role on Hugh Roe O'Donnell. Unfortunately, no letters from Maguire to O'Donnell were intercepted. However, in terms of military support to Maguire, O'Neill provided more assistance than O'Donnell against Willis and both gave an equal amount against the Binghams.[55] Moreover, the lord deputy pointed out that Maguire was related to the earl by blood and marriage and

---

49 Ibid. no. 23(15).
50 Ibid. nos 3, 18.
51 Ibid. no. 23(6).
52 CSPI, v. 119.
53 Ibid. 105, 108. The earl of Tyrone also held talks with O'Donnell at Derry on the last three days of May: PRO SP 63/170, no. 23(6).
54 Ibid. no. 23(15).
55 Ibid. no. 23(13); CSPI, v. 105.

'altogether at his devotion'.[56] Obviously, fundamental decisions had been taken at the Bannside conference. The instructions given to Maguire were part of a general strategy.

Immediately after Maguire's departure from Toome on 14 May, the earl had Phelim MacTurlough, the chief lord of Killetra, murdered by the O'Hagans.[57] Tyrone had only recently guaranteed Phelim's safety before the Irish council.[58] It now recalled that 'this gentleman was of the O'Neills and of great account and good force, one whom the earl feared and could never like of'.[59] His murder permitted the earl to complete the annexation of Killetra which he had been trying to take over since the late 1580s.[60] This district was strategically located on the western side of the confluence of the Lower Bann and Lough Neagh where Toome commanded the main crossing point from Tyrone into North Clandeboye. Furthermore, Phelim was a client of Bagenal through whose offices he had secured a royal pardon.[61] His murder was a signal warning to other wayward dependants, notably Henry óg the earl's son-in-law, who had contacts with Marshal Bagenal.[62] It is noteworthy that simultaneously with the attack on Sligo, Brian MacArt MacBaron, the earl's nephew, entered South Clandeboye with a large force and launched attacks on the Gaelic clients of Bagenal.[63] He was later described as 'wholly at the earl's direction'.[64] In early July, he was preventing soldiers of the Blackwater garrison from buying supplies in the nearby market town. Meanwhile, Niall MacHugh, the earl's man in North Clandeboye, was found less manageable following a meeting with his overlord.[65] The earl had evidently decided to wage war by proxy with his dependants as his instruments. The attacks were designed not simply to hurt Bagenal and Bingham but to force the state into the realisation that it could only govern the North through him. Thereby, the earl would achieve recognition of his provincial supremacy without a complete rupture in relations.

The implementation of this strategy had followed the meeting with Maguire at Toome. At the time of that meeting, O'Neill was not only concerned about government intentions towards Fermanagh but was also fearful of his own arrest and trial for treason. By the end of April, the council had received intelligence of a combination in Ulster. Hugh Dubh O'Donnell claimed that O'Donnell and Maguire were procured by O'Neill to revolt against the crown. Sir Hugh Magennis, with the assistance of Sir Henry Bagenal, offered further evidence against the earl's loyalty. The most damaging allegation came from Patrick MacArt Moile MacMahon, the sheriff of Monaghan. His story was that Mac-Gauran had persuaded Maguire and O'Donnell to forebear their allegiance to the state on the grounds that a fleet from the Pope and the king of Spain would

---

56 PRO SP 63/169, no. 41.
57 CSPI, v. 107–9.
58 PRO SP 63/170, nos 1, 57.
59 CSPI, v. 99.
60 Ibid; PRO SP 63/140, no. 61.
61 Ibid. 170, no. 1.
62 Ibid. 169, no. 49(5).
63 Ibid. 170, nos 5, 5(5–6).
64 Ibid. 174, no. 37(4).
65 CSPI, v. 126–7.

arrive by mid-May. As a result MacGauran and O'Donnell had written the same to the earl of Tyrone, Cormac MacBaron and Brian MacHugh óg Mac-Mahon. Afterwards at Dungannon, Maguire took an oath before the earl to aid the Spanish and at another meeting at Ballymascanlon Cormac MacBaron, Henry óg O'Neill, Brian MacHugh óg MacMahon, Ross Bann MacBrian Mac-Mahon, Rory MacHugh óg MacMahon, Art óg MacArt Moile MacMahon, Art MacRory MacBrian MacMahon, Hugh MacRory MacBrian MacMahon, and Brian Ne Sawagh MacMahon took similar oaths before the earl.[66] As Fitz-william later recollected in his *Memoir*: 'thereupon I had with the advice of that council laid a plot for his apprehension by drawing him to Dublin upon occa-sions pretended to compound differences between him and Magennis and others'.[67] Tyrone made excuses for not keeping this and a subsequent appoint-ment; as the council wrote 'he protracteth time to come to us'.[68] O'Neill was already well enough aware of the charges against him to fear the consequences of his going to Dublin. News of the allegations made by Patrick MacArt Moile before the commissioners at Monaghan would have reached him soon after-wards. Later, the rumours circulating about his treasonous intentions were retailed in letters from friends in England and the Pale.[69] In the face of such prevarication, the council decided to go to Dundalk to meet the earl with the recent agreement between him and Turlough as a further pretext.

The proceedings at Dundalk between 14 and 28 June, like the allegations of treason which prompted them, will never be fully explained. The council provided only one despatch on 30 June in spite of the serious issues under consideration. The council explained the delay on account of 'some differences and impediments falling out in the principal matters wherein we dealt'.[70] How-ever, it was not until mid-September that a more definite picture of events began to emerge.[71] The business at Dundalk was handled in two stages. Most of the time was spent in a preliminary examination of the evidence against the earl. In addition to the accusations of foreign conspiracy, which formed the centrepiece, the earl's part in the revolt of Maguire and the killing of Phelim MacTurlough was also examined. O'Neill managed to clear himself of these charges thereby avoiding arrest and trial for treason. Then in negotiations about the affairs of the North, he gained conciliar approval for his agreement with Turlough and a commission to deal with Maguire. This triumph was not simply because the earl could count Loftus, Jones and Gardiner on the council as well-disposed towards him, but because in Dundalk the council was directly threatened by his power.

The earl benefitted from a split in the council between Loftus, Jones and Gardiner who favoured a peaceful course and Tyrone and Fitzwilliam and Bagenal who favoured his arrest. Jones and Loftus believed that insufficient proof had been advanced to incriminate O'Neill as 'an actor, a consentor or

---

[66] Ibid. 94–5.
[67] BL Add. 12,503, fo. 394.
[68] PRO SP 63/169, nos 49, 49(1–2); *CSPI*, v. 100.
[69] PRO SP 63/170, no. 15.
[70] Ibid. no. 23.
[71] *CSPI*, v. 147–9.

concealor' in the matter of foreign conspiracy. They also cited mitigating circumstances for their decision. They had feared that the arrest of the earl would
have brought about an invasion of the Pale by at least five thousand men
headed by his brother, Cormac MacBaron. The government was singularly
unprepared for such an eventuality on account of the illness of the lord deputy
and the lack of men and money. Therefore, they had opted for the peaceful
course. Moreover, they hinted broadly at intimidation when they stated that
the forces of Tyrone had been massed between the Blackwater and Dundalk at
the time of the council's deliberations in the border town.[72] Later, the lord
deputy pointed out that the council had only been able to take 450 footsoldiers
and 120 horsemen with them to Dundalk.[73] It is unclear to what extent Fitzwilliam's illness affected events at Dundalk, but significantly he did request revocation from office towards the end of the proceedings.[74] In his *Memoir*, Fitzwilliam
claimed that Loftus, Jones and Gardiner had blocked his plan to arrest O'Neill.
They had re-examined the witnesses and had found inconsistencies in the
evidence. As a result, they had overruled Fitzwilliam in three points: in the case
of treason against the earl, in the despatch of the conflicting evidence to the
privy council and in the commission to deal with Maguire.[75] Later, Bagenal also
pointed out that his opinions had differed from those held by some other
councillors at Dundalk. He had desired the arrest of O'Neill on account of
policy not private malice. However, the contrary opinion had prevailed in the
council because of the fear of the tumultuous consequences of the earl's detention.[76] On his part, the earl of Tyrone objected to the charges and proceedings
at Dundalk on the grounds that Marshal Bagenal was seeking his overthrow by
suborning the lord deputy and concocting evidence against him.[77]

Foreign conspiracy was the main charge against O'Neill. The majority decision of the Irish council was to take no action against the earl on account of the
major inconsistencies in the evidence against him.[78] Scrutiny of the depositions
would appear to substantiate this view. The charge was derived from O'Neill's
alleged involvement with MacGauran and the subsequent taking of oaths. This
allegation had been made at Monaghan in April by Patrick MacArt Moile
MacMahon who was reputed 'an enemy to the earl'. When MacMahon was
re-examined on 15 June, his new statement differed markedly from his first. He
now alleged that during the previous winter the earl had adminstered oaths to
O'Donnell, Maguire and Cormac MacBaron at Dungannon and to Brian
MacHugh óg MacMahon, Art MacRory MacMahon and Cormac MacBaron at
Ballymascanlon with Brian MacHugh óg being deputised to adminster the same
oath to other MacMahons: 'Their oath was that they should be true to the earl
and that they would do as the earl would do.' These oaths appeared to relate to
the struggle for power in Ulster rather than a projected foreign invasion. It also
transpired that Patrick had not received his information directly from Henry

[72] PRO SP 63/171, no. 2.
[73] CSPI, v. 124.
[74] PRO SP 63/170, no. 17.
[75] BL Add. 12,503, fo. 394.
[76] PRO SP 63/170, no. 27.
[77] Ibid. no. 15.
[78] Ibid. no. 23.

óg, the earl's son-in-law, as he deposed initially but rather indirectly through a fosterbrother of both, Cú Uladh MacArdle. The second statement has a more authentic ring than the first but both Cú Uladh and Henry óg subsequently denied giving any such information and stated that their only communications with MacMahon concerned stolen pigs.[79] When this charge failed, new allegations were brought by Marshal Bagenal. The most serious was that the earl had held a secret conference at Strabane during the spring at which he, O'Donnell, Maguire and MacGauran had taken the sacrament together. However, these allegations were based on the information of others who, when examined, denied the stories or referred to other informants.[80] Furthermore the earl himself denied having any meetings or dealings with Archbishop MacGauran.[81] Clearly, as the evidence stood, it would have been unjustifiable to charge O'Neill with foreign conspiracy. Indeed, it looked as if he himself was the victim of a conspiracy mounted by his enemies.

Two aspects of the proceedings on this charge must be stressed. The fact that Marshal Bagenal had dredged up further allegations, after the original ones had failed, must have been highly irregular, though presumably admissible at the time. According to O'Neill: 'no man that was sent for to be examined could be heard, before the marshal or some of his, had taught him what to say. And he had dealing in all things, well known to be my malicious enemy'.[82] The council confirmed that the earl had made this complaint several times at Dundalk but pointed out that Bagenal had not been commissioned to confer with the witnesses. The council also recollected that the earl had objected to the marshal, one of his accusers, sitting as a judge over him.[83] In spite of his vociferous protestations, Tyrone's behaviour at Dundalk was not beyond reproach. Certain information suggests that O'Neill was putting pressure on key witnesses, especially Henry óg, to have them retract incriminating evidence.[84] As the queen subsequently observed: 'he aspiring to that tyrannical government as it seemeth by the depositions he doth, the informers shall for fear of him, have cause to go back on their confessions, or hereafter not to adventure to do the like'.[85]

Another serious charge against the earl was that he had been privy to the murder of Phelim MacTurlough O'Neill. Although this was obviously a political assassination plotted by the earl, he covered it up as revenge by the O'Hagans for the murder of one of their clan. Once again Bagenal was involved in the evidential process since the first declaration by an eye-witness, Ever MacRory O'Neill, had been given in his presence on 1 June.[86] The earl of Tyrone later protested that 'the complaint was preferred by one of Phelim's kinsmen, and after it had been once read to the lord deputy, it was delivered

---

[79] Ibid. no. 23(1–5).
[80] Ibid. no. 23(7–12).
[81] CSPI, v. 147–8. A Vatican source dated 1601 states that Neill swore an oath of confederation with other lords at the start of the war in the presence of Archbishop MacGuaran: 'Some papers relating to the Nine Years War', ed. J. Hagan, Archivium Hibernicum, ii (1913), 304.
[82] PRO SP 63/170, no. 53.
[83] CSPI, v. 147–9.
[84] PRO SP 63/169, no. 49(5); 170, no. 23(2).
[85] Ibid. 170, no. 36.
[86] Ibid. nos 1, 1(1).

back again to the clerk that wrote it, to make it more sharp and bitter against me'.[87] This was probably a reference to MacRory's initial declaration and the second one made by him together with Colla MacFerdoragh O'Neill. Although the second presented a fuller account, the substance was unchanged.[88] Tyrone swore by Her Majesty's hand that he had not been a party to the murder, although he still maintained his opinion that Phelim MacTurlough was a bad man and himself a murderer.[89] The majority of the council was satisfied with this since there was only circumstantial evidence against the earl. However, on this charge, 'I, the Deputy, was of another mind'.[90]

The earl was also charged with complicity in Maguire's activities against the government. A deposition from Moris O'Scanlon and an intercepted letter from Maguire to the earl clearly implicated him in the eviction of Willis from Fermanagh and the subsequent activities of Maguire in Connacht.[91] Further-more, two separate sources stated that Maguire and O'Neill had been in conference in mid-May.[92] Charged with sending Cormac MacBaron and Conn Mac an Íarla into Fermanagh to assist Maguire, the earl provided the ridiculous explanation that they had only gone into that country with a few men to discover the cause of the hubbub there. As such, this is reminiscent of the earl's facile excuse for Conn Mac an Íarla's attack on Monaghan the previous year. The earl also claimed that he had subsequently rescued Willis and his men from the wrath of Maguire.[93] O'Neill's involvement with Maguire was clear and on this count alone he should have been arrested. The privy council believed as much and later rounded on the Irish council for not doing so.[94]

After its failure to arrest the earl, the council was forced to negotiate with him. Maguire presented the most pressing problem. He had ignored the summons to appear at Dundalk on a protection.[95] No doubt, his interrogation would have further incriminated the earl. Recollection of the fate of Hugh Roe MacMahon would have provided another reason for absence. Instead, whilst the meeting at Dundalk was in progress, Maguire mounted another attack on Connacht, this time directed against county Roscommon. This raid proved less successful for Maguire: Archbishop MacGauran and certain chief lords of Fermanagh were killed.[96] The dead allegedly included some of the earl's kinsmen; one of whom was subsequently identified as Conn MacTurlough O'Neill.[97] News of this raid towards the end of June prompted the council to grant a commission to O'Neill – an idea which he had probably mooted during his own cross-examination. The earl's task was to disperse Maguire's forces and

[87] Ibid. no. 53.
[88] Ibid. no. 1(1); CSPI, v. 107–9.
[89] PRO SP 63/170, no. 53.
[90] CSPI, v. 148–9.
[91] PRO SP 63/170, nos 23(13, 15).
[92] CSPI, v. 105, 108.
[93] Ibid. 148.
[94] APC, xxiv. 364–9.
[95] PRO SP 63/170, no. 5.
[96] CSPI, v. 118–19, 136; PRO SP 63/170, no. 18.
[97] CSPI, v. 136; PRO SP 63/170, no. 27.

bring him to obedience.[98] Fitzwilliam was opposed to this decision but the state was in a weak position militarily.[99] Loftus and Jones later asserted that this was the only means of obtaining a peaceful settlement in Ulster 'without great and excessive charges to Her Majesty and very dangerous broils throughout that province'. They had hoped that the earl would perform a similar service as that of the previous year when Hugh Roe O'Donnell had submitted through his endeavours. Furthermore, it was hoped that the earl would confirm his loyalty to the crown by his present dealings with Maguire.[100] The commission granted to O'Neill is no longer extant but the privy council which received a copy complained about 'honouring the earl with such an ample commission as he might protect all others with whom he should treat as well as Maguire'.[101] This commission can be seen as a derogation of Bagenal's provincial authority and indeed the marshal was quick to point out that it only helped confirm O'Neill's standing in Ulster.[102] In taking up the commission at Dundalk, the earl promised to use armed force against Maguire if negotiations failed and even suggested a three-pronged attack on Fermanagh from Tyrone, Connacht and the Pale.[103]

The final settlement of the land dispute between the earl and Turlough Luineach and the establishment of civil government in Tyrone were also discussed. The lord deputy and council believed that the agreement already reached between the parties had been made under duress, with Art Mac-Turlough signing without his father's consent.[104] The earl of Tyrone admitted that Art MacTurlough had signed the agreement but claimed that he had been authorised to do so by his father. He also claimed that the initial agreement had been perfectly acceptable to Turlough and that it had been brought into question by the interference of the marshal and the lord deputy.[105] Yet the council had only acted on this matter as a result of the protests made by Turlough. Furthermore at Dundalk Turlough co-operated fully with the council in handing over letters intercepted from Maguire and letters written by the earl relating to the agreement.[106] The parties and their lawyers debated the land dispute before the council. The final agreement was probably much the same as the original.[107] Although the council had little room to manoeuvre on the matter, Bagenal saw its acceptance as a negation of government policy. Rather than destroying the absolute government of the O'Neills, that power was now simply transferred from one O'Neill to another.[108]

The future administration of the O'Neill lordship was now under scrutiny. Michaelmas 1592 had seen the first introduction of sheriffs with Cormac Mac-

98 Ibid. nos 15, 23.
99 BL Add. 12,503, fo. 394.
100 PRO SP 63/171, no. 2.
101 APC, xxiv. 364–9.
102 Fiants, 16th Report, no. 5552; PRO SP 63/170, no. 27.
103 Ibid. no. 44 (4).
104 Ibid. 169, no. 49(1).
105 Ibid. 170, no. 53.
106 Ibid. 169, nos 41, 49(1); 170, no. 23(15–18).
107 Ibid. no. 23; C, Carew, iii. 73–5.
108 PRO SP 63/170, no. 27.

Baron being appointed for Tyrone and Sir Oghy O'Hanlon for Armagh.[109] At Dundalk, the earl presented a memorandum to the council 'for the government and reformation of the country or territory of Tyrone'. He asserted that the territory was too impoverished to support the maintenance of two sheriffs and the construction of two shire halls and gaols. He wanted Tyrone reduced to one county with a countryman as sheriff assisted by two Palesmen as under-sheriffs. He promised to construct the necessary buildings as soon as possible and re-quested the introduction of common law procedures. This memorandum un-doubtedly represented O'Neill's absolute bottom line if English local government was going to be foisted upon him. The earl envisaged a single county roughly coterminous with the three modern units of Tyrone, Armagh and Derry. This district would have enjoyed a sort of palatinate status thereby leaving him a preponderant influence in the province at large. One intention was the exclusion of sheriffs, such as O'Hanlon, who were clients of Bagenal. The failure to account for the jurisdiction of the chief commissioner of Ulster and the establishment of freeholders was also significant. The state was unwill-ing to accord the earl such authority; the more so because his non-performance of the 1590 articles raised suspicions about his desire to implement genuine reform. Indeed, the memorandum was presented before the finalisation of the agreement with Turlough and as such it was probably a ploy to win the council's acquiescence.[110]

The handling of the news of events at Dundalk became a political issue. The Irish council's dispatch of 30 June contained only the depositions and, on this basis, the queen and her privy council administered an immediate and stinging rebuke to the Dublin government. The queen considered that the allegations in the depositions had been at least sufficient to arrest the earl. Certainly, there had been no cause to give him an ample commission 'to deal with Maguire, being his confederate in treasonable actions'. Furthermore, she rejected out of hand the agreement made between the earl and Turlough Luineach. The privy council underscored these objections. In addition, the privy councillors empha-sised the earl's manifest implication in Maguire's activities and wanted to know why no action had been taken against him over the murder of Phelim Mac-Turlough. Both the queen and the privy council wondered why the earl himself had not answered the charges made against him.[111] In spite of all this, a dra-matic change took place in the opinion of the authorities in London the following day. O'Neill's letters arrived; one to the privy council complained of 'extremity at the lord deputy's hands through the working of the marshal' and another to the earl of Essex requested his intercession with the queen.[112] No doubt, Essex's influence proved important at this juncture. O'Neill's proposal for the referral of his case to a commission of the chief justice, the chief baron, the chief justice of the common pleas and the master of the rolls was accepted.

[109] Ibid. no. 58.
[110] Ibid. 129, no. 3; 170, nos 15, 15(1), 58; ULC Kk 1 15 no. 5, fos 15–16.
[111] PRO SP 63/170, no. 36; APC, xxiv. 364–9.
[112] PRO SP 63/170, nos 15, 16.

The agreement with Turlough Luineach was referred for further consideration.[113]

At the end of July, the earl of Tyrone again felt impelled to write to the privy council when he discovered that his answers to the charges against him had not been sent to London with the depositions. He had given his answers in writing at the time and these had been accepted by the lord deputy and council.[114] O'Neill would have been gratified with the reply from London which showed the privy council well-disposed to him and distrustful of its own officials in Ireland.[115] It was not until mid-September that Fitzwilliam and his council provided the authorities in London with an adequate account of events at Dundalk and this was a result of direct prompting by O'Neill. Two important points emerged from this statement in relation to Fitzwilliam's conduct. First, the council did not know who had sent over the complaint made by the kinsmen of Phelim MacTurlough since it had decided against that course of action when it was unable to come to a decision on the case. However, annotations on the bill show that it was Fitzwilliam's doing. Secondly, the council had motioned Fitzwilliam on a number of occasions to send over the earl's answers but he had omitted to do so.[116] A subsequent letter to Burghley shows that Fitzwilliam continued to harbour doubts about O'Neill's loyalty.[117]

Some conclusions must be reached on this episode. Insufficient evidence was adduced to press charges of foreign conspiracy against O'Neill but he was clearly guilty of supporting Maguire. Divided and threatened, the council had decided not to arrest the earl. Afterwards, O'Neill's standing improved in the eyes of the privy council on account of the mishandling of the news of events at Dundalk which appeared to give credence to his allegations against Bagenal and Fitzwilliam. In the light of Bagenal's ambitions as would-be provincial governor, there are grounds to suspect his behaviour towards the earl. However, given the volatile state of Ulster, there would have been plenty of rumours on which to base his allegations against O'Neill. Fitzwilliam's behaviour is more difficult to assess. O'Neill, who was well aware of Fitzwilliam's susceptibility to bribery, claimed that he had been suborned by the marshal. However, it is more likely that the lord deputy acted for reasons of state. It is interesting that Sir James Perrot, who was not well-disposed towards Fitzwilliam, did not take the opportunity to condemn him on this point in *The chronicle of Ireland*.[118] Anyway it must be emphasised that both the lord deputy and the council had initially intended to arrest O'Neill on the basis of the allegations made in April. That consensus broke down in Dundalk. Yet, it was the actual handling of the news of Dundalk which brings suspicion upon the lord deputy. The only possible explanation is that Fitzwilliam by providing selective information hoped to incriminate O'Neill in the eyes of the privy council without detaching himself from the Irish council's line. However, for the benefit of government policy and

---

113 Ibid. no. 36; APC, xxiv. 364–9. In the event, this commission never reviewed the earl's case.
114 PRO SP 63/170, no. 57.
115 APC, xxiv. 461–6.
116 CSPI, v. 107–9, 147–9.
117 Ibid. 153–4.
118 Perrot, *Chronicle of Ireland*, 76.

the subsequent judgement of posterity, he should have separated himself from the majority view of the council by stating his opinion on O'Neill as he did eventually in his *Memoir*.

In Ulster, the immediate consequence of the Dundalk proceedings was two months of negotiations between Maguire and the government with O'Neill as mediator. In military and financial terms, the government's position was weak and it was therefore forced to grant a number of protections in the hope of reaching a peaceful settlement.[119] At the start of July, the Irish council granted Maguire a two month protection.[120] On receipt of this, Maguire demanded instead a six month protection, the inclusion of Brian óg O'Rourke and Connor óg MacDermot (Roscommon) and an assurance of Bingham's peaceful intentions. Maguire also claimed an inability to disperse his forces quickly, because he had hired them for a quarter of a year.[121] The earl's reports to the council are the only source of information for the events that followed. At the end of July he informed Maguire of the council's refusal to accede to the demands, and of his own promise to the council to use force against him. As a result, Maguire promised to accompany O'Neill to Dublin if another protection for three months could be secured. The council granted this request.[122] In the middle of August, O'Neill met Maguire at Lough Foyle. Here Maguire promised to submit by 15 September and order was taken 'for the present dispersing of his forces which I saw done before my face and their entertainment fully paid'.[123] However, at the start of September, Maguire and his forces invaded Monaghan with the assistance of those MacMahons who were disaffected with the settlement there. The main targets were John Talbott, the leasee of Farney, and the garrison forces at Monaghan town.[124] The earl warned the council about the raid on Monaghan only when it was actually taking place. If the greater part of Maguire's forces was actually dispersed at Lough Foyle, a good distance from Fermanagh, how were those forces able to reassemble there a fortnight later without his knowledge?[125] Either O'Neill was unable to control Maguire and hence repeat the success which he had achieved with O'Donnell the previous year or more likely the Monaghan raid took place with his approval and connivance but proved less successful than expected. At any rate, he was now committed to taking military action against Maguire in co-operation with the government. However, O'Neill's outward participation in this task was actually part of a holding operation designed to limit the government's advance.

The subsequent military campaign took place in the autumn of 1593. It began with the public proclamation of Maguire and his adherents as traitors in the middle of September.[126] Sir Henry Bagenal, as marshal of the army, drew up a journal of the campaign. First, the garrison forces under his command entered

119 *CSPI*, v. 129–130.
120 PRO SP 63/170, nos 38, 38(1).
121 *CSPI*, v. 127–8.
122 Ibid. 137–8.
123 PRO SP 63/171, nos 33(1, 3).
124 Ibid. no. 33.
125 Ibid. no. 33(3, 6); *CSPI*, v. 147.
126 PRO SP 63/171, no. 33.

the Dartry district of Monaghan and attacked Brian MacHugh óg, claimant to the MacMahon title, and his brother, Rory. Afterwards, these forces moved into Fermanagh where on 26 September they effected a rendezvous with those of the earl of Tyrone. As the lands on the north side of the Erne were ravaged, Maguire retreated westwards. On 10 October, Maguire made a stand at the ford of the Erne, near Beleek but was defeated by the forces of Bagenal and O'Neill, with the loss of at least 300 men. In spite of his earlier demands to intervene in Ulster, the forces of Bingham played little or no part in this campaign. After the success over Maguire, Bagenal left 300 troops under the command of Captain Dowdall to consolidate the government's position in Fermanagh.[127] This was achieved on 2 February the following year when Dowdall's men gained possession of Maguire's island stronghold of Enniskillen after a nine day siege.[128]

Although O'Neill's service against Maguire was voluntary, it was not undertaken with alacrity. With few exceptions, our information comes contrarily from O'Neill and Bagenal. Yet a close examination of O'Neill's correspondence lends validity to at least some of Bagenal's allegations. The earl was slow to assemble his forces and march into Fermanagh. In one case he claimed that his footsoldiers had been 'toiled with rain and the darkness of the night'; in another he complained about the tenuous lines of communication with the marshal.[129] Bagenal reported that O'Neill's first action was to take a prey from Connor Roe Maguire, the main rival to the ruling lord of Fermanagh and an ally of the government. It is obvious from O'Neill's own correspondence that his forces attacked and spoiled Connor Roe's lands until notification of his protection arrived from the marshal.[130] Two months later Connor Roe was still trying to obtain restitution of these preys from O'Neill.[131] When O'Neill eventually pitched camp inside Fermanagh, he had in his company, according to the marshal, 200 horse and 600 foot; this was half the complement of foot which he had originally promised the council in Dublin the previous month.[132] The information provided by the marshal and the earl concerning the events of the next fortnight shows a degree of concurrence. Both forces were uneasy and seem to have spent as much time watching each other as attacking the enemy. Both commanders disagreed over tactics.[133] In a conference the marshal favoured the separate deployment of their forces, 'yet doth his lord absolutely refuse to do the same, alleging his forces to be too slender to encounter the rebels'.[134] Only after a letter from the council complaining about his dilatory

---

[127] CSPI, v. 175–80.
[128] Dowdall claimed that the castle had been taken 'by boats, by engines, by sap and by scaling': CSPI, v. 207–9. Captain Thomas Lee claimed that it was 'yielded in the end upon composition. And Your Majesty's word being passed to the poor beggars that kept it, they were all notwithstanding put to the sword in a most miserable sort': BL Harleian 35, fos 258–65.
[129] PRO SP 63/171, nos 1, 1(2); CSPI, v. 157–8.
[130] Ibid. 156–8, 164; PRO SP 63/171, no. 1(2).
[131] CSPI, v. 185.
[132] Ibid. 177; PRO SP 63/170, no. 33.
[133] CSPI, v. 177–9; Lambeth, Carew 617, fos 206–8.
[134] PRO SP 63/172, no. 2(11).

conduct, did the earl undertake a separate expedition to the borders of Tircon-nell.[135]

The marshal and the earl, not surprisingly, gave conflicting reports on the battle of the Erne Ford. The earl later claimed that he had approached the marshal after the battle with a proposal for an agreed account of events. Ac-cording to the earl, the marshal had duped him by persuading him to make a favourable mention of his conduct in the battle which he then failed to recipro-cate.[136] In examining their respective accounts, it must be noted that the marshal gave a balanced overall account of a military engagement while the earl presented a more personalised view of events.[137] In his report to the Irish council, O'Neill not only gave a good mention of Bagenal's action but also praised the service of his own soldiers and friends, such as Henry Hovenden, Michael Marshall, Captain Lee and Dudley Loftus.[138] A separate report to Chancellor Loftus, in which he again praised the valiant actions of his son Dudley, earned the earl a letter of commendation to Burghley.[139] On his return to Dublin, Bagenal gave Fitzwilliam a private report on the earl's conduct. The morning before the battle most of his forces departed. The earl himself wished to leave claiming lack of supplies but in the end he was forced to participate with a small company of horse and foot.[140] This was partially confirmed by John Parker. He reported the earl's bravery in the battle as well as the subsequent scolding which he gave to his horsemen for their slowness in backing him up.[141] Afterwards, the earl wrote to the privy council in an attempt to allay suspicion and correct any misreports. He claimed that 'it was by my special advice that service was taken in hand, and I was one of the first that made an assault upon those rascals'. He also emphasised the fact that he had been wounded in the battle: 'not doubting that my blood now lost in this and other services hereto-fore will satisfy the queen's Majesty, and confirm her good opinion of me and also your lordships'.[142] In this regard Lughaidh Ó Cléirigh's wry comment is especially apt: 'Aodh Ó Neill was wounded there, and he was pleased thereat, so that the English should not have any suspicion of him'.[143]

During the Fermanagh campaign, reports were received that O'Neill was indirectly assisting Maguire and that a secret meeting had taken place between them. Matthew Smith, who was left in charge of the Monaghan garrison, alleged that 30–40,000 head of Maguire's cattle had been shifted by O'Neill to Tyrone for safekeeping.[144] Intelligence of the secret meeting came from two separate sources, though the fact that they were not made simultaneously weakens their claim to veracity. On 29 September Sir Richard Bingham re-ceived news from his spies that O'Neill, O'Donnell and Maguire had met

135 *CSPI*, v. 164, 178.
136 Lambeth, Carew 617, fos 207–8.
137 PRO SP 63/172, no. 4(1); *CSPI*, v. 166–8.
138 Ibid. 166.
139 Ibid. 167–8.
140 PRO SP 63/172, no. 19.
141 Ibid. no. 10.
142 *CSPI*, v. 170–1.
143 *Life*, i. 65.
144 *CSPI*, v. 164.

secretly. As Bingham informed Fitzwilliam: 'all men of judgement here, and such espials and beggars as I employ in Fermanagh doth wholly assure me that Maguire doth nothing without the earl's advice and consent, and that the earl may at his own pleasure rule both Maguire and Hugh Roe O'Donnell'. On receipt of this information, the council sought to verify it, presumably by writing to Bagenal.[145] However, it was not until November that Bagenal reported similar intelligence in a secret memorandum to Fitzwilliam, which he in turn sent to England for Burghley's perusal only.[146]

The indirect role played by Hugh Roe O'Donnell sheds more light on these developments. At the outset, the Irish council tried to ensure his neutrality. Rather than include O'Donnell in the proclamation of traitors, it had simply warned him not to permit the use of his lordship as a safe haven for Maguire's followers and herds.[147] This seemed to be working; after a meeting with O'Neill at Dungannon, O'Donnell wrote to the council distancing himself from the actions of Maguire and promising to do service against him. Even after news that some of Maguire's goods and cattle had been shifted into Tirconnell, the council was still trying to conciliate him. They instructed O'Donnell to seize Maguire's property for the queen's use, out of which he would be generously rewarded. However, by this stage, O'Neill was informing the council that he was no longer able to command O'Donnell.[148] O'Donnell was not personally involved in the battle of the Erne Ford but many of those killed were from Tirconnell, including galloglass leaders from all three MacSweeny septs.[149] Furthermore, a letter from O'Donnell was found on the corpse of a Scottish mercenary captain. This showed that the captain had been hired by O'Donnell and sent to aid Maguire.[150] After the battle, O'Donnell maintained this outward neutrality, permitting the government forces unimpeded use of the passes to Connacht and even sending Bagenal cattle for victualling purposes.[151] Ó Cléirigh's account of O'Donnell's participation in the battle of the Erne Ford is illuminating:

> As for Ó Domhnaill, it was a great affliction of spirit and mind to him that the English should thus return. But yet as they did not attack him, he did not atttack them, on account of the unprepared state in which he was, and he left a large body of his people at the aforesaid ford, which he gave for Maguidir's protection, though he withdrew himself by command of O'Neill, for there were messages between them secretly without the knowledge of the English.[152]

The crucial aspect of this account is Ó Cléirigh's lapse in according the

---

145 Ibid. 162–3.
146 Ibid. 181–2.
147 PRO SP 63/171, nos 33, 36.
148 CSPI, v. 164–5.
149 Ibid. 169–70; PRO SP 63/172, no. 18.
150 Ibid. no. 18(1).
151 Ibid. 172, 11(2); CSPI, v. 179.
152 Life, i. 67.

direction of events to O'Neill, in apparent contradiction of his insistent claim that O'Donnell was the promoter and commander of the Irish in the war.[153]

This major inconsistency in Ó Cléirigh's argument as well as the accumulation of government intelligence help us to form a conclusion concerning O'Neill's conduct. In the first instance, an undertaking to reduce Maguire by negotiation, if not by force, may have been the only means open to O'Neill to extricate himself from the imbroglio at Dundalk. By giving this undertaking, it could be argued that O'Neill acted genuinely on behalf of the government but in so doing proved unable to control his followers in preventing either Maguire's attack on Monaghan or the desertion of most of his own forces before the battle of the Erne Ford. Consequently, fearing the complete loss of his followers' support, he was forced to go to war on their side against the crown. Yet, this is unlikely given O'Neill's initial intrigues with Maguire, the suspicions at the time of the Fermanagh campaign and the sequel. The alternative is to regard this interlude as part of O'Neill's long term strategy. In obtaining a number of protections for Maguire, he held up military action until the harvest was gathered.[154] When the invasion of Fermanagh commenced, Maguire's cattle were moved to neighbouring lordships and his grain put in storage.[155] The late season would minimise the government's successes which it would be unable to consolidate. On a wider plane, had O'Neill refused to co-operate against Maguire, English reinforcements would have arrived in Ireland by the spring of 1594. As it turned out, the 300 troops garrisoned in Fermanagh put an enormous strain on the Dublin administration which had a small military establishment and a weak financial base. Furthermore, this outward display of loyalty ensured good relations with London at a time when the privy council was puzzled by the conduct of its Irish counterpart in the Dundalk proceedings. There was even a possibility of the Spanish embassy bearing fruit. Nevertheless, O'Neill took this course at the risk of suffering personal injury and of advancing government reform into the heart of Ulster.

On his return to Dublin, Bagenal proposed the settlement of Fermanagh along the lines of Monaghan: 'experience doth show what good hath grown in some parts of this realm by the division of seignories and reducing the uncertainty of the lords cuttings unto a rent certain'. The reorganisation of Monaghan had been an exemplary achievement. The successful introduction of 'Justice' there was such that the building where the court sessions took place 'is grown incapable of the press of suitors'. Furthermore, the freeholders of Monaghan had served willingly in the late campaign against Brian MacHugh óg who sought to tyrannise over them. Now, he believed, the people of Fermanagh were equally 'desirous to be delivered from the tyranny of their superiors'.[156] At the council table, Bagenal's proposals were keenly supported by Fitzwilliam and others but there were two obstacles. The first problem was that the annual

153 Ibid. 59–61.
154 PRO SP 63/171, no. 36.
155 CSPI, v. 159; PRO SP 63/172, no. 11.
156 Ibid. no. 16. Patrick MacArt Moile MacMahon was at this time demanding the redivision of Brian MacHugh óg's lands in his favour. However, Fitzwilliam did not wish to make one MacMahon 'to be great over the rest': ibid. no. 18(8).

rental of Fermanagh had been granted to Turlough Luineach O'Neill for life. For this reason and on account of the pressing military situation, an interim settlement with the chief lords was a priority. This presented another problem in that the chief law officers of the Irish council, by their interpretation of the proclamation of Maguire, were opposed to pardoning Maguire's followers.[157] Asked to decide the issue, the queen produced an ambiguous resolution which tended to favour the arguments of the lord deputy and marshal.[158] After the fall of Enniskillen in February 1594, an interim settlement began to emerge of its own accord. Captain Dowdall reached agreement with Connor Roe Maguire, the newly-appointed sheriff of Fermanagh, and the rest of the gentry of the county, most of whom had now submitted. By this, the chief lords agreed to maintain 120 government troops for four months at their own charges and to assist the crown against their former lord.[159] However, Fermanagh was spared replication of the Monaghan model by a further escalation in the crisis.

The months which followed O'Neill's participation in the Fermanagh campaign saw a dramatic change in his stance to one of non-co-operation with the government. At the beginning of November, the earl dismissed Lieutenant Michael Marshall, who had fought gallantly against Maguire, and the forty-four Englishmen amongst his footsoldiers.[160] By February of the following year, O'Neill had arrested and imprisoned the three surviving sons of Shane O'Neill. When the government requested their custody and promised not to use them as counterweights against him, the earl refused to hand them over.[161] Later in his *Memoir*, Fitzwilliam interpreted both these events as clear signs of O'Neill's disloyalty.[162] The same month Bagenal reported that the earl had made a proclamation in all the churches of Tyrone for the recruitment and maintenance of 1,900 men to defend his lordship.[163] The proxy warfare practised before the Fermanagh interlude resumed with the attacks on Bagenal's clients and property, the Monaghan settlement and the northern Pale.[164] The marshal's observation is important: 'he doth not in any way covertly procede in that he useth his son, his brethren and nephews as open instruments of his wicked designments'.[165] At the same time as these events, a litany of complaints, old and new, emanated from O'Neill.[166] The culmination was an inflammatory letter of 19 February in which O'Neill asserted that the real beneficiaries of his services on behalf of the crown were his enemies, in particular the marshal. However much he was beholden to Her Majesty, she had 'bestowed that upon me, which by descent I ought to have'. He accused the lord deputy and marshal of plotting his destruction.[167] Bagenal provided a different viewpoint: 'I have

---

[157] Ibid. nos 16, 18.
[158] ULC Kk 1 15 no. 15, fos 49–51.
[159] *CSPI*, v. 185; PRO SP 63/173, no. 34, 35(2).
[160] Ibid. 172, nos 20, 20(1).
[161] Ibid. 173, nos 64, 64(1, 7).
[162] BL Add. 12,503, fo. 396.
[163] PRO SP 63/173, no. 64(3).
[164] Ibid. nos 64(6, 11), 77, 79, 81, 92(5).
[165] Ibid. no. 97.
[166] *CSPI*, v. 171–2; PRO SP 63/172, no. 18(5); 173, no. 22(2).
[167] Ibid. no. 64(1).

known that usual device in men of evil affection to except against the persons of those who have had the charge or government over them, when they meant nothing else but to spurn against authority.'[168]

The crisis had come to a head over O'Donnell. After the Fermanagh campaign, the Irish council had found him 'deeply inculped in Maguire's treasons' and had requested the queen's resolution.[169] She decided that the earl of Tyrone could deal with O'Donnell on account of ties of marriage and dependence. If O'Donnell proved impervious to influence, Tyrone was to use force to obtain his submission.[170] On receipt of these instructions in February 1594, O'Neill refused to comply, complaining that his previous services on behalf of the crown had gone unrewarded.[171] The council then detailed Bagenal to parley with O'Donnell.[172] He sent a messenger to O'Donnell but O'Neill refused him passage beyond Dungannon. The earl claimed that Maguire's forces lying in western Tyrone constituted a danger to the man's life. He allegedly said that Tirconnell would not suffer the same fate as Fermanagh and returned the messenger to the marshal with a forthright letter.[173] 'I will deal plainly with you, me thinketh I have done too much in those matters seeing I have been so slenderly recompensed.' As for O'Donnell, the most he could offer was to arrange a meeting with commissioners. He indicated clearly who was in charge 'truly for my part, I will have no dealing with you in these behalf, neither shall O'Donnell by my consent or counsel'.[174] Subsequently, O'Neill stipulated two conditions on which he would arrange a meeting between O'Donnell and the commissioners: the exclusion of Bagenal from the commission and the postponement of military action against Tirconnell.[175] Given the deficiencies of the military establishment, the council had no option but to send a commission to the northern borders. It selected Loftus, Gardiner and St Leger for the task and agreed to put off action against O'Donnell, indicating that the earl himself should endeavour to prevent attacks on the Pale.[176] The commissioners were instructed 'to assure O'Donnell and draw him from all confederacy with the rebels'.[177] The state knew from intelligence reports that O'Donnell was preparing for war.[178] However, by the time the commission was made out on 7 March 1594, the priority was O'Neill, not O'Donnell. Therefore the commissioners were 'to discover the earl, what mind he beareth towards Her Majesty and her services, and what designs he hath to trouble the tranquillity of the state, by adhering to any rebels or practising or allowing to draw in Scots or other foreign forces, or any other whatsoever to contrary his duty to her Majesty'. In particular, they were to prevent the attacks from his lordship and to obtain

[168] Ibid. no. 64(3).
[169] Ibid. 172, no. 18.
[170] ULC Kk 1 15 no. 15, fos 49–51.
[171] PRO SP 63/173, no. 22(2).
[172] Ibid. no. 22.
[173] Ibid. nos 64(3–4).
[174] Ibid. no. 64(5).
[175] Ibid. no. 64(1).
[176] CSPI, v. 214; PRO SP 63/173, no. 64(2).
[177] Ibid. no. 91(2).
[178] Ibid. nos 45(1); 64(4); CSPI, v. 216–18.

restitution of spoils. In short, they were to do all within law, reason and discretion 'to stay and pacify these present broils'.[179]

In the journal of the proceedings at Dundalk and its vicinity between 8 and 15 March, the commissioners described their junketings, encounters and negotiations with O'Neill and O'Donnell.[180] Writing in the middle decades of this century, O'Faolain and Falls overdramatised and overpersonalised these events to give the impression of O'Neill caught between his loyalty to the crown and the pressure of his followers.[181] On close examination, this proves to be a misreading of the proceedings. At the outset, the earl refused to go into Dundalk alleging that his life was in danger. Instead, he sent Henry Hovenden to learn the commissioner's intentions towards the Ulster and Connachtmen already in action. Eventually, O'Neill and O'Donnell met one of the commissioners, Sir Robert Gardiner, outside Dundalk. O'Neill claimed that Fitzwilliam and Bagenal had procured a warrant out of England for his arrest and that they had sought his life since their last meeting at Dundalk. The marshal had been the chief beneficiary of his services on behalf of the crown. He disliked government policy: 'he perceived the plot intended by the executing of the late MacMahon, and next by the coming of Captain Willis with great force into Maguire's country, saying there would be the like course with others'. O'Neill evinced fear of conviction for the actions of his loose followers (a clear reference to the fate of Hugh Roe MacMahon). Gardiner then met O'Donnell and 'gathered by many his speeches that he would be ruled by the earl'. The subsequent events, involving Gardiner, O'Neill and the other Ulster lords, have been misconstrued. O'Neill's followers were not trying to force him to make a choice, rather, like the earl himself, they genuinely feared his arrest. Moreover, the tearful parting with his friend, Gardiner, was less about his 'disloyalty' to the crown than the highly problematic course on which he was embarking. Further meetings did take place in Dundalk town between O'Neill and the commissioners. These only occured after the issue of a protection to O'Neill; a significant departure in his relationship with the crown. The earl took the opportunity to draw up his grievances in writing. The commissioners disliked many of the articles, especially the first, but he refused to alter them.[182]

The grievances which O'Neill presented to the commissioners on 14 March consisted of seventeen articles; he sent a further article, which he had apparently forgotten, to his friend, Sir Henry Wallop, early the next month. These articles can be divided roughly into four categories: personal complaints against Fitzwilliam and Bagenal, jurisdictional rivalry with Bagenal, want of reward for services rendered and objections against current government policy. The commissioners had objected vehemently to the first article which concerned the proceedings at Dundalk the previous year. According to O'Neill, Bagenal had suborned Fitzwilliam 'with many bribes as well as plate as by giving him sundry warrants of great sums and other means'. Subsequently, the marshal had produced his enemies as witnesses to prove false accusations of treason against

[179] PRO SP 63/173, no. 91(2).
[180] CSPI, v. 221–6.
[181] O'Faolain, The Great O'Neill, 138–43; Falls, Elizabeth's Irish wars, 178–80.
[182] CSPI, v. 221–6; PRO SP 63/174, no. 2.

him. This allegation was part truth and part exaggeration. Bagenal's behaviour at Dundalk had been irregular and doubtless reflected his wish to remove O'Neill to further his own ambitions in the North. On the other hand, whatever Fitzwilliam's connections with Bagenal, his desire to arrest O'Neill was in the interests of the state. The earl asserted that Fitzwilliam and Bagenal were 'greatly befriended at Court' (i.e. by Burghley) whereas he was 'destitute of friends' since the deaths of Leicester, Hatton and Walsingham. Once again this was not the whole story: Essex was clearly willing to back O'Neill at Court and the same article referred to the honourable dealings of Loftus, Gardiner and more recently St Leger towards him. O'Neill's marriage with Mabel Bagenal was also a subject of enmity. Two years after the marriage, the marshal still withheld the dowry of £1,000 which Sir Nicholas Bagenal had left for his daughter.

The fifteenth article related to Bagenal's position as Chief Commissioner of Ulster. The earl insisted that Bagenal had, unbeknownst to the queen, obtained a commission under the broad seal of Ireland 'to end and determine all causes in the province of Ulster'. Bagenal had appointed a Chief Sergeant to execute his orders in the province 'whereat the earl is not well pleased, that the marshal (being his enemy and an open practiser of his overthrow) should bear that sway over him'. No mention was made of the privy council letter of 1591 which exempted Tyrone from the marshal's jurisdiction. Nevertheless, a bitter rivalry over the small lordships of south-east Ulster was evident. In the early 1580s O'Neill had reduced South Clandeboye, Killultagh, Kilwarlin, Kinelarty, Orior and Oriel. He made the outrageous claim that the queen had supported him in this. Since then he alleged that his supporters in these territories had been displaced by men of the marshal's faction. Furthermore, the earl and his countrymen hated the government officials, such as Henshaw, the seneschal of Monaghan, and Moate, the vice-constable of the Blackwater fort, whom they considered instruments of the marshal. O'Neill insisted that these men sought only his overthrow and their own private gain.[183] He demanded 'upright gentlemen' as replacements 'to stand indifferent between him and his adversaries'.

Articles four to eight concerned the earl's service on behalf of the crown. During the Armada crisis, his footmen under the leadership of his foster-brothers, Richard and Henry Hovenden, had killed 500–600 Spaniards in Tirconnell. The best men had been taken prisoner and the earl had turned them over to the authorities but no reward had been forthcoming. The earl had served voluntarily in the recent action against Maguire. This had cost him £3,000 and injury to his own person. In spite of this, he had received neither thanks nor recompense. Conversely, he claimed that the marshal had been paid a concordatum of £400. There is confirmation of this claim from other sources. The treasury accounts indicate that Bagenal was paid £86 for 43 days diet and travel against Maguire.[184] Tom Lee complained that Fitzwilliam had paid the marshall the sum of £400 out 'of Your Majesty's treasury and by defalks of the

---

[183] The earl pointed out that such officials 'always fleeceth and secretly robbeth the subject to fill their own purses and maintain their bribes'.
[184] PRO Audit Office 1/286/1078 m. 55d.

country' over and above the pay and perks of his office.[185] It is ironic that Bagenal himself complained that he had not received a letter of thanks from the queen for his service against Maguire even though he had been rewarded for doing his duty.[186] O'Neill produced three other articles to demonstrate how the marshal had sought to frustrate and misreport his actions in the Fermanagh campaign.

In the complaints about government policy, O'Neill revealed his antipathy towards the Monaghan settlement and exemplified the breakdown of 'trust' between the Gaelic lords and crown officials. The earl had obtained a privy council letter to settle his outstanding claims on the estate of the late Sir Ross MacMahon, his son-in-law; but this had no effect. In the division of Monaghan, the marshal had received a large grant; merchants and men of no account were also recipients but the earl's claims and services had been ignored. O'Neill commented on the fractured state of relations between the northern lords and government officials. Hugh Roe MacMahon had attended the lord deputy upon the word of certain gentlemen but afterwards had been executed as a traitor contrary to all justice 'for distraining for his right according to the usual custom'. In similar fashion, Sir Eoin O'Gallagher, a pensioner of the crown and the second best man in Tirconnell, had gone to Fitzwilliam on a promise of safe-conduct in 1588 but had been imprisoned ever since. Maguire had feared the example of MacMahon and the earl had worried that his word to him might be broken. The precedents coupled with the practises of Fitzwilliam and Bagenal had 'caused the earl to fear for his life in coming to the state upon security'. These broken promises were related to the use of bribery by the Gaelic lords to win over government officials. The extra article delivered to Wallop detailed how Maguire had bribed Fitzwilliam and Bagenal to keep sheriffs out of his lordship, yet an attempt was made to impose one nonetheless. These examples of broken promises and the use of bribery reveal a tendency on the part of the Gaelic lords to deal with crown employees as individuals rather than as officials in an administrative system.[187]

The result of the negotiations at Dundalk was the signing of a document entitled *The conclusion with the earl* on 15 March. In this the earl promised to do his best to discourage the raids by his countrymen on Her Majesty's subjects, to keep O'Donnell and his people in obedience and to prevent the ingress of Scots mercenaries. He agreed to suppress any rebellion that O'Donnell might lead against the crown. For their part, the commissioners promised that no violence would be perpetrated by Her Majesty's subjects and soldiers on O'Neill, O'Donnell and their countries until the earl's grievances had been made known to the queen and her resolution given.[188] On the face of it, this agreement achieved some of the objectives outlined in the instructions given to the commissioners but in actuality it was a truce with the northern lords headed by O'Neill. Indeed, the commissioners had little option but to conclude such an agreement. According to intelligence reports, the earl and O'Donnell had

---

185 BL Harleian 35, fos 258–65.
186 *CSPI*, v. 202.
187 O'Neill's grievances: Lambeth, Carew 617, fos 205–11; PRO SP 63/174, nos 2, 2(1).
188 Ibid. 173, no. 89(3).

mustered two thousand men between the towns of Dundalk and Armagh. On the other hand, the crown's forces were weak and the gentry of the northern Pale unwilling to serve.[189]

The most interesting document relating to these negotiations has been calendared in an unsatisfactory manner. This happens to be the covering letter to the privy council which the commissioners dispatched together with their journal of events, O'Neill's grievances and *The conclusion*. It gives the commissioner's opinion on why the confrontation with the Gaelic lords had arisen and their recommendations for resolving the crisis. This document is of seminal importance and must be quoted at length.

> By all which we do gather that there is at this instant amongst those chieftains of Ulster a general combination and that they all remain at the earl's commandment. The cause and ground whereof, so far as we can conceive is, that example and precedent of Monaghan (whereat they all do grudge), fearing it is meant and intended that now shortly Fermanagh, and consequently both Tirconnell and Tyrone will be reduced to the same estate. This undoubtedly, together with the rooted malice of the earl towards the marshal, is the cause of these great stirs and uprors in that province. For appeasing whereof, we see in our opinions two only means, either by pacification, or else by war, one of which must be attempted without delay, and the longer it is deferred the greater will be the danger. If pacification is liked, and thought convenient in this case, we see no means to effect the same, but by pardoning Maguire, after the scourges he hath already felt (for which we think there will be a very good fine yielded to Her Majesty), the revoking of Mr. Marshal's commission for the government of Ulster, the removing of Henshaw from the government of Monaghan, placing there some other sufficient servitor of wisdom and discretion, to hold a more temperate course towards the earl, then heretofore he complaineth to have been used, and that regard be had to give the earl some special credit in his country. By which means we think the earl and O'Donnell will be pacified; for we perceive that howsoever heretofore the earl and O'Donnell have coloured their abetting or favour to the traitor Maguire, they will be in the end of one faction and combination with him. If this course be liked, we wish that the commissioners which shall be appointed to deal in this pacification be named immediately from Her Majesty for their better credit to effect this service, wherein there is some hope to draw unto Her Majesty a good composition out of that province and induce them to receive sheriffs and Justice. And if this course be misliked then we see no remedy but Her Majesty must forthwith send over a good and sufficient number of soldiers under the direction of some man of action of good accompt to chastise them, which cannot but fall out to be an exceeding charge to Her Highness in this time of so great scarcity of corn and other victuals in this kingdom.[190]

The response of the authorities in London at the beginning of April was to

---

[189] Ibid. no. 89.
[190] *CSPI*, v. 221–2; PRO SP 63/173, no. 89.

ignore the urgency and content of the commissioners' letter and instead to put their own gloss on the events at Dundalk. The queen found the manner of proceedings with O'Neill, in particular Gardiner's private meetings and special pleadings with him, to be 'derogatory to our honour' and a 'disgrace to us in government'. The commissioners were condemned for not allaying some of the earl's suspicions on the spot, in particular his erroneous claim that a warrant had been obtained from England for his arrest. The queen's letter considered 'the whole ground of his articles to rest upon the allegations of a fear conceived of his life by the means of our deputy there and the marshal'. There was no cause for urgency. The earl's undertaking to restrain his followers and, if need be, to prosecute O'Donnell was found acceptable. The crown had now decided to recall Fitzwilliam and to warn Bagenal not to interfere with the earl.[191] If the earl's fears were not in fact a cloak for disloyalty, the situation thus created would facilitate his appearance before the Irish council in the near future. Given the crisis facing crown policy in the north of Ireland, this reaction from London was misconceived and inadequate.[192]

In the space of a year a dangerous confrontation had developed in Ulster. Even with the assistance of the primary source material, it is a difficult task to give a full explanation of this development. The conspiracy of Catholic bishops, as befits their role as social props of the Gaelic political system, must be relegated to the background. O'Donnell was the main backer of the subsequent embassy to Spain; O'Neill was pulling the strings behind the scene. At any rate, it was O'Neill who was the principal supporter of Maguire in his early military actions. The attempt to impose a sheriff on Fermanagh had sparked off the conflict. In the longer term, the settlement of Monaghan, which distracted the minds of all the Gaelic lords, was to blame. The main beneficiaries of this policy were Gaelic freeholders and government officials, especially Bagenal as chief commissioner of Ulster. The intended victims were Gaelic lordship in general and the hegemony of the O'Neills in particular. The crisis deepened with the accusations of treason against Tyrone and the ensuing examinations at Dundalk. Although he was guilty of more than one offence, the earl evaded arrest and turned the affair into a propaganda campaign against Bagenal and Fitzwilliam. After Dundalk, he was forced into military action against Maguire but did so in such a way as to minimise the government's success. The earl was not being pressurised by his followers into confrontation. In fact, the lords, who needed his leadership to resist English encroachment, were more susceptible than ever before to his influence. The earl had no wish to see a reformed Ulster. He wanted the traditional hegemony enjoyed by his forefathers in the province. This conservative objective was tempered by the need to compromise with a centralising state. O'Neill's actions on behalf of the state, most recently against his own cousin and son-in-law, had shown his desire to remain loyal. Yet, this continued loyalty was plainly conditional on the concession of regional

---

191 Fitzwilliam's revocation was on account of his grave illness. On 21 March he had written of 'being now out of hope to have ever an able body for travail and service of this state in a politic function, much less in a martial persecution . . . So as it is more than time I cast mine eye to matters spiritual only, and nothing temporal': ibid. no. 92.
192 ULC Kk 1 15 no. 17, fos 58–9.

autonomy. Because of the nature of the state and his own position as an earl, he could not ask directly for what he wanted. He decided to fight proxy wars with his dependants as instruments to achieve this and to avoid a complete rupture. It seemed a good opportunity: a weak regime in Dublin facing the old dilemma that it could not secure consent in the North without the support of the dominant O'Neill. However, the division of sovereignty which concessions necessarily entailed was anathema to the Tudor state.

8

The Outbreak of War

The critical situation which pertained in the early months of 1594 had developed into open war by the middle of the following year. However predictable, this outcome was by no means inevitable. The earl of Tyrone feigned inability to control a confederacy of Gaelic lords who were in fact applying political and military pressure on his behalf. The queen, with her honour and sovereign claims at stake, found it impossible to compromise. The escalating spiral of events into which the opposing parties were locked eventually resulted in Tyrone's proclamation as a traitor. The war was already general before it was made official. O'Neill trained an Ulster army which was more than a match for the dispirited and disorganised forces of the crown. The resultant territorial gains revealed the ambitions of O'Neill and O'Donnell to hold regalian rights in Ulster and Connacht. Clearly, this was a structural crisis between consolidating magnates and a centralising monarchy. The following analysis explains in detail the path from confrontation to war and the early stages of the conflict.

The Elizabethan regime, plagued by bitter rivalry between the Burghley and Essex factions, beset by economic difficulties at home and committed financially and militarily on the continent, was negligent in its approach to the crisis in Ireland.[1] In the spring of 1594 it ignored not only the grave news from Dublin but also the reports of two experienced Ireland hands, Sir George Carew and Captain Nicholas Dawtrey. These concurred in their respective assessments of confederate capabilities and the military strategy to be adopted against them. Dawtrey noted the persistence of Gaelic political customs whilst Carew spoke of the earl of Tyrone's 'thirsty desire to be called O'Neill, a name more in price to him than to be entitled Caesar'. Both men reminded the government that Hugh O'Neill was the most capable and valiant military commander of his nation and that the forces of Ulster were better trained and armed than they had been in the time of Shane O'Neill. They were certain that a war against the Ulster confederates would be the most costly and troublesome which the queen had yet fought in Ireland. Both asserted that a garrison policy was the only effective way to reduce the North of Ireland to submission.[2] Dawtrey also discerned O'Neill's Machiavellian nature: 'And yet if I shall deliver unto Your Highness the outward show of the man: I never saw an Irishman of more plausible behaviour to content all men.'[3]

In March 1594 the queen decided to replace the ailing lord deputy by Sir

---

1 A. G. R. Smith, *The emergence of a nation state*, Harlow 1984, 233–9.
2 PRO SP 63/174, nos 13, 13(1), 62, 62(1).
3 Ibid. no. 62(1). This coincides with the character-sketch of O'Neill given by Lombard in his *Commentarius*: Byrne, *Irish war of defence*, 29.

Richard Bingham and Sir Robert Gardiner as lords justice.[4] However, Fitzwilliam, who had long been a suitor for revocation, now refused to hand over the reins of power. He seized upon a clause in the queen's letter relating to a recovery in his health. He also insisted that the appointment of a new lord deputy was the most expedient course in such a troubled time.[5] There is a plausible explanation of Fitzwilliam's paradoxical behaviour. He feared that Bingham and Gardiner would accuse him of maladministration and disgrace him in the same fashion as he himself had done Perrot. Bingham had been involved in bitter jurisdictional disputes with Fitzwilliam, and Gardiner was regarded as Sir Richard's 'partial supporter' in the central administration.[6] When Fitzwilliam announced his decision to the Irish council, a row developed with Gardiner. The chief justice claimed that Fitzwilliam's acceptance of bribes had caused the crisis in the North and demanded an investigation into O'Neill's allegations on the issue. Fitzwilliam reported his fears to Burghley: 'your lord may conceive what he is like to do when his authority is enlarged and my back turned'. He went on to complain about Gardiner's clandestine negotiations with Tyrone and their use of Captain Thomas Lee as a go-between.[7] Whatever Fitzwilliam's motivations, his decision to remain in office was a major impediment to the crown's dealings with the earl of Tyrone. Secretary Fenton realised that the earl had been given a pretext to excuse himself from the Irish council and an opportunity to consolidate his hold on the North.[8] At the end of April the queen was in a fury at Fitzwilliam's action. He had no right either to elect governors or to upset policies which were predicated upon his recall. She announced that Sir William Russell was to succeed him as lord deputy.[9]

Fitzwilliam was now a worried man. In May when Tom Lee left for England, he wrote again to the lord treasurer: 'I wish in a trembling fear he shall be barred all access to her royal sacred person.' The outgoing lord deputy obviously feared that Tyrone and Gardiner had sent Lee with incriminating evidence against him.[10] In fact, the document which Lee addressed to the queen reflected his own views as much as those of possible backers. He had personal grievances against the old lord deputy. He alleged that Sir William had taken away lands and troops alloted to him in Leinster and he had ignored his valiant services against Maguire in favour of the propaganda of the cowardly Sir Henry Bagenal. Lee denounced Fitzwilliam as a disgrace to his office: 'this instrument so chosen by Your Majesty, being royally and with great bounty, enabled to do you great and honourable service, without extortion, bribery or such like dishonourable gettings, hath for his own lucre, used his place to the great dishonour of Your Majesty and the public discomfort of your subjects in that Realm; which is the chiefest cause of this rebellion that now is there'. He castigated Fitzwilliam's official journeys into the interior in his private search for Armada gold, preys of cattle and other men's goods. He instanced his arbitrary treatment of Sir Eoin

---

4   ULC Kk 1 15 no. 18, fos 59–60.
5   BL Harleian 7004, no. 120.
6   Lee, 'Brief declaration', 98–9; PRO SP 63/183, no. 44.
7   Ibid. 174, no. 18.
8   Ibid. no. 14.
9   ULC Kk 1 15 no. 18, fos 59–60.
10 PRO SP 63/174, no. 38.

O'Gallagher and the 'vile practice and device used to that MacMahon, that was executed'. He cited the prevalence of bribery used by the English to secure preferment and by the Irish to secure deferment. Lee did reiterate Tyrone's complaint about the large concordatum of £400 given to Bagenal as well as his abusive remarks about the lowly status of those appointed freeholders in Monaghan. But he was not Tyrone's puppet: he denounced the earl's execution of Hugh Gavelach MacShane as 'a most monstrous and cruel murder' and advertised his constant use of bribery. As immediate measures, Lee advised the removal of Sir Henry Bagenal whom he referred to as 'the coward' from the marshal's office and the appointment of Gardiner, St Leger and Bingham as commissioners to assist Sir William Russell in the investigation of Fitzwilliam's crimes.[11] But Russell was not instructed by the queen to carry out such an investigation. Indeed the queen had failed not only to provide sufficient and speedy measures to reach a peaceful resolution, she had also failed to appoint an experienced leader with adequate forces to do otherwise.

Russell's deputyship must rate, together with that of his patron the earl of Essex, as one of the most disastrous of the century. In the 1580s he had spent a year in Ireland as a commander of a cavalry troop and subsequently served four years in the Low Countries first as lieutenant of the horse and then as governor of Flushing. Sir William had held no public office since 1589 and had no real experience of government at executive level.[12] One product of his visit to Ireland in 1580–1 had been a rather incoherent reform treatise. 'Touching the redress of these enormities', he advised the privy council, 'surely all this world shall never redress the same nor subdue the Irish captains and make them obedient to Her Majesty's laws but by force and strength and that the sword be bent naked over their heads'.[13] In 1594 Russell's advocacy of a military solution was supported in print by the Munster planter and administrator, Richard Beacon. In the allegorical work *Solon his folie*, Beacon argued that the corruptions of past governors and the subtle intrigues of the earl of Tyrone had caused the present impasse. He believed that only the resolute application of force by Russell could reform Ireland.[14] However much Russell may have favoured this approach, no troops were sent over with him. The privy council probably hoped that the presence of a lord deputy from the ranks of the nobility – he was second son of the earl of Bedford – would be sufficient to quell the status-conscious Irish lords.[15]

In spite of the urgency of the situation, Russell did not arrive in Ireland until

11 BL Harleian 35, fos 258–65.
12 P. W. Hasler, *The Commons, 1558–1603*, 3 vols, London 1981, iii. 310–12.
13 BL Cotton Titus B xii. fo. 352. The fact that Russell was a puritan (Hasler, *The Commons*, iii. 310–12) may have led him to regard coercion as the only solution to England's problems in Ireland. For discussion of this issue see Brendan Bradshaw, 'The Elizabethans and the Irish', *Studies*, lxvii (1977), 38–50.
14 Richard Beacon, *Solon his folie or a politique discourse touching the reformation of common weales conquered, declined or corrupted*, Oxford 1594, 1–2, 43–4, 97–112; DNB, ii. 92; PRO SP 63/178, no. 12.
15 The Irish did expect more from the blue-blooded Russell than his predecessor. 'The goodly fame I hear of Sir William Russell's gentle dealings and nobility of personage above all deputies doth put me [O'Donnell] in trust he will take good order for all these countries': ibid. 176, no. 11(2). Similar views were expressed by O'Neill: ibid. 175, no. 56(5).

1 August and did not take the sword of state until ten days later.[16] On 7 August a government column sent to the relief of Enniskillen Castle was driven back by confederate forces under Cormac MacBaron O'Neill and Hugh Maguire in an engagement known in the Irish annals as the battle of the Ford of the Biscuits.[17] The earl of Tyrone held a meeting with the victors at which he informed them of his decision to visit the new lord deputy and instructed them to ravage the borders of the Pale to assist his negotiations.[18] The earl's entry into the lion's den was as calculated as it was audacious. The military defeat had weakened the government's position. The fact that Russell had brought no reinforcements may have caused O'Neill to believe that the new lord deputy had plenary powers. According to Secretary Fenton, the earl expected to be 'heard and redressed' when Russell arrived; furthermore he had recently notified the council of O'Donnell's demands on behalf of the confederates.[19] At the very least, a meeting could win him valuable time. Although the earl came to Dublin without the grant of a protection, he seems to have had adequate assurances from Loftus, Gardiner and Ormond for his safe-return.[20] According to William Warren, the new lord deputy had also given his word to O'Neill.[21] The earl's confidence was such that he offered to answer any allegations that Fitzwilliam and Bagenal could make against his loyalty. Fitzwilliam refused this offer, fearing no doubt that it might become a trial of his own conduct. He departed for England the day before the earl's arrival in Dublin.[22]

On 17 August O'Neill made a formal submission before the lord deputy and council.[23] With a view to strengthening its position, the council forced the earl to admit that he had broken his agreement of the previous March by failing to prevent the 'Irish treasons' of his followers. The council had begun to put certain articles to him when the proceedings were disrupted by Bagenal.[24] The marshal had chosen this moment to present a long list of accusations impugning Tyrone's loyalty. He later claimed that this was in line with the earl's original offer and that he had cleared it with Russell beforehand.[25] The council nevertheless expressed surprise at Bagenal's action and decided to defer his charges since they had been made 'without proof or time when the things were done'.[26] Secretary Fenton felt this incident had perturbed the earl to such an extent that his subsequent answers to the other articles 'were not direct, but uncertain and wavering and his consent far more difficult'.[27] However, it is worth recollecting that O'Neill had been equally diffident in answering similar

---

[16] C, Carew, iii. 221.
[17] Life, i. 75; PRO SP 63/175, nos 45, 47, 47(1). The battle is so called because the English forces led by Duke and Herbert lost the supplies which they were carrying to Enniskillen when attempting to cross a ford on the river Arney: AFM, vi. 1951–4.
[18] Ibid. 176, no. 60(10).
[19] Ibid. 175, nos 12(1), 43(1).
[20] Ibid. no. 71; 179, no. 5(1); Lee, 'Brief Declaration', 112–13, 117–18.
[21] CSPI, vii. 50.
[22] PRO SP 63/175, no. 55; 179, no. 5(1).
[23] Lambeth, Carew 612, fo. 10.
[24] PRO SP 63/175, nos 56, 68.
[25] Ibid. nos 71, 71(1).
[26] Ibid. nos 56, 56(5).
[27] Ibid. 175, no. 68.

articles in London four years earlier: on this occasion the marshal's outburst simply provided a convenient pretext for his normal equivocation.[28] In the articles Tyrone promised to recall his brother, Cormac MacBaron, and the rest of the forces of Tyrone and to do his best to control O'Donnell. He also agreed to the introduction of English law and administration into his territory and to the handing over of his eldest son for education at university.[29] Two days later O'Neill returned to the North promising to do service against invading Scots.[30]

Whatever Russell's predilections, it is quite clear that he had deferred to the majority decision of the Irish council in not detaining the earl of Tyrone.[31] At least seven members – Loftus, Jones, Ormond, Gardiner, St Leger, Dillon and Bourchier – of the thirteen man council can be described as friends or associates of the earl, some may even have been in his pay.[32] Many had landed interests and did not want the war to spread outside Ulster. In the view of Fenton, Ormond had 'a special interest in the earl'.[33] Besides these private concerns, there was also the general situation. In mid-August the near-defenceless government was confronted by 'Cormac the earl's brother, a person stirring, ill-affected and apt to work troubles in the country having in readiness all the earl's forces'. Therefore they decided to dismiss the earl to avoid 'more dangerous sequels'. With Fitzwilliam gone and Bagenal overruled, the council hoped that O'Neill would be content with an agreement which resembled that of 1590 and that consequently he would do his best to reduce the North to obedience.[34] The assessment of Bagenal, who chose to dissociate himself from the council's decision, was very different. The apprehension of O'Neill, he averred, would have split the confederates into factions 'which are now all suppressed by the earl his greatness'. In the marshal's eyes, Hugh O'Neill had called the council's bluff and would go back to Ulster in triumph.[35]

The events in Dublin were not only a propaganda coup for O'Neill but also gained him valuable time in the harvest season. The agreement acknowledged that the crown could not govern Ulster without his assistance and indeed the queen subsequently complained that he had been dismissed with 'authority, trust and countenance'.[36] O'Neill was doubtless disappointed that Russell had brought no directive from London to constitute his special role in Ulster into legitimate authority. Nor did Russell have anything new to offer those lords already proclaimed. For Tyrone the most important achievement was that his submission now permitted him to re-open communications with London. He wrote to the privy council and to the lord treasurer imputing his past faults wholly to the malice of Fitzwilliam and Bagenal in the hope of gaining inter-

---

[28] ULC Kk 1 15 no. 4, fos 11–13.
[29] PRO SP 63/175, no. 56(3).
[30] Ibid. no. 65.
[31] Ibid. 176, nos 33, 40.
[32] Ibid. 175, no. 56; Lee, 'Brief declaration', 101–2, 115–16. On bribery see Life, i. 27; PRO SP 63/176, no. 60(11).
[33] Ibid. no. 15.
[34] Ibid. 175, no. 56.
[35] Ibid. no. 71.
[36] ULC Kk 1 15 no. 27, fos 79–80; no. 28, fos 81–2.

cession with the queen.[37] He also prompted Ormond to write on his behalf to Burghley. Ormond suggested O'Neill's return to favour so that he might be made 'an instrument to help to suppress and appease the northern stirs that otherwise may be chargeable to Her Majesty'.[38]

Elizabeth was infuriated when she heard that her council in Ireland had not taken the opportunity to arrest the earl of Tyrone. In the queen's opinion 'this slight manner of proceeding both eclipsed the greatness of our estate there and served to glorify him, to the comfort of all his followers and to the amazement of those who have opposed themselves against him'.[39] She accused the council of 'as foul an oversight as ever was committed in that kingdom' and attributed their decision to 'fear, faction or corruption'.[40] In a separate letter to the lord deputy, she reminded him that he had been specifically instructed before his departure to beware of the earl's promises and not to dismiss him without adequate answers. Russell was given a lesson in statecraft: all treasons were necessarily contrived in secret and it was his duty to uphold the dignity of the sovereign's rule. Nevertheless, the queen was willing to give Russell the benefit of the doubt. She recognised that he had probably yielded to the experience of others and advised him in the future to be wary of those councillors 'tied by nature or country's bond'.[41] For months afterwards the queen harped on in her letters about this missed opportunity. As a result of the earl's dismissal, the queen lost confidence in a large section of her council. Consequently, when a council of war was established the following year, she excluded the councillors of the long robe much to their displeasure.[42]

O'Neill's return to the North did not herald the establishment of the tranquillity which the government wished for but rather marked an escalation in the crisis. The earl feigned inability to hand over his eldest son as a hostage claiming that his sons had been stolen away by their foster-parents in his absence.[43] The disgruntled council informed him that 'this manner of dealing in all congruent construction savoureth of an evasion in you' and that even his friends considered it a 'weak and frivolous excuse'.[44] More importantly, the earl claimed that he was now unable to rule his followers and that the chief men of his lordship had confederated themselves with O'Donnell to hold out for a settlement embracing all those who had been proclaimed. Until this was arranged, he saw no point in further meetings with the council.[45] In fact, the earl was directing a Gaelic confederacy from behind the scenes. Fenton first remarked on this in April 1594 and later offered the following explanation: 'they have secretly contracted a strong league amongst themselves, leaving out the name of the earl, that in his own person he might stand clear, to be an

37 PRO SP 63/175, nos 57, 58.
38 Ibid. no. 65.
39 ULC Kk 1 15 no. 29, fos 82–3.
40 Ibid. no. 31, fos 87–9; no. 28, fos 81–2.
41 Ibid. no. 29, fos 82–3.
42 Ibid. no. 37, fos 95–6; no. 38, fos 97–8; CSPI, v. 323–6.
43 PRO SP 63/176, no. 11(1).
44 Ibid. no. 11(7).
45 Ibid. no. 11(9).

instrument to work for them when opportunity would serve'.[46] When forced to explain the behaviour of the confederates, O'Neill claimed that they were out of his control when actually they were pressurising the government on his behalf. Towards the end of 1594 even this smokescreen was becoming increasingly transparent and the earl was forced to fall back on the claim that Fitzwilliam and Bagenal were plotting his destruction.[47]

The earl's alleged inability to control his followers necessitates a look at his brother, Cormac MacBaron, the principal commander of the forces of Tyrone at this time. Lord Deputy Russell later attempted to justify the dismissal of O'Neill in August 1594 on the grounds that Cormac was seeking to displace his brother by custom of tanistry.[48] Not enough is known about this important figure. Under the patent of 1587 the earldom had been remaindered to Cormac and in 1590 he was left in charge of Tyrone during his brother's visit to Court.[49] In spite of Cormac's strength within Tyrone, a number of factors militated against an attempted usurpation of power by him. Although he shared the same blood relations as the earl, it was the latter's marriage alliances with O'Donnell, Maguire, Art MacTurlough and Henry óg which held the confederacy together. For instance, Art MacTurlough and Henry óg were parties, together with Cormac, to the confederate ultimatum of 2 February 1595. If Cormac had been making a bid for supremacy in Tyrone, these individuals would hardly have backed him since they were claimants in their own right to the O'Neillship.[50] Indeed, all three would have emerged as substantial landowners under a Monaghan-style settlement in Tyrone. Furthermore, the state had appointed Cormac the first sheriff of the county. And if, as Russell suggested, Cormac so coveted his brother's place, why did he not leave the earl in the lurch either in June 1593 at Dundalk or in August 1594 at Dublin by withdrawing the forces which were threatening the government? The only plausible explanation is an orchestrated campaign of disinformation by the earl, which was in turn seized by the government to cover its own mistakes. One intelligence report of November 1594 is especially interesting in this regard. It details a quarrel between Hugh and Cormac and shows that Cormac resented the dangerous role which his brother was forcing him to play.[51] In fact, other intelligence sources demonstrate the earl's actual involvement in military operations in spite of his outward show of neutrality.

During the summer of 1594, the government received reports that the earl was travelling regularly to the confines of his lordship with Fermanagh to give orders to the forces besieging Enniskillen Castle.[52] The most convincing evidence relates to the battle of the Ford of the Biscuits. On 17 August the council dismissed Bagenal's claim that the earl had conferred with Cormac MacBaron

[46] Ibid. 174, no. 14; 175, no. 36. According to Fenton, Hugh O'Neill could 'command and rule' O'Donnell at will while Cormac MacBaron, Turlough MacHenry, Conn Mac an Íarla and Henry óg were all 'most dear and inward with the earl': ibid. 175, no. 36.
[47] Ibid. 177, nos 30(2), 40(1).
[48] Ibid. 179, no. 6.
[49] CPCRI, ii. 123; PRO SP 63/151, no. 39(1).
[50] Ibid. 178, no. 36(4).
[51] Ibid. 177, no. 9(1).
[52] Ibid. 175, nos 13(5), 35(1).

and Hugh O'Donnell before the battle and that many members of his household had taken part.[53] However, the earl's involvement was subsequently confirmed by the sworn confession of Joan Kelly, a camp-follower in the relief column, who had been captured by the confederates. Two days after the engagement the earl arrived nearby and Joan was called before him to give an account of government losses. She overheard O'Neill's conversations and saw him receive his share of the booty. She also provided a comprehensive list of those members of O'Neill's household who had participated in the battle. She knew these people because she had been brought up at Dungannon in the house of Art Braddagh O'Hagan, the seneschal of Tyrone.[54] The earl was orchestrating these military actions to strengthen the negotiating position of the confederates whose demands were being made by Hugh O'Donnell, Cormac MacBaron and others. The earl was forwarding their petitions and playing the role of intermediary even though he had the 'power to sway them, as he listeth, either to war or peace'.[55]

The objective of the confederacy was the restoration of the *status quo ante*. In August 1594, O'Donnell opened direct communications with Dublin with a request on behalf of the lords living in exile in his lordship.[56] A fuller articulation of the confederates' demands came in their petitions of November 1594 and February 1595. The first petition dealt mainly with Tirconnell and was couched in conciliatory language. O'Donnell wanted a remission from rent payments until his country had recovered sufficiently from the 'oppressions' to which it had been subjected by the state. He demanded the restoration of O'Rourke and the other Connacht men at the nominal rents and services paid by their ancestors. O'Donnell's claims of overlordship surfaced in his proposed exemption of these lords from Bingham's jurisdiction and his offer to 'undertake for them'. By contrast, the confederates offered to see the full rents of Monaghan paid both to the queen and to the earl of Essex after the restoration of the MacMahons. O'Donnell and MacBaron also offered to assist the crown in collecting its rents from the territories of the Route and Clandeboye.[57] The demands of February 1595 marked an advance on those of the previous November. Amongst those declaring themselves 'now in rebellion' were James MacSorley MacDonald, Shane MacBrian O'Neill and Niall MacHugh O'Neill from east Ulster and certain of the MacWilliam Bourkes from north Connacht. The confederates petitioned for the removal of the seneschal and garrison of Monaghan and for the appointment of a leading MacMahon to take up the queen's rents in the county. O'Donnell openly demanded the restoration of the

[53] Ibid. no. 71(1).

[54] Ibid. 176, no. 60(10). Further intelligence about O'Neill suggests that he was anxious that no mercy be shown to government troops. When Conn Mac an Iarla and Henry óg botched an attack on crown forces, the earl was angry that the English churls had not been wiped out and told Conn that he was not fit to be called his son: ibid. 175, no. 13(5). After the capture of the Blackwater fort in February 1595 by Art MacBaron, the earl arrived on the scene with a corps of pioneers to raze the fortifications and to urge his half-brother without success to execute the defenders who had been promised safe-conduct: ibid. 178, nos 53(5), 70, 70(1), 81.

[55] Ibid. 177, nos 12(1), 48(1); 178, no. 36(3–4); 176, no. 15 (Fenton to Burghley).

[56] Ibid. no. 11(2, 5).

[57] Ibid. 177, no. 48(1).

lands and rents which his ancestors had formerly enjoyed in Connacht. Although the demands became more numerous and strident over time, general themes can be discerned. The confederates were willing to pay customary rents. The exception was Monaghan where they promised to continue with the high rents agreed under the 1591 settlement. The lords wished to collect and forward this tribute themselves rather than have it collected by interfering and rapacious officials. Obviously, O'Neill and O'Donnell wanted the neighbouring lords restored to their patrimonies as buffers against the further encroachment of reform government. The petitions revealed in the case of O'Donnell and disguised in the case of O'Neill claims of overlordship in Connacht and Ulster respectively. The substantiation of such claims would necessarily have entailed the English crown abandoning its claims to undivided sovereignty in the north of Ireland.[58]

The confederates attempted to negotiate on these terms over a six month period. From the beginning of his involvement in direct negotiations in August 1594, O'Donnell refused to take a pardon for himself and his country until the exiles were satisfied. Furthermore, he reserved the right to use force by refusing to dismiss his Scots mercenaries until a definite answer was forthcoming.[59] Tyrone fortified this by reminding the council of the danger inherent in O'Donnell's hiring of mercenaries and suggested a general protection until such time as the queen's resolution was known.[60] The council was unable to meet O'Donnell's demands without the queen's warrant. The fact that his offer of submission was conditional upon the inclusion of proclaimed rebels was unacceptable; indeed his negotiations on their behalf suggested that he was in the same predicament.[61] As its military position deteriorated, the Dublin government was left with little room for manoeuvre. In spite of its refusal to grant a general protection, on 15 September the council was forced to conclude a truce. Although this was ostensibly agreed between O'Donnell and MacBaron for the confederates and Sir Edward Moore for the government, the earl of Tyrone was closely involved in the negotiations and in the subsequent restitution of stolen goods from the confederate side.[62] Towards the end of September the council decided to send Sir Robert Gardiner to Court in order to detail the situation in Ireland and to solicit a decision for peace or war.[63] This decision was to O'Neill's liking:

> My special hope is in him that now repairing over he will work some means with Her Majesty, whereby all things that are so far out of order here in the North may be straightened and put in good course again, that we may enjoy peace and Her Majesty have such duties performed towards her as from subjects are due.[64]

---

[58] Ibid. 178, no. 36(4).
[59] Ibid. 176, no. 11(2, 5).
[60] Ibid. 171, no. 11(9). One intelligence report suggests that O'Neill himself had paid for some of the Scots mercenaries in service with O'Donnell: ibid. 176, no. 60(4).
[61] Ibid. no. 11(11).
[62] C, *Carew*, iii. 223; PRO SP 63/176, no. 60(1); BL Harleian 7004, no. 123.
[63] PRO SP 63/176, nos 32, 37.
[64] Ibid. no. 60(1).

If confederate hopes rested on Gardiner's mission to England, they were soon dashed. He was at first prevented from taking ship by easterly winds in the Irish sea and then by direct orders from the queen. She was opposed to 'a person of that quality and place' being absent at such a time and wondered at the earl's interest in his mission.[65] There followed a drift towards open war. In November, O'Neill sought Ormond's assistance and sent him a confederate petition. Although Ormond forwarded this document to Burghley, he warned the earl that a display of dutiful behaviour on his part was now 'the only course left for you to preserve your house and posterity from utter ruin'.[66] By 5 December, after the earl's persistent evasions and repeated refusals to obey their summons, the Irish council deemed him to be 'a person corrupted in loyalty' and broke off 'all manner of temporising courses' with him.[67] At the start of January 1595, O'Donnell rejected the overtures of a government messenger offering a separate pardon for himself and his country. Instead, he referred to the binding oath which he and the other lords had taken.[68] On 2 February, the confederates met at Dungannon and drew up an ultimatum to present to the government. They demanded a meeting with the lord deputy at Dundalk within a fortnight and the grant either of a general pardon or a protection until Halloween during which time their grievances might be redressed. They also demanded the same terms for Feagh MacHugh O'Byrne.[69] With the inclusion of O'Byrne, the confederates threatened to widen the scope of their struggle by joining forces with the Gaelic dissidents in Leinster. This was designed to force the government into making concessions.

The confederates did have an advocate at Court in these critical months – the impoverished adventurer, Captain Thomas Lee. He regarded himself as the man to solve the crisis. He even had a portrait painted of himself as an Irish kerne complete with a citation from Livy referring to a Roman who entered an Etruscan camp and obtained a peace settlement.[70] On a second trip to England in the winter of 1594/5, Lee presented a treatise to the queen entitled A brief declaration of the government of Ireland.[71] Thomas Lee blamed the Irish crisis on Fitzwilliam's employment of 'the baser sort' such as Willis to be sheriffs and seneschals in Monaghan, Fermanagh and Donegal.[72] He wanted a trial of Fitzwilliam for maladministration.[73] His proposed solution was the result of discussions with the Ulster lords in March 1594 and was in many respects reminiscent of the compromise put forward by the commissioners at that time.[74] According to Lee, the lords were not opposed to the introduction of English

[65] Ibid.; ULC Kk 1 15 no. 30, fo. 85; no. 31, fos 87–8.
[66] PRO SP 63/177, nos 12, 12(1–2).
[67] Ibid. nos 30, 37.
[68] Ibid. 178, no. 3(1).
[69] Ibid. no. 36(1–4). The confederates may have felt obliged to support O'Byrne on account of the assistance which he had rendered O'Donnell during his escape from Dublin four years earlier.
[70] de Breffny, 'An Elizabethan political painting', 39–41.
[71] PRO SP 63/177, no. 22; 188, no. 2.
[72] Lee, 'Brief declaration', 96–8, 106, 119.
[73] Ibid. 122–3, 126–30.
[74] Ibid, 89–90; CSPI, v. 225–6; PRO SP 63/173, no. 89; 174, no. 18.

law and the payment of crown rents. Moreover, they would accept the presence of garrisons if the soldiers were commanded by honest servitors. Future garrisons could be maintained by grants of monastic land. Lee insisted that a lasting settlement must be founded on the earl of Tyrone. The sheriffs and seneschals proposed by him were 'near friends of the earl'. He recommended establishing Tyrone as one county instead of two and granting the earl the exercise of martial law within it.[75] Lee's scheme would have left O'Neill supreme in the North with the Gaelic lords tied to him by blood and marriage and the English servitors tied to him by patronage – a bastard feudal arrangement. However, Lee had not seen the earl since March 1594 and the crisis had escalated and confederate demands had multiplied in the interim. Lee advised the dispatch of Chief Justice Gardiner and proposed himself as a messenger between the queen and the earl. The alternative, in Lee's view, was a more expensive and dangerous war than that fought against Shane O'Neill.[76]

The English government was indeed reluctant to fight a major war in Ireland. The Cecils favoured a peaceful solution and Burghley even indicated a willingness to intercede on O'Neill's behalf as a result of his submission to Russell.[77] Sir Robert referred to 'the unfitness to make war'. His father regretted that the queen was unwilling to concede a grant of authority to the earl linked to payment of the revenues due to her in Ulster.[78] The criterion which dictated the queen's decision was the matter of honour; or put more explicitly, the standing of her monarchy in the world. At the end of October, the queen was enraged that a subject such as O'Neill should talk in terms of 'truce and peace' and she instructed the Irish council to make one final demand for his submission in person or else he would be proclaimed a traitor.[79] The queen's disposition was made plain in the council's subsequent letter to the earl of Tyrone: 'Her Majesty finding in her princely wisdom how far her honour is touched in the eye of the world, with these foul disorders of Ulster and your bad course holden therein'.[80] In mid-November the queen decided to redeploy in Ireland 2,000 of her troops then serving under Sir John Norris in Brittany.[81] The transfer of these troops was subject to countless delays and it was not until 18 March that the first companies arrived in Ireland.[82] Although there was mounting concern that Spain might be involved with the confederates, the queen's reasoning remained consistent: 'we are constrained (for our honour's

---

[75] Lee, 'Brief declaration', 89–90, 98–102, 107–8, 115–16.
[76] Ibid. 140–5, 149–50. In 1596 Captain Lee and his kinsman, Sir Ralph Lane, proposed that the crown should grant the earl a 'Lieutenancy of the North': PRO SP 63/189, nos 41–2; 190, no. 18. Though not ventured by the proponents, this plan makes an interesting comparison with the role of the head of the Campbell family in Scotland. He was both a feudal lord (earl of Argyll) and a clan chief (MacCaillin Mór) and held a commission of lieutenancy in the south-western Highlands and Islands: Gregory, *History of the western highlands and isles of Scotland*, 94–5, 136–9, 185, 286, 312, 340.
[77] PRO SP 63/176, no. 1.
[78] ULC Kk 1 15 no. 30, fo. 85; Ee 3 56, no. 32.
[79] Ibid. Kk 1 15 no. 31, fos 87–8.
[80] PRO SP 63/177, no. 30(1).
[81] CSPD, iii. 564.
[82] ULC Ee 3 56, no. 37; C, *Carew*, iii. 228.

sake) to be at the charge of sending over new great forces'.[83] However, the decision to dispatch these forces to Ireland did not entail a final break with the earl of Tyrone. Despite the earlier declaration of intent, the queen continued her characteristic indecision. In January she still held out some hopes of the earl's loyalty.[84] By 20 March, she was using the term 'the traitor Tyrone'.[85] The next day Burghley still wanted to open negotiations through Ormond's mediation, but was unable to obtain his mistress's approval.[86] This possibility had already evaporated when the confederates took pre-emptive action before the arrival of the Brittany forces.[87] According to Fenton, the earl of Tyrone still held himself aloof from the actions of the confederates in expectation of some resolution in his favour out of England.[88] Nevertheless, he was clearly involved in the latest developments, in particular the taking of the Blackwater fort, and so the Irish council demanded directions from London for his proclamation.[89] These demands from Dublin finally forced the queen into making a decision.

The proclamation of the earl of Tyrone was drafted by Lord Burghley in April 1595.[90] Like the proclamation of Shane O'Neill in 1566, it was a justification of the military action which the crown was about to take.[91] The document reflected the contradictions in Elizabethan policy towards Ulster. In spite of the exemplification which Hugh O'Neill had obtained in 1567, his father was now deemed a bastard. Turlough Luineach O'Neill, who had for many years been the object of official odium, was now described as 'a very loyal noble subject'. The proclamation claimed that Hugh O'Neill had been advanced by the queen's bounty to the largest earldom in Ireland and that he had been maintained financially in his position by her. Contrary to law, he had murdered Hugh Gavelach MacShane and had since imprisoned two of his brothers. Furthermore, Hugh O'Neill had seduced O'Donnell and other Ulster lords from their allegiance and had used his brothers and bastard sons to support such traitors as Maguire and O'Rourke. He was cited as 'a known practiser with Spain and other Her Majesty's enemies'. His real objective was to usurp sovereign power and to be, in effect, 'a prince of Ulster'. Those willing to desert the earl's cause were offered pardon for their lives and lands.[92] Unlike the proclamation of Shane O'Neill, no money was put on the earl's head.[93] The proclamation was printed in Dublin on 12 June in both English and Irish and was read out at Dundalk twelve days later and subsequently at other corporate towns throughout Ireland.[94] The issuing of the proclamation was delayed to coincide with the march of the queen's army into Ulster, thereby giving military support to those

---

83 *The Edmondes Papers*, ed. G. G. Butler, London 1913, 209; ULC Kk 1 15 no. 38, fos 97–8.
84 HMC *Salisbury MSS*, v. 80–1.
85 ULC Kk 1 15 no. 36, fos 92–4.
86 PRO SP 63/179, no. 13.
87 Ibid. 178, no. 54.
88 Ibid. no. 81.
89 Ibid. nos 53(5), 68, 84, 100.
90 Ibid. 179, no. 20. In drafting this, Burghley probably used notes which the Irish secretary had recently sent to him for the purpose: ibid. 178, no. 102.
91 HMC *Haliday MSS*, 172–4.
92 ULC Kk 1 15 no. 39, fos 98–9.
93 HMC *Haliday MSS*, 172–4.
94 PRO SP 63/179, no. 82; 180, nos 48, 48(2).

who wished to submit under its terms. By then the earl of Tyrone had himself been in action against government forces in the battle of Clontibret. This was pointed out in an addition to the final version of the proclamation.[95]

The battle of Clontibret shocked the Dublin government. Marshal Bagenal's mixed force of garrison troops, continental veterans and raw recruits had the task of relieving Monaghan town with fresh men and supplies from the coastal settlement at Newry. The relief column was harried on the march to Monaghan and nearly met disaster on the return journey. Afterwards, it was beleaguered for a time in Newry. In the engagement, the earl of Tyrone had deployed combinations of cavalry and shot to telling effect.[96] English commanders with continental experience compared his ability with that of the Prince of Parma.[97] In assessing the new situation, the Irish council declared that 'these traitors are increased to a greater strength in numbers and wonderfully altered from their Irish manner of arms and weapons, and the use thereof, besides their order and discipline in governing their men'.[98] Clontibret exemplifies the military encounters of Russell's deputyship and serves as a convenient starting-point for a comparative analysis of the crown and confederate forces.[99]

An Irish administration which could not operate without subventions from England in peacetime, inevitably suffered severe financial difficulties in wartime. To cover its outlay, the Dublin government was forced to negotiate short-term loans from Irish merchants pending the arrival of money from England. When money did arrive, it was often needed to pay off these creditors.[100] At the end of September 1595, Wallop, the treasurer-at-wars, was still awaiting the arrival of funds to enable him to pay the army for part of July and the whole of August.[101] Although the Cecils proved responsive to Irish needs, the queen was incensed at 'the excessive greatness of her charge'.[102] The cost of the confederate war-effort was equally onerous. The earl of Tyrone was described by Sir George Carew as 'the greatest man of territory and revenue in that kingdom'.[103] Yet most of this revenue was in kind whereas the confederate lords needed ready cash to recruit Scots mercenaries and purchase munitions. In 1594 O'Neill and O'Donnell were reportedly offering the earl of Argyll £8–10,000 Scots to obtain the employment of 2,000 highlanders in Ireland.[104] When Argyll proved unco-operative, the confederates turned to Angus and

---

[95] Ibid. no. 48(2).
[96] Hayes-McCoy, *Irish battles*, ch. vii.
[97] PRO SP 63/180, no. 23.
[98] Ibid. no. 5.
[99] Hayes-McCoy has written extensively and at times brilliantly on Gaelic military organisation in this period, see especially 'The army of Ulster, 1593–1601', *Irish Sword*, i (1950), 105–17 and 'Strategy and tactics in Irish warfare, 1593–1601', *IHS*, ii (1941), 255–79; also *Scots mercenary forces, passim* and *Irish battles*, chs vii–x. For English military organisation see Falls, *Elizabeth's Irish wars*, chs ii, iii and John McGurk: 'The recruitment and transportation of Elizabethan troops and their service in Ireland, 1594–1603', unpubl. PhD thesis, University of Liverpool 1982.
[100] PRO SP 63/175, no. 52; 178 nos 8, 83; 179, no. 42.
[101] *CSPI*, v. 402.
[102] ULC Kk 1 15 no. 30, fo. 85; Ee 3 56 no. 37; *CSPI*, v. 402.
[103] PRO SP 63/174, no. 13(1).
[104] *CSP, Scot.* xi. 457–8, 476–7.

Donal Gorm MacDonald and gave them advance payments in silver to bring over mercenaries.[105] This cash must have been obtained by taxing salmon fishing and exporting grain and cattle to western Scotland. In this early phase of the war, the forces of the crown were outnumbered by those of the confederates.[106] At the beginning of Russell's deputyship, Elizabeth had a 1,000 strong garrison in Ireland as well as 500 native troops raised for the emergency.[107] The arrival of the Brittany troops the following March was the first major reinforcement but they came about one third under their purported strength of 2,000 men and hence more soldiers were required from England.[108] In Ireland, the ranks of the queen's army suffered continual thinning through death and desertion.[109] Many fresh recruits from England were simply unfit for military service; one company being described as 'refuse people'.[110] The soldiers were expected to campaign in the summer months when the warmer weather made the boggy countryside a malarial environment. Hence the need for 'seasoning'.[111] Cramped and dirty camps caused dysentery and typhus.[112] The nutritional deficiencies of the limited army diet made the troops more prone to disease. Sir Henry Wallop described Ulster as 'a country that yieldeth him [the English soldier] least relief of meat, drink, lodging or both of any country that I know in Europe'.[113] It was said of the experienced Brittany forces who were reduced by disease and especially by desertion that 'they like not this country service'.[114] Some officials blamed the high rates of desertion on corruption amongst the officers.[115] In this crisis, the Pale was of little military help to the crown. The 'hosting of the Englishry' was now only used to defend the colony in the absence of normal forces.[116] Even in this it was defective; when the army was in Ulster in the late summer of 1595 instead of a levy of 1,000 foot and 300 horse, the Pale could only turn out four weak companies of foot and less than sixty horse.[117] By contrast, the confederates had no shortage of hardy fighting men. In 1595 their army numbered roughly 6,000 men.[118] The Ulster lords relied more on hired troops than upon the traditional risings-out.[119] In 1595 the lords

---

105 Ibid. 581, 650.
106 PRO SP 63/180, no. 17.
107 Ibid. 175, no. 35. English commanders questioned the reliability of the Irish troops whom they were forced to levy: ibid. 175, no. 38; 185, no. 12. There is an example of the earl of Tyrone making offers of land to Irish soldiers in the hope of winning them over: ibid. 182, no. 10(5).
108 Ibid. 178, nos 58, 100; 179, no. 5.
109 Ibid. 181, no. 42; CSPI, v. 401–2.
110 PRO SP 63/178, no. 100.
111 James C. Riley, 'Insects and the European mortality decline', American Historical Review, xci (1986), 846–9.
112 Patrick Logan, 'Pestilence in the Irish wars: the early phase', Irish Sword, vii (1966), 280–1.
113 PRO SP 63/183, no. 12.
114 CSPI, v. 351–2. As a solution, the crown seriously considered recruiting hardy Scots mercenaries for service in Ireland, but never implemented the plan: PRO SP 63/185, no. 31; Hayes-McCoy, Scots mercenary forces, 263–9, 329–30.
115 CSPI, v. 348–50; PRO SP 63/182, no. 63.
116 BL Add. 4792, fo. 143.
117 PRO SP 63/183, no. 23.
118 Ibid. 180, no. 43(1); 183, no. 49.
119 Hayes-McCoy, 'Army of Ulster', 106–10.

suffered a setback when a flotilla of galleys, replete with mercenaries, was intercepted off the Copeland Islands by English warships and sent back across the North Channel.[120] However, Scotland was not the only source of mercenaries: O'Neill was able to hire local men and swordsmen displaced from Munster and Connacht.[121]

Even under favourable circumstances, the victualling of a royal army in Ireland presented logistical problems. Most supplies had to come from England and their passage across the Irish sea was hindered by the predominant westerly winds. This situation was now exacerbated by a series of bad harvests which caused food shortages in England and Ireland between 1594 and 1597.[122] Furthermore, distribution in Ireland was hampered by the failure of the Palesmen to provide the army with enough carts and pack-horses.[123] Although the poor harvests would also have affected the confederate food-supply, the logistics of war were more straightforward in the North of Ireland. The risings-out were supplied from the demesne lands. More importantly, the maintenance of mercenaries reached a peak of development under Hugh O'Neill. Contracts of bonnaght service normally lasted three months. The mercenaries were paid by the lord and victualled by the country people. At the beginning of a contract, the bonnaghts were given a specified length of time to go to designated districts to collect their food supplies.[124] Certain districts may have given cash payments in lieu and in such cases the lord would have provided the supplies.[125] With the exception of the household lands, all parts of Tyrone were obliged to support bonnaghts.[126] The overrunning of neighbouring lordships permitted the extension of the system. In the autumn of 1594 Cormac MacBaron marched along the Ulster borders imposing bonnaght on the MacMahons, O'Hanlons and Clandeboye O'Neills. This boosted confederate strength in foot by some 700 men.[127]

Both sides in the war had to import munitions. English counties were obliged to equip the companies which they recruited with arms and armour. In the many cases where the English counties failed to provide equipment, it could be easily imported by the Dublin government.[128] The confederates had greater problems. It is well attested in a number of sources that the earl of Tyrone used the lead roofing of his castle at Dungannon to make bullets but this quantity would hardly have sufficed for long.[129] Until his proclamation as a traitor, the earl remained in a technical sense a commander of crown forces and he

---

[120] PRO SP 63/182, no. 43(1–4). Elizabeth always had the advantage of naval power in her Irish wars: T. Glasgow, 'The Elizabethan navy in Ireland', *Irish Sword*, vii (1966), 291–307.

[121] PRO SP 63/177, no. 66(4–5); 174, nos 18(1), 55, 62(1); *CSPI*, v. 235–6.

[122] PRO SP 63/178, no. 100; 179, nos 15, 42; 181, nos 4, 48; 182, no. 43. See also R. B. Outhwaite, 'Dearth, the English crown and the "crisis of the 1590s" ', in Peter Clark (ed.), *The European crisis of the 1590s*, London 1985, 23–43.

[123] PRO SP 63/180, nos 53–4.

[124] C, *Carew*, iv. 210–12.

[125] RIA, Miscellaneous O'Donovan MS, 14/B/7.

[126] *CSPI*, iii. 332; PRO SP 63/180, no. 48(1).

[127] Ibid. 176, no. 60(4, 10, 11); 177, no. 5(5); 180, no. 48(1).

[128] Ibid. 177, no. 48; 178, no. 100; 179, no. 23.

[129] Moryson, *An itinerary*, II/i, 12; Perrot, *Chronicle of Ireland*, 68; Byrne, *Irish war of defence*, 30–1; PRO SP 63/175, no. 83; *CSP, Scot.* xi. 618–21.

exploited that technicality to purchase munitions from Irish merchants.[130] At the end of 1594 Secretary Fenton obtained documentary proof that O'Neill had been buying up and transporting large quantities of powder to Dungannon under this pretext since the Fermanagh campaign.[131] Later, the government issued a proclamation forbidding merchants of the corporate towns from selling munitions to traitors.[132] The Ulster lords were also supplied from the west coast ports of Scotland. Fenton noted that 'the earl of Tyrone hath all his provision of powder from Scotland, being brought to Glasgow from Dansk and other easterly parts'.[133] A good part of this trade was undertaken by John Bath, a Palesman and close associate of the earl. He had established himself as 'a great merchant of Strabane' and owned a ship to expedite his business.[134] In July 1595 English diplomats in Scotland persuaded the government of James VI to issue a proclamation banning the western port towns from selling munitions to Irish rebels.[135] In spite of the proclamations, Irish and Scottish merchants continued to sell armaments to the confederates.[136] A regular supply of munitions was critical to the Gaelic lords because they were now dependent on firearms. In 1595 at least a third of the Ulster army fought with guns compared with only an eighth in 1562.[137] This transformation had taken place during the lordship of Turlough Luineach.[138] Most soldiers thus armed came from Tyrone and as a result the earl employed Scottish gunsmiths at Dungannon.[139] It is interesting to find that the MacDonnell Galloglass septs now provided 'shot and pikemen' rather than the traditional heavy infantry.[140] By contrast, the forces of Tirconnell lagged behind in armament at the start of the war.[141]

Modern weaponry was useless without adequate training. In theory, the English recruits received instruction in their home counties and during transit to Ireland. Yet a severe reversal in county Mayo prompted Bingham to remark that 'our new soldiers for the most part could not tell how to handle their pieces [guns], so that the captains were driven to take away their bullet and powder and give the same to the Irish shot, which stood us in best stead that day'.[142] The earl of Tyrone, on the other hand, excelled at training and organisation. Lombard, the Catholic propagandist, asserted that Hugh O'Neill took a special interest in training his countrymen in the use of firearms.[143] This is verified from a contemporary Scottish source: 'he has long prepared for this war, training children as he does now with wood shaped like pieces for lightness and

---

130 Byrne, *Irish war of defence*, 30–3.
131 PRO SP 63/177, no. 28.
132 Ibid. 178, no. 57(1); Perrot, *Chronicle of Ireland*, 110.
133 PRO SP 63/182, no. 63.
134 Ibid. 178, nos 53(5), 86, 87; *CSP, Scot.* xi. 586, 664–5.
135 Ibid. 642, 665, 691.
136 BL Add. 34,313 fo. 54; ULC Kk 1 15 no. 71, fos 200–5; Hayes-McCoy, *Scots mercenary forces*, 284, 307–8.
137 PRO SP 63/180, no. 48(1); BLO, Carte 55, no. 282.
138 PRO SP 63/65, no. 4; 137, no. 10(2); *CSPI*, iii. 516–17; BL Lansdowne 111, no. 46.
139 PRO SP 63/190, no. 42(1).
140 Ibid. 180, no. 48(1).
141 Ibid. 179, no. 51; 180, no. 48(1); 182, no. 42(1).
142 *CSPI*, v. 418–19.
143 Byrne, *Irish war of defence*, 30–3.

training them for shooting and giving pay for it'.[144] The use of firearms by the confederates was well-suited to their defensive style of warfare.[145] Fynes Moryson, in his history of the war, claimed that 600 composition troops trained by six 'butter' captains had formed the nucleus of the earl's forces.[146] However, the government had never permitted Tyrone to keep more than 200 composition soldiers and besides these units were now disbanded.[147] Whatever the long-term preparations, most of the training needed to weld together an effective army would have taken place during 1594 and one intelligence report gives us the vivid picture of O'Neill mustering his own troops and beating those who were not ready with a truncheon.[148] Irish veterans from the Low Countries also provided assistance. The highly-regarded Hugh Boye MacDavitt, who had served as an ensign under Stanley, returned on a request from the earl.[149] He was a special adviser on military matters who brought the latest ideas from Flanders to the battlefields of Ireland.[150]

The crown managed to weaken itself in the crucial area of military command. At first, the normal hierarchy pertained in the queen's army with the lord deputy as commander-in-chief and the provincial presidents and marshal of the army as his subordinates. However, as the situation escalated into full-scale war, the authorities in London decided to divide the command. In April 1595 the queen announced the dispatch of Sir John Norris to act as general in the lord deputy's absence.[151] Sir Robert Cecil described this appointment as 'a matter of form' to place Norris over the other military men in Ireland.[152] Russell had requested the assistance of a 'martial man' but he and the Lord Chancellor would have preferred Bingham to Norris.[153] In Loftus' view, Bingham was better suited 'for this broken and running service', more easily managed and not likely to demand a large stipend for himself and an entourage.[154] Russell and Loftus did not mention the crucial factional alignment; like themselves Bingham depended on Essex while Norris had strong connections with the Cecils.[155] Norris received his commission as lord general in June. He was empowered to exercise full martial law, parley with rebels and grant protections and pardons.[156] Not surprisingly, the drafting of this commission occasioned a quarrel. According to Norris, Russell at first refused to sign the fiat claiming that 'it was

---

[144] CSP, Scot. xi. 620.
[145] BL Lansdowne 111 no. 46.
[146] Moryson, An itinerary, II/i. 12.
[147] PRO SP 63/112, no. 23; 137, no. 10(3); 151, no. 43; 173, no. 83.
[148] Ibid. 174, no. 48; 175, no. 83.
[149] Ibid. 180, no. 61; CSP, Sp. iv. 642; HMC Salisbury MSS, v. 440, 515; ULC Kk 1 15 no. 71, fos 200–5; Brendan Jennings, 'Irish swordsmen in Flanders, 1586–1610', Studies, xxxvi (1947), 402–10; ibid. xxxvii (1948), 189–202.
[150] AGS Estado 839, fos 104–5.
[151] ULC Kk 1 15 no. 37, fos 95–6. Norris was not anxious to take up his new assignment. Cecil had to warn him not to dally in England and when he did go over, he spent three weeks in Munster before travelling to meet the council in Dublin: PRO SP 63/179, nos 36, 78, 82, 91; ULC Kk 1 15 no. 41, fo. 100.
[152] ULC Kk 1 15 no. 40, fos 99–100.
[153] PRO SP 63/178, nos 82, 98, 130.
[154] Ibid. 178, no. 98.
[155] CSPI, v. 124; Hasler, The Commons, iii. 138–9.
[156] Fiants, 16th report, no. 5932; Lambeth, Carew 612, fos 49–50.

prejudicial to his patent'.[157] By turns, Russell blamed the row on Norris's discontent with the terms of his commission.[158] Whatever the incidental details, the real fault lay with the original decision of the queen and her privy council in London to divide the command. Precedents should have demonstrated the dangers inherent in this. In the early 1570s Fitzwilliam as lord deputy had rendered the first earl of Essex little assistance when the latter had possessed similar powers in Ulster.[159] There was also the example of the quarrels which had plagued the service in the Netherlands when the earl of Leicester and Norris himself had been expected to fulfil comparable roles.[160] The confederates had no such command problems. O'Neill was in overall control with O'Donnell as a subordinate general on the less important western front.

The respective commands needed good intelligence on which to base their decisions. Government commanders on the borders such as Sir Henry Duke passed on intelligence which they received from local people.[161] Occasionally spies were sent into the North.[162] It was the job of Fenton, as Irish secretary, to collate such information. He maintained his own informers of whom the most important was Richard Weston, one of Tyrone's secretaries.[163] The earl himself maintained an effective intelligence network which kept him abreast of government intentions. One memorandum stated: 'there is nothing consulted or concluded with the state in Ireland but thereof he hath quick flying intelligence'.[164] O'Neill had sufficient forewarning of government troop movements to marshal his forces for the battles of the Ford of the Biscuits and Clontibret.[165] When a ship was sent round the Ulster coast to sound out some of the minor lords, its captain reported that the earl had knowledge of his mission even before the ship sailed from Carlingford and had therefore dispatched O'Donnell, O'Doherty and O'Cahan to guard their countries.[166] The earl of Argyll held the opinion that O'Neill was receiving information from his friends on the council.[167] To prevent this eventuality, the lord deputy kept the news of the dispatch of the Brittany forces secret from his fellow councillors for nearly three months. Yet O'Neill had details direct from court about the Brittany forces, their numbers and commander even before the full council was informed![168]

During hostilities, the crown maintained an offensive strategy and the confederates a defensive one. The confederates benefitted from a dreadful strategic blunder even before the proclamation of Tyrone made the war official. Russell began his deputyship by marching into Ulster to the relief of Enniskillen.

---

[157] PRO SP 63/181, no. 43.
[158] Ibid. 181, no. 48.
[159] Fiants, 12th report, no. 2462; T. W. Moody, F. X. Martin and F. J. Byrne, A new history of Ireland, Oxford 1976, iii. 97.
[160] Hasler, The Commons, iii. 138–9.
[161] PRO SP 63/176, nos 60(5–8, 10); 178, nos 53(5).
[162] Ibid. 177, nos 43, 51; 178, no. 30.
[163] Ibid. no. 28; 180, nos 48, 48(1).
[164] Ibid. 175, no. 83.
[165] ULC Kk 1 15 no. 25, fos 75–8; PRO SP 63/175, no. 83; 180, no. 17(2).
[166] Ibid. 181, no. 37.
[167] CSP, Scot. xi. 676–8.
[168] PRO SP 63/177, no. 45; 178, nos 54, 58, 84.

Afterwards a truce was concluded with the confederates.[169] Had the outlying garrisons and the borders of the Pale been properly defended, this action may have sufficed until the arrival of reinforcements. However, in the middle of January 1595 Russell made a surprise attack on Feagh MacHugh O'Byrne, captured his stronghold and proclaimed him and his adherents traitors.[170] This was an unprovoked attack on O'Byrne who had in fact made recent overtures to the government to obtain letters patent for his lordship.[171] As a pretext, the lord deputy alleged that O'Byrne had secretly combined with the Ulstermen.[172] Yet the confessions of Walter Reagh Fitzgerald and his brother made on their capture suggest that the first substantive contact only took place after the January attack when Feagh sent a messenger to O'Neill requesting assistance.[173] In fact, this was a result of programmatic government. Russell's first service in Ireland during 1580–1 had also been in Wicklow and this action was in line with his treatise of that time which envisaged the elimination of O'Byrne and the reform of Leinster as the first step to reducing the whole kingdom.[174] Not surprisingly, Russell's attack on Feagh MacHugh received timely praise from his supporter, Richard Beacon.[175] This attack was only the beginning of a major prosecution of O'Byrne. Two subsequent campaigns in the Wicklow mountains occupied the lord deputy for the greater part of the spring.[176] This was a questionable use of scarce resources. The queen complained about the first campaign and during the second Russell deployed three of the newly-arrived Brittany companies.[177] This military adventure also entailed building fortifications and stationing troops in garrison.[178] Although outlying strongholds such as the Blackwater fort and Enniskillen castle may still have been lost, undoubtedly the time, men and money expended in Wicklow could have been more profitably used on the northern front.[179] Indeed, one of the reasons for the confederates' termination of their truce with the government so early in the year was to take advantage of Russell's foolish distraction with O'Byrne.[180] Furthermore, this military activity failed to achieve its objectives. Although some of O'Byrne's principal associates were killed and his strength in men reduced, the crown was soon forced to grant him a truce.[181]

In the summer of 1595 the state finally directed its military power northwards. The lord deputy had favoured the establishment of two armies to attack Ulster simultaneously from Connacht and the Pale. Too few troops were

---

[169] CSPI, v. 267–9; C, Carew, iii. 222–3.
[170] Ibid. 225.
[171] PRO SP 63/177, nos 5, 5(1–4).
[172] Ibid. nos 31, 45; 178, no. 36.
[173] Ibid. no. 53(6); 179, no. 23(2).
[174] Hasler, The Commons, iii. 310–12; BL Cotton Titus B xii. fo. 355.
[175] PRO SP 63/178, no. 13.
[176] C, Carew, iii. 226–30.
[177] PRO SP 63/178, no. 101; 179, no. 23.
[178] Ibid. 178, no. 54; 179, no. 82.
[179] Ibid. 178, no. 70; 179, no. 90.
[180] Ibid. 178, nos 38, 54.
[181] Ibid. 179, no. 82; 180, nos 31, 31(1); ULC Kk 1 15 no. 44, fo. 105. Russell finally managed to eliminate Feagh MacHugh just before the end of his deputyship in 1597. In spite of this, the O'Byrnes remained a focus of discontent in south Leinster: C, Carew, iii. 258–9.

available for this purpose. Therefore, the government had to be content with a single army marching into Ulster from the South-east in the hope of re-establishing a garrison on the Blackwater and capturing Dungannon.[182] This proved over-optimistic but a forward garrison was established at Armagh.[183] It was now hoped that Norris would be able to advance further into Tyrone, establish more garrisons and destroy the harvest.[184] Norris himself realised that this was not feasible. From the outset, he had wanted the establishment of a garrison at Lough Foyle in the rear of the enemy by means of a seaborne expedition direct from England. Russell was unwilling to back this plan, prob-ably because Norris wanted his brother, Henry, put in charge of the oper-ation.[185] During this offensive, the earl had demolished his own castle at Dungannon as well as those of O'Hagan and O'Quinn lest they should be taken and garrisoned. His failure to demolish Armagh Cathedral was a serious error. The government now possessed a base to contest his control of the eastern third of Tyrone.[186] Yet garrisons, once established, had to be victualled. The earlier attempts to revictual Enniskillen and Monaghan had given the confederates opportunities at the Ford of the Biscuits and Clontibret. Likewise, O'Neill attacked Norris's force as it returned southwards after resupplying Armagh in the late summer.[187]

The strengths and weaknesses of the opposing armies were reflected in politi-cal developments. By the second half of 1595 the military weaknesses of the crown, in particular its divided command, were beginning to paralyse the governmental process itself. The problems began when Russell withdrew to the Pale leaving Norris in charge of the war in Ulster.[188] Although this was auth-orised by an act in council, it is clear that the lord deputy took the decision against the advice of his fellow councillors.[189] After the fraught expedition to Armagh, Norris complained that the lord deputy was refusing to forward any of the reinforcements and little of the treasure newly-arrived from England.[190] Only a few months after his appointment, Norris was demanding revocation from office.[191] There is no doubt that the status-conscious Norris was a difficult subordinate, but the main blame must lie with the lord deputy. He remained inactive on the borders of the Pale and let others become scapegoats in the deteriorating war situation, thereby saving face himself. This was even more pronounced in the case of Connacht where Bingham's authority had collapsed. Russell would not march his forces into that province in spite of the pleas of

182 CSPI, v. 323–6; PRO SP 63/180, no. 48.
183 Ibid. 181, nos 4–5.
184 Ibid. 182, no. 13.
185 Ibid. 180, no. 34; 181, no. 43; 182, nos 13(1), 28.
186 Ibid. 181, nos 28, 42; 182, no. 7(1). In the spring of 1594, O'Donnell had demolished certain forts in his lordship fearing their attack and occupation by the government: ibid. 173, nos 45(1), 78. In the autumn of 1595, he broke down Sligo Castle for the same reason: ibid. 183, no. 32.
187 CSPI, v. 387–90; PRO SP 63/183, no. 12.
188 Ibid. 181, no. 28; 182, no. 7(1).
189 Ibid. nos 7(1), 13, 45; 183, nos 44, 48, 48(1); 185, no. 30.
190 CSPI, v. 387–90; PRO SP 63/183, no. 21.
191 Ibid. 181, no. 43; CSPI, v. 403.

Fenton and the judges.[192] By the same token, the lord deputy wished to avoid any part of the negotiations which the government was now forced to resume with the earl of Tyrone. He wanted Norris to undertake these, thereby maintaining his own dignity in the matter.[193] In both war and peace, the division of executive authority was frustrating the queen's service. Fenton urgently requested the despatch of explicit instructions from London to both Russell and Norris that 'there might be no opposition but a direct correspondency in all things between them'.[194] In the event, the queen wrote only to the lord deputy condemning 'such causeless formalities' between the two men. She reassured Russell that it had not been intended 'to give any authority divided from you, to any second minister whomsover', only to provide an able councillor and a military commander in his absence.[195] Russell made sure Norris saw this letter. The lord general believed that this interpretation effectively nullified his commission. He imputed it to the intrigues of Russell's associates at Court. On this pretext, he decided to retire to Munster and a personal letter from the queen was required to oblige him to return.[196] In this administrative crisis, Sir Geoffrey Fenton, the experienced secretary of the Irish council, was the lynch-pin of the government. He was prompting the lord deputy with ideas and utilising his connection with Lord Burghley to secure directives from London.[197]

The political consequences of confederate superiority in numbers and organisation were massive increases in the power of O'Neill and O'Donnell as regional overlords. Neighbouring lordships had been weakened militarily by recent government intrusion and hence the process of aggrandisement was rapid. The Gaelic lords, subjected to their power, were forced to give hostages, promise risings-out and support bonnaghts as signs of dependency or at least give buyings to obtain a respite.[198] The extension of O'Neill's power took place mainly during 1594 when the government could put few men into the field. The most dramatic results were achieved in east Ulster where Brian MacArt MacBaron was militarily active on his uncle's behalf. Marshal Bagenal asserted that these activities reflected the earl's 'ambitious desire of sovereignty' in the region.[199] Those who resisted the earl's requests to join his alliance were dealt with ruthlessly. At first Niall MacBrian Fertagh, the lord of South Clandeboye, was only willing to offer a buying.[200] When he persisted in his refusal to submit, he was deposed in favour of a competitor, Eoin MacHugh MacNeill óg. However, Niall was restored after a full submission and Eoin put in charge of the adjacent lordship of the Dufferin where the English lessee, Randal Brereton, had lost control.[201] Ever MacRory Magennis was driven out of his small lordship

---

192 PRO SP 63/183, nos 10, 23, 42, 48, 48(1).
193 Ibid. nos 42, 44.
194 Ibid. no. 44.
195 ULC Kk 1 15 no. 56, fos 121–2.
196 CSPI, v. 427–8; PRO SP 63/184, no. 14; ULC Kk 1 15 no. 59, fos 123–4; PRO SP 63/185, no. 8.
197 DNB, vi. 1187–88; PRO SP 63/183, nos 44, 105, 109, 112, 113.
198 Ibid. 177, no. 30(7); 182, nos 7, 42(1); ULC Kk 1 15 no. 22, fos 70–2.
199 PRO SP 63/174, no. 18(9).
200 Ibid. no. 37(6); ULC Kk 1 15 no. 22, fos 70–2.
201 PRO SP 63/175, no. 5(19); 177, no. 30(7).

of Kilwarlin in the Lagan valley when he refused to submit. The government compensated him with a maintenance allowance but he was murdered by the earl of Tyrone's nephews on his return to the North.[202] Sir Hugh Magennis and Sir Oghy O'Hanlon were also under threat. Although forced to give buyings, they remained loyal to the crown because of the proximity and support of Marshal Bagenal.[203] After the battle of the Ford of the Biscuits, O'Neill re-established the *uirríthe* in south Ulster. At the beginning of September, he guaranteed an agreement under which Connor Roe, the government's erstwhile supporter in Fermanagh, submitted to Hugh Maguire.[204] Later the same month Cormac MacBaron and Art Braddagh O'Hagan marched into Oriel and pro-claimed Brian MacHugh óg 'the MacMahon'. They continued to the Farney district where they placed Ever Mac Con Uladh and his sons in their inherit-ance which had been taken from them by John Talbot, the earl of Essex's lessee.[205] The O'Reillys in the neighbouring lordship of East Breifne now came under pressure but it was not until the capture of Monaghan town in December 1595 that their leading men joined the confederacy.[206]

The earl of Tyrone's military power gave him a measure of political authority throughout the North. His exercise of such authority is well-exemplified by his dealings at Edenduffcarrick [now Shane's Castle] in June 1594. There he con-cluded agreements in the land disputes between Shane MacBrian and Niall MacHugh for North Clandeboye and Niall MacBrian Fertagh and Eoin MacHugh for South Clandeboye. The earl was *sláinte* for the performance of these agreements. On his departure to settle a similar dispute between MacQuillan and James MacSorley MacDonald, he requested that the parties remain obedient to the queen. Lord Burghley glossed the letter relating these events with the wry comment: 'a busy officer without a warrant'.[207] Another report on the earl of Tyrone stated: 'all the proclaimed rebels and others resort to him to redress their private wrongs among themselves as subjects do to the state'.[208] The title of O'Neill was required to confirm the earl's assumption of regalian rights. This was attained in September 1595 on the death of Turlough Luineach. The earl travelled to the stone at Tullaghoge to be inaugurated in the time-honoured fashion.[209] The new O'Neill later claimed that he had only taken the title to prevent other claimants being appointed and causing trouble in the North.[210] Yet, there is little doubt that Hugh O'Neill preferred his Gaelic title. He used it soon after his inauguration in a letter to the lord deputy and where its use was not politically sensitive in his correspondence with the Spanish court, he chose to sign 'O'Neill'.[211] The assumption of this title

202 ULC Kk 1 15 no. 22, fos 70–2; PRO SP 63/174, no. 37(4); 176, no. 40.
203 ULC Kk 1 15 no. 22, fos 70–2; PRO SP 63/175, no. 5(12); 178, no. 70; 182, no. 7(1).
204 Ibid. 176, no. 40.
205 Ibid. no. 60(5, 10–11).
206 Ibid. no. 60(7); 178, no. 53(5); 185, no. 28; ULC Kk 1 15 no. 63, fos 136–41.
207 PRO SP 63/175, no. 19(1).
208 Ibid. no. 83.
209 *CSPI*, v. 394.
210 Lambeth, Carew 612, fo. 47.
211 *CSPI*, v. 408–9. It is a reflection of his anglicisation that he signed 'O'Neill, H.' in long hand while his ally's signature was 'Aodh O Domhnaill' in Irish script. This is well-spotted by Cyril Falls in *Elizabeth's Irish wars*, 195.

potentially transformed the nature of the conflict by highlighting the issue of sovereignty. The bishop of Limerick wrote a few months later: 'The priests and bishops confess that Tyrone was a traitor, but yet lawful for him to rebel: both they and the whole Irishry are taught now a new lesson: O'Neill is no traitor. Tyrone was one, but O'Neill none.'[212]

O'Donnell also sought to establish a dependent clientage in Connacht to substantiate his claims to sovereignty in that province. In the first half of 1595, he mounted devastating raids on the counties of Roscommon and Longford.[213] The real breakthrough was not of his making. In June Ulick Burke slew his commanding officer, Captain George Bingham, and took control of Sligo Castle.[214] Ulick wanted the support of O'Neill and O'Donnell against his uncle, the earl of Clanrickard.[215] Sligo Castle was described by Sir Richard Bingham, the chief commissioner of Connacht, as 'the very key of the province and passage from Tirconnell'.[216] With its loss, the Connacht exiles in Ulster were able to return to ferment revolt in their own countries.[217] O'Donnell could now enter the province without interference and Bingham expected him 'to build up a commonwealth' there.[218] By August, only the counties of Galway and Clare were free from revolt.[219] In meeting this crisis, Bingham's forces were insufficient in number and mostly Irish in composition and the spread of the revolt prevented the collection of rent which maintained them.[220] It is hard to accept the view of contemporaries that the cause of revolt in Connacht was arbitrary government by Richard Bingham. The officials in Dublin Castle who blamed him resented his autonomous jurisdiction. In particular, he suffered the unrelenting hostility of Geoffrey Fenton. These jealousies were fuelled by reports from opponents amongst the colonists as much as by the complaints of the indigenous landholders.[221] Likewise, Hugh Roe O'Donnell hated Bingham, and his biographer, Ó Cléirigh, described the chief commissioner as 'the greatest monster of all the English that were then in Ireland'.[222] In short, the Irish feared Bingham's success and the English were jealous of it. Although he was ambitious, Bingham's rule can be characterised as firm but fair. The real cause of the revolt was the desire to revert to the Gaelic mode of lordship in north Connacht where Bingham had done so much to root it out. This preference was especially strong amongst the Lower MacWilliam Bourkes.[223] As Bingham pointed out, it was not the rents agreed under the composition which caused grievance but 'the tenor of the composition which cuts off the Macs and Oes

[212] CSPI, v. 435–6.
[213] PRO SP 63/178, no. 85; 179, nos 51, 68, 72(1); Life, i. 79–93.
[214] PRO SP 63/180, no. 16.
[215] Ibid. 182, no. 10(5).
[216] Ibid. 180, no. 16.
[217] Ibid. 181, nos 47, 48(1); 182, no. 42(1).
[218] Ibid. 181, no. 48(1).
[219] Ibid. 182, nos 35, 42, 42(1).
[220] Ibid. 181, no. 48; 182, no. 42(1).
[221] Ibid. 183, no. 44; 184, no. 31; 185, nos 10, 12. Although it is possible to exonerate Bingham himself, the rapacious activities of the kinsmen who followed him to Connacht as soldiers and local officials cannot be explained away.
[222] Ibid. 185, no. 10(1); Life, i. 101.
[223] PRO SP 63/184, no. 31.

and all Irish customs'.[224] Had the key fortress of Sligo not been betrayed, Bingham argued, his control could have been maintained in the normal way and this outbreak prevented.[225]

This preference for the Gaelic mode of lordship at first assisted O'Donnell's ambitious designs on Connacht which became patently obvious during his progress through its northern counties in December 1595. Anthony Brabazon, a government commissioner, met O'Donnell and reported his demand for the lordship of Sligo as swordland and his acknowledgement of the queen as little more than a suzerain. The gloss put on O'Donnell's reported speeches was 'he doth aspire to absolute sovereignty over the whole country'.[226] The summation of this was O'Donnell's conferment of Gaelic titles on a number of Connacht nobles around Christmas time, most notably that of Tibbot Fitzwalter Kittagh Bourke as the Lower MacWilliam. O'Donnell had the ceremonial rath surrounded by soldiers when he made his choice and subsequently took hostages from the unsuccessful candidates and their supporters. The right of inauguration was a symbolic demonstration of sovereignty.[227] In making these appointments, O'Donnell was pursuing his own ambitions, irrespective of those of his father-in-law, Hugh O'Neill. Nevertheless, it is significant that Cormac MacBaron, the *tánaiste* of Tyrone, and Conn Mac an Íarla were in the company of O'Donnell as representatives of the senior partner in the alliance.[228]

The confederacy headed by O'Neill and O'Donnell was a weak construction based on main force. O'Neill had to keep the hostages of his chief lords and *uirríthe* 'in close prison clogged with irons enough'.[229] The proclamation and show of force by the government in the summer of 1595 demonstrated the superficial nature of his support. During military operations the creaghts of the *uirríthe* were retained in the fastnesses of Tyrone to prevent desertions.[230] Another precaution was the imprisonment of the earl's unreliable son-in-law, Henry óg, on an island.[231] The first defections came in east Ulster. In August Niall MacHugh opened negotiations with the government. This individual had long been a client of the earl's but was now disgruntled at his patron's division of North Clandeboye between himself and his cousin, Shane MacBrian. He asked for a grant of his competitor's lands and the government offered to make him custodian.[232] As a result of Niall's overtures, Shane was also forced to tender his submission the following month.[233] Both of these lords travelled to Dublin in November and received protections for ten weeks.[234] James MacSorley MacDonald also indicated a desire to submit but was still under

---

[224] Ibid. 183, no. 65. A secondary cause of conflict in Connacht was the search for concealed lands. This programme had been promoted by Burghley and implemented by Fitzwilliam without effective control over potential abuses: Ranger, 'Richard Boyle', 257–82.

[225] Ibid. 184, no. 31; *CSPI*, v. 423–4.

[226] PRO SP 63/185, nos 10, 10(1).

[227] Ibid. 186, no. 10; *CSPI*, v. 448; *Life*, i. 115–19.

[228] PRO SP 63/185, no. 10(3).

[229] Ibid. 174, no. 55; 175, no. 83.

[230] Ibid. 181, no. 28.

[231] Ibid. 182, no. 50(1).

[232] Ibid. no. 47.

[233] Ibid. 183, no. 71(1).

[234] Ibid. 184, no. 37.

military obligations to the earl of Tyrone.[235] The government even made contact with Hugh Maguire. He was willing to accept a pardon if granted a
temporary freedom from sheriffs and a company of horsemen in pay. A major
stumbling block was the government's demand that he should first do service
against the traitors as a sign of loyalty.[236] When the earl's nephew, Niall MacArt
MacBaron, defected in October, the government probably hoped that his father
would follow suit.[237] The state failed to back these waverers with actual military
assistance and therefore we find Art MacBaron, Hugh Maguire and Shane
MacBrian in the earl's camp during the 1596 negotiations.[238]

O'Donnell had similar problems in controlling his *uirríthe*, both old and new.
He imprisoned Sir John O'Doherty for a time, apparently at the request of
O'Neill. Afterwards, O'Doherty rejected overtures from the government to
defect from the confederates.[239] O'Donnell's position in Connacht did not go
unchallenged. In the winter of 1595, Russell, Loftus and Fenton journeyed into
Connacht in the hope of quietening the province. They managed to obtain the
submissions of some nobles, mainly from Sligo and Roscommon, but the
presence of O'Donnell and the possible interference of Bingham hindered their
work.[240] The weak points which subsequently emerged in O'Donnell's alliance
were of his own creation. His appointments to Gaelic titles were fundamentally
flawed: 'not making his choice of any that were nearest to those places by their
law and custom, but raised such as were of his own partiality and faction, being
persons base and far off that dignity'.[241] In so doing, O'Donnell squandered a
golden opportunity to create a genuine alliance in Connacht based on a mutual
preference for 'tanist law'.[242] In the important case of the Lower MacWilliamship, he antagonised the leading Bourkes by appointing a man who had been
exiled in Tirconnell. The government realised that he had sowed the seeds of
division and were immediately interested in backing Tibbot na Long Bourke as
a counterweight.[243] This was in stark contrast to O'Neill's willingness to drop
his client, Niall MacHugh, in favour of a more powerful rival in North
Clandeboye.

It would be unwise to conclude this analysis of the outbreak of hostilities
without highlighting the predominant factor – the issue of sovereignty. O'Neill
presents a more ambiguous case than O'Donnell in this regard. He preferred his
prohibited Gaelic title. Yet he acted as 'a busy officer without a warrant' to
disguise his role of Gaelic overlord in the hope of obtaining devolved authority
from the crown. He even tried to conceal his leadership of the confederates.
This charade has since made O'Neill an historical enigma but at the time it cut
no ice with the queen. She was unwilling to dilute her claims to sovereignty.
Concessions would have affected her standing as a monarch in the world.

235 *CSPI*, v. 413–14, 416–17.
236 PRO SP 63/178, no. 30; 182, no. 26(2).
237 *CSPI*, v. 416; PRO SP 63/182, no. 47.
238 ULC Kk 1 15 no. 63, fo. 136.
239 PRO SP 63/174, no. 55; 181, no. 37.
240 Ibid. 184, no. 30; 185, nos 2, 10, 13, 13(1), 15, 30.
241 Ibid. 186, no. 10.
242 Ibid. 185, no. 16(1).
243 Ibid. 186, no. 10; *CSPI*, v. 448; Chambers, *Chieftain to knight*, 78–82.

Moreover, the confederates had been forced by rapid English encroachment to seek their objectives through military action and this made compromise by a queen anxious to defend 'our honour' doubly difficult. In deciding to fight this war, the English government ignored to its peril the warnings about the improvement in military organisation and leadership in Ulster. Worse still, to meet the crisis the queen chose the inexperienced Sir William Russell and then to fight the war Sir John Norris, whom the former saw as a threat to his authority. The queen's decisions in these matters no doubt reflected the different counsels which she received from the factions of Burghley and Essex. This is not to say that all was rosy on the confederate side. The northern alliance which had been forced into being to defend the Gaelic mode of lordship was soon revealed as a stalking horse for the dynastic claims of O'Neill and O'Donnell.

9

The Aborted Peace

The negotiations which followed the first phase of armed conflict mark a watershed in the course of the Nine Years War. Disagreements in the Irish executive and delaying tactics by the Gaelic lords held up the beginning of these negotiations. When talks did eventually take place, the crown was willing to make concessions but wished to do so without losing face. Conversely, the confederates needed a settlement which would guarantee their control of local affairs. Concessions were forced upon the crown by increasing fears of Spanish intervention. However, it was raised expectations of the same eventuality on the confederate side which wrecked the peace initiative. The result was a nationwide struggle culminating in the decisive battle of Kinsale.

Submissions by the confederates and a formal truce were prerequisites for negotiations with the crown. O'Neill had made overtures at the time of his proclamation in June 1595 but the government returned his letters unopened, regarding them as an attempt to frustrate its military operations.[1] The queen believed that these letters should have been read secretly. Therefore O'Neill's offers could not be overlooked when he contacted Sir John Norris two months later. The earl sent Norris a short submission for himself, his followers and allies. The lord general rejected this submission. He disliked the implicit claim of jurisdiction over the other Ulster lords and saw it as a ploy to gain a breathing-space during the harvest season.[2] The earl of Tyrone did not produce the contrite submission required by the state until 18 October. In this the earl acknowledged his offences, requested pardon only for himself, his kinsmen and followers of Tyrone and renounced the prohibited title of O'Neill. O'Donnell also tendered his submission the same day.[3] Ten days later a truce was arranged in spite of disagreement over the victualling of the Armagh garrison. It would be operative 'til the first of January next, according to the computation of the Church of England'. To ensure its performance, the earl promised to deliver four of the O'Hagans as hostages.[4]

In London, the crown's negotiating position was already under consideration. The queen was anxious to uphold her dignity, as she told the lord deputy: 'the less we afford to such traitors, the more honour our ministers do to us and our estate'. Since the success of the revolt had already entailed a loss of face, the

---

[1] PRO SP 63/180, no. 53.
[2] Ibid. 182, nos 57, 57(1), 62, 65.
[3] Lambeth, Carew 617, fos 46–7. Cecil sent a copy of Tyrone's submission to Edmondes, the English ambassador in France, so that it could be publicised abroad to discourage foreign interference: *Edmondes papers*, 285; ULC Kk. 1 15 no. 54, fos 119–20. Norris arranged the despatch of another copy from Waterford to Spain: PRO SP 63/185, no. 32.
[4] Lambeth, Carew 617, fo. 47.

terms which the queen now demanded were much harsher than simply a return to the *status quo ante*. The price, which she intended to exact for full admission to her grace, was the reduction of O'Neill's status and wealth. Only the lands and title of the baron of Dungannon were to be regranted to O'Neill. The lands and title of earl of Tyrone were to be withheld from him until such time as he had proved himself worthy of holding them by a display of good behaviour.[5] Following the submissions of 18 October, Sir Robert Cecil drew up *A memorial of certain conditions to be offered to the earl of Tyrone*. For the most part, these conditions replicated the articles to which O'Neill had subscribed in 1590 with the addition of a clause securing the release of the MacShanes. Cecil's memorial also tackled the question of reparations. The state wanted the earl to rebuild the Blackwater fort, to make full restitution of the spoils done since his entry into rebellion and to submit to a special tax on his lordship for the upkeep of neighbouring garrisons.[6] When their pardons had been delivered, O'Neill and O'Donnell were expected to make personal submissions to the lord deputy 'that thereby our honour may be satisfied in the world'.[7] In contrast to the leaders, the queen intended to make examples of some of the minor lords; she had singled out Maguire for execution 'because he was the first in actual rebellion'.[8]

The crown was soon forced to abandon many of these demands as unrealistic. This climb-down was dictated not only by the deteriorating military situation in Ireland but also by legal difficulties and by increasing fears of foreign invasion. The lord deputy, with the advice of the chief justice, summarised the legal position. The earl of Tyrone was a proclaimed traitor and, while he remained so, a pardon would simply return him to his former state. The deprivation of lands and title would necessitate his outlawry by attainder. Indictments had in fact already been taken in pursuit of this objective at court sessions held near Tyrone. However, to proceed now with the case would only make the earl less conformable and besides, it could not be recommended until Hilary term when the current truce would have elapsed. There was another loophole. The earl held his lands by patent for life with remainders to his sons, Hugh and Henry, and his brother, Cormac. If he was now attainted by judicial process, the crown would gain possession during his lifetime only and then the remainders would have to be fulfilled.[9] For these reasons, the plan to reduce O'Neill's status and wealth had to be dropped.

The crown moderated its line when it discovered the confederate approach to Spain. At the end of September 1595, a priest called Piers O'Cullen was captured in Drogheda while awaiting passage.[10] He was carrying letters addressed to Philip II, to Prince Carlos and to Don Juan del Águila. In their letter to the Spanish king, O'Neill and O'Donnell claimed to be fighting for the

5 Ibid. 612, fos 34–5.
6 PRO SP 63/183, nos 112–13.
7 ULC Kk 1 15 no. 57, fos 122–3.
8 Ibid. nos 55, fo. 120; 60, fos 124–5.
9 *CSPI*, v. 431–2.
10 PRO SP 63/183, no. 71. O'Cullen's capture resulted from information supplied by Richard Weston, one of the secretaries of the earl of Tyrone. It would not be too far-fetched to suppose that O'Neill wanted the priest to be captured, knowing that the despatch he was carrying would frighten the government: *CSPI*, v. 450–1.

establishment of the Catholic religion and made an offer of the kingdom of Ireland to Philip. They requested military support by the feast of St Philip and St James the following year. If the confederates received adequate assurances, they promised not to make peace with the heretics.[11] It was also clear from the letters and from the interrogation of O'Cullen that this was not the first occasion on which O'Neill and O'Donnell had written to the Spanish government.[12] Soon afterwards, intelligence reached the government that Francis Montford, an English seminary priest in the earl's entourage, was on his way to Spain via Scotland.[13] O'Neill later claimed that Montford had been dispatched with letters to the same effect as those which had been intercepted.[14] Consequently, a note of urgency can be found in the queen's letter of 16 October. Since the traitors wanted Spanish assistance by May 1596, Russell and Norris were to proceed with full-scale negotiations as soon as possible. A shift of emphasis is detectable in her instruction to bargain with O'Neill rather than simply force terms upon him.[15] Thus the queen was retreating from the high ground even before receiving O'Neill's submission.

The English authorities were further alarmed by the confession extracted from a Spanish pilot captured by the earl of Cumberland. An armada was allegedly gathering at Lisbon for descent on Ireland. The privy council reacted by reminding the lord deputy of the contingency plans for a Spanish invasion and by informing him of the queen's decision to send over another 1,000 troops.[16] Not surprisingly, the subsequent dispatches from London concerning the Irish war reflect a keener sense of urgency and a more obvious willingness to compromise. The Irish council was told to stand by the main conditions drawn up by Cecil and to use discretion with the rest.[17] Even if all the conditions could not be fulfilled, pardons were to be issued to O'Neill and O'Donnell and their hostages obtained so as to prevent their further intrigues with Spain or any strengthening of their position.[18] On receipt of these dispatches, the queen and her privy council demanded prompt and concerted action by the Irish administration in the negotiations without any referral back to London.[19]

With time at a premium, the queen was understandably displeased about the delay in starting negotiations with the confederates. She imputed this situation to the disagreements between Russell and Norris and to the unwillingness of the council as a whole to shoulder the burden of responsibility.[20] Although Norris took umbrage and went off to Munster at one stage, Russell was more at fault. For instance, the lord deputy knew of the queen's acceptance of the submissions and her willingness to grant pardons by 1 December but he waited

11 Lambeth, Carew 612, fos 45–6.
12 Ibid; CSPI, v. 409–10.
13 CSP, Scot. xii. 38; CSPI, v. 412–13: Godfrey Anstruther, The seminary priests, 4 vols, Great Wakering 1968–77, i, 232.
14 PRO SP 63/184, no. 6.
15 ULC Kk 1 15 no. 56, fos 121–2.
16 APC, xxv. 37–8.
17 ULC Kk 1 15 no. 60, fos 124–5.
18 Ibid. no. 58, fo. 123.
19 Ibid. nos 57, 58, fos 122–3.
20 Ibid. nos 57–9, fos 122–4.

until a meeting of the council eighteen days later before notifying O'Neill and O'Donnell.[21] Russell did admit to Burghley that he had not been anxious to deal with Tyrone. In mitigation, he claimed that the conduct of Ulster affairs had been handed over to Norris and that O'Neill had shown himself completely untrustworthy in the past.[22] A good example of the lack of co-ordination between the state's principal officers is their holding of preliminary talks through different intermediaries. The lord deputy sent Captain Henry Warren back and forth to O'Neill; the lord general dealt through Captains Warham St Leger and William Warren.[23] It was less fair to blame the delays on the Irish council as a whole. The English privy council accused the members of its counterpart of occupying 'the room of dumb councillors' because they constantly referred matters to London.[24] In fact, it was the queen's past criticisms which had made the Irish council, as a body and as individuals, so tentative in their dealings with Tyrone.

In his turn, the lord deputy blamed the delays on a deliberate confederate strategy to exploit the government's desire for a peaceful settlement.[25] O'Neill's *volte-face* in December 1595 seems to vindicate this viewpoint. Over the two previous months, the earl had displayed a readiness to conform to the tough terms, which the intermediaries proposed to him. After one such meeting, he wrote to the lord deputy offering to yield a fine of 20,000 cows, levied upon himself and his allies, and to discuss the issues of the Blackwater fort and the MacShanes.[26] On 20 December, O'Neill received notification of his appointment to meet the Irish council on 8 January at Drogheda, for which purposes a protection was granted and the cease-fire duly extended to 1 February. His response was to seek a postponement until he had conferred with O'Donnell. Captain Henry Warren subsequently revealed to the council that O'Neill was reluctant to come to Drogheda because of the precedent of other Gaelic lords who had suffered death in spite of the pardons which they possessed. However, he also reported the earl's willingness to perform reasonable conditions if his pardon was sent to him and the earl's guarantee that O'Donnell would do likewise.[27] It is clear that O'Neill had duped the government and this is reflected in the exasperated tone of the queen's letters early in January.[28] By his humble submission and his feigned willingness to accept harsh terms, he had won the promise of a pardon. Now he could afford to adopt a more flexible approach. The confederates had already taken advantage of the cease-fire to strengthen their position. The fort of Monaghan had been betrayed to them and O'Donnell was making triumphant progress through Connacht.[29] Given this situation, the

21 PRO SP 63/185, nos 1, 28(1–2).
22 Ibid. no. 30.
23 Ibid. 183, no. 88; 185, no. 8; *CSPI*, v. 414–16, 442–3. William Warren later claimed that the lord deputy had sent his brother, Henry, without his knowledge, as a part of a deliberate spoiling operation: *CSPI*, vii. 49.
24 ULC Kk 1 15 no. 60, fos 124–5.
25 PRO SP 63/183, no. 108; 185, no. 30.
26 Ibid. 183, nos 108, 108(3); *CSPI*, v. 442–3.
27 PRO SP 63/185, no. 28(1); *CSPI*, v. 441–2.
28 ULC Kk 1 15 nos 61–2, fos 126–9.
29 PRO SP 63/185, no. 28; 186, no. 10.

Irish administration now wanted the inclusion of the minor lords from Connacht and the Ulster borders in a peace settlement. They feared that O'Neill and O'Donnell, having secured their pardons, would revert to a proxy war with such men as their instruments.[30] As a result, the queen was forced to abandon her desire to make examples of the minor lords and instead she requested a general peace with 'all the conditions as good and honourable as you may, and specially that our revenue in Monaghan be still continued'.[31] By the start of January 1596, the crown's plans for an honourable peace were in ruins and O'Neill and O'Donnell were able to dictate a meeting on the Ulster borders to which the Irish council capitulated with the appointment of commissioners.[32]

Wallop and Gardiner were the councillors selected for the unenviable task of negotiating with the confederates. The commissioners' task was to gain acceptance of as many of the crown's conditions as possible, to find out the extent of confederate involvement with Spain and to obtain an extension of the truce.[33] The confederates held the initiative throughout the negotiations. In spite of the pleas of Wallop and Gardiner, the earl refused to come to Dundalk, deeming it unsafe to do so, and instead sought a meeting in the countryside nearby. To avoid deadlock, the commissioners requested the confederates to send in their terms. These proved 'such insolent demands' that Wallop and Gardiner were forced to agree to meeting in the open field in the hope of moderating them.[34] The result was two inconclusive meetings on horseback on 20 and 22 of January. O'Neill and O'Donnell were the only confederate leaders involved in direct talks. As was normal on such occasions, the earl adopted a dissembling tone; Hugh Roe with his more forthright manner provided the perfect foil.[35] More important business was transacted by the secretaries of O'Neill and Wallop carrying documents back and forth between the confederates and the commissioners.[36] The commissioners had requested that each lord now send in his 'griefs, petitions, and offers'.[37] O'Neill and O'Donnell reiterated the complaints which they had made in the past. For the first time, the MacMahons were able to voice their objections to Fitzwilliam's settlement of Monaghan. Hugh Maguire catalogued the death and destruction wrought by crown officials in Fermanagh.[38] As for the separate demands, Wallop and Gardiner concluded that they were 'not in substance any ways varying from the former general'.[39] Only after the conclusion of a new cease-fire at a third meeting on 26 January,

30 Ibid. 185, no. 28.
31 ULC Kk 1 15 no. 62, fos 128–9.
32 CSPI, v. 450; PRO SP 63/186, no. 12.
33 Lambeth, Carew 612, fo. 50; ULC Kk 1 15 no. 63, fos 130–73: 'A jornal of the proceedings of us, Sir Henry Wallop and Sir Robert Gardiner, knights, appointed commissioners by a commission under the greate seale of Ireland, dated 8th of January 1595 to treat and parlee with the earl of Tyrone, Odonnell and other northerne chiefteynes, by vertue of which commission we sett forward from Dublin on Monday, the twelfe of January 1595 and came to Dundalke on Thursday the XV of the same.'
34 Ibid. fos 132–5.
35 Ibid. fos 135–6, 140–3.
36 Ibid. fos 143–73.
37 Ibid. fo. 141.
38 Ibid. fos 150–9.
39 Ibid. fo. 149.

did the commissioners put the crown's conditions to the confederates. To have done so at an earlier stage would have caused extreme difficulties in renewing the cease-fire, if not a complete rupture in relations.[40] The negotiations as a whole took place against an acrimonious background. In Iveagh, the crown was trying to prevent the confederates imposing Glasny MacAgholy, who claimed the lordship by tanistry, as an alternative to Arthur, the eldest son of the deceased patentee.[41] In a similar vein, O'Neill and his newest allies, the O'Reillys, accused the government of violating the truce by moving troops into East Breifne to garrison Cavan castle.[42]

The most dramatic of the confederate demands was for liberty of conscience.[43] The religious outlook of O'Neill and O'Donnell was conditioned by the Counter-Reformation. For instance, Lombard relates their attempt to enforce clerical celibacy by the circuitous method of issuing decrees against women co-habiting with priests.[44] However, none of the complaints, which the confederates had made hitherto, related to religious persecution. The reason why they now chose to make this demand must therefore have been primarily political rather than devotional. Two political criteria were involved. First, the proposition of this demand in the actual negotiations was a gambit to force concessions from the crown in other areas. Secondly, it was the expedient adoption of an ideology to attract potential allies. This probability and its possible ramifications had been anticipated by Fenton. He knew that the clarion call of religion was intended to strengthen the confederates' request for Spanish assistance and to widen their appeal at home.[45] Ironically, the same viewpoint was later expressed by Peter Lombard. He wrote that O'Neill had first revolted against English oppression, but, finding religion and politics intermeshed, had subsequently adopted the demand for liberty of conscience to ensure the success of his endeavour.[46] The time was indeed opportune to place religious freedom at the head of the confederate manifesto: by the mid-1590s the early successes of the Reformation in many Anglo-Irish districts were ebbing away with the arrival of a new wave of Catholic clergy trained on the continent. Not surprisingly, the demand for liberty of conscience alarmed the ramshackle Irish administration which was increasingly aware of its own failure in the religious sphere.[47] Wallop and Gardiner were taken aback by this demand. They reminded the Ulster lords that their religious practices had been tolerated unofficially in the past and that this situation was likely to continue.[48]

---

[40] Ibid. fos 162–3, 170–1.
[41] Ibid. fos 131, 143. In this succession struggle among the Magennises, Glasny MacAgholy and Arthur later switched sides: McCall, 'The Gaelic background to the settlement of Antrim and Down', 43–4.
[42] ULC Kk 1 15 no. 63, fos 138–9, 142, 145.
[43] Ibid. fos 134, 151, 154.
[44] Byrne, *Irish war of defence*, 34–9. Since Lombard's claims about O'Neill's military organisation can be verified, his claims about religion, though propagandist, may also be true.
[45] PRO SP 63/185, no. 33.
[46] Byrne, *Irish war of defence*, 38–41.
[47] PRO SP 63/183, nos 47, 47(1); *CSPI*, v. 487–8. For discussion of these religious developments see Alan Ford, *The protestant reformation in Ireland, 1590–1641*, Frankfurt am Main 1985, chs i, ii.
[48] ULC, Kk 1 15 no. 63, fos 147, 151.

The commissioners found the other demands equally unacceptable, deeming them an attack on royal claims to sovereignty and property.[49] O'Neill and O'Donnell made claims to regional hegemony. The earl requested pardon not only for himself and the inhabitants of Tyrone but also for the lords of eastern and southern Ulster who had taken part with him in the war. These lords would 'depend upon the earl's peace, he the earl yielding for them unto Her Majesty from henceforth such rents, services and risings-out as their several ancestors have paid unto Her Majesty's predecessors'. In the same fashion, O'Donnell asked for pardon on behalf of O'Rourke, the Bourkes and the other Connacht-men who had taken part with him and promised to ensure the payment of the rents and services which they owed to the queen.[50] Moreover, O'Donnell de-manded and subsequently specified the rights which his ancestors had enjoyed in the lordship of Sligo.[51] The confederate leaders would permit no garrison, sheriff or officer in their own lordships or in those of their adherents. They were prepared to accept the continuance of the garrisons only at Newry and Carrick-fergus.[52] O'Neill was especially anxious for the removal of the most recent garrison in Tyrone; he told Philip Hore, Wallop's secretary, that 'he would have no peace as long as any soldiers remained in Armagh'.[53] To prevent further encroachment and to reverse the process where it had occurred, the confeder-ates wanted the grant of spiritual lands within their respective lordships.[54] The earl himself was determined to retain control over the lands of the archbishop of Armagh.[55] Finally, the lords were only willing to pay nominal rents to the crown and many wanted a respite from payment until their countries had recovered from the war.[56]

Rather than marking progress towards a peace settlement, the conclusion to the January negotiations reflected a stalemate in which both sides restated their positions. A new cease-fire was an immediate necessity. The earl of Tyrone proposed a truce until Michaelmas or Halloween. The commissioners on the other hand had been authorised to grant a two months period during which time the queen's resolution was to be obtained.[57] At a meeting on 26 January, a cease-fire was duly signed, tenable until 1 April with the possibility of an extension until 1 May. There was disagreement about the articles of the truce. Wallop and Gardiner wanted O'Neill and O'Donnell to promise not to enlarge their confederacy by withdrawing subjects from their due allegiance. They refused to consent to this unless the crown reciprocated with the promise not to attempt the same with their adherents. Moreover, O'Donnell refused to give hostages, claiming that his country was too far off and that he would have insufficient time to collect them.[58] The truce agreed, the commissioners

49 Ibid. fo. 148.
50 Ibid. fo. 134.
51 PRO SP 63/186, no. 22(15); ULC Kk 1 15 no. 63, fos 134, 155.
52 ULC Kk 1 15 no. 63, fo. 134.
53 Ibid. fos 140, 152, 166.
54 Ibid. fos 142, 149.
55 Ibid. fos 149, 164, 166; NLI MS 669, fos 52–3.
56 ULC Kk 1 15 no. 63, fos 154, 156–7, 159.
57 Ibid. fo. 146.
58 Ibid. fos 149–50, 170–1.

proposed the crown's conditions to O'Neill and O'Donnell. Since Cecil's memorial covered only the earl of Tyrone, Wallop and Gardiner had themselves to draw up terms for O'Donnell.[59] Conditional on the grant of their pardons, both men agreed to certain of the articles. However, the earl refused to permit the establishment of a provincial governor over him or to release the Mac-Shanes. O'Neill and O'Donnell adopted the same contrasting but complementary styles in their answers as they had done previously in direct talks. The matter of reparations provides a good example. When asked to rebuild the Blackwater fort at his own expense, the earl evinced a willingness to pay a sum decided by indifferent commissoners. Yet from his subsequent answer about Armagh, it is clear that he wanted no garrisons in his territories. As regards a special tax in reparation to be levied upon his lordship, the earl was agreeable but said he could not answer for his kinsmen and followers. O'Donnell was more forthright. He refused to rebuild and return Sligo Castle to the queen's possession claiming it to be his property to dispose of as he wished.[60] O'Neill and O'Donnell concluded with a reminder of the oath of general combination. Unless their adherents in Leinster, Connacht and Breifne were granted pardon for lives, lands and goods, they refused to perform anything previously agreed, except the truce.[61]

Not surprisingly, the Irish administration reacted negatively to the January negotiations. The councillors were displeased that the 'proud and immoderate demands' of the confederates varied so radically from their voluntary submissions of the previous autumn.[62] The failure of negotiations in turn fuelled the militaristic views of the lord deputy: 'I have been long of opinion that this realm would not be reduced to any good state but by force'.[63] The collapse of government control in hitherto settled areas strengthened his case. All Connacht was in revolt with the exceptions of county Clare and the part of county Galway held by the earl of Clanrickard. Disaffection had now spread from Breifne to engulf the neighbouring lordship of the O'Farrells.[64] Secretary Fenton was worried that food shortages and the burden of the war would provoke trouble in the Pale.[65] The sudden manifestation of religious zeal on the part of the confederates could only exacerbate matters. In these circumstances, the lord deputy was able to persuade the majority of the council that the prosecution of a vigorous war was necessary even to achieve honourable terms from O'Neill and O'Donnell.[66] To this end, the council of war had already drawn up a scheme for the invasion of Ulster and the establishment of a garrison at Lough Foyle to the rear of the enemy. It was estimated that 10,000 men would be required; these would have to be recruited and supplied almost entirely from England.[67] In London, the military option was also under scrutiny.

[59] Ibid. fos 170–1.
[60] Ibid. fos 161–7.
[61] Ibid. fos 167–8.
[62] PRO SP 63/186, no. 51.
[63] Ibid. no. 22.
[64] Ibid. no. 51.
[65] CSPI, v. 458–9.
[66] PRO SP 63/186, no. 51.
[67] Ibid. no. 44(1).

The privy council decided that the use of garrisons on the Foyle at Lifford or Derry, at Beleek and at Armagh would be better than the invasion of Ulster by a single army. It considered the employment of Scots mercenaries along with various reforms to the military and financial establishments.[68] Three days later Sir Henry Bagenal, who was then at Court, backed up these proposals and stated plainly that their implementation would entail a scorched earth policy to reduce the rebels to starvation in the wintertime.[69]

Ironically, the Irish administration had selected the pacifically-inclined Sir Robert Gardiner to brief the queen and privy council on the course of the negotiations and the state of the kingdom.[70] The queen refused to admit Gardiner into her presence because of the dishonourable way in which he and Wallop had conducted the negotiations. She frowned upon her privy councillors taking part in meetings in open country at the behest of rebels and disliked their use of the subscriptions 'Your Loving Friends' and 'Your Very Good Lord' in letters to rebels. Most of all, she was displeased that they had condescended to conclude a truce, let alone meet with rebels, after they had sent in such insolent demands.[71] In the queen's view, the actions of her commissioners were 'utterly repugnant to all royal considerations'.[72] Yet Gardiner's mission proved successful in spite of the queen's public stance. The Irish chief justice acquitted himself well before the privy council and as a result his views were relayed to the queen.[73] Gardiner took this opportunity to blame the Irish crisis on the corrupt dealings of Fitzwilliam. Sir James Perrot claims that Lord Burghley saved the retired lord deputy from the wrath of the queen on this occasion by advising him to stay away from Court on account of illness.[74] A visit to Court by Gardiner had been a potential threat to Fitzwilliam ever since the dispute over the appointment of lords justice in 1594. Furthermore, he was now armed with the complaints presented in the recent negotiations. A privy council letter to Fitzwilliam on 3 March lends authenticity to Perrot's story. Before she learned of his illness, the queen had wanted Fitzwilliam summoned to Court. Now she would be content with written answers to the complaints of the Ulster lords which suggested provocation to disloyalty 'by great extremities and most hard courses offered unto them by you'.[75]

Retribution for past maladministration could not solve the current crisis and therefore Elizabeth was now prepared to make major concessions to the confederates. She favoured a peaceful solution for three reasons. In the first place, the new proposals for a full-scale military campaign in Ireland would involve enormous costs.[76] Instead, she sent over 1,500 infantry and 300 cavalry as a

68 Ibid. no. 70.
69 Ibid. no. 76.
70 Ibid. no. 51.
71 Ibid. 187, nos 20, 25.
72 ULC Kk 1 15 no. 64, fo. 177.
73 PRO SP 63/187, nos 20, 24.
74 Perrot, Chronicle of Ireland, 101–2.
75 APC, xxv. 260–1. For the answers to these allegations see BL Add. 12,503, fos 389–97: 'The memoir of Sir William Fitzwilliam, addressed to the queen'. This document is incorrectly dated 1601; Fitzwilliam had died in 1599.
76 Lambeth, Carew 612, fo. 67.

stop-gap measure.[77] Secondly, a prolongation of the war would invite the possibility of Spanish intervention. This difficult situation was compounded by the
fear that France was about to conclude a separate peace with the enemy.[78] By 9
March, the queen had decided to commission Norris, seconded by Fenton, 'to
proceed with them to some final end'.[79] While the commissioners could use
considerable latitude in reaching an agreement, they were to uphold the
queen's honour to the utmost. In a letter to Norris, the queen demanded 'that
the place and manner may as little derogate from us, as you can devise,
considering you and the rest are sent from a Sovereign to a pack of rebels'.[80] At
the same time, Cecil wrote to encourage a positive attitude in Norris. Since he
had been the original author of Tyrone's submission, it would now redound to
his honour and confound his critics, if he could achieve an agreement. Cecil
believed that, if the rebels ever intended obedience, they must accept the latest
conditions in which only the matter of religion was denied.[81]

The conditions contained in the queen's instructions to the commissioners
were indeed propitiatory. They were probably penned by Cecil with the advice
of Sir Robert Gardiner.[82] Liberty of conscience was considered 'a matter meet
for no subject to require'; the demand was deemed extraordinary since there
had been no proceedings against any of the confederate lords on this issue in
the past. The jurisdictional claims of O'Neill and O'Donnell were avoided, the
queen 'not allowing that one rebel should obtain pardon for another'. With
regard to the earl of Tyrone, the crown was willing to withdraw its garrisons
from his territories, if the inhabitants would live peaceably. It would permit
Armagh and Tyrone to be one county with a countryman as sheriff. There was a
possibility of compromise over the imprisonment of the MacShanes if the earl
could make out a convincing case for his retention of them. However, the
crown still wanted an end to his interference in the lands and rights of the
archbishop of Armagh. The queen was willing to accept the rest of the earl's
answers to the terms presented to him by Wallop and Gardiner.[83] Despite the
arrogance of O'Donnell's demands, there was to be an investigation into his
claims for rents out of Sligo.[84] The conditions were most conciliatory in relation
to MacMahon and Maguire. Hitherto, the queen had no inkling of their mal-
treatment by officials. Their complaints would be examined and, if they proved
true, recompense would be made. In Monaghan the grant of termon lands to
servitors would be revoked and regrants made to inhabitants; in Fermanagh the
possibility of granting the spiritual lands to locals was also to be considered. The
queen's greatest dislike amongst their demands was the derisory rent offered by
Brian MacMahon for the whole of Monaghan which was less than he had
formerly paid for one of its constituent baronies. On the contrary, the queen

[77] APC, xxv. 267–70.
[78] Conyers Read, *Lord Burghley and Queen Elizabeth*, London 1959, 501, 513–14.
[79] Lambeth, Carew 612, fo. 67.
[80] ULC Kk 1 15 no. 64, fo. 177.
[81] PRO SP 63/187, no. 24.
[82] ULC Kk 1 15 no. 65, fos 178–84; PRO SP 63/186, no. 97; 187, no. 29.
[83] ULC Kk 1 15 no. 65, fos 179–80.
[84] Ibid. fos 180–1.

wished to maintain the former revenue and political division of Monaghan.[85] Gardiner's influence on these instructions is shown in an additional article in his own hand which advised the commissioners to use their discretion to prevent the pacification from breaking down.[86]

The preliminaries to the second round of negotiations were in many respects a repetition of the run-up to the first round. The confederates continued to break the truce when it suited them. They did their utmost to stymie government attempts to revictual the remaining garrisons in Ulster and Connacht. Their most notable success was the winning of Cavan Castle.[87] In his letters and meetings with messengers, Tyrone again promised conformity and obedience. He expressed a willingness to pay a fine, to relinquish control over the *uirríthe* and did in fact exchange his original hostages for more acceptable ones.[88] Once more, O'Neill refused to partake in negotiations until he had consulted with O'Donnell, his brothers and other associates and thereby delayed proceedings.[89] Norris alleged that the lord deputy again held up the business in hand by retention of the commissioners' instructions until his return from the Midlands and by failing to inform Tyrone about the queen's decision to send out another commission.[90] The commissioners now feared opposition from certain elements in Dublin and London in the event of an agreement. Fenton wanted Cecil to act as 'our defence' in case they were forced to overstep their instructions on particular points.[91] The realisation of this fear was already evident at the last meeting of the council before the departure of the commissioners towards the Ulster borders. They requested that the lord deputy and the other councillors clarify and amplify those articles in the queen's instructions which were obscure or in which difficulties might emerge. The council refused, leaving the interpretation up to Norris and Fenton who had been given full authority in the negotiations.[92] The commissioners made further requests for elaboration upon the queen's instructions during the actual talks but the council maintained the same stance.[93] By this, the lord deputy and the other councillors dissociated themselves at the outset from a treaty which might be unacceptable to the queen or be broken by the confederates.

The treaty negotiations took place in the third week of April. True to form, the confederates refused to enter walled towns and this time the commissioners 'eshewed their barbarous manner of parleying in the fields at places of their choice'. The only method which could be devised was the employment of Captains William Warren and Warham St Leger as intermediaries with Norris and Fenton based in Dundalk and the confederates camped somewhere in the vicinity. After many days spent in bargaining through these intermediaries, only O'Neill, O'Donnell and MacMahon remained dissatisfied with the articles

---

[85] Ibid. fos 181–3.
[86] Ibid. fo. 183; PRO SP 63/187, no. 29.
[87] Ibid. 186, nos 86, 86(5–18), 89, 90; 187, nos 9, 9(1).
[88] *CSPI*, v. 493–6, 504–5; PRO SP 63/187, no. 66; 188, no. 6; ULC Kk 1 15 no. 67, fo. 191.
[89] *CSPI*, v. 505; ULC Kk 1 15 no. 67, fo. 191.
[90] *CSPI*, v. 498–9, 501–2.
[91] Ibid. v. 493–4; PRO SP 63/188, no. 6.
[92] Ibid. no. 23.
[93] Ibid. nos 54, 54(1–4).

proposed to them. Eventually their qualifications to objectionable articles were allowed to stand with the commissioners' remarks appended to them. These articles, which were then signed by the commissioners and the individual parties, formed the essential component of the treaty. The articled agreements with O'Donnell and MacMahon are no longer extant though presumably the points at issue were Sligo in the first case and the rents and political division of Monaghan in the second.[94] Fortunately, the most important agreement has survived.

The crown's treaty with the earl of Tyrone was a classic exercise in ambiguity and sophistry. In these arts, it surpassed previous government agreements with the O'Neills. The treaty maintained the nominal sovereignty of the state but conceded substantial local control to O'Neill. The earl agreed to drop the demand for liberty of conscience, but it is clear from the final article of the agreement that unofficial toleration would continue. This article required the earl to arrest and hand over any disloyal persons entering his territories. His acceptance was qualified by an unwillingness to 'apprehend any spiritual man that cometh into the country for his conscience sake'. The commissioners' gloss was crucial: 'this is not required by the article'. When he again refused to hand over the MacShanes, the commissioners promised to make a suit to the queen on the point at issue. By judicious wording, the treaty left the earl in control of the *uirríthe* previously under Turlough Luineach. Moreover, he was allowed to retain any leases or lands held outside his own lordship.[95] Tyrone renounced his Gaelic title but as Philip O'Reilly pointed out soon afterwards: 'howsoever he denied it to you, he retained it amongst us'.[96] The major stumbling block in the whole proceedings was the garrison at Armagh. The earl hated its presence in his territory; according to Norris, 'the continuance of the garrison at Armagh hath been the hardest morsel for him to swallow'.[97] The queen's instructions did allow for the withdrawal of the garrison but had linked the same to the peaceable disposition of the inhabitants and the shiring of the earl's lordship.[98] Even though the garrison's upkeep was burdensome to the government, it would have been military folly to withdraw it at this stage. Therefore, the commissioners and the earl agreed to disagree. Until it was removed, the earl refused to permit his territories to be shired or the archbishop of Armagh to enjoy his lands and rights. No doubt, the earl would have conveniently forgotten the *quid pro quo* in the event of the garrison's removal.[99]

Another thorny issue was the crown's demand for reparations. O'Neill had promised to pay a fine on a number of occasions – in his conversations with messengers, in his letters and in his answers to the conditions proposed by Wallop and Gardiner. Yet, he now managed to evade payment in a devious manner. When Norris and Fenton demanded the payment of reparations, the

[94] Ibid. nos 53, 54(1).
[95] ULC Kk 1 15 no. 66, fos 187–9. Norris and Fenton had asked Tyrone only to renounce his claims over the lords of eastern Ulster and over 'Her Majesty's urriaghs' (those in south-eastern Ulster).
[96] Ibid.; PRO SP 63/190, no. 44(9).
[97] Ibid. 188, nos 54(3), 55, 56.
[98] ULC Kk 1 15 no. 65, fos 178–9.
[99] Ibid. no. 66, fos 187–9.

confederates referred them to a sum agreed with Wallop and Gardiner. The commissioners could find no reference to this in the notes given to them by Wallop. The commissioners also challenged the earl about the offer of 20,000 cows which he had made in a letter to the lord deputy. O'Neill claimed that the party who had procured the letter had assured him that such an offer was only intended to 'show his conformity thereby than of any meaning that he should be charged with it'. Norris and Fenton then requested further information from the council in Dublin.[100] In reply, the lord deputy pointed out that Sir Henry Warren, the procurer of the letter, had not been authorised to give such an assurance to the earl.[101] Warren had been called before the council on this occasion. Subsequently, he wrote to O'Neill desiring to be cleared of the imputations against him. The earl did so but in his usual equivocal fashion.[102] He later informed Norris that Warren had actually given him the assurance and that he had written in his favour only to save him from blame.[103]

The treaty negotiations concluded with the signing of instruments signifying submission on the part of the confederates and promising pardon on the part of the government.[104] Afterwards, Hugh Maguire, Brian MacMahon, Sir John and Philip O'Reilly, Shane MacBrian O'Neill and Ross O'Farrell came into Dundalk and made personal submissions before the commissioners in the market place. O'Rourke had also signed the final agreement but rather than submit he now returned suddenly to his lordship. O'Neill and O'Donnell showed outward displeasure at O'Rourke's behaviour. Yet the commissioners feared that he had been chosen as a 'Robin Hood', a proxy to act militarily on behalf of the rest. The lords who did submit were then directed back to their countries to send in hostages to guarantee the agreement. Unlike the minor lords, O'Neill and O'Donnell did not make personal submissions. The commissioners had initially demanded that Tyrone hand over one of his sons as a hostage.[105] Instead, he delivered over two of his nephews. One nephew was the eldest son of Cormac MacBaron who at the age of sixteen was already the captain of a band of thirty horse. Turlough MacHenry was supposed to send in his eldest son but in the end only his second son was produced. Secretary Fenton claimed these hostages to be 'good ties' not only upon the earl but also upon Cormac and Turlough whose countries bordered the Pale.[106] Norris and Fenton now suggested two separate commissions to settle matters in eastern Ulster and Connacht. O'Neill and O'Donnell wanted Norris and Fenton to undertake the difficult task of settling Connacht and O'Donnell promised to assist them in doing so.[107] In fact, the stance of O'Neill and O'Donnell on Connacht was reminiscent of their rejoinder at the close of the first negotiations. They now

---

[100] PRO SP 63/188, no. 54(3).
[101] Ibid. no. 54(4).
[102] Ibid. 189, nos 5, 18, 18(1–3).
[103] Ibid. 190, no. 1(4).
[104] These documents are not extant.
[105] PRO SP 63/188, no. 53.
[106] Ibid. no. 69.
[107] Ibid. nos 48, 53.

warned the intermediaries that the peace could not be maintained or finalised 'unless those of Connacht were reconciled'.[108]

The council in Dublin accepted the plans for further peace commissions to eastern Ulster and Connacht but Norris found 'that our conclusion receiveth no favourable interpretation here and is as much sought to be disgraced as may be'.[109] Certainly, the lord deputy's reaction was negative. At first, he complained to Burghley about the treaty being accomplished by mediation rather than by direct meetings and about the erratic behaviour of O'Rourke. The lord deputy backed up this unfavourable opinion with intelligence from the Basque country and the reported sighting of a Spanish vessel off the coast of Kerry.[110] When the arrival of Spanish shipping was confirmed the following month, Russell was able to address a damning letter to the queen in which he voiced the opinion that the peace would not last. He termed the treaty 'a kind of conclusion', no doubt a reference to the many loose ends in its articles.[111] But the peace treaty had been welcomed in London. The queen congratulated Norris and Fenton, though it was patently obvious that their attempt to maintain her honour belied the extent of concessions.[112] The queen wanted outstanding matters expedited quickly. The personal submissions of O'Neill and O'Donnell were to be obtained as soon as possible. Norris and Fenton were to address themselves to the pacification of Connacht and, if Bingham was guilty of maladministration, he was to be tried and removed. Confidence in the peace settlement was reflected in a demand for troop reductions.[113] At the same time the privy council wrote to Sir Henry Bagenal who was on his way back to Ireland. It warned him to avoid further quarrels with the earl of Tyrone which might disturb the progress towards a general peace.[114] By then, late in May, the authorities in London were also aware of the arrival of Spanish shipping in Ulster and were requesting more information on what had taken place.[115] This Spanish interference was to wreck the peace process.

O'Neill and O'Donnell had in fact received news from Spain before the final round of talks. Their dispatches written to the Spanish court in 1595 had miscarried but their military successes were well-known there.[116] Furthermore Edmund óg MacDonnell was still in Madrid – he had stayed behind when O'Hely left on his fateful voyage. An intercepted letter shows that he was still active in May 1595 even though he had lost contact with home. MacDonnell claimed to be working not on behalf of the church but on behalf of the earl in whose favour he had submitted a strong report to the king and council.[117] More influential than the dean of Armagh were two exiled Catholic bishops, Tadhg O'Farrell of Clonfert, based at Burgos, and Connor O'Mulrian of Killaloe, based

---

108 Ibid. no. 62.
109 C, *Carew*, iii. 180–1; PRO SP 63/188, no. 73; 189, no. 5.
110 Ibid. 188, nos 67, 67(2–3).
111 HMC *Salisbury MSS*, vi. 185–6.
112 ULC Kk 1 15 no. 69, fo. 196.
113 PRO SP 63/189, no. 43.
114 APC, xxv. 416–17; PRO SP 63/189, nos 49, 52.
115 ULC Kk 1 15 no. 69, fo. 196; PRO SP 63/189, no. 43.
116 Ibid. 186, no. 22(2); C, *Carew*, iii. 171–2; PRO SP 63/183, no. 109; *CSPI*, v. 192–3.
117 O Lochlainn, *Irish chief and leaders*, 81–2.

at Lisbon. They had set themselves up to act as agents for the Irish confederates and were in contact with Juan de Idiáquez.[118] It was through the efforts of O'Farrell and O'Mulrian that the confederates were eventually informed of the prospect of Spanish aid. After a meeting in Madrid, the bishops sent a priest called Bernard O'Donnell to assure the confederate lords of Spanish support and to urge them not to make peace with the English. Henry Hovenden interviewed the messenger on his arrival in Ulster in March 1596. As a result, he advised his master, the earl of Tyrone, on the pros and cons of concluding a peace settlement at this juncture.[119] The subsequent dispatch of another messenger from Ulster shows a continuing interest in Spanish aid. This messenger travelled in disguise through Dublin and arrived successfully at the Spanish court in May. He gave an exaggerated account of confederate successes in the first quarter of 1596 and requested munitions, in particular artillery to enable the confederates to capture towns.[120]

Although the news brought from the bishops was encouraging, it would not have been concrete enough to prevent O'Neill and O'Donnell negotiating seriously with the crown's commissioners the following month. Yet, the subsequent agreement and its ambiguities would have left them with great misgivings. The presence of the garrison at Armagh, a location which dominated the eastern third of his lordship, still rankled with the earl. Nor was there any guarantee that his rival, Marshal Bagenal, would remain absent from his patrimony in south Down.[121] As yet, no formal recognition had been given to O'Donnell's claims in Connacht. Despite these specific difficulties, O'Neill and O'Donnell were faced with the more serious problem of whether the crown could be trusted to keep to the agreement. The precedent of Shane O'Neill was not reassuring. He had achieved a more conclusive agreement in 1563, than that which the confederates now possessed, only to see it set aside by the government a few years later.[122] The confederates would have been well aware of Russell's militaristic outlook and would have worried about the maintenance of a peace under his deputyship. Nor would they have been surprised to learn that Norris and Fenton were proposing that the peace be 'managed' to the advantage of the crown, presumably with the object of fragmenting the confederacy.[123] Under normal circumstances, such a response would have inevitably followed the humiliation of the crown at the hands of those it regarded as rebels. However, circumstances were abnormal; the Tudor regime in the

[118] PRO SP 63/186, no. 22(2). O'Mulrian had written to Philip II in October 1588 after the failure of Armada. Allegedly acting on behalf of the Irish nobility, he advised the king to mount another attack on Elizabeth through Ireland using Waterford as a point of entry and to appoint a Habsburg prince as ruler of Ireland: AGS Estado 431 (Portugal), fo. 55.
[119] We know of Hovenden's advice to the earl because the letter in which he gave it was intercepted: C, Carew, iii. 171–2. We know of Bernard O'Donnell's activities because of his subsequent capture in France, imprisonment in England and banishment by James I: CSPI vi. 351–2; viii. 451–2; PRO SP 63/189, no. 46(1); 200, no. 51; M. Walsh, 'Destruction by peace', 163–4.
[120] CSP, Sp. iv. 617–19.
[121] PRO SP 63/188, nos 56, 74.
[122] Brady, 'Government of Ireland', 162–71, 183–92.
[123] CSPI, v. 493–5; PRO SP 63/187, no. 58.

mid-1590s was under acute pressure at home and abroad and may therefore have been willing to tolerate an agreement with the confederates longer than it had done with Shane O'Neill three decades before.

In May 1596 three Spanish ships arrived in Ireland in close succession. These had come independently of each other and as such constituted separate expeditions. The first expedition sailed under the command of Ensign Alonso Cobos from Santander, the second under Captains Cisneros and Medinilla from Lisbon and the third under Ensigns Montero and Jimenez from La Coruña.[124] All three expeditions shared the same objectives: to encourage the confederates in their war against the English crown, to survey the coasts and harbours of Ireland for a possible Spanish invasion and to assess the military strength of the Irish lords.[125] These ships had been sent out separately by Philip II to ensure the success of their mission. During the previous winter, he had finally heeded the pleas of the Irish bishops and had decided, for reasons of his own, to attempt to block the English peace initiative in Ireland.[126]

Alonso Cobos landed at Killybegs in Tirconnell and travelled to O'Donnell's castle at Lifford.[127] Ó Cléirigh gives Hugh Roe O'Donnell the credit of dealing with Cobos on behalf of O'Neill and the other lords.[128] This claim was a deliberate fabrication on the part of the biographer. Although Cobos did not wish to remain long, O'Donnell reportedly informed him that he would do nothing without O'Neill's consent.[129] In fact, he had already written to O'Neill, Cormac MacBaron and Conn Mac an Íarla about the arrival of the Spanish delegation.[130] In a similar vein, George Cawell, an English observer of these events, tells us that a list of the confederate lords in order of importance had to be amended. Santiago, the secretary of Alonso Cobos, had at first placed O'Donnell before the earl and O'Doherty before the rest. This was changed and the final version read O'Neill, O'Donnell, Maguire, O'Rourke, MacWilliam Bourke, Cormac MacBaron, O'Doherty and O'Cahan.[131]

Cawell recorded a speech made by Alonso Cobos during a dinner at Lifford after the arrival of O'Neill and his entourage. This speech was tailored to meet the ideological needs of the assembled company. Cobos reminded the Irish lords 'that their first and original ancestors came out of Biskay'.[132] This was a reference to Leabhar Gabhála (The Book of Invasions) which asserted that the Gaelic inhabitants of Ireland were descendants of the sons of King Milesius from the Iberian peninsula.[133] This idea was not lost on O'Neill and O'Donnell, who in their desire to become vassals of the Spanish crown, mentioned the

124 Ibid. 190, no. 11(9); CSPI, v. 538; CSP, Sp. iv. 619–27.
125 Ibid.
126 M. Walsh, 'Destruction by peace', 8–9.
127 AGS Estado, 839, fos 104–5: 'Relacion del alferez Alonso Cobos'. I would like to thank Professor Colin Smith of St Catharine's College, Cambridge, for his assistance in translating this document.
128 Life, i, 123.
129 PRO SP 63/189, no. 40.
130 Ibid. no. 18(4).
131 Ibid. 190, no. 42(1); AGS Estado, 839, fos 104–5.
132 PRO SP 63/190, no. 42(1).
133 Ó Cléirigh also refers to the Milesian myth at this point: Life, i. 121.

Iberian origins of the Irish race in letters to Philip II.[134] Cobos also made a reference to Pope Adrian IV's donation of Ireland to Henry II of England and his successors under the bull *Laudabiliter* in the twelfth century. He contended that

> Her Majesty had no title to the realm of Ireland, and that the defence and trust thereof was committed by Popes in former times to the princes of England for their defence and establishment of religion. And now since the succeeding princes were digressed from the true Catholic faith, His Holiness purposed to free them from the usurpation of their government.[135]

The confederates were already interested in Papal donation as a mechanism to transfer sovereignty but the ensign was lying when he claimed that the pope was of a similar mind.[136] In his report to Philip II, Cobos recorded what was either a different speech or a more crucial part of the one noted by Cawell. Since his arrival, Cobos had learnt that a treaty with the English queen was already agreed and that only the grant of her pardon and the swearing of fealty by the lords was lacking. He told the confederates that the peace treaty was prejudicial to their interests. Most importantly, to be sure of winning them over, he informed them that the king had already raised soldiers and prepared a fleet to succour them. This was untrue and, in doing so, he exceeded his brief.[137] This tactic was doubtless assisted by Philip's letter to O'Neill which had given a vague promise of assistance and entrusted the rest to his messenger.[138]

An agreement followed secret talks between Cobos on the one side and O'Neill, O'Donnell and Cormac MacBaron on the other in a small house near Lifford Castle. Hugh Boye MacDavitt acted as interpreter.[139] The confederates, who 'had almost concluded peace with the queen on terms satisfactory to themselves', now agreed to abandon the attempt and to become instead vassals of the king of Spain.[140] The letter written by O'Neill and O'Donnell to Philip II on this occasion is of obvious import. They gave the impression that they were doing Philip II a good turn when in reality they were dissatisfied with the terms they had obtained from the English crown. They said that they had been offered freedom of worship and peaceful occupation of their countries but now

---

[134] AGS Estado, 839, fos 104–5; 2604 (unfoliated); *CSPI*, vi. 353. In a memorial sent to Philip III in 1608, Hugh O'Neill and Rory O'Donnell traced their genealogical origins in accordance with *Leabhar Gabhála*: M. Walsh, 'Destruction by peace', 207–9. The Milesian tradition also enabled Irish exiles in Spain to claim equal rights of citizenship: Walsh, 'The military order of St Patrick', footnote on pp. 280–1. In short, *Leabhar Gabhála* served as an ideological *vade-mecum* for the Gaelic elite: Cunningham, 'Native culture and political change in Ireland, 1580–1640', in Brady and Gillespie, *Natives and Newcomers*, 155–7, 167.
[135] PRO SP 63/190, no. 42(1).
[136] F. M. Jones, 'The Counter-Reformation' in P. J. Corish (ed.), *The history of Irish Catholicism*, 7 vols, Dublin 1967, iii. 45. At this time the Papacy, which was pursuing an independent foreign policy under Clement VIII, would have been averse to using its powers of donation to further Spanish machinations in Ireland: J. J. Silke, *Ireland and Europe, 1559–1607*, Dublin 1966, 22.
[137] AGS Estado, 839, fos 104–5.
[138] C, *Carew*, iii. 141.
[139] PRO SP 63/190, no. 42(1).
[140] *CSP, Sp.* iv. 619.

in the hope only of Philip's benevolence they were willing to forego these honourable conditions and renew the war. They calculated that 6,000 soldiers and arms for 10,000 more were needed to sustain a successful campaign in Ireland and requested the immediate dispatch of 1,000 soldiers as an interim measure. O'Neill and O'Donnell also wanted a new monarch.

> Since, to our great and unspeakable detriment, we have experienced acts of injustice and wrongdoing on the part of the officials whom the ruler of England used to send to us, we pray and beseech Your Majesty to designate as king over this island someone who is close to you, a man who is completely honourable and gifted, for Your Majesty's own benefit and that of the commonwealth of Ireland, a man who will not in the least disdain to rule over us, but also to be among us and to rule and advise our people with kindness and wisdom.

As a result they took the advice proffered in a letter from the bishop of Clonfert and petitioned Philip II to have Cardinal Archduke Albert appointed their prince.[141] In the light of the decisions taken at Lifford, it is hard to overstate the importance of the mission of Alonso Cobos. Petitions addressed to Philip III by Hugh O'Neill during his continental exile show clearly that this event had altered, indeed determined the course of the war.[142]

Just as Cobos was setting sail, the second expedition arrived in Tirconnell escorted by MacWilliam Bourke.[143] Another conference was held at Donegal between the emissaries of the Spanish crown and the confederates. Cisneros and Medinilla found the lords united; O'Neill and O'Donnell acted like one man and they were respected by the rest. This time the discussions went into greater detail about possible landing sites for an armada, with Galway and Limerick being selected as the most suitable for the purpose. In further letters to Philip II, O'Neill and O'Donnell reiterated their demands and insisted that, without prompt assistance, they would be forced to make peace with the English.[144] In a letter delivered on this occasion, the bishop of Killaloe urged O'Rourke to write to the pope. O'Rourke was advised to ask the pope to separate Ireland for ever from the English empire by appointing the earl of Tyrone, the scion of a royal house, as its king.[145] However, the confederates stuck to their first choice of Archduke Albert which was clearly more politic since they were seeking the support of the Spanish crown.[146] Unlike the first expedition, Cisneros and Medinilla brought the lords a supply of munitions which was divided out amongst them.[147] According to one intelligence report reaching the government, O'Neill received twenty firkins of powder, O'Donnell fifteen, MacWilliam Bourke five and the others smaller portions.[148]

---

[141] AGS Estado 839, fo. 107. I am grateful to Dr Brian Scott of Queen's University, Belfast for his translation of this letter. *CSP, Sp.* iv. 620; *CSPI*, viii. 451.
[142] M. Walsh, *'Destruction by peace'*, 205, 251–2.
[143] AGS Estado 839, fos 104–5.
[144] *CSP, Sp.* iv. 620–5.
[145] PRO SP 63/186, no. 38.
[146] *CSP, Sp.* iv. 623.
[147] PRO SP 63/190, no. 42(1).
[148] Ibid. 189, no. 53.

Captain Medinilla and two experienced soldiers had been instructed to remain in Ireland as military advisers but the confederates decided that it was too risky for them to stay behind.[149] The success of the first two expeditions rendered the third under Montero and Jimenez relatively unimportant and it was left to Hugh Boye MacDavitt to deal with it.[150]

O'Neill and O'Donnell did their utmost to conceal the events at Lifford and Donegal from the Dublin administration. For instance, Sarah O'Neill and her party who were present at Lifford were sworn to silence.[151] A public statement made by the earl at Lifford repudiating Spanish assistance formed the basis of early reports obtained from men travelling out of the North and from spies specially sent for the purpose.[152] O'Neill and O'Donnell had themselves written to Norris from Lifford. They said that they had informed the Spanish messenger of their readmission to the favour of their own prince and of their consequent inability to satisfy his requests.[153] Later in May they notified Norris about a similar rebuff which they had allegedly given to two other Spanish gentlemen.[154] The most elaborate attempt to cover up came when Captain William Warren was sent to the earl to find out more about the Spanish embassy. To demonstrate his renewed fidelity to the queen, Hugh O'Neill forwarded to the council the letter which Cobos had brought to him from Philip II after extracting a promise from Warren that the letter would be either returned or destroyed without a copy being made. Of course, O'Neill knew the likely outcome – the council decided to retain the letter for transmission to London.[155] As a result, he was able to accuse Warren of abusing his friendship and more importantly to accuse the Dublin government of acting dishonourably.[156] In subsequent correspondence with Philip II, O'Neill explained that he had handed over the letter to deceive the English and thereby to disguise his true dealings with the Spanish.[157] This ploy by O'Neill was not sufficient to convince even the moderate members on the Irish council.[158] It was now receiving good intelligence about the second Spanish expedition from sources in Connacht.[159] Later, on 7 June an Italian merchant who had come to Ireland on board the third ship of Ensigns Montero and Jimenez reported in person to the council.[160] In a casual meeting with an official at Newry, MacDonnell Galloglass remarked that the peace was likely to break down on the question of religion and that the Spaniards had promised assistance by the end of the

---

[149] CSP, Sp. iv. 621, 624.
[150] AGS Estado 839, fo. 118.
[151] PRO SP 63/189, no. 46(8). Sarah was wife of Arthur Magennis and daughter of Hugh O'Neill.
[152] Ibid. nos 27, 28, 37, 40, 46(6).
[153] Ibid. no. 14.
[154] Ibid. 190, no. 1(2).
[155] Ibid. nos 1, 5.
[156] Ibid. nos 20, 44(3), 44(7).
[157] CSP, Sp. iv. 638, 642; M. Walsh, 'Destruction by peace', 9–10.
[158] PRO SP 63/190, nos 1, 2(1), 5, 30(5).
[159] Ibid. 189, nos 46(6), 53.
[160] Ibid. 190, no. 11(9).

summer.[161] Finally at the end of June George Cawell provided a full account of what he had seen and heard at Lifford and additional information on the second embassy. From this, the government could easily determine that O'Neill and O'Donnell had decided to accept the offer of Spanish aid.[162]

After their agreement with the Spanish agents, O'Neill and O'Donnell embarked on a deliberate attempt to frustrate the peace process and to provoke revolt in hitherto unaffected parts of the kingdom. The work of the various peace commissions was stymied.[163] A commission had been sent northwards to deliver Tyrone's pardon and to settle the affairs of eastern Ulster. Alleging the need to deal with certain Scottish marauders, O'Neill put off meeting the commissioners for a number of weeks.[164] He only condescended to take his pardon from them in July two months after its enrolment in chancery.[165] When the affairs of eastern Ulster were eventually considered, the earl prevented the local lords from dealing independently with the commissioners.[166] Another commission was sent to settle the affairs of the O'Reillys and O'Farrells and to take up the pledges promised by them. This commission was also frustrated and the parties now refused to send in their hostages.[167] The interception of letters from O'Neill proved that he was trying to exercise overlordship in the Midlands.[168] The confederate lords of Connacht refused to discuss peace terms with Norris and Fenton until the arrival of O'Donnell who was delayed by the apparent need to fend off some Scottish mercenaries demanding employment.[169] No progress was made when he did arrive towards the end of June. Indeed, O'Donnell refused to hand over his own hostages until Connacht itself was settled.[170] O'Neill had sent Henry Hovenden ostensibly to assist in the pacification of Connacht but an intercepted letter exposed the true nature of confederate dealings with Norris and Fenton. Hovenden boasted to his foster-brother: 'All the delays that could possibly be used for prolonging the causes here have not been omitted.'[171] And without a settlement in Connacht, O'Neill was threatening to send back his pardon and to demand the restoration of his hostages; in fact there had already been an abortive attempt to rescue Cormac MacBaron's son.[172] A meeting at Strabane marked a new departure in confederate policy. O'Neill, O'Donnell, O'Rourke and MacWilliam Bourke dispatched a circular letter to lords in other parts of Ireland, in particular Munster, requesting their adhesion to the confederacy in a war on behalf of 'Christ's Catholic religion'.[173] The authorities in London were disappointed at

---

[161] Ibid. no. 44(1). The leader of O'Neill's galloglasses was reportedly worried about the possibility of Spanish intervention having 'heard much of their cruelty and brutality'.
[162] Ibid. 190, nos 42, 42(1).
[163] Ibid. no. 32.
[164] Ibid. no. 11(1–2).
[165] CPCRI, ii. 373; CSPI, vi. 41–2.
[166] C, Carew, iii. 180–1.
[167] PRO SP 63/190, no. 11(4), 30(1–2), 44(9).
[168] Ibid. no. 30(11–12).
[169] Ibid. nos 1(3), 25, 25(2–3).
[170] Ibid. no. 44(14–16).
[171] Ibid. 189, no. 28(2); C, Carew, iii. 178–9.
[172] PRO SP 63/190, nos 42(1), 44(10); CSPI, vi. 42; C, Carew, iii. 178–9.
[173] Ibid. 179.

the turn of Irish events. Lord Burghley saw no likelihood of peace, only renewed war and increased expenditure.[174] As it turned out, the military assistance which the confederates expected in 1596 did not materialise. A Spanish fleet left Lisbon for Ireland in October under Don Martin del Padilla but it was wrecked in a storm off Cape Finisterre.[175]

In the spring of 1596 Hugh O'Neill took a momentous decision. He reneged on a peace treaty with the English crown and committed the confederacy to an alliance with Spain. As a by-product of this decision, the confederates had to couch their struggle in religious and national terms in order to broaden their support. Its actual objective was only realised five years later when a Spanish army landed at Kinsale. The result was the decisive defeat of the confederate cause. In hindsight, it is easy to regard the confederate repudiation of peace in 1596 as a disastrous mistake. Yet, in that year the chances of complete victory must have appeared bright when weighed against adverse precedents and uncertain portents. Though temporarily buoyed up by success at Cadiz, the future of the English regime seemed bleak. It was lumbered with an ageing Queen, a fractured elite and a war generalised throughout western Europe. In succeeding years, its prospects became bleaker still. In the end, it was only through the expedient of currency debasement and the strength of its institutions that the regime avoided insolvency and staged a military recovery in Ireland.

[174] ULC Ee 3 56 no. 99.
[175] Cesareo Fernández Duro, *Armada Española*, 9 vols, Madrid 1895–1903, iii. 129–31.

Conclusion

I want to conclude this book with two historiograpical points; by reassessing the early career of Hugh O'Neill and by examining the nature of the conflict in which he was involved.

It is high time that Hugh O'Neill was restored to his rightful place at the centre of developments leading up to the Nine Years War and indeed acknowledged as one of the most adept politicians in Irish history. Any reassessment of this hitherto enigmatic figure must start with his upbringing. Hugh O'Neill was born about 1550. In his earliest years he was fostered amongst the household families of the O'Neills in his native Tyrone. After his father Matthew was killed by Shane O'Neill, he became a ward of the crown. His wardship was granted to Giles Hovenden, a New Englishman, who already had a business connection with Hugh's grandfather, Conn. As a result Hugh came to live in the Pale. In 1562 his elder brother, Brian, was killed by Turlough Luineach, leaving Hugh and Cormac as the surviving legitimate sons. However it was only when war broke out between the crown and Shane O'Neill in 1566 that Hugh acquired any importance in the political arena. Prior to that time there was every likelihood that Shane would make good his claim to the earldom of Tyrone as Conn's eldest legitimate son thereby extinguishing the claims of the heirs of the affiliated Matthew Kelly. It was only at this stage that Lord Deputy Sidney would have paid any attention to Hugh and may have entertained him in the viceregal household. It cannot be stressed enough that Hugh O'Neill was not brought up at the home of the Sidneys at Penshurst to adorn the court of Elizabeth. Far from being trained in the refined graces of a courtier, he probably received a basic education by attending grammar school or by getting lessons from a private tutor. He was of course anglicised. Yet many other young Gaelic noblemen were being exposed to similar anglicising influences as a result of being educated, being held hostage or being imprisoned in the Pale. This did not necessarily lead to a crisis of identity by creating individuals caught between opposing Gaelic and English cultures. The situation was not that black and white and anyhow the preoccupation with the problem of identity is a distinctly modern one. Hugh O'Neill's main preoccupation was the pursuit of power and his upbringing in this regard was a great advantage because it gave him a facility with both cultures in a period of transition.[1]

Had O'Neill been brought up at Penshurst, he would almost certainly have been a Protestant of the puritan variety like Sir Philip Sidney. This was not the case. His fosterers, the Hovendens, were amongst the earliest and therefore the least Protestant of the New English settlers. Giles Hovenden had come over

[1] Hiram Morgan, 'The end of Gaelic Ulster: a thematic interpretation of events between 1534 and 1610', *IHS*, xxvi (1988), 26.

with St Leger and by marrying Elizabeth Cheevers, he had begun the integration of his family into the established gentry of the Pale.[2] As with the rest of the Palesmen, the Hovendens probably conformed initially to the established church but then became progressively alienated from it in the 1570s and 1580s. In 1584 O'Neill signalled his adherence to the Counter-Reformation by celebrating Easter according to Pope Gregory's new style calendar.[3] In fact O'Neill maintained his outward conformity longer than most of the Palesmen. In 1594 Tom Lee described Hugh and his wife, Mabel, as well-known Papists who kept seminary priests and went on to explain how O'Neill on visits to Dublin would accompany the lord deputy to church and attend the service whereas the Palesmen would go only as far as the church door.[4] The state had already seen through O'Neill's antics characterising him in 1590 as a man 'rooted in superstition' who was not be trusted in the event of a foreign invasion.[5] Of course, actual conformity to Protestantism would not have made political sense for Gaelic lords such as O'Neill because an important adjunct to their power was the influence they exercised over the local church. O'Neill was hardly going to permit the Ulster church to be overrun by Protestant careerists from England and Wales who would have diminished that influence.

Obviously the government never considered Hugh O'Neill's religious affiliation a serious impediment in supporting him in the years before 1587. When it came to a fight, the crown felt cheated by a hitherto insignificant individual who had ridden to power on its shoulders. Had this analysis been wholly correct O'Neill's authority and ability to resist would have crumbled in no time. O'Neill also felt slighted. Since the late 1560s he had contained Turlough Luineach and the MacShanes; he had protected the northern approaches to the Pale; he had kept the North quiet, indeed he claimed to have civilised it. Now his efforts were being overlooked in favour of money-grabbing English officials. O'Neill proposed a compromise whereby Armagh and Tyrone (which included O'Cahan's country) would be established as one county palatine. He would in turn control the North through a combination of trusted army officers in his pay and Gaelic noblemen in his extended family. This situation would have been analogous to the role played by the head of the Campbell family who as both feudal magnate – earl of Argyll – and Gaelic lord – MacCaillin Mór – kept the Western Highlands and Islands quiet for the kings of Scotland. Such a compromise was not on the cards. Tudor reform policy was inimical to derogating sovereignty in this neo-feudal fashion and the reformers would have abolished Ormond's palatinate of Tipperary if they could have had their way. Nor was there any chance of O'Neill himself becoming Lord President of Ulster; Irishmen in the persons of the earl of Clanrickard in Connacht and the earl of Thomond in Munster were given these jobs only when the state was forced to fall back on bastard feudalism after those presidencies had been

---

[2] John Marshall, 'The Hovendens: fosterbrothers of Hugh O'Neill, prince of Ulster', *Ulster Journal of Archaeology*, 2nd ser. xiii (1907), 5.
[3] PRO SP 63/108, no. 56.
[4] Lee, 'Brief declaration', 111.
[5] PRO SP 63/152, no. 4.

destablised by the Nine Years War.[6] As an insurance policy against the future, O'Neill started to make overtures to Spain – unfortunately we cannot establish the exact date for the inception of his secret diplomacy. O'Neill also tried to hold back the deluge by bribing royal officials, most notably Lord Deputy Fitzwilliam. Nevertheless, Tudor policy in Ulster did reach its logical conclusion in the Monaghan settlement which threatened the basis of Gaelic lordship on which O'Neill's power rested. In the spring of 1593 it became plain that the next domino would be Fermanagh when an attempt was made to impose a sheriff there. As a result O'Neill decided to let the boys loose to demonstrate that the government could not rule the North without him whilst holding himself in reserve should full-scale war become a necessity and Spanish intervention a real possibility.

The struggle for power in Ulster was personalised in the characters of Hugh O'Neill and Sir Henry Bagenal. In 1591 Bagenal became chief commissioner of Ulster, a post which the steady advance of crown government would eventually transform into a provincial presidency. For forty years the Bagenal family had been the principal standard-bearers of English civility in the North of Ireland. Sir Henry himself had attended Oxford, had deputised as marshal of the army for his aged father and had established a political connection with Lord Burghley. Instead of using dependable Englishmen such as himself, successive governments had used Hugh O'Neill in an attempt to reform Ulster and had thereby helped him gain the very marks of Gaelic sovereignty which it wanted to stamp out. Bagenal now had his opportunity in the deputyship of Fitzwilliam. To thwart Bagenal's aggrandisement, O'Neill asked for the hand of his sister, Mabel, in order to neutralise the Bagenals as he had done the O'Donnells by enmeshing them in a marriage alliance. When he was refused, he persuaded Mabel to elope with him. This was a matter of power politics, not love. In this case Hugh O'Neill used his great personal charm to inveigle a woman half his age into his confidence and then into his bed. Hugh was mistaken if he believed that his new brother-in-law would accept the accomplished fact because the latter refused to recognise the marriage and the whole episode served only to embitter relations between the two men.

It is noteworthy that Hugh O'Donnell had similar unexecuted plans in 1595 to kidnap the daughter of the earl of Clanrickard with a view to neutralising his power in Connacht. This would have involved O'Donnell divorcing O'Neill's daughter. But the very fact that O'Donnell took Rose O'Neill back and remained in a barren marriage is symbolic of his dependence on her father.[7] O'Donnell's deathbed will in Spain in 1602 does show that a formal treaty was made between himself and the earl at some point during the war making the two men equal in everything right down to equal shares of Spanish munitions.[8] However, the evidence adduced here for the early years of the war suggests the contrary. In general, Hugh Roe O'Donnell deferred to Hugh O'Neill. He made

6 Bernadette Cunningham, 'Political and social change in the lordships of Clanricard and Thomond, 1569–1641', unpubl. MA thesis, University College, Galway, 1979, ch. i.
7 PRO SP 63/185, nos 10, 10(1); CPSI, vi, 260.
8 J. J. Silke, 'The last will of Red Hugh O'Donnell', Archivium Hibernicum, xxiv (1984–8), 50–60.

the running in opening up contacts with Spain but he was merely a frontman for O'Neill. When the first Spanish agents arrived in 1596 he reportedly refused to deal with them alone answering that 'there was one above him, naming O'Neill, which if he would consent unto it, he would do the same'.[9] Undoubtedly, O'Donnell was an arrogant and warlike individual whereas O'Neill was dissembling and meditative. Yet they made a successful double-act which continued to mystify the state. In fact it was in the mutual interest of both men to act together because the one could not succeed without the backing of the other. And while O'Neill had the predominant voice in the councils of the Gaelic confederacy, he also kept a firm and directive rein on his own kinsmen and followers. He exemplifies the exercise of lordship and indeed the centrality of lordship in the Gaelic political system. This point is brought home most strikingly by the sorry state of Gaelic society in Ulster after the Flight of the Earls in 1607. Gaelic society was left leaderless; the poets squealed in anguish, renewed conspiracies proved ineffectual and an actual rebellion in 1641 quickly turned into a sectarian massacre.[10]

The successes of O'Neill's early career depended on the political skills he could bring to bear on a given situation. He lacked the charisma of O'Donnell yet was possessed of considerable personal charm. For instance, he made a favourable impression on the queen on his visit to Court in 1587. He inspired loyalty in his servants to such an extent that he would trust them as double-agents. Most of all, he was a consummate liar. His dissembling manner deceived some government officials, others allowed themselves to be deceived by taking his bribes. Thereby he made himself the enigma he is today because the elaborate campaign of disinformation he waged was so successful that it confounded subsequent historians as well. There are many examples of his political acumen in the early stages of the conflict. He used his kinsmen as proxies to wage war on the state and, when challenged, claimed that they were refusing to do his bidding. When he did not wish to meet officials face to face, he evinced a fear of treachery. This may have been a genuine fear given the assassination of Shane O'Neill in the 1560s and the more recent executions of Hugh Roe MacMahon and Brian O'Rourke. But what else did he expect for defying his former masters? On the other hand, he was willing to gamble his own personal safety to buy time as when he fought at the battle of the Ford of the Erne or when he went to Dublin to explain himself to the new lord deputy. O'Neill himself was not averse to murdering political opponents such as Hugh Gavelach MacShane and Phelim MacTurlough O'Neill and he even managed to fob off the government with excuses. Nor can his compromise proposals for palatinate status be taken seriously given that he subsequently raised the stakes at each successive stage of the negotiations. O'Neill was a very ambitious man; indeed far too ambitious because he lacked experience in the vital area on which ultimate success depended. He did not have the formal training in regular warfare which he might have acquired had he been brought up at Court

9   PRO SP 63/189, no. 40.
10 Raymond Gillespie, *Conspiracy: Ulster plots and plotters in 1615*, Belfast 1987, *passim*; Cunningham, 'Native Culture and political change', 158; Gillespie, 'Ulster and the 1641 rising', in Brady and Gillespie, *Natives and Newcomers*, 210–11.

or visited the continent as a young man. He was beaten decisively in the two pitched battles in which he fought, at Carricklea in 1588 and at Kinsale in 1601. All his experience was of the guerrilla-style border warfare of Ireland. His victories were Irish ambushes executed on a grand scale. Furthermore, these victories were gained over Sir Henry Bagenal. Bagenal was given the job of the marshal of the queen's army in Ireland in spite of reverses against the Scots in the Glens of Antrim which in retrospect are not dissimilar to the battles he subsequently lost to O'Neill at Clontibret and at the Yellow Ford. His only qualifications were that he knew the right people and that his father had been marshal before him. In a sense Hugh O'Neill got as far as he did because of the ineptitude of his inveterate rival, Sir Henry Bagenal.

Having looked at the career of Hugh O'Neill, it is worthwhile reflecting on the nature of the conflict in general. Supporters of the Tudor regime described the war in Ireland as rebellion. In contemporary usage, the word rebellion was synonymous with treason. It covered all manner of revolts against one's natural superiors – of the servant against his master, of the wife against her husband and of the subject against the monarch. Here it meant levying war against the sovereign. Since Tyrone was a subject of Queen Elizabeth, it follows that he was in rebellion against her.[11] His revolt furthermore exhibited many of the features common to rebellion in England. For instance, the defence of the Catholic religion was made a keynote as it had been in the Pilgrimage of Grace (1536), the Western rebellion (1549) and the Northern rebellion (1569).[12] It was also a commonplace to rail against the evil ministers of the crown rather than the policy or person of the monarch. In this case, O'Neill directed his animus at Fitzwilliam, Bagenal and a host of petty officials rather than against the queen.[13] Nor was the duplicitous behaviour of O'Neill in the early stages of the conflict so unusual. In the rebellions cited above Lord Hussey, the earl of Arundel and the earl of Northumberland used their kinsmen and followers to put pressure on the government while remaining neutral themselves. The object of this ma-noeuvre was to protect estates from confiscation and to leave the magnate sufficient leeway to negotiate. However, when the crown in turn demanded that the magnate act against the rebels, the latter was put in an awkward position. To mitigate his ambiguous stance, he argued that his followers were out of control or that the rebels were simply a rabble of rioting commoners. Given this background, it is surely symptomatic of the political divisions and military impotence of the English government in Ireland that it gave O'Neill the benefit of the doubt for so long.[14] As such the conflict was not just a rebellion, it was the Tudor rebellion *par excellence* because it was the most dangerous and most costly one they faced.

Even so it was not a straightforward Tudor rebellion which the English crown

[11] William Rastell (ed.), A collection in English of the statutes now in force, London 1588, 389, 494.

[12] Anthony Fletcher, Tudor rebellions, Harlow 1983, chs iv, v, viii.

[13] Mervyn James, English politics and the concept of honour, Past and Present supplement, no. 3, Oxford 1978, 35.

[14] Ibid. 17, 41–3, and idem. 'Obedience and dissent in Henrician England: the Lincolnshire rebellion, 1536', Past and Present, xlviii (1970), 9, 59–61.

faced in Ireland at the turn of the sixteenth century. O'Neill was in no sense excluded from the Court as a point of contact as was the case in certain English rebellions. Although not present in person, he had access to the monarch via the two factions competing for her favour; he could deal directly with the earl of Essex and indirectly with Lord Burghley through the medium of the earl of Ormond.[15] The real problem was the ambiguous constitutional relationship between the Gaelic lords and the English crown, not the degree of contact between the opposing parties. In the North of Ireland full English sovereignty, that is the feudal mode of land tenure and the panoply of civil government, either was not in operation or was only in the process of introduction. Under these circumstances, the lords in action against the crown can not be strictly categorised as rebels. Instead, another term in contemporary usage – confederates – has been employed to denote them. This term was not pejorative and simply implied a group of individuals banded together for a particular purpose.

The crisis which eventually led to war was caused by attempted centralisation. To achieve its aim, the state had to abolish the Gaelic instituion of lordship and the military power which underpinned it. This meant confronting Hugh O'Neill whose strength rested on Gaelic lordship even though he possessed a feudal title. The favoured methods were the establishment of freeholders to undermine the Gaelic lords as a class and the shift to administration through provincial presidents to remove the hegemonic claims of O'Neill and O'Donnell. Although it is debatable whether Gaelic lordships represented sovereign entities, they certainly did count as 'ancient liberties' which the English crown had deigned to recognise in the past. The policy of centralisation was now endangering these liberties. The problem was the Renaissance concept of sovereignty which the Tudors were seeking to deploy in Ireland. Their idea of sovereignty was both integrative and penetrative – they wanted their writ to run in all parts of the country and to be effective at all levels of society. It is plain that the Gaelic lords still entertained a medieval system of overlapping sovereignties in which authority was divided between them and the queen and her representative, the lord deputy. And even though they willingly took advantage of the reform process, their concept of obedience did not change. It never became the absolute loyalty of the subject but remained the self-serving and conditional support of the tribal lord. As a result once their local power was threatened with extinction they abandoned one monarch and sought another. What may or may not have been a rebellion in the first instance became a war of liberation. Towards the end of 1598 the Irish council warned its English counterpart: 'this rebellion is now thoroughly sorted to an Irish war, whose drifts and pretences are, to shake off all English government, and subtract the kingdom from Her Majesty, as much as in them listeth'.[16]

Seen in this light, the crisis facing England in Ireland merits serious comparison with the crisis facing Spain in the Netherlands. Both crises began with attacks on entrenched liberties by centralising regimes. In turn, these developments produced demands from the aggrieved parties for constitutional

---

[15] G.R. Elton, *Studies in Tudor and Stuart politics and government*, 3 vols, Cambridge, 1974–83, iii. 50; Williams, *The Tudor regime*, 345.
[16] *CPSI*, vii. 305.

guarantees to underwrite their old privileges. In Ireland as in the Netherlands both sets of dissidents demanded liberty of conscience. The monarchs involved found it difficult to compromise; their standing in the world was at stake. Elizabeth feared the besmirching of 'our honour' in the same way as Philip II feared the loss of 'nuestra reputación'. Therefore they refused to countenance dilution of sovereignty or any deviation from the state religion. Both England and Spain strove to prevent any foreign intervention in what they regarded as purely domestic matters. Paradoxically, both powers were constrained by foreign commitments – England in the Netherlands and France, Spain in the Mediterranean and France – from deploying the resources needed to crush their own revolts. Also, each state had the problem of financing and supplying an army overseas for a long duration and the possibility of alienating the civilian population by doing so.[17]

The opponents of state centralisation reacted in a similar way during hostilities. The earl of Tyrone can be readily compared with both William the Silent and Maurice of Nassau. Like William, he was a shrewd politician who raised the stakes while simultaneously obstructing and deceiving his enemies; like him, he was denigrated by the state as a devious, disloyal, ungrateful hypocrite because of his previous connection with it.[18] Like Maurice, he was a skillful military commander who enjoyed conspicuous success in defensive warfare. From a strategic viewpoint, Ulster and the northern Netherlands were perfectly suited for defensive warfare. Ulster was a veritable fortress, having two passes on its eastern and western extremes as the principal points of entry with hilly and watery terrain in between. The United Provinces were shielded by a westward-flowing river system.

In ideological terms, the dissidents in both countries were conservatives interested in protecting their own privileges. When they failed to prise constitutional guarantees from their respective suzerains, they sought new protectors. The Irish confederates hoped to secure a transfer of sovereignty through invitation and Papal donation. The United Provinces also sought a new sovereign; overtures were made to Elizabeth and Henry III but neither was anxious to take on board somebody else's rebellious subjects.[19] These opponents of centralisation lacked legitimising authority but the reluctance, slowness and inadequacy of their chosen protectors forced them to assume authority for reasons of functional expediency. The dissident Dutch provinces eventually assumed regalian rights themselves. In Ireland O'Neill and O'Donnell used Gaelic overlordship within their respective spheres of influence. In Munster O'Neill established James Fitzthomas Fitzgerald as earl of Desmond by proxy and inaugurated Florence MacCarthy as the MacCarthy Mór in person to legitimise the

---

17 Geoffrey Parker, *Spain and the Netherlands, 1559–1659*, London 1979, chs i–ii. For a more general treatment of the concept of honour held by Renaissance princes see Paula Fichtner, 'The politics of honour: Renaissance chivalry and Habsburg dynasticism', *Bibliothèque d'Humanisme et Renaissance*, xxix (1967), 567–80.
18 H. Wansink (ed.), *The apologie of Prince of Orange against the proclamation of the king of Spain*, Leiden 1969, 155–60.
19 Geoffrey Parker, *The Dutch revolt*, London 1977, 196–207; Charles Wilson, *Queen Elizabeth and the revolt of the Netherlands*, London 1970, ch. ii; E. H. Kossman and A. F. Mellink (eds), *Texts relating to the revolt of the Netherlands*, Cambridge 1974, 42–5.

confederate position.[20] The opponents of the crown in both countries used a faith and fatherland ideology to transcend regional particularism, ethnic divisions and factional loyalties and to galvanise the war effort against foreign oppressors.[21] Only the dictates of success and failure ensured that William the Silent became *pater patriae* and that Hugh O'Neill did not.[22]

This comparison demands attention. After all, monarchies in the early modern period were, by nature, centralising institutions. Their drive towards administrative uniformity was constrained politically by the strength of vested interests, socially by the prevalence of religious controversy and militarily by technological advances in defensive warfare. As a result, major wars broke out in the Netherlands and in Ireland in the second half of the sixteenth century. These wars had international repercussions and both countries emerged as separate theatres in a wider European conflict. Of course, the United Provinces succeeded against Spain whereas the Irish confederates lost against England. But the explanation is not hard to find. The failure of the Irish and Spanish forces at the battle of Kinsale ensured English victory as well as Dutch survival.

---

[20] *CPSI*, vii. 300, 317; ix. 38.
[21] Alastair Duke, 'From king and country to king or country? Loyalty and treason in the revolt of the Netherlands', *Transactions of the Royal Historical Society*, 5th ser. xxxii (1982), 113–35.
[22] Using the comparative case of the Netherlands, I have developed these themes further in 'Hugh O'Neill and the Nine Years War in Tudor Ireland', *Historical Journal*, xxxvi (1993), 1–17.

APPENDIX

Cormac MacBaron O'Neill played a crucial but silent part in the events described in this book. Fortunately in May 1596 he took advantage of the intervention of Spanish agents to write to Philip II. The object of his letter was to ensure for himself a grant of lands in south Down and north Louth when the war had been won. To make his case he gave an account of how the war had begun and of his role in it. His letter provides substantive proof for the argument propounded in this book. The following translation from Latin has been executed by Dr Brian Scott.

Text of AGS Estado 839, fo. 97.

I, Cormac O'Neill, full brother of the lord O'Neill, promise truly, most serene monarch, that I will obey and serve (God Almighty only excepted) you alone, nevertheless deferring to my aforesaid brother, who in this realm of Ireland is more powerful than the person who calls himself deputy to the queen of the English. For this deputy in his administration of this commonwealth is attempting, under orders, to put the faithful to death and root out the church (if any spark of life remains in it) and utterly and unceasingly to overthrow it to the best of his abilities. And this is happening more or less daily. For they have afflicted by a cruel death the earl of Desmond and several other Irish nobles, whom they have not exiled. They have, indeed, sent into exile the lords O'Connor, O'Rourke and MacMahon. They have seized their goods, movable and immovable, so much so thay they have forced the said O'Rourke, a man of considerable standing among us, to cross into Scotland accompanied only by a few followers, due to the tyrannical behaviour of the English. Indeed the Scots handed him over to the queen of England by treachery and he was consigned to a wretched death.

At this time, the English made the whole of Ireland subject to themselves, save only this fifth part of Ireland called Ulster, in which O'Neill and myself live. We were accorded great respect among the English, lest we should withdraw ourselves from their state, or rather tyranny, and attack it as has now occurred. For when we realised that almost the whole kingdom was thus being made subject to the English, I thought that I should choose rather to obey God and you, king Philip, if ever, as an indication of your illustrious mercy, you should deign to encourage me with your gracious favour, rather than to prosper, fighting against God and the Roman church, aided by the forces of the said queen and other heretics, granted to me, and by the wealth promised to me. So I took up arms against the enemies of Christ. Those from other parts of Ireland whom I found to be outlawed, I brought over to join me as allies and men well versed in arms. When they had been equipped to fight, I supplied them with all that was necessary to build up their military strength. We must be thankful to God the Father that nowhere did I attempt to join battle with the heretics (for I have fought them in many more than just one battle) without getting the

223

better of the fighting, by the favour of the powers above. So much so that those
beggarly, untrained and exiled Irish, whom I gathered together and enlisted,
now have been disciplined and hardened in war **** the heretics, whether
they like it or not, who are dwelling in and cultivating their lands.

O'Neill has been possessed of so much authority and glory by the queen of
the English that he was unwilling to be considered to be stirring up war lest he
should appear to be acting imprudently or in a manner inconsistent with his
office. He entrusted to me, his brother, the plan which he had devised a little
earlier, using me as the agent. For he was always of the opinion that a garrison
and regiments of soldiers was being sent by you to help him against the hordes
of Lutheran enemies who ceaselessly, night and day, deceive the Catholics
under the pretext of peace. In order that this military help should come across
the seas quickly, O'Neill has instructed me to write to Your Majesty. For three
times messengers have been sent to you with letters and, having been captured
by the heretics, have been removed from among us by an unspeakably cruel
death. When O'Neill heard this, and the news had been confirmed to him, he
did not brook it lightly and revealed himself an enemy and declared war. When
war had been thus proclaimed, he ordered O'Donnell, a lord with a power that
rested on a noble rank, the lord O'Reilly and other noble Irish, to come to him
as soon as they could to quell and hold back the onslaught of the heretics. At
that time, coming together, touching the Holy Gospel and giving their solemn
oaths, they swore mutually to pursue that all-out war, wholeheartedly, against
all the enemies of the Catholic church, especially the English Protestants.

For all the Irish obey O'Neill, as sails obey the wind. For they have as much
love for him as sons do for their parents, both for his own sake as for hatred of
the English. Thanks be to the powers above and to Your Highness (led by
expectation of whose help we have initiated this war), the English in Ireland
were not fewer in number this past fifty years, nor weaker and less versed in war
than they are at the present time. And over all those years, there has never
been any time at which Your Majesty may with greater ease be able to make
subject to himself the kingdom of Ireland than the present. Only cause to be
sent to O'Neill and myself (that which we need most and most desire) without
delay, a very large number of regiments and no small supply of arms.

If it pleases you, in return for the loyal service which I promise to perform for
you my prince, that is my king Philip, I ask you to appoint me leader of 500 men
under command, to prosecute this action with the resources of your military
treasury, and also ask that you may not disdain to give the same authority to my
heirs. But in that matter let whatever seems fit to you be done. And if it is not
tiresome for you, I would like Your Highness to grant me the ability to live with
honour, that is to grant me certain lands which I ought to possess by right, and
which the English possess, namely Lethcathayl and the lands of Mudharnayr
and the castle of Fuirionnath and the lands of Cuaylgne with the castle of
Carlynford, the lands of Beyllcogay and Baylenacloyche and Baylenaraince.
And now I urge you, whatever troops you may wish to grant me command over,
you may inform me about them along with the most senior of the troops whom
you are sending to my brother O'Neill. And if you think that I am worthy of the
things I have asked for, do not value me more highly than that. I believe also
that it will be no harm if you send to Ireland quantities of gold and silver coin

to pay the soldiers along with engineers to work guns. There we have many men, and are unable to satisfy their needs for arms and pay, unless you are willing to help us. For it is a great power that is opposing us. At the end of the day, it must be feared that we cannot resist it without speedy help from you. However we still continue and are victorious, I pray and beg you to order large numbers of troops to cross over to us without delay after you have seen this letter and send me with the first fleet the lands which I humbly await, by letters patent under your hand and that of your son and heir, with your seal. And as I said formerly, even if all the Irish (which God forbid) were to abandon you, I, as long as I shall live, will not desert Your Majesty. May Your Most Invincible Majesty prevail forever. Augher, 20 May 1596.

Obedient to Your Most Excellent Highness
cormok onell

Bibliography

Guides and Bibliographies

Edwards, R. W. Dudley and Mary O'Dowd, *Sources for early modern Irish history, 1534–1641*, Cambridge 1985.

Hayes, R. J., *The manuscript sources for the study of Irish civilisation*, 11 vols, Boston 1965.

Lee, Joseph, *Irish historiography*, Cork 1981.

Moody, T. W. (ed.), *Irish historiography*, Dublin 1971.

Read, Conyers, *Bibliography of British history, Tudor period, 1485–1603*, 2nd edn, Oxford 1959.

Ware, James, *Two books of the writers of Ireland*, Dublin 1704.

Primary Sources

Alnwick Castle
Letters and papers, vol iii: Miscellaneous, 1567–87
Letters and papers, vol vi: Perrot's defence papers
MS 476: 'Treatise of Ireland'

Archivo General de Simancas
Estado, lejagos 176, 431, 596, 839 and 2604

Bedford Estates, London
HMC Bedford 12: Correspondence of Sir William Russell, 1594–7
HMC Bedford 13: Sir William Russell's journal of his deputyship

Bodleian Library, Oxford
Carte MS 55–58, 131: Papers of Sir William Fitzwilliam
Perrot MS 1: Sir John Perrot's letter-book, 1584–6
University College, MS 103: Bagenal's rental, 1575
Willis MS 58: English historical treatises
   MS 30237: Waterhouse's papers

British Library
Additional MS:
   4783–4801: Papers of Sir James Ware
   4819: Collection made by Sir James Perrot
   5754: Ireland affairs, miscellaneous
   12,503: Papers of Sir Julius Caesar
   19,837: recognizances
   31,878: Two tracts on Ireland

33,743: 'The discovery and recoverye of Ireland', by Thomas Lee
34,313: Tracts on Ireland
48,015 and 48,017: Yelverton papers relating to sixteenth century Ireland
Cottonian MS
    Titus B xii: Miscellaneous Irish state papers
    Titus C vii: Miscellaneous state papers
    Titus F v: Irish state papers, 1582–87
Egerton MS
    75: Abstracts of enrolments of Crown grants
    3048: Privy Council precedent-book
Harleian MS
    35: Miscellaneous tracts
    3292: Miscellaneous state papers relating to Ireland
    7004: State papers relating to Scotland and Ireland
Lansdowne MS
    111: Miscellaneous state papers
Stowe MS
    160: Privy Council letters, Elizabeth

College of Arms
  Betham MS
    Wards, Liveries and alienations
    Repertory of Exchequer records

Hatfield House
  Cecil papers, vol. 163

Lambeth Palace
  Carew Papers:
    MS 600: Miscellaneous state papers
    MS 601: Miscellaneous state papers
    MS 605: Carew correspondence
    MS 611: Instructions and agreements
    MS 612: Russell papers
    MS 614: Miscellaneous state papers
    MS 617: Official papers, 1594–1602
    MS 618: Letters and warrants of Sir George Carew
    MS 627: Miscellaneous state papers
    MS 632: Miscellaneous state papers

National Library of Ireland
  MS 669: Treatise of Ireland

Northampton Record Office
  Fitzwilliam Papers (Ireland)
  Finch Hatton Papers

Public Record Office, Chancery Lane, London

SP 63: Irish state papers from Eliz. to Geo. III
SP 65: Miscellaneous Irish papers

Public Record Office, Kew, London
Audit Office 284–87: Irish Treasury accounts of Sir Henry Wallop

Public Record Office of Northern Ireland
D 686: Ellis papers

Royal Irish Academy
Miscellaneous O'Donovan MS 14/B/7: 'Old Customs of O'Donnell', a translation of ULC. Add. MS 2766 (20) (7)

Syon House
MS Y III 1: Papers of Sir John Perrot

Trinity College, Dublin
MS 743: Treatise of Ireland

Ulster Museum
Accession no. 282 1913: Patent for Calvach O'Donnell

University Library, Cambridge,
Additional MS
2766 (20) (7): Fragments in Irish
4246: Miscellaneous Irish papers
Dd 3 20(D): Latin letters of Queen Elizabeth
Dd 3 84: Miscellaneous tracts; first tract originally part of BLO MS 30237
Ee 3 56: Burghley's letters to his son, Robert
Kk 1 15: Papers on Nine Years War copied for Robert Cecil

Primary Printed Sources

Acts of the Privy Council of England, ed. J. R. Dasent, 32 vols, London 1890–1907.
'Additional Sidney state papers, 1566–70', ed. D. B. Quinn, *Analecta Hibernica*, xxvi (1970), 89–102.
'Agreement between O Domhnaill and Tadhg O Conchobar concerning Sligo castle (23 June 1539)', trans. Maura Carney, *IHS*, iii (1943), 282–96.
Calendar of the Carew Manuscripts preserved in the archiepiscopal library at Lambeth, 1515–1624, ed. J. S. Brewer and W. Bullen, 6 vols, London 1867–73.
'Calendar of the Irish council book: 1 March 1581 to 1 July 1586, made by John P. Prendergast between 1867 and 1869', ed. D. B. Quinn, *Analecta Hibernica*, xxiv (1967), 91–180.
Calendar of Patent and Close Rolls of chancery in Ireland, ed. J. Morrin, 3 vols, Dublin 1861–3.
Calendar of Patent Rolls, Elizabeth, 1558–80, 8 vols, London 1939–86.

Calendar of State Papers, Domestic, ed. R. Lemon and M. A. E. Green, 12 vols, London 1856–72.

Calendar of State Papers, Ireland, ed. H. C. Hamilton, E. G. Atkinson and R. P. Mahaffy, 24 vols, London 1860–1912.

Calendar of State Papers relating to Scotland and Mary, Queen of Scots, 1547–1603, 13 vols, Edinburgh and Glasgow, 1898–1969.

Calendar of State Papers, Spanish, Elizabeth, ed. M. A. S. Hume, 4 vols, London 1892–9.

'Ceart Uí Néill', trans. Myles Dillon, *Studia Celtica*, i (1966), 1–18.

'Ceart Uí Néill', trans. with commentary by Eamon Ó Doibhlin, *Seanchas Ard Mhacha*, v (1970), 324–59.

'Cios Mhios Mhathghamhna', trans. Seosamh Ó Dufaigh, *Clogher Record* (1960), 125–33.

The compossicion booke of Conought, ed. A. Martin Freeman, Dublin 1936.

Criminal trials and other proceedings before the High Court of Justiciary in Scotland, ed. Robert Pitcairn, 3 vols, Edinburgh 1833.

Desiderata curiosa Hibernica or a collection of state papers, ed. John Lodge, 2 vols, Dublin 1772.

The Edmondes papers, ed. G. G. Butler, London 1913.

Egerton papers, ed. J. Collier and J. Payne, London 1840.

Facsimiles of the national manuscripts of Ireland, ed. J. T. Gilbert, 4 vols, Dublin, 1874–84.

Fitzwilliam Accounts, 1560–65, ed. Ada Longfield, Dublin 1960.

'Fitzwilliam MSS at Milton, England', ed. Charles McNeill, *Analecta Hibernica*, iv (1932), 287–326.

Highland papers, ed. J. R. N. MacPhail, 4 vols, Edinburgh 1914–34.

Historical Manuscript Commission reports:
  6th Report, London 1877.
  Bath MSS, 5 vols, London 1904–80.
  De L'Isle and Dudley MSS, 6 vols, London 1925–66.
  Haliday MSS, London 1897.
  Hastings MSS, 4 vols, London 1928–47.
  Laing MSS, 2 vols, London 1914–25.
  Rutland MSS, 4 vols, London 1888–1905.
  Salisbury MSS, 23 vols, London 1883–1973.

Inquisitionum in officio rotulorum cancellariae Hiberniae asservatarum repertorium, ed. J. Hardiman, 2 vols, Dublin 1826–9.

Irish patent rolls of James I: a facsimile of the Irish Record Commissioners' calendar prepared prior to 1830, introduced by M. C. Griffith, Dublin 1966.

Letters and memorials of state, ed. Arthur Collins, 2 vols, London 1746.

'Ó Domhnaill's claims for military service', trans. Colm Ó Lochlainn, *Irish Sword*, v (1961–2), 117–18.

'Original letters of Shan O'Neill in Irish and Latin', trans. John O'Donovan, *Ulster Journal of Archaeology*, 1st ser. v (1857), 259–74.

'The Perrot papers: the letter-book of Lord Deputy Sir John Perrot between 9 July 1584 and 26 May 1586', ed. Charles McNeill, *Analecta Hibernica*, xii (1943), 1–67.

The reports of the deputy keeper of the public records in Ireland, Dublin 1875–90.

'Reports on Manuscripts in the Bodleian Library, Oxford', ed. Charles McNeill, *Analecta Hibernica*, i (1930), 1–178.

Sidney State papers, 1565–70, ed. Tomás Ó Laidhin, Dublin 1962.

'Some papers relating to the Nine Years War', ed. J. Hagan, *Archivium Hibernicum*, ii (1913), 274–320.

Statutes at large passed in the parliaments held in Ireland, ed. W. Ball, 21 vols, Dublin 1786–1804.

The Tanner Papers, ed. Charles McNeill, Dublin 1943.

Ulster and other Irish maps c. 1600, compiled by G. A. Hayes-McCoy, Dublin 1964.

The Walsingham letter-book or register of Ireland, May 1578 to December 1579, ed. J. Hogan and N. McNeill O'Farrell, Dublin 1959.

Contemporary Writings

Beacon, Richard, *Solon his folie or a politique discourse touching the reformation of common weales conquered, declined or corrupted*, Oxford 1594.

Bodley, Josias, 'Descriptio itineris d. Josias Bodleii ad Lecaliam in Ultonia, anno 1602', *Ulster Journal of Archaeology*, 1st ser. ii (1854), 73–99.

Breactach, Padraig (ed.), 'Select document xl: an address to Aodh Ruadh Ó Domhnaill in captivity, 1590', *IHS*, xxv (1986), 198–213.

Byrne, M. J. (trans.), *The Irish war of defence, 1598–1600: extracts from the 'De Hibernia Insula commentarius' of Peter Lombard, archbishop of Armagh*, Cork 1930.

———— (trans.), *Ireland under Elizabeth . . . being a portion of the history of Catholic Ireland by Don Philip O'Sullivan Beare*, Dublin 1903.

Camden, William, *History of the most renowned and victorious princess Elizabeth, late Queen of England*, London 1675.

de Cuellar, Francisco, *A letter written on October 4 1589 to king Philip II, recounting his misadventures in Ireland and elsewhere after the wreck of his ship*, trans. H. D. Sedgwick, London 1896.

Davies, John, *A discovery of the true causes why Ireland was never entirely subdued . . . until . . . his majesty's happy reign*, London 1612.

Derrick, John, *The image of Ireland*, London 1581.

E. C. S, *The government of Ireland under Sir John Perrot, 1584–1588*, London 1626.

Farmer, William, 'Chronicles of Ireland from 1594 to 1613', ed. C. L. Falkiner, *English Historical Review*, xxii (1907), 104–30, 527–52.

Gainsford, Thomas, *The true, exemplary and remarkable history of the earle of Tyrone*, London 1619.

Greene, David (ed.), *Duanaire Mhéig Uidhir*, Dublin 1972.

Harrison, G. B. and R. A. Jones (trans), *A journal of all that was accomplished by Monsieur de Maisse ambassador in England from King Henri IV to Queen Elizabeth, anno domini 1597*, London 1931.

Hennessy, W. M. (ed.), *The annals of Loch Cé: a chronicle of Irish affairs, 1014–1590*, 2 vols, London 1871.

Holinshed, Raphael, *Chronicles*, ed. Henry Ellis, 6 vols, London 1807–8.

Knott, Eleanor (ed.), *The bardic poems of Tadhg Dall Ó Huiginn*, 2 pts, London 1922–6.

Kossman, E. H. and A. F. Mellink (eds), *Texts relating to the revolt of the Netherlands*, Cambridge 1974.

Lee, Thomas, 'A brief declaration of the government of Ireland . . . 1594', in *Desiderata curiosa Hibernica*, Dublin 1772, i, 87–150.

Lombard, Peter, *De regno Hiberniae, sanctorum insula, commentarius*, ed. P. F. Moran, Dublin 1868.

Mooney, Donagh, 'De provincia Hiberniae S. Francisci', ed. Brendan Jennings, *Analecta Hibernica*, vi (1934), 12–138.

Moryson, Fynes, *An itinerary*, 3 pts, London 1617.

Naunton, Sir Robert, *Fragmenta regalia or observations on the late Queen Elizabeth her times and her favourites*, 3rd edn, London 1653 in *English reprints*, ed. Edward Amber, London, 1870.

O Cianain, Tadhg, *The flight of the earls*, trans. Paul Walsh, Dublin 1916.

Ó Cléirigh, Lughaidh, *The life of Aodh Ruadh Ó Domhnaill*, ed. Paul Walsh, 2 pts, Dublin 1948–57.

O'Donovan, John (ed. and trans.), *Annála rioghachta Éireann: Annals of the kingdom of Ireland by the Four Masters from the earliest times to the year 1616*, 7 vols, Dublin 1856.

O'Sullevan Beare, Philip, *Historiae catholicae Iberniae compendium*, Lisbon 1621, ed. Matthew Kelly, Dublin 1850.

Perrot, James, *The chronicle of Ireland, 1584–1608*, ed. Herbert Wood, Dublin 1933.

Rastell, William (ed.), *A collection in English of the statutes now in force*, London 1588.

Rawlinson, Richard (ed.), *The life, deedes and death of Sir John Perrot*, London 1727.

Rich, Barnaby, *A new description of Ireland*, London 1610.

Scott, H. S. (ed.), 'The journal of Sir Roger Wilbraham, 1593–1616', *Camden Society Miscellany*, x (1902).

Sidney, Henry, 'Memoir of government in Ireland', *Ulster Journal of Archaeology*, 1st ser. iii (1855), 33–44, 85–90, 336–57; v (1857), 299–315; viii (1860), 179–95.

Spenser, Edmund, *A view of the state of Ireland*, ed. W. L. Renwick, London 1934.

Stafford, Thomas, *Pacata Hibernica*, London 1633, ed. Standish O'Grady, 2 vols, London 1896.

Stow, John, *The Annales of England*, London 1605.

Walsh, Paul (trans.), *Leabhar Chlainne Suibhne*, Dublin 1920.

Ware, James (ed.), *Ancient Irish histories: the works of Spenser, Campion, Hanmer and Marleburrough*, Dublin 1633.

Ussher, James, *A discourse of the religion anciently professed by the Irish and British*, 4th edn, London 1687.

Wansink, H. (ed.), *The apologie of Prince of Orange against the proclamation of the king of Spain*, Leiden 1969.

Secondary Sources

Andrews, K. R., N. P. Canny and P. F. H. Hair, *The westward enterprise: English activities in Ireland, the Atlantic and America, 1460–1650*, Liverpool 1978.

Anstruther, Godfrey, *The seminary priests*, 4 vols, Great Wakering 1968–77.

Appleby, J. and Mary O'Dowd, 'The Irish admiralty: its organisation and development, c. 1570–1640', *IHS*, xxiv (1985), 300–1.

Ashton, Robert, *Reformation and revolution, 1558–1660*, London 1984.

Bagenal, P. H., *Vicissitudes of an Anglo-Irish family, 1530–1800*, London 1925.

Bagwell, Richard, *Ireland under the Tudors*, 3 vols, London 1885–90.

Bindoff, S. T., Joel Hurstfield and C. H. Williams, *Elizabethan government and society*, London 1961.

Bossy, John, 'The Counter-Reformation and the people of Catholic Ireland, 1596–1641', *Historical Studies*, viii (1971), 155–69.

Bradshaw, Brendan, *The dissolution of the religious orders in Ireland under Henry VIII*, Cambridge 1974.

——— 'The Elizabethans and the Irish', *Studies*, lxvii (1977), 38–50.

——— 'Sword, word, and strategy in the Reformation in Ireland', *Historical Journal*, xxi (1978), 478–502.

——— *The Irish constitutional revolution of the sixteenth century*, Cambridge 1979.

——— 'Manus "the magnificent": O'Donnell as Renaissance Prince', in Art Cosgrove and D. McCartney (eds), *Studies in Irish History, presented to R. Dudley Edwards*, Dublin 1979, 15–36.

Brady, Ciarán, 'Faction and the origins of the Desmond rebellion of 1579', *IHS*, xxii (1981), 289–312.

——— 'The killing of Shane O'Neill: some new evidence', *Irish Sword*, xv (1982), 116–23.

——— 'The O'Reillys of East Breifne and the problem of "surrender and regrant" ', *Breifne*, vi (1985), 233–62.

——— 'Spenser's Irish crisis: humanism and experience in the 1590s', *Past and Present*, cxi (1986), 17–49.

——— *Worsted in the game: losers in Irish history*, Dublin 1989.

——— 'Court, castle and country: the framework of government in Tudor Ireland', in Ciarán Brady and Raymond Gillespie (eds), *Natives and newcomers: essays on the making of Irish colonial society, 1534–1641*, Dublin 1986, 22–49.

de Breffny, Brian, 'An Elizabethan political painting', *Irish Arts Review*, i (1984), 39–41.

Brown, Peter Hume (ed.), *The collected essays and reviews of Thomas Graves Law*, Edinburgh 1904.

Butler, W. F. T., *Gleanings from Irish history*, London 1925.

Canny, Nicholas, 'The treaty of Mellifont and the reorganisation of Ulster, 1603', *Irish Sword*, ix (1969), 249–62.

——— 'Hugh O'Neill, earl of Tyrone, and the changing face of Gaelic Ulster', *Studia Hibernica*, x (1970), 7–35.

——— 'The flight of the earls, 1607', *IHS*, xvii (1971), 380–99.

——— *The Elizabethan conquest of Ireland: a pattern established, 1565–76*, Hassocks 1976.

——— 'Why the Reformation failed in Ireland: une question mal posée', *Journal of Ecclesiastical History*, xxx (1979), 423–50.

——— 'The formation of the Irish mind: religion, politics and Gaelic Irish literature, 1580–1750', *Past and Present*, xcv (1982), 91–116.

——— 'Edmund Spenser and the development of an Anglo-Irish identity', *The Yearbook of English Studies*, xiii (1983), 1–19.

——— *From Reformation to Restoration: Ireland, 1534–1660*, Dublin 1987.

Carney, James, *The Irish bardic poet*, Dublin 1967.

Chambers, Anne, *Granuaile: the life and times of Grace O'Malley c.1530–1603*, Dublin 1979.

——— *Chieftain to knight: Tibbot Bourke, 1567–1629, first viscount Mayo*, Dublin 1983.

Clark, Peter (ed.), *The European crisis of the 1590s*, London 1985.

Colles, Ramsey, *The history of Ulster from the earliest times to the present day*, 4 vols, London 1919–20.

Collier, William Francis, *History of Ireland for schools*, London 1884.

Collins, M. E., *Ireland, 1478–1610*, Dublin 1980.

Conaghen, Charles, 'Intrepid Donegal ecclesiastic of the sixteenth century: the most reverent Donald McGonagle D.D., bishop of Raphoe, 1562–89', *Capuchin Annual* (1976), 179–83.

Corish, P. J. (ed.), *The History of Irish Catholicism*, 7 vols, Dublin 1967– .

Cowan, Edward J., 'Clanship, kinship and the Campbell acquisition of Islay', *Scottish Historical Review*, lviii (1979), 132–57.

Cox, Richard, *Hibernia Anglicana or the history of Ireland from the conquest thereof by the English to this present time*, London 1689.

Cruickshank, C. G., *Elizabeth's army*, 2nd edn, Oxford 1966.

Cuninghame, Richard, *The broken sword of Ulster*, Dublin 1904.

Cunnningham, Bernadette, 'The composition of Connacht in the lordships of Clanricard and Thomond, 1577–1641', *IHS*, xxiv (1984), 1–14.

——— 'Native culture and political change in Ireland, 1580–1640', in Ciarán Brady and Raymond Gillespie (eds), *Natives and Newcomers: essays in the making of Irish colonial society, 1534–1641*, Dublin 1986, 148–170.

Curry, John, *An historical and critical review of the civil wars in Ireland from the reign of Elizabeth to the settlement under king William*, London 1786.

Dawtrey, John, *The Falstaff saga*, London 1927.

Duffy, P. J., 'The territorial organisation of Gaelic landownership and its transformation in county Monaghan, 1591–1640', *Irish Geography*, xiv (1981), 1–26.

Duke, Alastair, 'From king and country to king or country? Loyalty and treason in the revolt of the Netherlands', *Transactions of the Royal Historical Society*, 5th ser. xxxii (1982), 113–35.

Dunne, T. J., 'The Gaelic response to conquest and colonisation: the evidence of the poetry', *Studia Hibernica*, xx (1980), 7–30.

Edwards, R. W. Dudley, *Church and state in Tudor Ireland*, Dublin 1935.

——— *Ireland in the age of the Tudors*, London 1977.

Ellis, Steven, G., *Tudor Ireland: crown, community and the conflict of cultures, 1470–1603*, London 1985.

—— *Reform and revival: English government in Ireland, 1470–1534*, Woodbridge 1986.

Elton, G. R., *Studies in Tudor and Stuart politics and government*, 3 vols, Cambridge 1974–83.

Fallon, Niall, *The Armada in Ireland*, London 1978.

Falls, Cyril, *Elizabeth's Irish wars*, London 1950.

—— *Mountjoy, Elizabethan general*, London 1955.

—— 'Black Tom of Ormonde', *Irish Sword*, v (1960–1), 10–22.

—— 'Hugh O'Neill the great', *Irish Sword*, vi (1963), 94–102.

Farrell, Brian (ed.), *The Irish parliamentary tradition*, Dublin 1973.

Fernández Duro, Cesareo, *Armada Española*, 9 vols, Madrid 1895–1903.

Fichtner, Paula, 'The politics of honour: Renaissance chivalry and Habsburg dynasticism', *Bibliothèque d'Humanisme et Renaissance*, xxix (1967), 567–80.

Finch, M. E., *The wealth of five Northamptonshire families, 1540–1640*, Northampton 1956.

Ford, Alan, *The protestant reformation in Ireland, 1590–1641*, Frankfurt am Main 1985.

Fletcher, Anthony, *Tudor rebellions*, Harlow 1983.

Friel, Brian, *Making History*, London 1989.

Froude, J. A., *History of England from the fall of Wolsey to the defeat of the Spanish Armada*, 12 vols, London 1856–70.

—— *The English in Ireland in the eighteenth century*, 2 vols, London, 1872–4.

Gillespie, Raymond, *Conspiracy: Ulster plots and plotters in 1615*, Belfast, 1987.

—— 'Ulster and the 1641 rising', in Ciarán Brady and Raymond Gillespie (eds), *Natives and Newcomers: essays in the making of Irish colonial society, 1534–1641*, Dublin 1986, 191–213.

Glasgow, T., 'The Elizabethan navy in Ireland', *Irish Sword*, vii (1966), 291–307.

Graham, J. K., 'The birth-date of Hugh O'Neill, second earl of Tyrone', *IHS*, i (1938–9), 58–9.

Gregg, W. Stephenson, *Irish history for English readers*, London 1886.

Gregory, Donald, *The history of the western highlands and isles of Scotland from A.D. 1493 to A.D. 1625*, 2nd edn, Edinburgh 1881.

Guénot, C., *Le comte de Tyrone*, Tours 1863.

Gwynn, Aubrey, *The medieval province of Armagh*, Dundalk 1946.

Hamilton, Ernest, *Elizabethan Ulster*, London 1919.

—— *The Irish rebellion of 1641*, London 1920.

Hammerstein, Helga, 'Aspects of the continental education of Irish students in the reign of Queen Elizabeth I', *Historical Studies*, viii (1971), 137–54.

Hasler, P. W., *The Commons, 1558–1603*, 3 vols, London 1981.

Haverty, M., *History of Ireland, ancient and modern, derived from our native annals, from the most recent researches of eminent Irish scholars and antiquaries, from the state papers and from all the resources of Irish history now available*, Dublin 1860.

Hayes-McCoy, G. A., *Scots mercenary forces in Ireland, 1565–1603*, Dublin 1937.

————— 'Strategy and tactics in Irish warfare, 1593–1601', *IHS*, ii (1941), 255–79.

————— 'The army of Ulster, 1593–1601', *Irish Sword*, i (1950), 105–17.

————— 'Gaelic society in Ireland in the late sixteenth century', *Historical Studies*, iv (1963), 45–61.

————— 'A note on Hugh O'Neill', *Irish Sword*, ix (1969), 147–9.

————— *Irish battles*, London 1969.

————— 'The making of an O'Neill: a view of the ceremony at Tullaghoge, Co. Tyrone', *Ulster Journal of Archaeology*, 3rd ser. xxxiii (1970), 89–94.

Henley, Pauline, 'The treason of Sir John Perrot', *Studies*, xxi (1932), 404–22.

Hepburn, A. C., *Minorities in history*, London 1978.

Hill, George, *An historical account of the MacDonnells of Antrim*, Belfast 1873.

Hogan, James, 'The Irish law of kingship with special reference to Ailech and Cenél Eoghain', *PRIA*, xl (1932), sect. C, 186–258.

Hurstfield, Joel, *Freedom, corruption and government in Elizabethan England*, London 1973.

Jackson, Donald, *Intermarriage in Ireland, 1550–1650*, Montreal 1970.

Jackson, Robert Wyse, *Archbishop Magrath: the scoundrel of Cashel*, Dublin 1974.

James, Mervin, 'Obedience and dissent in Henrician England: the Lincolnshire rebellion, 1536', *Past and Present*, xlviii (1970), 3–78.

————— *English politics and the concept of honour*, Past and Present supplement, no. 3, Oxford 1978.

Jennings, Brendan, *Michael O'Cleirigh and his associates*, Dublin 1936.

————— 'Irish swordsmen in Flanders, 1586–1610', *Studies*, xxxvi (1947), 402–10; ibid. xxxvii (1948) 189–202.

Johnston, Dorothy, 'Richard II and the submission of Gaelic Ireland', *IHS*, xxii (1981), 1–20.

Lacy, Brian *et al.*, *Archaeological survey of county Donegal*, Lifford 1983.

Lawless, Emily, *Ireland*, London 1888.

Leland, Thomas, *A history of Ireland from the invasion of Henry II*, 3 vols, Dublin 1773.

Lennon, Colm, *Richard Stanihurst: the Dubliner, 1547–1618*, Dublin 1981.

Leslie, J. B., *Armagh clergy and parishes*, Dundalk, 1911.

Lloyd, Howell A., 'The Essex inheritance', *Welsh Historical Review*, vii (1974), 13–59.

Lloyd, Rachel, *Elizabethan adventurer: a life of Captain Christopher Carleill*, London 1974.

Logan, Patrick, 'Pestilence in the Irish wars: the early phase', *Irish Sword*, vii (1966), 279–90.

Longfield, A. K., *Anglo-Irish trade in the sixteenth century*, London 1929.

MacCarthy, Justin, *An outline of Irish history*, London 1883.

MacCarthy-Morrogh, Michael, *The Munster plantation*, Oxford 1986.

MacDermot, Martin, *A new and impartial history of Ireland from the earliest accounts to the present time*, 4 vols, London 1823.

MacDuinnshleibhe, Peadar, 'The legal murder of Aodh Rua MacMahon, 1590', *Clogher Record*, i (1955), 39–52.

McGee, Thomas D'Arcy, *A popular history of Ireland from the earliest period to the emancipation of the Catholics*, 2 vols, Glasgow 1869.

Macgeoghegan, James, *Histoire de l'Irelande, ancienne et moderne*, 3 vols, Paris 1758–62.

McGurk, John, 'William Camden: civil historian or Gloriana's propagandist', *History Today*, xxxviii (1988), 47–53.

Mckerral, Andrew, 'West Highland mercenaries in Ireland', *Scottish Historical Review*, xxx (1951), 1–14.

Marshall, John, 'The Hovendens: fosterbrothers of Hugh O'Neill, prince of Ulster', *Ulster Journal of Archaeology*, 2nd ser. xiii (1907), 4–12, 73–83.

Matthew, David, *The Celtic peoples and Renaissance Europe*, London 1933.

Mitchel, John, *The life and times of Aodh O'Neill, prince of Ulster*, Dublin 1846.

Moody, T. W., F. X. Martin, and F. J. Byrne, *A new history of Ireland*, vols iii, ix, Oxford 1976, 1984.

Moore, Philip, 'The MacMahons of Monaghan', *Clogher Record* (1955), 22–38; (1956), 85–107; (1957), 148–69.

Moore, Thomas, *The history of Ireland from the earliest kings of that realm down to its last chief*, 4 vols, London 1835–46.

Morgan, Hiram, 'The colonial venture of Sir Thomas Smith in Ulster, 1571–5', *Historical Journal*, xxviii (1985), 261–78.

——— 'Extradition and treason-trial of a Gaelic lord: the case of Brian O'Rourke, *Irish Jurist*, xxii (1987), 285–301.

——— 'The end of Gaelic Ulster: a thematic interpretation of events between 1534 and 1610', *IHS*, xxvi (1988), 8–32.

——— 'Writing up early Modern Ireland', *Historical Journal*, xxxi (1988), 701–11.

——— 'Making History, a criticism and a manifesto', *Text and Context*, iv (1990), 61–5.

——— 'Hugh O'Neill and the Nine Years War in Tudor Ireland', *Historical Journal*, xxxvi (1993), 1–17.

Morris, William O'Connor, *Ireland, 1494–1868*, Cambridge 1898.

Morrissey, Thomas J., *James Archer of Kilkenny: an Elizabethan Jesuit*, Dublin 1979.

Nicholls, Kenneth, *Gaelic and gaelicised Ireland in the later Middle Ages*, Dublin 1972.

——— *Land, law and society in sixteenth century Ireland*, National University of Ireland, O'Donnell lecture, Dublin 1976.

O'Brien, Eoin (ed.), *Essays in honour of J. D. H. Widdess*, Dublin 1978.

Ó Doibhlin, Eamonn, ' "O'Neill's own country" and its families', *Seanchas Ard Mhacha*, vi (1971), 3–23.

O'Dowd, Mary, 'Land inheritance in early modern county Sligo', *Irish Economic and Social History*, x (1983), 5–18.

O'Faolain, Sean, *The Great O'Neill*, London 1942.

Ó Fiaich, Tomas, 'The O'Neills of the Fews', *Seanchas Ard Mhacha*, vii (1972), 1–64, 263–315.

O'Grady, Standish, *Red Hugh's captivity*, London 1889.

——— *The flight of the eagle*, London 1897.

O'Hallaron, Sylvester, *An introduction to the study of the history and antiquities of Ireland*, 3 vols, Dublin 1810.

Ó Lochlainn, Colm (ed.), *Irish chiefs and leaders: studies by Father Paul Walsh*, Dublin 1960.

O'Rorke, T., *The history of Sligo, town and county*, 2 vols, Dublin 1889.

Otway-Ruthven, A. J., *History of medieval Ireland*, London 1968.

Parker, Geoffrey, *The Dutch revolt*, London 1977.

────── *Spain and the Netherlands, 1559–1659*, London 1979.

Pawlisch, Hans S., *Sir John Davies and the conquest of Ireland: a study in legal imperialism*, Cambridge 1985.

Quinn, D. B., *The Elizabethans and the Irish*, Ithaca, NY 1966.

Ranger, T. O., 'Richard Boyle and the making of an Irish fortune, 1588–1614', *IHS*, x (1957), 257–97.

Read, Conyers, *Lord Burghley and Queen Elizabeth*, London 1959.

Richey, Alexander G., *Lectures on the history of Ireland from A.D. 1534 to the date of the plantation of Ulster*, London 1870.

Riley, James C., 'Insects and the European mortality decline', *American Historical Review*, xci (1986), 833–58.

Robinson, Philip, *The plantation of Ulster*, Dublin 1984.

Schlegal, Donald, 'The MacDonnells of Tyrone and Armagh: a genealogical study', *Seanchas Ard Mhacha*, x (1980–1), 193–219.

Sheehan, Anthony, 'The overthrow of the plantation of Munster in October 1588', *Irish Sword*, xv (1982), 11–22.

────── 'The recusancy revolt of 1603: a re-interpretation', *Archivium Hibernicum*, xxxviii (1983), 3–14.

Shirley, E. P., *Some account of the territory or dominion of Farney*, London 1845.

Silke, J. J., 'The Irish appeal of 1593 to Spain: some light on the genesis of the Nine Years War', *Irish Ecclesiastical Record*, 5th ser. xcii (1959), 279–90, 362–71.

────── 'Hugh O'Neill, the Catholic question and the papacy', *Irish Ecclesiastical Record*, 5th ser. civ (1965), 65–79.

────── *Ireland and Europe, 1559–1607*, Dublin 1966.

────── *Kinsale*, Liverpool, 1970.

────── 'The last will of Red Hugh O'Donnell', *Archivium Hibernicum*, xxiv (1984–8), 50–60.

Simms, M. Katherine, 'The archbishops of Armagh and the O'Neills, 1347–1471', *IHS*, xix (1974), 38–55.

Smith, A. G. R., *Servant of the Cecils*, London 1977.

────── *The emergence of a nation state*, Harlow 1984.

Stephen, Leslie and Lee, Sidney, *Dictionary of national biography*, 22 vols, London 1917.

Stephens, N, and Glasscock, R. E., *Irish geographical studies*, Belfast 1970.

Taafe, Denis, *An impartial history of Ireland*, 4 vols, Dublin 1809–11.

Taylor, W. C., *History of the civil wars of Ireland*, 2 vols, Edinburgh, 1831.

Treadwell, Victor, 'The Irish parliament of 1596–71', *PRIA*, lxv (1966), sect. C, 55–89.

────── 'Sir John Perrot and the Irish parliament of 1585–6', ibid., lxxxv (1985), sect. C, 259–308.

Walpole, Charles, *A short history of the kingdom of Ireland*, London 1885.

Walsh, Micheline, 'The military order of St Patrick, 1593', *Seanchas Ard Mhacha*, ix (1979), 274–85.

—— *'Destruction by peace'*: *Hugh O'Neill after Kinsale*, Armagh 1986.

—— 'Archbishop Maguaran and his return to Ireland, October 1592', *Seanchas Ard Mhacha*, xiv (1990), 68–79.

Walsh, Paul, *The will and family of Hugh O'Neill, earl of Tyrone*, Dublin 1930.

—— 'The septs of Muintear Ghallchabhair', *Irish Book Lover*, xxvii (1940), 194–200.

Ware, Sir James, *The annals of Ireland*, Dublin 1705.

Williams, Neville, *All the queen's men*, London 1972.

Williams, Penry, *The Tudor regime*, London 1979.

Williams, Ronald, *The lords of the Isles*, London 1984.

Wills, James, *Lives of illustrious and distinguished Irishmen from the earliest times to the present period, arranged in chronological order and embodying a history of Ireland in the lives of Irishmen*, 6 vols, Dublin, 1840–7.

Wilson, Charles, *Queen Elizabeth and the revolt of the Netherlands*, London 1970.

Wormald, Jenny, *Court, kirk and community: Scotland, 1470–1625*, London 1981.

Zagorin, Perez, *Rebels and rulers, 1550–1660*, 2 vols, Cambridge 1982.

Unpublished Theses

Brady, Ciarán, 'The government of Ireland, c. 1540–1583', PhD, Trinity College, Dublin 1981.

Canny, Nicholas, 'The government reorganisation of Ulster (1603–7)', MA, University College, Galway 1967.

Costello, Joseph, 'Turlough Luineach O'Neill, the uirríthe and the government', MA, University College, Dublin 1973.

Cunningham, Bernadette, 'Political and social change in the lordships of Clanricard and Thomond, 1569–1641', MA, University College, Galway 1979.

Graham, J. K., 'An historical study of the career of Hugh O'Neill, 2nd earl of Tyrone, c. 1550–1616', MA, Queen's University, Belfast 1938.

McCall, Timothy, 'The Gaelic background to the settlement of Antrim and Down, 1580–1641', MA, Queen's University, Belfast 1983.

McGurk, John, 'The recruitment and transportation of Elizabethan troops and their service in Ireland', PhD, University of Liverpool 1982.

Simms, M. Katherine, 'Gaelic lordships in Ulster in the late Middle Ages', PhD, Trinity College, Dublin 1976.

Singleton, Retta, 'The earl of Tyrone's rebellion', MA, University of Liverpool 1915.

Glossary

Act of Attainder	the declaration by parliamentary statute without recourse to a trial that a man was a traitor
Ballybetagh	a unit of land division in Gaelic Ulster, supposed to contain 960 acres. A unit of assessment rather than mensuration
Barony	the administrative division of an Irish county, corresponding to the English 'hundred'
Brehon law	name given to the legal system operative in Gaelic parts, derived from *breitheamh*/brehon(judge)
Buannacht/Bonnaght	the wages and provisions of a mercenary soldier levied as tax upon a district. By extension, a mercenary soldier
Buying/*Ceannuigheact*	protection money paid to a Gaelic lord to gain a respite from marauding soldiers
Cess	a range of government impositions, originally a prerogative right to provisions for the viceroy's household, later used to maintain the garrison
Clan/*Clann*	literally 'children, offspring'; a corporate family with political and legal functions descended from a single male ancestor
Coign and livery	also referred to as cutting and spending; a range of Gaelic exactions which facilitated the free quartering of a lord's dependents upon his tenantry
Composition	an agreement; a formal arrangement for taxation purposes
Concealments	land (often former monastic land) which was rightfully forfeited or escheated by common law but secretly detained
Concordatum	a single payment by the crown for services rendered.
Creaghts	the anglicised form of the collective noun *Caoruigheacht* (pl. *Caoruigheacta*) meaning a herd of cattle with its keepers.
Defalks	short for 'defalcations'; financial terminology meaning deductions.
Demesne	lands directly exploited by an individual
Deposition	sworn statement given in evidence
Ensign	a standard of an army company; the standard bearer
Erenagh	the occupant of termon lands, possessing quasi-clerical status, whose office was the inheritance of a single clan.
Escheat	the return of lands to the feudal superior in default of an heir or on conviction of felony
Exemplification	a document obtained from the crown clarifying a legal point.
Fosterage	Gaelic custom whereby nobles committed the upbringing of their children to others with the aim of establishing a political connection
Freeholders	in Gaelic parts, those individuals who held rights to demesne lands

Galloglass/*Gallóglach*	literally 'foreign warrior'; a professional footsoldier, armed with double-headed axe, originally from Scotland
Horseboy	horseman's attendant or gillie
Hosting	military expedition, especially by a royal army, which included militia contingents; a feudal obligation upon able-bodied males to give unpaid military service to defend the kingdom
Indenture	document used to record a contract or lease between two parties
Inquisition	formal inquiry by sworn evidence before a jury
Lucht Tighe	literally 'people of the household', referred to as 'mensal land' by English commentators. A special tract of land, held by certain families and free of normal exactions, which supplied the basic commodities of a lord's household.
Lordship	the territory ruled by a Gaelic lord; the mode of Gaelic rule; the duration of a Gaelic lord's rule
Kerne/*Ceithearn*	Gaelic light infantrymen
Mark	a unit of account, being two-thirds of a pound or 13s. 4d.
Marshal (of the Army)	head of the military establishment and commander of government forces in the absence of the lord deputy or provincial presidents
Muster-master	officer responsible for a regular assembly or muster of troops, usually quarterly, to check that numbers were up to strength
Official	the title given to the judge of the diocesan court who had jurisdiction in cases involving wills, marriages etc
Palatinate	a territory, also known as a liberty, in which the crown had delegated many of its jurisdictional rights to the local lord
Pale	an area of exclusive English control, originally defended by a palisade. In Ireland, Dublin and its hinterland
Pledge	person (hostage), goods or land retained as a surety for performance of an agreement by the donor; also a mortgage of lands in Gaelic parts
prey/*creagh*	a cattle-raid
Primogeniture	system of inheritance by which the eldest son succeeds to all his father's landed property
Protection	a safe-conduct granted by the Crown
Provincial presidencies	administrative councils with the task of establishing law and order in the outlying regions of the Tudor dominions.
Pursuivant	a messenger of the state who wore a distinctive red livery.
Quarter	land division, being a quarter of a ballybetagh
Recognisance	an obligation, under penalty, entered into before a court or magistrate to do or refrain from a particular act; the sum pledged as surety
Rising(s)-out	the military service(s) due to a Gaelic lord from dependant areas
Sept/*Sliocht*	literally 'section'; the branch of a clan
Shot	a collective term for infantrymen bearing firearms
Sláinte	'Guarantee, indemnification'; by extension (1) protection given by a greater man to a lesser one (2) the suretyship of a

	third party for observance of an agreement (3) the person extending such suretyship
Subinfeudation	the process by which land tenures were feudalised within a Gaelic lordship
Surrender and regrant	modern name given to the policy begun during the reign of Henry VIII which entailed the surrender of Gaelic lordships and their regrant as feudal fiefs
Tail male	the reservation of estates for the direct male descendants of the original grantee; as distinct from tail general
Tanist/*Tánaiste*	successor-designate in a Gaelic lordship. Tanistry: the Gaelic method of political succession
Termon	lands, attached to a church, which enjoyed privileges of sanctuary and protection
Urriagh(s)/ *Urrí (Uirríthe)*	literally sub-king(s); the lords of distinct lordships over whom other lords claimed suzerainty
Victualling	the provision of food to the army
Wardship	feudal right of guardianship exercised by the crown over those who succeeded to their lands as minors, involving the administration of the lands and the right to arrange their marriages

Index

Águila, Juan del 194
Albanagh, Donnell 145
Albert, Archduke 210
Anglo-Irish reformers 16, 31, 42
annals 8, 9, 13, 139
Ap Hugh, Rice 58
Árbol, Baltasar del 106
Argyll, earl of 119, 177n, 179, 184, 215
Armada 71, 73, 105–6, 122, 131, 162, 168
Armagh 95, 186, 193, 199, 200, 201, 204, 207, 215
army, *see* crown forces
assizes 79, 81
Athlone 30, 34

Bagenal, Dudley 40, 46n
Bagenal, Sir Henry 34, 36, 37, 40, 46–8, 51, 60, 61n, 65, 66, 70, 71, 76–80, 103, 140, 146, 147, 148, 149, 151, 152, 153, 154–65, 168, 169, 170, 171, 173, 179, 187, 200, 206, 207, 216, 218, 224
Bagenal, Mabel 6, 10, 79, 162, 215, 216
Bagenal, Sir Nicholas 30, 34, 35, 39, 40, 43, 45–8, 51, 52, 53, 96, 99, 162
Bagwell, Richard 9–10
Ballimote 144
Ballygawley 89
Ballymascanlon 147, 148
Banagh 116–17, 130
bardic poetry 13, 88, 116, 118, 120, 129
Barkley, Edward 37
Barkley, Francis 33
Barnes, Nicholas 128
Barnesmore 113, 130
bastard feudalism 17, 20, 22, 51, 97, 177, 215
Bath, John 182
Beacon, Richard 169, 185
Beleek 155, 201
Belfast 99
Berwick, treaty of 43
Beverley, George 38

Bingham, Sir George 128n, 144
Bingham, Captain George 189
Bingham, Sir Richard 30, 33–4, 47, 51, 52, 53, 56, 60, 72–3, 134, 140, 141, 145, 146, 154, 156, 157, 168, 174, 182, 183, 186, 191, 206
Bird, Henry 57
Blackwater 21, 24, 39, 51, 76, 99, 146, 162, 174, 178, 186, 194, 196, 200
Blanco, Pedro 106
Bourchier, Sir George 171
Bourke, Lower MacWilliam 49–50, 72–3, 134, 141, 174, 189, 190, 191, 199
Bourke, Tibbot Fitzwalter Kittagh 190, 208, 210, 212
Bourke, Tibbot na Long Bourke 191
Bourke, William 50
Bowen, Captain 122, 127
Boylagh 116, 130
Brabazon, Anthony 190
Bradshaw, Brendan 12
Brady, Ciarán 12, 17n, 29
Brehon law 108
Brereton, Randal 187
buannacht 89, 109, 116, 144, 145, 181, 187
Bundrowes 120
Burghley, *see* Cecil, William
Burke, Ulick 189
Butlers 17, 97
Butler, Thomas (earl of Ormond) 17, 29–30, 33, 43, 51, 97, 171–2, 176, 178, 215, 219

Calthorpe, Sir Charles 31, 45, 57, 58
Camden, William 3–5, 139
Campbell, Agnes 91, 99, 124
Canny, Nicholas 12
Carew, Sir George 7, 70, 167, 179
Carleill, Christopher 30–1
Carlos, Prince 194
Carrickfergus 19, 40, 199
Carricklea, battle of 105, 129, 218

Carrigans 124
Castle Chamber 45, 143
Castle Roe 88
Cavan castle 198, 203
Cavan, county of 40, 70, 79
Cawell, George 208, 209, 212
Ceart Uí Néill 85, 89
Cecil, Sir Robert 183, 194, 195, 202, 203
Cecil, Sir Thomas 56, 57
Cecil, William (Lord Burghley) 3, 7, 32, 33, 35, 36, 41, 45, 46, 51, 56, 57, 59, 71n, 72, 74, 75, 132, 153, 162, 167, 168, 172, 177–8, 186, 188, 190n, 192, 196, 201, 206, 213, 216, 219
Cheevers, Elizabeth 215
Chichester, Sir Arthur 77, 78
Cisneros, Captain 208, 210
Clanbrassilagh 95
Clancarne 90
Clancarvell 68
Clandeboye 19, 23, 38, 40, 41, 71, 81, 146, 162, 174, 181, 188, 190
Clanrickard, earl of 50, 189, 200, 215, 216
Clement VIII 209n
Clontibret, battle of 179, 184, 218
Cobos, Alonso 208–11
Coke, Sir Edward 78
Colclough, Thomas 45
Coleraine, county of 76
colonisation 20–1, 23, 30, 72
Common law 40, 41, 45, 47, 62–4, 74, 75, 79, 152, 158, 171, 177, 194
composition 33, 37–9, 46–9, 60, 66, 67, 71–3, 74, 75, 101, 122, 128, 183, 189–90
concealed lands 59, 70n, 190n
confederacy 15, 140–9, 156–7, 160, 164, 172, 176–7, 185, 196–200, 203–212, 223–5
Connacht 33–4, 49–50, 59, 71–2, 120, 127, 150, 157, 174–5, 182, 186, 189–90, 191, 199, 200, 205–6, 212, 215, 216
Connalan, John 69
Connill, John 122, 123, 130, 133
Corruption 162n
Cox, Richard 5
Cremone 68
crown forces 34–9, 48, 61, 63, 79–80, 94, 105, 154–8, 179–87

Dartry 67, 155
Davies, Sir John 65, 77, 78
Dawtrey, Nicholas 17, 37, 40, 47, 53, 103, 167
Delvin, Lord 109
Denmark 182
Derry 117, 127, 201
Desmond wars 24, 29, 94, 118, 121, 223
Devereux, Robert (second earl of Essex) 65, 68, 97, 152, 162, 167, 183, 192, 219
Devereux, Walter (first earl of Essex) 21, 24, 50, 68, 93, 184
Dillon, Sir Lucas 31, 35, 43, 49, 56, 57, 58
Dillon, Sir Robert 32, 45, 63, 83, 171
Dillon, Tibbot 33
Doire Leathan 130
Donamayne 68, 69
Donegal castle 13, 117, 210–11
Donegal, county of 40, 123
Dowdell, Captain 155
Dublin castle 13, 43, 55, 56–7, 58, 61, 101, 128, 131–3
Dudley, Robert (earl of Leicester) 97, 105, 131n, 162, 184
Dufferin 187
Duffy, P. J. 67
Duke, Sir Henry 52, 55–6, 58, 104, 170n, 184
Dundalk 147–54, 161–5, 203
Dungannon 76, 89, 90, 91, 147, 148, 157, 174, 181, 182, 186
Dunlop, Robert 8
Dunluce 35, 48
Dunnalong 107
Dyer, Lady 57, 59, 62

East Breifne 20, 21, 40–3, 46, 49, 51, 92, 188, 198, 212
Edenduffcarrick 188
Edwards, R. W. Dudley 11
Elizabeth I 17, 35–7, 44, 57, 71, 72, 102, 152, 159, 160, 164, 168, 176, 177, 179, 184, 187, 193, 195, 197, 201–2, 217, 220
Ellis, Steven 12
Enniskillen castle 170, 173, 184
Erne ford, battle of 155, 156, 157, 158
Essex, earls of: first earl *see* Devereux, Walter; second earl *see* Devereux, Robert

Falls, Cyril 12, 139, 161
Farney 22, 68, 154, 188
Fenton, Sir Geoffrey 30, 31, 32, 43–4,
    45, 52, 58, 72, 75, 168, 170, 171–2,
    178, 182, 184, 187, 189, 191, 198,
    200, 202–7
Fermanagh 22, 111, 142–59, 216
Fernan, Solomon 103, 106
Fews 96, 102
Finn 125, 127
firearms 182–3
fisheries 88, 113
Fitzgerald, James 132
Fitzgerald, James Fitzmaurice 29
Fitzgerald, James Fitzthomas 220
Fitzgerald, Walter Reagh 132, 185
Fitzwilliam, Sir William: Armada
    106–7; corruption 59–60, 62, 66–7,
    74–5, 80, 107, 131–3, 134, 143, 161,
    163, 168–9, 176, 190n, 201;
    factionalism 55–8; family 57, 59;
    finance 59, 60, 66, 72; first
    deputyship 16, 55, 184;
    historiography 4–7, 10; Monaghan
    settlement 61–71; Ulster policy
    60–80, 122, 130, 131, 147–65, 170
Fleming, Thomas 91, 121
Ford of the Biscuits, battle of 170,
    173–4, 184, 188
fosterage 90–2, 123, 124, 125, 214
France 193n, 202, 220
Freeholders 18, 21, 42, 43, 65, 66–7, 72,
    77, 158, 165, 169
Friel, Brian 12n
Froude, James Anthony 8–9, 10

Gaelic society 18–19, 67, 80–1, 85–127,
    219
Gainsford, Thomas 4, 92
Gardiner, Sir Robert 45, 52, 75, 76,
    147, 148, 160, 161, 168, 170, 171,
    175–7, 197–202
Garvey, John (archbishop of Armagh)
    95
Geraldines 17, 20, 22, 51, 97
Girona 106
Glasgow 182
Glenaule 95
Glens (of Antrim) 36, 37, 48, 218
Gormanston, lord 73
Graham, J. K. 11, 139
Grey, Arthur (lord deputy) 94, 121

Hamilton, Lord Ernest 10
Harpole, Robert 97
Harrington, Sir Henry 97, 108
Hatton, Sir Christopher 57, 97, 162
Haverty, Martin 8
Hayes-McCoy, G. A. 12
Henry III 220
Henshaw, Thomas 66, 68, 162
historiography 3–13, 15, 29, 55, 85,
    91–2, 131–2, 139, 213–21
Hore, Philip 199
hostages 47, 53, 76, 89, 98, 100, 104,
    107, 108, 120, 122, 125, 128, 129,
    187, 190, 193, 199, 203, 205
Hovenden, Giles 93, 214
Hovenden, Henry 97, 106, 156, 161,
    162, 207
Hovenden, Piers 97, 102
Hovenden, Richard 97, 106, 107, 162
Hovenden, Walter 97
Hume, M. A. S. 7

Idiáquez, Juan de 141, 142, 207
Ineen Dubh, see Finola MacDonald
Inishowen 119, 123
Irish Council, see Privy Council of
    Ireland
Islandmagee 68
Iveagh 21, 41, 199

James VI 37, 43, 71, 182
Jimenez, Ensign 208, 211
Jones, Thomas (bishop of Meath) 32,
    45, 57, 58, 147, 148, 151, 171

Kelly, Joan 174
Kelly, Matthew, see Matthew O'Neill
Kildare, earls of 16–17, 21–2, 97, 109
Kilkenny 33
Killetra 18, 146
Killibegs 116
Killultragh 99, 162
Kilmacrenan 116, 117, 133
Kilwarlin 99, 162
Kinelarty 162

Laggan 113, 118
Lambert, Oliver 100
Lane, Sir Ralph 144, 177n
Laudabiliter 209
Leabhar Gabhála 208, 209n

Lee, Thomas 5, 60, 65, 75, 80, 97, 134, 155n, 156, 162, 168–9, 176–7, 215
Legg, Robert 59–60, 64
Leicester, earl of, *see* Robert Dudley
Leitrim, county of 40, 65, 71, 72
Leland, Thomas 5–6
Le Strange, Thomas 34
Lifford 98, 110, 125, 127, 201, 208–13
Lodge, John 5
Loftus, Adam 32–4, 43, 44–6, 48, 49, 51, 52, 53, 56, 59, 75, 105, 108, 147, 148, 151, 156, 160, 170, 171, 183, 191
Loftus, Dudley 156
Lombard, Peter (archbishop of Armagh) 4–5, 182, 198
Long, John (archbishop of Armagh) 40, 43, 51
Longford, county of 70
Lough Foyle 35, 100, 115, 116, 155, 186, 200
Lovell, Francis 33
Luzon, Alonso de 106

Mac an Bhaird 118, 129
MacArdle, Cú Uladh 63, 67, 149
MacCann 24, 95, 101
MacCartan 22
MacCarthy, Florence 220
MacCollas 68, 69
MacCroddan, William 145
MacDavitt, Hugh Boye 183, 209, 211
MacDermot, Connor óg 154
MacDonald 20, 36, 48, 74, 106
MacDonald, Alexander MacSorley 48, 49, 129
MacDonald, Angus 37, 44, 48, 91, 104, 109, 180
MacDonald, Catherine 92
MacDonald, Donnell Gorm 37, 91, 180
MacDonald, Finola 124, 130, 131, 133
MacDonald, James MacSorley 174, 188, 190
MacDonald, Sorley Boye 35, 37, 44, 48, 91, 96, 107
MacDonnell galloglass 89–90, 96, 182, 211
MacDonnell, Art 90
MacDonnell, Edmund óg 140–1, 206
MacGauran, Edmund (archbishop of Armagh) 141, 145, 146, 147, 148, 149
McGee, Thomas D'Arcy 8

MacGeoghegan, James 5
MacGonigle 118
MacGonigle, Donnell 117
MacLean 37, 74, 107, 120
MacLean, Catherine 92
MacLean, Lachlan 96, 100, 104, 106, 110
MacLinchy, Tadhg 117, 118
MacMahon 147, 148, 154, 174, 181, 197
MacMahon, Brian MacHugh óg 61–7, 68, 81, 96, 147, 148, 155, 158, 188, 202, 203, 204, 205
MacMahon, Ever MacCon Uladh 63, 65, 68–9, 96, 188
MacMahon, Hugh Roe 3, 6, 10, 61–4, 70, 161, 163, 169, 217, 223
MacMahon, Patrick MacArt Moile 142, 146, 147, 158n
MacMahon, Sir Ross 61, 68–9, 96, 104, 105, 163
MacMurrehy, Cormac 108
MacMurrehy, Melaughlin 108
MacQuillan 96, 105, 188
MacShanes, *see* O'Neill, Shane: sons of
MacSweeny 48, 116–17, 122, 124, 127, 128, 130, 133, 157
MacSweeny, Alexander MacDonnell óg 144
MacSweeny, Donnell 116
MacSweeny, Donough 117, 129
MacSweeny, Eoin óg 116
Magennis, Arthur 198
Magennis, Ever MacRory 187–8
Magennis, Glasney MacAgholy 198
Magennis, Sir Hugh 21, 34, 39, 47, 61n, 147, 188, 197
Magrath, Miler (archbishop of Cashel) 70, 88, 90, 92, 123, 124, 125, 126, 143
Maguire 24, 49, 52, 91, 96, 101, 103, 106, 111
Maguire, Connor Roe 96, 155, 188
Maguire, Hugh 119, 128n, 141, 142–59, 170, 188, 191, 194, 202, 205, 208
Malby, Sir Nicholas 127
Manrique, Antonio 106, 109
Maplesden, John 132–3
Marshall, Michael 156, 159
Marshalsea jail 45
Matthew 129
Mayo 49–50, 72–3, 182
Medinilla, Captain 208, 210, 211

Merbury, John 72
Meredith, Richard (bishop of Leighlin) 57–8
Merryman, Nicholas 49, 106
Milesian myth 208–9
Mince, Captain 121
Mitchell, John 7
Moira 99
Monaghan settlement 61–71, 76–7, 80–1, 158, 163, 164, 169, 174, 175, 197, 202–3, 204, 216
Monaghan town 66, 68, 156, 179, 186, 188, 196
Mongavlin 124, 127, 130
Montero, Ensign 208, 211
Montford, Francis 195
Moody, T. W. 11
Moore, Sir Edward 56, 57, 58, 60, 97, 175
Moore, Garrett 132
Moore, Tom 6–7
Moryson, Fynes 3, 139, 183
Mostian, William 40, 52, 106, 122
Mountjoy, Lord 88
Muckno 69, 70, 95
Muintir Luinigh 91
munitions 181–2, 207, 210, 216
Munster 29–30, 59, 94, 181, 212, 215

Nassau, Maurice 220
Naunton, Sir Robert 4, 29
Netherlands 15, 36, 43, 49, 169, 183, 219–21
New English 31–2, 45, 97, 214
Newry 34, 47, 68, 199
Nonsuch, treaty of 43
Norris, Sir Henry 186
Norris, Sir John 30, 34, 38, 43, 100, 177, 183–4, 186–7, 193, 195, 202–7, 212

O'Boyle 116, 133
O'Boyle, Niall 134
O'Boyle, Tadhg 122
O'Byrne, Feagh MacHugh 110, 132, 176, 185
O'Cahan 19, 41, 49, 76, 85, 88, 96, 100, 102, 103, 110, 111, 124, 184, 208, 215
Ó Cléirigh 118
Ó Cléirigh, Lugdaidh 6, 8, 103, 110, 123, 129, 132, 139, 156, 157–8, 189, 208
O'Connor Sligo, Donough 34, 53

O'Connor Sligo, Tadhg 120
O'Crean, James 141
O'Cullen, Patrick 45, 47
O'Cullen, Piers 194–5
O'Devlin 89
O'Doherty 19, 96, 111, 119, 127, 130
O'Doherty, Sir John 123, 129, 130, 133, 134, 184, 191, 208
O'Donnell (title) 123, 133–4
O'Donnell, Bernard 207
O'Donnell, Calvach 92, 116, 117, 119, 121, 123, 125
O'Donnell, Cathbarr MacManus 126
O'Donnell, Conn 24, 98, 120, 124, 125, 127, 129, 130
O'Donnell, Donnell 107, 119, 123–4, 130, 131
O'Donnell, Sir Hugh 23, 24, 38, 40, 41, 49, 52, 98, 99, 104, 117, 118, 120, 121–35
O'Donnell, Hugh Dubh 123, 124, 126, 128, 133–4, 146
O'Donnell, Hugh Roe: confederacy 145–9, 157, 160, 161, 163–4, 170, 172, 174, 175, 176, 196–200, 203–12, 224; escape 78, 81, 110, 131–33; grievances 174–5; historiography 6, 8, 10–11, 13; kidnapping 52, 53, 104, 128–9; marriage 96, 124, 135, 216; military policy 179, 182, 184, 186n, 196, 197; overlordship 167, 174–5, 189–93, 199, 200, 202, 207, 219; rise to power 123–35; Spanish contacts 141–3, 194, 207–13, 216–17; submission 193, 194
O'Donnell, Manus 19, 22, 117, 121
O'Donnnell, Niall Garbh 106, 123, 125, 133–4
O'Donnell, Rory 121n, 128, 131, 135, 209n
O'Donnell, Siobhán 93, 96, 135
O'Donnelly 89, 96, 99, 100, 107
O'Donnelly, James Carragh 96
O'Donovan, John 8
O'Duffy, Eoin 70
O'Faolain, Sean 12, 92, 139, 161
O'Farrell 21, 200, 212
O'Farrell, Ross 205
O'Farrell, Tadhg 206–7, 210
O'Freel 117, 133
O'Gallagher 91, 118, 125–6
O'Gallagher, Art MacPhelim 117

O'Gallagher, Donnell 117
O'Gallagher, Sir Eoin 96, 118, 124,
125, 130, 163, 168–9
O'Gallagher, Hugh MacEdegany 106,
125–6, 127, 130–1
O'Gallagher, Redmond 118
O'Grady, Standish 10–11, 132
O'Hagan 85, 89, 96, 107, 144, 146, 149,
186, 193
O'Hagan, Art Braddagh 174, 188
O'Hagan, Turlough Boye 132
O'Hallaron, Sylvester 6
O'Hanlon, Sir Oghy 34, 52, 61n, 96,
104, 105, 152, 181, 186
O'Hely, Dr James 134, 140, 141–3, 206
Ó Huiginn, Tadhg Dall 88, 116, 120
Oidhreacht-Uí-Chatháin 111
O'Kenny, Turlough 141
Omagh 91
O'Mulrian, Connor 206–7, 210
O'Neill (title) 19, 20, 21–4, 51, 76, 85,
88, 90, 98, 109, 110, 167, 188–9, 193,
204
O'Neill, Art MacBaron 174n, 191
O'Neill, Art MacShane 92, 95, 100,
101, 132
O'Neill, Sir Art MacTurlough 77–8, 91,
101, 102, 103, 107, 129, 151, 173
O'Neill, Art óg 90
O'Neill, Brian MacArt MacBaron 146,
187
O'Neill, Brian MacBaron 214
O'Neill, Brian MacShane 92, 100, 108
O'Neill, Colla MacFerdoragh 150
O'Neill, Conn 19, 21–3, 25, 50, 51, 77,
91, 93, 102, 214
O'Neill, Conn Mac an Íarla 69–70,
150, 173n, 174n, 190, 208
O'Neill, Conn MacShane 92, 100, 101,
107, 108, 109, 132
O'Neill, Conn MacTurlough 150
O'Neill, Cormac MacBaron 143, 145,
147, 148, 150, 151–2, 170, 171,
173–4, 175, 181, 188, 190, 194, 205,
208, 209, 212, 214, 223–5
O'Neill, Cormac MacTurlough 91, 104
O'Neill, Edmond MacShane 92, 109
O'Neill, Eoin MacHugh MacNeill mór
132
O'Neill, Eoin MacHugh MacNeill óg
187, 188
O'Neill, Ever MacRory 149–50

O'Neill, Henry MacShane 92, 98, 100,
132
O'Neill, Sir Henry óg 78, 145, 146, 147,
149, 173, 190
O'Neill, Hugh (earl of Tyrone):
alliances 79, 93, 96, 97, 124, 128,
131–3, 135, 160, 171, 173, 177, 194,
211n, 215, 216–17; confederacy
145–9, 165, 172, 175–6, 196–200,
201–12, 216, 223–4; earldom 23, 24,
46, 50–1, 101–3; grievances 161–4;
historiography 3–13, 92–3, 139–40,
214–18; lands 69–70, 95; military
policy 167, 179–88; Monaghan
settlement 61, 68–70, 161, 163, 164;
overlordship 34, 39, 61, 69, 96, 140,
162, 167, 175, 177, 178, 187–8,
190–1, 193, 199, 202, 212, 219;
proclamation 178; proxy warfare
143–51, 154–5, 159, 166, 171–5, 196,
198, 205, 216, 217, 223–4; rise to
power 85, 98–112; rivalry with
Bagenals 46–8, 78–9, 140, 146, 149,
151, 153, 154–65, 168–9, 170–1, 204,
216, 218; Spanish contacts 106,
140–3, 194–5, 207–13, 216, 223–5;
submission 193, 194; upbringing 85,
92–3, 94, 188n, 214–15; use of
bribery 74–5, 80, 103–4, 105, 107,
169, 216
O'Neill, Hugh Gavelach MacShane
73–5, 92, 95, 100, 101, 106, 107, 108,
109, 169, 178, 217
O'Neill, Hugh MacNeill MacCoyne 91
O'Neill, Matthew (né Matthew Kelly)
19–20, 22–3, 118, 214
O'Neill, Niall Connallach 18, 22, 23,
77, 90, 102
O'Neill, Niall MacArt MacBaron 191
O'Neill, Niall MacArt MacHenry 91, 96
O'Neill, Niall MacBrian Fertagh 187,
188
O'Neill, Niall MacHugh 71, 146, 174,
188, 190, 191
O'Neill, Phelim MacTurlough 18, 146,
147, 152, 153, 217
O'Neill, Phelim Roe 22
O'Neill, Rose 124, 128, 135, 216
O'Neill, Sarah 211
O'Neill, Shane 18, 19–20, 118, 121,
177, 178, 207, 214, 217: attainder of;
20, 23, 50, 68, 74, 88; sons of; 35, 73,

74, 75, 81, 92, 94–6, 97, 105, 159,
194, 196, 200, 202, 204
O'Neill, Shane MacBrian 19, 71, 174,
188, 190, 191, 205
O'Neill, Shane óg MacShane 92
O'Neill, Turlough Breasalach 91, 94–6,
98
O'Neill, Turlough Luineach 18, 23–5,
34, 35, 38, 39, 46, 49, 51, 52, 53, 56,
73–9, 90–1, 92, 93–4, 97–112, 117,
118, 124, 125, 127, 129, 130, 134,
151, 152, 153, 159, 178, 182, 188,
214, 215
O'Neill, Turlough MacArt 78
O'Neill, Turlough MacHenry 96, 205
Oneilland 95, 96
O'Nolan, Tadhg 145
O'Quinn 89, 96, 186
Orange, William of 220–1
O'Reilly 20, 21, 40–3, 212
O'Reilly, Sir John 42–3, 205
O'Reilly, Philip 43, 134, 204, 205, 224
Oriel 52, 61, 95, 104, 109, 162
Orior 105, 109, 162
Ormond, earl of, see Butler, Thomas
O'Roughan, Sir Denis 56–8
O'Rourke, Sir Brian 33, 41, 53, 56, 58,
70–1, 217, 223
O'Rourke, Brian óg 73, 81, 128n, 141,
144–5, 154, 174, 205, 206, 208, 210,
212
O'Rourke, Hugh Galt 145
O'Scanlon, Moris 142, 150
O'Sullevan Beare, Philip 5, 139
O'Toole 21

Padilla, Martin del 213
Pale, Palesmen 41, 42, 43, 44, 49, 53,
57, 66, 68, 69, 75, 76, 79, 91, 94, 97,
102, 110, 147, 148, 158, 159, 166,
180, 182, 185, 186, 198, 200, 205, 214
Parker, John 156
Parliament of England 36
Parliament of Ireland 16, 20, 30–1, 43,
50, 71, 93, 102
Pelham, Sir William 94
Perrot, Sir James 29, 51, 139, 153, 201
Perrot, Sir John: early career 29–30;
factionalism 30–3, 43–6, 55–8;
finance 36, 38, 41, 44, 49, 52, 59;
historiography 4–6, 29;
imprisonment & trial 56–8;

patronage 31, 44, 52, 55–6;
propaganda 51–2, provincial
presidencies 33–4; Scottish policy
34–5, 48–9, 53; Ulster policy 34–44,
48–52, 62, 65, 75, 76, 100, 101, 105,
121–2, 128
Philip II 140, 141, 142, 194–5, 208,
209–10, 211, 223–5
Philip III 209, 210
Pittes, William 140
plantation, see colonisation
pledges, see hostages
Plunket, Captain 63
Porterlare 69
Privy Council of England 21, 35, 43,
50, 51, 55, 65, 69, 75, 76, 99, 109,
142, 152, 153, 158, 167, 183–4, 195,
196, 200
Privy Council of Ireland 30–2, 44–6,
50, 56–8, 74, 109, 111, 147–54, 157,
160, 170–2, 175, 184, 187, 195, 196,
197, 200, 201, 211
provincial presidencies 20, 29–30,
33–4, 47, 75, 79, 140, 151, 162, 164,
165, 200, 215, 216

Quinn, D. B. 11

Radcliffe, Thomas (earl of Sussex) 16,
20, 23, 30
Rawlinson, Richard 5
Rathmullan 128
rebellion 174, 178, 193–4, 218–19
religion 4–8, 13, 24, 134, 139–42, 165,
169n, 195, 198, 202, 204, 209, 211,
212, 215, 220, 223–4
Richey, Alexander 9
Route 38, 48, 174
Russell, Sir William: appointment 168;
early career 169; military policy
179–87, 192, 200, 203, 207;
negotiating stance 170–2, 173, 191,
195–6, 206

St Columba 116, 143n
St Leger, Sir Anthony 16, 21, 22, 41,
55, 215
St Leger, Warham 97, 160, 171, 196,
203
Santiago 208
Scottish mercenaries 18, 19, 22, 23, 25,
35, 36–7, 38, 39, 44, 46, 49, 62, 63,

73, 74, 75, 98, 99, 104, 120, 124, 130,
133, 157, 162–3, 175, 179–80, 181,
212
Seager, Philip 55, 58, 133
Shee, Richard 33
sheriffs 40, 44, 59, 61, 69, 75, 76, 109,
127, 130, 143, 151–2, 164, 165, 176,
177, 199, 202
shiring 40, 71
Sidney, Sir Henry 16, 20, 21, 24, 29, 30,
34, 37, 40, 41, 50, 55, 93, 95, 121,
122, 123, 214
Sidney, Sir Philip 214
Silke, John 12, 139, 140
Slane, Lord 57
Sligo 20, 38, 41, 60, 120, 122–3, 127,
186n, 189, 190, 199, 200, 202, 204
Sliocht Art 18, 110, 111
Smith, Matthew 156
Smith, Sir Thomas 21
Spain 8, 12, 35, 36, 43, 60, 105–6,
140–3, 177, 178, 195, 197, 202,
206–7, 208–13, 220, 223–5
Stanihurst, Richard 142n
Stanley, Sir William 38, 40, 183
Star Chamber 58
state papers 8, 10, 13, 164
Strabane 90, 91, 98, 110, 111, 182, 212
subinfeudation 18, 21, 42, 43, 65
surrender and regrant 16, 20, 41–3, 52,
61, 62, 64–5, 71
Sussex, earl of, see Radcliffe, Thomas

Taaffe, Nicholas 42
Talbott, John 69, 154, 188
tanistry 18, 20, 41, 42, 49, 61, 64, 72,
93, 126, 167, 187–92, 198, 219
termon land 66, 70, 89, 117, 202
Termon Magrath 70
Termonmagurk 104
Thomond, earl of 50, 215
Tipperary, liberty of 30, 32
Tiranny 95
Tir Breasil 117
Tirconnell, earldom of 121
Tirconnell, lordship of 49, 91, 113–35,
174

Tirenda 117
Tirhugh 117–18, 124
Toome 145–6
Treadwell, Victor 29
Treatise of Ireland 40, 46, 119, 128
Trinidad Valencera 131
Trough 68
Tuatha 116
Tullaghoge 85, 88, 89, 98, 101, 188
Tyrone, county of 76, 151–2, 177, 202,
215
Tyrone, earl of, see O'Neill, Hugh
Tyrone, earldom of 19, 23, 50, 88, 102,
173, 178, 194
Tyrone, lordship of 18, 19, 49, 85–112

Ulster, geography of 17–18. *See also*
maps
uirríthe 18, 19, 21, 23, 39, 47, 67, 75, 77,
85, 93, 96, 99, 102, 103, 104, 105,
106, 118–20, 122–3, 167, 187, 203,
204

Wallop, Sir Henry 31, 32, 33, 36, 45,
46, 49, 52, 76, 108, 161, 179, 180,
197–202
Walshe, Edward 45, 57
Walsingham, Sir Francis 31, 35, 38,
43–4, 51, 57, 75, 162
Ware, Sir James 5
Warren, Henry 97, 108, 132, 196, 205
Warren, William 48, 97n, 108, 170,
196, 203, 211
Waterhouse, Sir Edward 31, 44, 46, 47
West Breifne 33, 40, 41, 71–3, 127
Weston, Richard 103, 132, 184, 194n
White, Sir Nicholas 31, 33, 46, 49, 53,
56, 58, 60, 74, 75, 99, 107
Wilbraham, Sir Roger 45, 59, 63, 65–6,
70, 76–8
Williams, Philip 32, 45
Willis, Humphrey 63, 122, 130, 132,
143, 144, 145, 150, 161, 176
Wills, James 6
Wood, Owen 108, 140